# Waging War
# in Waziristan

# Waging War in Waziristan

## The British Struggle in the Land of Bin Laden, 1849–1947

Andrew M. Roe

UNIVERSITY PRESS OF KANSAS

All photographs, unless otherwise noted, are courtesy of The Green Howards Museum in Richmond, North Yorkshire, United Kingdom.

Published by the University Press of Kansas (Lawrence, Kansas 66045), which was organized by the Kansas Board of Regents and is operated and funded by Emporia State University, Fort Hays State University, Kansas State University, Pittsburg State University, the University of Kansas, and Wichita State University

ISBN-13: 978-0-7006-1699-2

Printed in the United States of America

# CONTENTS

Preface, *vii*

Acknowledgments, *ix*

Introduction, *1*

1 The Lay of the Land: Waziristan's People, History, and Terrain, *15*

2 Blood for Blood: The Tribal Culture of Code, *39*

3 Securing the Frontier: Politics, Policy, and Tribal Realities, *60*

4 The Forward Policies: British Influence, Political Control, and the *Maliki* System, *83*

5 1930s Waziristan: The British Administrative Apparatus, *104*

6 The Mailed Fist in the Velvet Glove: The Army of India and the Royal Air Force, *123*

7 A Cause Célèbre, the Fakir of Ipi, and the British Response: The Trial Case of Islam Bibi and the 1936–1937 Campaign, *155*

8 Keeping the Flame of Insurrection Alight, 1938–1947, *178*

9 The Hard-Earned Lessons and Realities of the British Experience in Waziristan, Part 1, *193*

10 The Hard-Earned Lessons and Realities of the British Experience in Waziristan, Part 2, *215*

11 Contemporary Parallels and Prognostications, *241*

Notes, *257*

Selected Glossary, *293*

Bibliography, *295*

Index, *309*

*A photograph section appears after page 143*

At the time of this writing, the U.S.-led coalition of armed forces has been in Afghanistan for almost a decade. Despite initial successes in efforts to ensure that al-Qaeda could never again build training camps, current policy makers face a mutating, vigorous, and elusive Taliban insurgency. Notwithstanding the proposed surge of 17,000 extra troops in the summer of 2009—driven principally by U.S. counterinsurgency doctrine to "clear, hold, and build" populated areas—politicians and military commanders are now increasingly cautious about Afghanistan's long-term future. Moreover, there is mounting unease over Pakistan's instability, particularly within the Federally Administered Tribal Areas (FATA) bordering southern Afghanistan.

To help meet these challenges, policy makers might look to the earlier British efforts to manage the North-West Frontier of India, which relied on a variety of mature political and military structures to successfully control and appease the tribal areas. The pertinent lessons to be learned from the British experience in the region—especially in Waziristan, the storm center of the frontier—have undoubted utility in helping address present-day challenges in the same geographical area. Indeed, as resources flux and priorities change, new and inventive measures—plus tried and tested ones—will be needed to help control the region's belligerent tribes. This book zeroes in on the issue of colonial control and provides a historical model that deserves study.

Moreover, the British experience in Waziristan has resonance in the daily news stories about the problems of coping with Pakistan's FATA and its links to the Afghan insurgency. This is the same area where al-Qaeda is resident today, the area where Osama bin Laden is probably hiding, and the area where the Taliban is regrouping. For today's policy makers grappling with the challenges of the FATA and southern Afghanistan, the British experience in Waziristan will not always make for happy reading; nonetheless, it is a story that must be told. The fact that the infamous Fakir of Ipi evaded capture, despite the employment of more than 40,000 troops to locate his whereabouts in Waziristan, is something from which Osama bin Laden can draw some comfort. Of note, the Fakir of Ipi died of natural causes in 1960; he never faced the magistrate's bench.

The British colonial approach, however successful, remains deeply controversial. Despite attempts to leave tribal structures largely intact, punitive raids and allowances, which the British employed in the service of imperial policies, had a profound influence on tribal behavior. Tribal encounters with British officialdom must have felt like a clash of civilizations: two fundamentally different worlds seemingly at loggerheads. The present challenge, therefore, is to place the gambit of tested colonial measures into a contemporary context to help inform today's policy makers.

## ACKNOWLEDGMENTS

My sincere appreciation and gratitude go to my wife, Pippa, for her patience, encouragement, and sacrificed evenings, weekends, and holidays. Particular thanks must also go to Mr. Les Grau of the Foreign Military Studies Office, Fort Leavenworth, Kansas. His untiring support, constructive criticism, and perceptive guidance have proved invaluable to the development of this work at every stage. I am also indebted to Dr. Alice Butler-Smith, Colonel Mike Scott, Colonel (Retired) Khushwaqt Ulmulk, Lieutenant Colonel Paul Corden, Major (Retired) John Badgery, Major John Greenacre, and the librarians at Prince Consort's Library, Aldershot, the Royal United Service Institution, Whitehall, and the Combined Arms Research Library, Fort Leavenworth, Kansas. All were generous with their time and wise counsel. I also wish to thank the British army for their backing and continued interest in this important and relevant area of historical study.

I would also like to acknowledge and thank Professor Efraim Karsh, head of the Mediterranean Studies Programme, and Dr. Rory Miller, also of the Mediterranean Studies Programme, King's College, London. The latter provided untiring support, clear guidance, and welcome criticism. His help was decisive, but all mistakes, misinterpretations, and errors are mine.

Additionally, I would like to thank the staff of the University Press of Kansas for their assistance and encouragement, in particular Mike Briggs, acquisitions editor, Susan Schott, marketing director, Jennifer Dropkin, production editor, and Monica Phillips, copyeditor extraordinaire.

My profits from this book will go to H4H: Help for Heroes (www .helpforheroes.org.uk), a registered charity that serves British Navy, Army, and Royal Air Force wounded.

Or what king, going to encounter another king in war, will not sit down
first and take counsel whether he is able with ten thousand to meet him
who comes against him with twenty thousand?

—Luke 14:31

## India's Volatile Border: The North-West Frontier and Waziristan

The British Empire was the most well known and diverse kingdom in
modern history. At its zenith in the late nineteenth century, the Empire
incorporated territories on all continents, including roughly one-quar-
ter of the world's population. Sir Rennell Rodd, diplomat, poet, and
politician, captured the magnitude of the Empire in the British psyche
when he wrote, "There has never been anything so great in the world's
history as the British Empire, so great as an instrument for the good of
humanity. We must devote all our energies and our lives to maintaining
it."[1] Within this vast domain, the Indian Subcontinent, comprising present-day Bangladesh, India, and Pakistan, sparkled as the brightest jewel
in Britain's Imperial Crown. Possession afforded Britain status, wealth,
and regional authority. It also offered a burgeoning market for British
trade. Predictably, this highly prized possession was guarded jealously
against foreign attack or interference.

Although Afghanistan and Persia presented recurrent challenges to
India's security, of particular concern during the nineteenth and early
twentieth centuries were imperial Russian advances into central Asia.[2]
These threatening moves, part of the "Great Game,"[3] preoccupied the
administration and brought the two European powers closer geographically.[4] In 1846, 2,000 miles separated the distant regions of czarist Russia and British India. By 1885, this gap was less than 500 miles.[5] An
official report of the time notes: "To-day Russia is our near neighbour;
her every movement is watched with the keenest interest from Peshawar to Cape Comorin; and the chance of her being able to attack us is
discussed in every bazaar in India."[6] Protecting the approach to India
from the northwest and separating the two powers was the landlocked

country of Afghanistan, which the British feared would become a staging post for a Russian invasion of India. Sir Alfred Lyall, member of the Indian Council from 1888 to 1902, summarized the importance of Afghanistan's role in Britain's imperial defense when he wrote, "During the nineteenth century Afghanistan has been a foreign kingdom which the English, who have no desire to possess, are nevertheless imperatively compelled to protect, and which must be retained at all risks and costs within the orbit of British influence, since its independence is essential to the security of any rule or dynasty in India."[7]

Unintentionally, Afghanistan, sitting at the crossroads of central, west, and south Asia, found itself between two ambitious competing powers. Simplifying the complex state of affairs, Lord Lytton, viceroy of India from 1876 to 1878, referred to Afghanistan as "an earthen pipkin between two iron posts"; Abdur Rahman Khan, the *amir* (king) of Afghanistan from 1880 to 1901, spoke of his country as "a goat between two lions, or a grain of wheat between two millstones."[8] Indeed, the British invasions of Afghanistan in 1838 (the First Anglo-Afghan War) and 1878 (the Second Anglo-Afghan War) were stimulated by fears of Russian imperial expansion from central Asia through Afghanistan into India.[9] Throughout the nineteenth and twentieth centuries, policy makers in London and Calcutta faced a difficult choice of leaving Afghanistan as a buffer state or of controlling the country completely and pushing British outposts into central Asia.[10] However, by the end of the nineteenth century, the British realized that Russia was using her threat of intervention in Afghanistan as a means of furthering her policies in Turkey and Europe. Furthermore, in 1907 the growth and danger of Germany made both powers realize that they had common strategic interests in Asia and Europe.

While the defense of India remained paramount to the British government, border management and the security of the frontier provided an equally complex dilemma. The pressing challenges of tribal control routinely overshadowed the threat of Russian advances. From the annexation of the Punjab in 1849 to a change in organization and policy in 1901, the territory up to the administrative border came under the administration of the Punjab government in Lahore. However, beyond the boundary sat a narrow piece of mountainous tribal territory separating Afghanistan from India. This ungoverned space, inhabited predominantly by Pashtun tribesmen, constituted the mainstay of the frontier problem. Although the *amir* of Afghanistan claimed suzerainty over the tribesmen, the reality was that he possessed little influence or physical control over the territory. Despite the area being vital to India's security, the British left the hill tribesmen largely to their own devices, unless events determined the administration of punishment for tribal misbehavior.[11]

The establishment of a common border between Afghanistan and India in 1896 by the Durand Commission aggravated the independent tribesmen of the region and did little to establish a clear and acceptable partition. Many in the Afghan government refused to recognize the border as a legal frontier. Likewise, the arbitrary topographical line divided the tribal area between two countries, with little or no consideration for ethnographical realities.[12] Tribal insurrection followed, and it took until 1901 for the British government to restore full order in the region. Moreover, 26,000 square miles of complex mountainous terrain, with a tribal population of approximately 2.5 million, now fell under the so-called British sphere of influence.[13] This included the regions of Chitral, Bajaur, Swat, Buner, Dir, the Khyber, Kurram, and Waziristan. Unsurprisingly, the demarcation of the Durand Line required a revised policy to influence and control the tribesmen.

In November 1901 Lord Curzon, the viceroy, created a new administrative area known as the North-West Frontier Province. Placed under the political control of a chief commissioner, but directly responsible to the government of India, Curzon hoped that the new province would focus attention on the region after extensive tribal uprisings resulting from the establishment of the Durand Line.[14] The province was divided into five settled districts (Hazara, Peshawar, Kohat, Bannu, and Dera Ismail Khan) and seven loosely controlled political agencies (Dir, Swat, Chitral, Khyber, Kurram, Tochi, and Wana), which included additional tribal territory up to the Durand Line. The administration of both the settled districts and political agencies, while different in approach, became unavoidably linked. This political structure was to remain largely in place until the British departed India in 1947.

Despite the sympathetic efforts of the British, the transborder tribes were highly sensitive to the presence of foreign troops in tribal territory and to any form of outside influence. Shaped by uncompromising

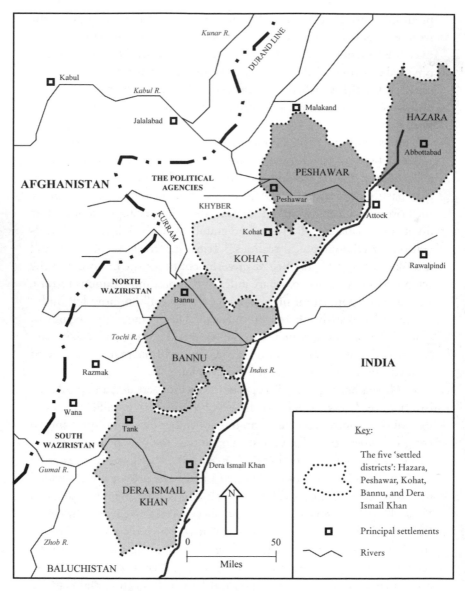

North-West Frontier Province, 1901. (Based on a map in C. C. Trench, *The Frontier Scouts* [London: Jonathan Cape, 1985])

conditions, religious fervor, and a stern code of moral conduct, in which revenge and self-preservation reigned supreme, the warlike tribes of the mountains proved difficult to control. To help address these realities, the British adopted a number of frontier policies and basing strategies during the colonial period.[15] This included the employment of a sliding scale of negative and positive incentives to pacify and control the region. As chapters 3 and 4 show, constrained by limited financial resources and available military forces,[16] routine control evolved into the distribution of allowances to sympathetic *maliks* (tribal representatives or elders), and by the employment of a frontline of resident civil armed forces based on locally recruited *kassadars* (tribal policemen), indigenous militias (known as scouts), and the frontier constabulary. Each played a vital role in discouraging tribal disorder and relieving regular troops of the expensive work of garrisoning remote frontier outposts. However, as the tribes behaved in unpredictable ways, this approach often achieved mixed results. In the event of a situation escalating out of control, the Army of India and the Royal Air Force (RAF) were used to punish the tribes.

As this book highlights, the storm center of the frontier and main focus for the government from 1919 onward was the remote political agency of Waziristan. From widespread tribal insurrection, following the fallout from the Third Afghan War,[17] during which the British briefly lost control of Waziristan, to the tribal revolt of 1936–1937,[18] headed by the redoubtable Fakir of Ipi, the mountainous region oscillated in and out of major tribal rebellion. Inhabited by the warlike Wazir and Mahsud tribes,[19] who were well known for their endurance, resistance skills, and love of independence, the region proved to be an intractable problem for the government and frustrated all attempts at pacification. Significant to this book is that this remote geographical area was routinely and effectively controlled by a relatively small but highly trained British administrative and military apparatus. When the British departed the region in 1947, proven colonial methods of control, including the employment of allowances, indigenous scouts, and *kassadars*, continued to be employed by the Pakistani authorities to pacify the tribesmen.

Waziristan is once again the storm center of the frontier. Currently, the Taliban and al-Qaeda use the remote region both as a sanctuary and as an impregnable base from which to launch attacks against targets in

Afghanistan and Pakistan. Moreover, the region may also be sheltering Osama bin Laden and many of his key lieutenants. With Pakistan and the international community short of ideas on how best to deal with this troubled region, investigating the successes and failures of British political and military structures employed in Waziristan may produce some useful and relevant parallels that could have application to contemporary challenges. Indeed, as resources are restricted, old as well as new imaginative measures will be needed to control Pakistan's frontier tribes. This book argues that looking at British institutional responses to similar problems in the same geographical area, albeit from a past era, has considerable value.

## The Book's Relevance

A detailed study of the British colonial response to Waziristan is needed because at present there is a lack of contemporary literature on the subject.[20] Although Michael Crawshaw's "Running a Country: The British Colonial Experience and Its Relevance to Present Day Concerns," published in April 2007, makes inroads into the wider principles and practice of British colonial and other forms of overseas governance, it fails to address the unique challenges of the North-West Frontier of India or the core of the frontier problem, Waziristan.[21] Understandably, the official publications and colonial records of the region concentrate almost exclusively on military activity. The routine political aspects of the period are often mistreated, downplayed, or ignored. This book will attempt to address this lacuna.

Alan Warren, one of the few military historians to have written on the region's past, points to three reasons why Waziristan has been overlooked in recent times: the dramas of the nationalist movement, partition, and the two world wars.[22] However, this is only part of the explanation. Technological advances have questioned the utility of historical frontier experiences, and the information explosion has broadened exponentially the areas in which a politician or military commander has to be knowledgeable. Perceived areas of greater utility and the selective use of history in education are also at the heart of this oversight. But despite George Santayana's admonition that those who fail to learn the lessons of history are doomed to repeat them, it is arguably the fear of a return to a quasi-imperial approach to the region that has been the greatest obstacle to the renewed study and contemporary analysis of the subject.[23]

However, a historical review of Waziristan is important because the period 1849–1947 (from the annexation of the Punjab to partition), and specifically 1936–1947 (the period of political and military activities against the Fakir of Ipi), contain the only reliable records available to draw patterns of tribal behavior.[24] Such material also permits a degree of contemporary analysis to distinguish between which approaches worked and which fell short of expectations (and why). In a speech on cultural understanding delivered to the Defence Academy, Shrivenham, on 11 June 2008, Major General Jonathan Shaw, chief of Staff Headquarters Land Forces, asked, "What is our education in *Pashtunwali* [the tribal code of honor]? Better we get it before embarking from those who spent years penetrating this obscure and harsh culture, rather than learn by deadly personal experience."[25] But the reality is that there is a paucity of contemporary analysis of the colonial methods of controlling Waziristan's warlike tribes. Moreover, knowledge of historical frontier experiences is also extremely limited.[26] It is hardly surprising that Shaw concluded his speech by quoting a Russian observer in Afghanistan who stated, "You've got a great history [in the region], it's just a pity you don't read it."[27]

But there is another equally pressing reason to study the British experience of Waziristan. There is a concern among some senior military officers that the United Kingdom is falling behind the United States in counterinsurgency doctrine,[28] despite the release of a heavily revised draft of an army doctrine publication titled *Counter Insurgency—A Guide for Commanders*.[29] The worry is that the staple works on counterinsurgency, which inform current doctrine, now appear too straightforward and unsophisticated for contemporary challenges.[30] Additionally, there is some unease that the United Kingdom may not be preparing commanders and forces adequately for counterinsurgency operations. Such criticism falls into three broad areas: British counterinsurgency doctrine; the teaching of doctrine during individual training; and specific preparation of forces for operational deployments. But the problem is not just confined to those committed to military operations. For example, how does one address the lack of historical and contemporary

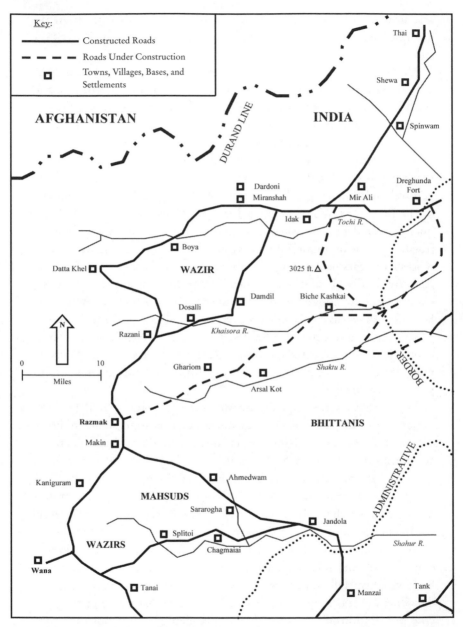

Waziristan, 1936–1937. (Based on a map in C. C. Trench, *The Frontier Scouts* [London: Jonathan Cape, 1985])

counterinsurgency knowledge amongst politicians charged with directing and delivering outcomes at the strategic and operational levels of
war? It is with this challenge in mind that this book attempts to provide
a detailed examination of the British political and military apparatus of
control in Waziristan and how they fared against the Fakir of Ipi.

Moreover, as this book seeks to show, the historical British approach
to Waziristan offers a number of valuable insights and practical measures worthy of consideration.[31] Therefore, at a minimum, policy makers and military commanders would do well to read the monographs
and memoirs of those who served in the region during colonial times;
however, the prerequisite for such a recommendation is the availability
of good material, which for the military is not always easy to access. In
addition, this book attempts to illustrate that the British experience in
Waziristan remains pertinent and that many of the British lessons of
Waziristan can be effectively incorporated into a contemporary strategy
to meet the present-day challenges of the Pashtun tribal belt.

## Sources

Given the depth of available information and analysis on the North-
West Frontier of India, this book is based on a combination of primary
and secondary sources. Official reports, compiled by British officials on
the frontier, provide a foundation and offer an invaluable insight into
colonial mentality and policy. Two of the most comprehensive collec-
tions can be found at the National Archives and the India Office Records. However, valuable and wide-ranging records can be found at the
Centre of South Asian Studies, University of Cambridge; the National
Army Museum, London; and the Salmond Papers, located at the Royal
Air Force (RAF) Museum, Hendon. Unfortunately, the *Official History
of Operations on the North-West Frontier of India 1936–37*, written in
1943, concentrates on military activities and is of limited utility for this
study. The wider political initiatives of the period appear unobserved or
neglected. Moreover, due to the finite period of this official history, the
report provides only a small part of the overall competency of British
methods of frontier control. Interestingly, no official history was written to cover the period between 1937 and 1947.

There are many secondary monographs, memoirs, and regimental histories about the North-West Frontier and the colonial campaigns in Waziristan. The themes and quality vary widely, ranging from general overviews to those more specific and comprehensive in scope. Many of the older British works, written when the Empire still existed, appear biased and lack balance and objectivity. This predisposition is understandable, as these works sold the virtues of the Empire, bowdlerizing shortfalls for popular appeal. This is arguably the case with A. P. Newton's *A Hundred Years of the British Empire* and, to some degree, H. L. Nevill's *North-West Frontier: British and Indian Army Campaigns on the North-West Frontier of India, 1849–1908*. The challenge, therefore, is placing such works in their appropriate context.

However, *Imperial Policing*, written by Major General Sir Charles W. Gwynn, is far more balanced and candid in its criticism of military support to the civil power. Likewise, balanced, detailed, and revealing insights appear in William Barton's *India's North-West Frontier*, C. E. Bruce's *Waziristan 1936–1937*, Olaf Caroe's *The Pathans, 550 B.C.–A.D. 1957*, John Master's *Bugles and a Tiger*, Geoffrey Moore's *Just as Good as the Rest*, H. R. C. Pettigrew's *Frontier Scouts*, John Prendergast's *Prender's Progress*,[32] and Charles Chenevix Trench's *The Frontier Scouts* and *Viceroy's Agent*. The same is also true of Frank Leeson's *Frontier Legion*. Completed in 1950 and donated to the National Army Museum ten years later, the manuscript was lost for more than forty years before being tracked down in 2001. Leeson, who was one of four British officers belatedly seconded to the North Waziristan *kassadars*, provides a well-balanced and underused account of life on the frontier with the tribal police.

Recent works also offer a more rounded description of events, analyzing both published primary and secondary sources. Of particular note are Michael Barthorp's *The North-West Frontier*, Hugh Beattie's *Imperial Frontier*, T. R. Moreman's *The Army in India and the Development of Frontier Warfare, 1849–1947*, Arthur Swinson's *North-West Frontier*, and Alan Warren's *Waziristan, the Faqir of Ipi, and the Indian Army* (a particularly well-researched account of the pursuit of the Fakir of Ipi and the 1936–1937 Waziristan revolt). *The Evolution of India and Pakistan, 1858–1947: Selected Documents on the History of India and Pakistan*, compiled by C. H. Philips, with the cooperation of H. L. Singh and B. N. Pandey, has also proved helpful. These source materials allow for an objective, detailed, and balanced understanding of the main political and military lines of development.

A few works challenge the success of British governorship on the North-West Frontier. "An Aspect of the Colonial Encounter in the North-West Frontier Province," by British-trained social anthropologist Akbar Ahmed (a former member of the civil service of Pakistan and political agent in South Waziristan from 1978 to 1980), for example, stresses the failure in communication between the two cultures. Such works provide useful balance but are frustratingly few in number. Perhaps unsurprisingly, the virtually illiterate and traditionalist nature of Pashtun society means that there are few tribal source documents available. In a culture where storytelling and folklore go hand in hand, selective memory, creative imagination, and tribal pride routinely usurp historical accuracy. Second- and thirdhand accounts offer little utility. However, there are a small number of tribesmen alive today who conducted government operations on the frontier in colonial times. Colonel Khushwaqt Ulmulk, for example, who served in the South Waziristan Scouts from 1941 to 1946, and returned to command the unit in 1948, has, despite the passage of time, been invaluable in confirming claims in the literature and in providing a further degree of authority.

Although suffering from the same limitations as the books mentioned above, a number of journals and periodicals give firsthand accounts of frontier military actions and offer opposing views of topical issues, such as the introduction of new technologies as a means to control the tribes. For example, the *Journal of the Royal Central Asian Society, Journal of the United Services Institution of India, Army Review, Asiatic Review*, and *Fortnightly Review* all possess historical works of relevance, although the wider political means of tribal control receive limited attention. Likewise, supplements to the *London Gazette* and articles in the *Times* are also useful in casting light on key events.

Unsurprisingly, there is no shortage of books, magazines, scholarly journals, and government documents on the current and future problems facing Afghanistan and Pakistan. Of particular relevance to this thesis are David Edwards's *Before the Taliban: Genealogies of the Afghan Jihad* and *Heroes of the Age: Moral Fault Lines on the Afghan Border*, Kurt Lohbeck's *Holy War, Unholy Victory*, and Abdulkader Sinno's *Organizations at War in Afghanistan and Beyond*. Also invaluable has been *Afghanistan: A Short History of Its People and Politics,* written by Sir Martin Ewans, a former head of Chancery in Kabul, Afghanistan. This book clearly describes the unique challenges faced by Afghanistan and provides a frank insight into the immense task of political and economic reconstruction. Two further books worthy of note are *Afghanistan* by Amalendu Misra and *In the Line of Fire* by President Pervez Musharraf. Predictably, access to current knowledge about military operations in southern Afghanistan and Pakistan's federally administered tribal areas is limited to open source reporting.

## Structure

This book is divided into eleven chapters. The first describes Waziristan's terrain, historical complexities, and centers of population. The second looks closely at the region's inhabitants, code of honor, and standards of behavior. The first two chapters set the geographical and cultural foundation for the remainder of the thesis. Chapters 3 and 4 examine the many twists and turns of British policy in the region. By showing events along a historical continuum, commencing pre-1849 and highlighting the influence of individuals and resource constraints, it emphasizes that to have any hope of success frontier policy must be consistent, culturally sustainable, and based on actual capacity. Chapter 4 posits that only if these interlinked tenets are met in the round will the political balance have any chance of favoring the government.

Chapter 5 investigates the roles and interactions of the political cornerstones of frontier control: the Indian Political Service, the tribal *kassadars,* and the frontier scouts. Chapter 6 describes the complementary functions and limitations of the Army of India and the RAF in tribal control. In so doing, both chapters point to the importance of using force as a last resort and of harmonizing political and military activities from the outset. Chapter 6 concludes by noting that the routine management of the tribesmen sat best under a flexible political framework. This management had to be capable of containing and quickly resolving tribal disorder based on a small number of empowered individuals and supported by indigenous forces, but always backed up by military capability.

During the period in question, the political and military apparatus of control were arguably given their greatest test of competence and suitability. Chapter 7 provides a review of British successes (and failures) against the notorious Fakir of Ipi over the troublesome period 1936–1937. Chapter 8 looks at the British responses to the *fakir's* decentralized campaign from 1938 until India's independence in 1947. Chapters 9 and 10, in an effort to emphasize the challenges of tribal control, build on this case study by examining the hard-earned lessons of the British experience of this period. These chapters close by suggesting that many of the lessons of the British involvement in Waziristan continue to have modern-day relevance.

The final chapter investigates the contemporary parallels between the colonial approach to managing Waziristan and the present-day challenges along the Afghan-Pakistani border. It suggests that if the past is prologue the British experience in Waziristan points to a complex and frustrating road ahead for Pakistan and the coalition. The chapter concludes by advocating that the practical measures and valuable insights into the British experience in Waziristan remain relevant and worthy of consideration by today's policy makers.

*Summary*

After decades of unwanted and costly experimentation, the British response to the complexities of Waziristan was containment. Control, as in the Indian States, was neither necessary, desirable, nor practical. Indirect rule, through the employment of political officers and indigenous security structures, routinely and relatively successfully controlled the frontier using a sliding scale of incentives and force to encourage tribes to control themselves. This approach was based on a light touch, commitment, and continuity but was underpinned by an early and firm response if the tribes stepped out of line.

Despite injecting large numbers of military reinforcements into tribal territory during 1936–1937 in pursuit of the wily Fakir of Ipi, the British never sought full control in the latter years of the colonial period. Military operations were finite in duration and localized in their employment. Against a fiercely independent and fanatical foe, any enduring occupation of tribal territory by foreigners was hotly contested. Political primacy remained paramount, and routine control occurred via the locally recruited scouts and *kassadars*. Working with the forces in society and grounding policy in regional realities offered the only hope of controlling the unpredictable and confrontational tribesmen.

Yet the agility and structures of the British response to Waziristan appear all but forgotten today.[33] Despite many parallels between the British historical approach to the region and the contemporary challenges in southern Afghanistan, the colonial approach to the region remains largely unknown, underlining Aldous Huxley's maxim that the most important thing we learn from history is that we never learn from history. This important oversight is in part due to a fear of a quasi-imperial occupation of the region as well as being a consequence of the dearth of contemporary analysis into the methods of British colonial control.

It is within this context that this book attempts to identify the enduring lessons of the British colonial experience and endeavors to draw contemporary parallels, general truths, or approximate precedents for today's policy makers and military commanders.[34] The underlying assertion of this book is that the British approach worked well in the past and many of the hard-earned lessons from Waziristan can be adopted as part of a contemporary solution for the troublesome Pashtun tribal belt today.

# 1

# The Lay of the Land: Waziristan's People, History, and Terrain

> The historian of great events is always oppressed by the difficulty of tracing the silent, subtle influences, which in all communities precede and prepare the way for violent outbursts and uprisings.
> —Winston S. Churchill, *The Story of the Malakand Field Force*, 1898

## Terra Incognita

Waziristan is a remote, complex, and austere district of modern-day Pakistan. Independent of central authority, it lies at the geographic, economic, and social extremity of Pakistani society. It has evolved little over recent centuries. Characterized by the rugged Sulaiman Range, the region is a tangled mass of inaccessible khaki-colored mountains and deep twisting valleys. The highest peaks are Pier Ghal (11,556 feet) and Shuidar (10,936 feet). Both are found in the northwest region. About 120 miles long and almost 60 miles wide at one point, Waziristan is a rough quadrilateral totaling 4,500 square miles, stretching from the Kurram Valley in the north to the River Gomal in the south. The region is bounded by the high mountains and jagged skyline of the Afghan border to the west, known since 1893 as the Durand Line—a theoretical legal construct, largely ignored by the inhabitants—and the wide expanse of the Bannu basin and rich trans-Indus plains to the east.[1] Its products are few and unimportant and its population is meager and dispersed. "The country is, in reality, largely unpopulated, the tribesmen all congregating in villages and hamlets situated in the less arid positions of the valleys, or in such as lie within reach of the grazing grounds."[2]

For political and administrative purposes, the region is divided into North and South Waziristan.

The region's transportation network is limited and restrictive. There are only a small number of narrow-gauge railways in Waziristan due to the severity of the terrain. The major broad-gauge railway network stops short on the flatlands below. Only a partial and unsatisfactory road network exists, which was constructed by the British to permit the rapid deployment of military assets and to facilitate tribal trade and civilizing influences. The network was also essential in speeding up and lessening the challenges of supply by motorized vehicles. Despite periodic growth in the late nineteenth and early twentieth century, many areas, particularly those close to the border, have no road network. Animal transport, both pack and draft, remain a common sight throughout Waziristan. Camel and mule tracks are ubiquitous in the region. The two principal thoroughfares in the region follow the channels of the rivers Tochi and Gomal respectively. Ravines and watercourses form the only natural means of communication in the region.

The terrain in the south of the region is precipitous, arid, and stony, with hills rising from east to west via a series of parallel ranges.[3] The hills attain heights of over 10,000 feet close to the Afghan border. The valleys are often deep waterless tracts that are difficult to negotiate on foot and are even trickier for the region's pack animals. Only small strips of mountainous terrain are suitable for subsistence agriculture. The northern area of Waziristan is equally barren and rock-strewn but is physically less severe. Large sections of land are inaccessible and must be covered on foot. Valleys are generally broader, rounded, and more navigable. Irrigation, drainage, and a rudimentary system of terraced fields—by means of retaining walls—are usual around the principal waterways. The main river in the north is the Tochi, which has two tributaries: the Kazha and Margha—both start life in Afghanistan. Thick scrub is commonplace around these watercourses and to a lesser extent on the surrounding hillsides. Many of the larger valleys have established tracks that permit routine vehicle movement. The route of these rocky trails is contiguous with the course of the streams and rivers. Punctuating the rock-strewn basins are towering steep-sided hills.[4] A small number of these contain forests of mature pines. Waziristan's unforgiving and barren terrain contributes to separating the region's tribes into distinct geographical entities. It also provides a natural barrier from the flatlands below and engenders in its inhabitants a psychological independence. The hill tribesmen had little cultural or social unity with the tribes of the flatlands or the wider Indian subcontinent below.

Not all of Waziristan's terrain was so uninviting in recent history. In the late 1800s, the western part of Waziristan contained significant forests of cedar and ilex. Other areas were equally green and fertile, especially the hills over 4,000 feet.[5] R. I. Bruce, a former political officer in Baluchistan and late commissioner and superintendent of the Darajat Division of the Punjab, recalls:

> The Shawal valley, as regards climate, forest, and grazing is the choicest valley of the Derwesh-Khels, and it certainly deserves the high praise which I have often heard bestowed upon it by them. It is about sixteen miles long and eight miles broad, measuring between the high ranges which surround it. Low broken hills and ridges descend from the mountains to within a quarter of a mile of the river bed. Numerous valleys pass through and join the main stream from the mountains. The Bosh-Nerai and the Dare-Nashtar valleys have magnificent timber. I have seen no place in the Waziri hills more suitable for a sanatorium than this valley.[6]

Birmal, close to the Afghan border, was another example of a productive vale. Containing several hamlets and significant areas of cultivable land, the western slopes also possessed an abundance of chilgoza pines.[7] However, these green anomalies were an exception in an otherwise harsh and unforgiving environment. The constant demand for firewood, both for personal use and as a means of revenue, resulted in a rapid decline in the expanse of forested areas throughout the region. "In Sibi alone more than 11,000 acres of juniper were completely denuded of trees in two years; in Pishin acres upon acres fairly covered with pistacia became bare."[8] Without the trees and flora to bind the earth, rich topsoil was either washed away in severe downpours or blown away in strong mountain winds. Areas that were once mature woodland—containing game and edible plant life—transitioned, over time, into barren tracts of unrecognizable earth. Deforestation, exacerbated by the various British garrisons' demands for a constant supply of firewood and by tribal overgrazing, had a far-reaching effect on the region. Lieutenant

Colonel Bruce points to a wider effect of deforestation when he questions, "What has been done to conserve these forests and to stop this wasteful denudation which is very probably one of the main reasons for the decrease in the water supply."[9] With no control over Waziristan's natural resources, the tribesmen continued to exploit the dwindling forests unchecked.

But some factors, shaped by Waziristan's severe topography, remain unchanged. The principal means of passage to and from Afghanistan is still via a small number of remote river valley passes. For millennia, such trading routes have connected south Asia to central and west Asia. These unique gorges start life in Afghan territory and develop in an easterly direction toward Pakistan. Historically, the British favored the strategic Bolan and Khojak Passes near Quetta and the infamous Khyber Pass, geographically the most direct route between Kabul and the plains of the Punjab. However, Waziristan also contains a number of important breaches of the frontier. In the north, the Kaitu River Pass transits through the rugged district of Khost toward Bannu. In the center, the Tochi River, the arterial watercourse in Waziristan, affords a direct route from Ghazni in eastern Afghanistan to Bannu. In the south, the Gomal Pass, derived from the Pashtu word *ghwa* (cow) and *lara* (road), is a challenging four-mile gorge that is almost constantly in flood. This barren and rocky pass links Ghazni and Dera Ismail Khan and is the oldest trade route in the area. It was also a challenging and dangerous route. The official record of *Operations in Waziristan, 1919–1920* states: "The country [around the pass] is difficult, affording great opportunities for a few riflemen to hold up whole convoys; also, the stages are long and the climate unhealthy."[10] But there are also other less recognized points of ingress, known only to the local populace. Depressions in the mountains, linked by steep grazing tracks, permit unlimited options to cross the border to those with local knowledge. These, like the acknowledged passes, are only traversable in the summer months and in clement weather conditions.

The climate of Waziristan varies in severity according to the altitude. In the mid-mountains, typical weather conditions are severe and oppressive with a low annual rainfall.[11] Summer starts in May and ends by September. June is the hottest month, with temperatures reaching over one hundred degrees Fahrenheit.[12] Dust clouds and sandstorms are common, and the entire region is covered consistently in a thin layer of fine gray powder.[13] Respite from the debilitating heat can be achieved only by attaining elevation. Winter starts in October and lasts until April. Temperatures fall routinely below freezing for extended periods, with significant snow accumulating on high ground. Hard spells of frost are frequent. With little available firewood, the unforgiving winters of the region pose a significant threat to the inhabitants. To negate this, winter migration to the lowlands is commonplace.[14] But even on the plains little comfort from the hostile environment exists.

Most areas of Waziristan average six inches of rainfall a year, and spectacular electrical storms are a common occurrence. Precipitation occurs in short, violent, and irregular downpours. This is the result of two climatic events: the monsoon period (August to September), when moisture is brought up by the winds of the Arabian Sea and Bay of Bengal, and the western disturbance (November to March). Both result in heavy showers that are absorbed by the arid ground or lost in surface run-off. The heaviest rainfall occurs in the northeastern part of the region. Such extreme climatic conditions frustrate routine subsistence agriculture reliant on a consistent source of water. They also challenge movement. The numerous waterways in the region are variable in volume. In the winter months, smaller rivers decrease to meager streams or dry up altogether. When the mountain snow melts or it rains, half-dry streams and rivers, fed by countless small tributaries, become powerful torrents and formidable obstacles.[15] All rivers in the region flow west to east into the River Indus in the Bannu basin.

Agriculture is carried out where possible and is dependant on the fertility of the soil. In broken ground, this normally occurs in thin bordered strips of well-tended land. Geoffrey Moore, a platoon commander and part-time brigade intelligence officer of the Razmak Brigade in 1936, recalls how "cultivation was restricted to occasional breaks in the arid valleys, terraced with infinite labour and irrigated only by strenuous effort."[16] Maize, barley, wheat, *jowar* (Indian millet), and rice are the staple crops of the region. Apart from the River Tochi and the Wana plain, which benefit from rich floodwater alluvial deposits (known as *kaches*), there is little cultivable land in Waziristan. In the early 1900s, the mountainous tribesmen survived on a meager diet of rice, buttermilk, bread, and water. Meat and wheaten bread were uncommon and infrequent luxuries.[17] Due to the extreme topography and weather, only limited tracts of land yielded sufficient returns. In the spring, tribesmen took refuge in the mountain pastures to graze their herds of livestock on sparse but dependable grazing lands. Although trade was limited with the Indus Valley below, wood, wool, hides, and fibrous products were all traded on a regular basis. To help compensate for nutritional and agricultural deficiencies, grain, salt, and other necessities of life were imported back into Waziristan.

## Raids, Robberies, and Abductions

Despite concerted efforts, subsistence agriculture fell short of providing for individual and tribal necessity. For centuries, this habitual deficit was supplemented by raids on nomadic caravans passing through the area and looting forays into villages and towns on the fertile flatlands below. In the case of the latter, these prosperous areas were populated mostly by agriculturalists who spoke the same language — Pashtu. These tribesmen were psychologically different from those of the mountains of Waziristan and were seen as fair game. Raids sought to attain money, livestock, fodder, and goods, but indirectly they also exacerbated the area's poverty. H. L. Nevill summarized the unavoidable realities of the situation when he posited, "The effect of the inability of the soil to support the inhabitants is that they have to find other means of supplying themselves with the necessaries and all the luxuries of life, and plunder and robbery under arms are the result."[18] Raids were the primary source of revenue for the tribesmen, and no dishonor was attached to their endeavors.[19] But such activities, much praised by the tribesmen, were strictly forbidden by the British. The infamous Jalal-Khel-Mahsud raider Khonia Khel provides a useful insight into the rationale behind his actions.

I have three wives and five strapping sons like myself, and several sisters with large families. You have stopped me raiding in the Dera Ismail Khan and Bannu Districts, as well as the Tochi Valley. Now I hear you are going to stop me raiding in the Khaisora . . . You will not even allow me to raid in Birmal or Khost, although these valleys are in Afghanistan. There has been no rain and so no grazing for my flocks. How, then, am I to live?[20]

But the reality was often considerably more complex. For generations, the tribesmen had supplemented the region's meager resources with imports from across the Durand Line and from the fertile plains below. Moreover, the area's natural products, aided by village stores of grain and food, were sufficient to enable the tribesman to endure successfully long-standing blockades.[21]

Not all raids were designed to compensate for food shortages or to achieve material gains. Raiding took place for political reasons or to settle disputes. It was an activity that suited the tribesmen's martial ethos. Robberies, abductions, and murders were also a common attribute of tribal existence and a constant threat to those who transited through tribal territory. In 1921, for example, an American geologist was killed and a caravan of Nasars, part of the nomadic Powindah tribe, were massacred without cause by the Suleiman Khel.[22] Raids routinely targeted vulnerable mountain passes, low-lying villages, towns, and government establishments. Kidnappings of rich Hindu or prosperous merchants for ransom were also commonplace. Soldiers operating in tribal territory were also likely to be abducted. In 1942, the London *Times* reported the capture of a Madrassi signaler in Waziristan. Momentarily separated from his unit, the signaler was seized by tribesmen and led to a large concealed cave. The article recounts that "it was filled with rifles, ammunition, and stores of food and about 1,000 tribesmen."[23] The soldier was offered money, land, and a wife if he chose to join the outlaws in their cause. Repeatedly turning down the offer, the signaler was beaten severely after each refusal. After four days of captivity and continual suffering, the signaler managed to free himself from the straps securing his arms and escaped.

Such lucky escapes were exceptional. John Masters, who served in Waziristan with the Gurkhas, recounts in *Bugles and a Tiger* of a more usual and expected outcome. Describing the state of a British officer's body after a short time in tribal hands, he recalls: "He had been castrated and flayed, probably whilst still alive and his skin lay pegged out on the rocks not far from the camp."[24] Beheadings were also a common practice. Lieutenant Colonel Bruce recounts a "very ghastly spectacle." Whilst riding out to Hurrund, Robert Sandeman, deputy commissioner of Dera Ghazi Khan, was intercepted by a tribesman, known as Gurchani Sowar, in a great state of excitement. Stating that he had the head of Gholam Hosein, a notorious murderer and robber, the tribesman held "up the end of his mare's nosebag, [and] out rolled the head of a man on to the road."[25] Such a fate was not uncommon for captured government forces, nor was the practice of removing a man's genitalia.[26] This was often repositioned to the victim's mouth and was a solemn reminder of tribal cruelty for those charged with recovering bodies. It was also known for a wounded man to be pegged to the floor and his jaws forced open to prevent him from swallowing. A woman of the tribe would then urinate in his mouth until the individual in captivity drowned.[27] Unsurprisingly, it was an unwritten rule never to abandon a wounded soldier.[28]

Raiding parties were frequently accompanied or led by local district outlaws. These were wanted individuals who had committed an offense in British territory and who had escaped across the porous border into Waziristan for sanctuary. Under the safeguard of the headman, the outlaw attained a position of *hamsaya,* or "one who dwells beneath the headman's shade."[29] However, contrary to popular belief, these individuals were not given protection and shelter free of charge. Instead, the outlaw had to find a means of regular payment to preserve his protected rights. This resulted customarily in unlawful activities, either individually or as part of a larger raiding gang guiding incursions into known villages. On average, an important headman could have a dozen *hamsayas* under his charge at any one time. Lieutenant Colonel C. E. Bruce, a veteran of thirty-five years on the North-West Frontier declares, "It is because nearly every tribal raiding gang is accompanied by local district outlaws that they often prove so successful."[30] Bruce recognized that the outlaws possessed many unique qualities. They enjoyed firsthand knowledge of many of the flatland villages to be raided and were able to avoid fortified posts or permanent picquets, where opposition might be expected. Likewise, local district outlaws could rely on associates and relations for up-to-date information and wider support in extremis. It was not uncommon for villagers to harbor outlaws or to shield them to secure their protection. Such traits were exploited forcefully by the tribesmen. But the relationship was not just one-sided. Villagers also used *hamsayas* for illegitimate purposes. Sir William Barton recalls tribesmen in "British villages" using outlaws to eradicate local adversaries.[31]

There were also other dynamics at play in Waziristan. Regular and relatively uninterrupted contact with the settled areas had an economic, social, and political effect on the structure of fragile tribal societies. Thomas Thornton, a former secretary to the Punjab government, notes that far from the tribesmen keeping their distance from the flatlands, "The bazaars of the frontier stations teemed with hill-men, and Powindahs from Ghazni."[32] Further outside pressures included the spread of education, religious diversity in the form of missionaries, and medicine. Dispensaries and hospitals were resented in the region, although medical assistance, including vaccinations and the treatment of chronic diseases, was received readily by the tribesmen and their families. Each taste of the previously unknown posed a dilemma for tribal society. But like other medieval-like societies encountering outside influences, the perils of economic development proved to be a dominating and unpredictable factor in Waziristan's instability.[33] Over time, the aspirations and standard of living of the tribesmen increased.[34] Unrestricted trade improved the economic position of many and spending power also grew.[35] Access to a wider range of products, a better diet, and the availability of basic medicines also improved the lot of many tribesmen. This resulted in a steady growth of the tribal population, previously subdued by starvation, infighting, and endemic diseases — although malaria, scurvy, dysentery, and sandfly fever continued to take their toll.

## The Frontier Arms Race

An improved economic position also meant that modern rifles, including breechloaders and magazine rifles, became a realistic goal and demand increased. In 1901 W. R. Merk, commissioner of the Darajat Division, provided a useful insight into the tribesmen's psyche regarding the acquisition of rifles:

> Now as to rifles: with some notable exceptions a rifle to a hill Pathan is literally the breath of life, if for instance I have a breechloader and my enemy with whom I am at a blood feud has none he must get it or go under. There are no two ways about it. This is the chief and most common motive for the acquisition of breech-loaders, the fierce struggle for existence which is ever being waged in the hills. A subsidiary reason is no doubt also the feeling that the

more rifles a tribe has, the better it can hold its own if its independence is threatened. But the primary cause remains the instinct of individual, or family, or sub-section or even clan preservation.[36]

The modern rifle became the ultimate symbol of individual prestige in Waziristan and a tangible trophy of daring. It helped permit the successful prosecution of blood feuds and became a decisive factor in intertribal warfare. It also provided an effective means to raid the rich and fertile flatlands below and narrowed the gap between the armament of government forces and the tribesmen. To meet the growing demand for new weapons, a string of arms factories were established in the tribal areas selling inexpensive but crudely made rifles. The most renowned were the Afridi factories within the Kohat Pass, situated in the strip of independent territory that separates Peshawar from Kohat. In the early 1900s, Edward Cadogan, part of a study group transiting the region, visited a remote village factory. He notes with some curiosity that the method of manufacture was unconventional and that the craftsmen appeared to be fashioning armaments from iron railings.[37] But such unexpected raw materials seemed of little concern to the purchasers. "A number of Waziris, the wildest-looking men imaginable, were buying them, and seemed satisfied as to their adequacy for the purpose for which they were intended."[38] But these hand-crafted imitations of European weapons, complete with serial and regimental numbers, had a number of practical limitations. The craftsmanship was often substandard and the accuracy of the weapons uncertain. Moreover, since the barrels and breechblocks were constructed from unhardened steel, repeated use further degraded the weapon's performance.

Such inadequacies were short-lived. Improved raw materials came from Afghanistan and India and small village factories procured high-quality precast barrels and other machined working parts of hardened steel from many of the larger factories. This left the village smiths, mostly ex-armorers trained in the Indian army, the task of assembling the remainder of the weapon; a relatively straightforward undertaking using hand tools and foot-operated lathes.[39] But key rifle components also came from condemned government rifles. Whilst the barrels were cut into sections to prevent further use, the working parts, including bolt, were sold for their scrap value. During the late 1800s, these part-worn components were bought by traders and sold to the tribal rifle factories. Over time, the increased production of improved weapons in tribal arms factories caused prices to slump. In the Kohat area a European .303 sold for Rs. 500–600 in 1924. Only nine years later this had fallen to Rs. 300–400. Likewise, a tribal Martini .303 that was worth Rs. 100–120 in 1924 dropped to under Rs. 50 in 1933.[40]

Additional modern weapons came from Europe. A standard movement saw arms shipped from Antwerp to Muscat, across the Gulf of Oman to the Persian Coast in dhows. The final leg of the journey was by camel caravan. Smooth transit through Waziristan's tribal areas relied on the local chiefs. They were rewarded financially to ensure safe passage. It is telling that in spite of heavy transportation costs the profits derived from such activities were sufficiently large that gunrunning continued relatively unabated. This was despite the threat of British raids to secure weapons in tribal territory and greater efforts to interdict arm shipments in the Gulf of Oman by the Royal Navy.[41] It was not until 1910 that the British established a robust blockade of the Gulf. Within six months, more than 200,000 rifles lay undelivered in Muscat godowns, "but the damage had been done."[42]

There were also other means of gaining modern rifles. From 1919 to 1921 government arms and ammunition were issued to the villages along the border to counter raiding, without any form of registration or control.[43] Rather than being used for self-protection, many were sold for financial gain or stolen during intertribal raiding. Rifles were also abundant across the permeable border in Afghanistan, and others came from the Middle East, supplied initially by the British and Turkish governments to Arab tribesmen in return for loyalty. More usually, modern weapons were captured during bloody engagements with government forces. Tribesmen became adept at seizing weapons from the bodies of the dead and wounded.[44] Geoffrey Moore was aware of this when he noted, "The hillmen were primarily after the sport of battle; how else can it be explained? And the trophies they sought were rifles of the Government pattern, so superior to their own from the Kohat Pass, and ammunition."[45] Larger attacks often yielded impressive returns. The evacuation of Wana under concerted pressure resulted in the capture of 1,200 modern rifles and nearly a million rounds of small arms ammunition in 1919.[46] Raids against police armories, designed to capture modern rifles and accoutrements, were also frequent.

The constant demand and elevated prices of service rifles made the risks of stealing rifles and ammunition from the military a worthwhile, if dangerous, undertaking.[47] Professional rifle thieves (known as *loose-wallahs*) determined to exploit the burgeoning demand were active in the Punjab and throughout India. These individuals targeted unsuspecting government forces in sedentary areas. Simple measures to alleviate the threat were introduced. Rifles were chained together and the working parts were stored separately. Soldiers whose rifles were stolen were fined heavily and it became a matter of unit or subunit pride not to lose a rifle. Dogs were kept also as a means of early warning and protection. But the cunning *loose-wallahs* found a way to mitigate this protection. "These animals would be 'neutralised' as defences by the *loose-wallahs* greasing themselves with leopard or cheetah fat."[48] The scent of these animals reduced the boldest dogs to a state of fear. Stolen weapons and ammunition were moved rapidly to the frontier for a quick profit. Ingenious measures were often employed to smuggle stolen weapons across the border.

> Some years ago a coffin, in which apparently some Pathans were taking the remains of a dead fellow-countryman back to his native land for interment, became an object of suspicion to the police. In spite of the protestations of the heart-broken relations, the police insisted upon opening it, and found that, instead of a corpse, it was full of stolen rifles.[49]

Monies gained from other illegal activities were also used to buy armaments. It is telling that tribesmen continued to spend excessively on weapons, as opposed to long-term agriculture and infrastructure investment initiatives.[50] The desire for modern weapons acted as an obstacle to tribal political and economic progression.

The constant flow of arms across the border into Waziristan posed a serious menace to the region and a wider threat to the Indian Subcontinent. The qualitative and quantitative enhancement of the tribal armory was a regular cause of concern to the Indian military and political authorities. Initiatives to interdict the gun trade faced significant challenges. A lack of local knowledge, a permeable border, difficult terrain, and an insatiable demand were all strong contributing factors. But the *amir* of Afghanistan, Amanullah, whose position gave him the religious standing of a king of Islam amongst the tribes, also had a role to play.

He was central to maintaining the good conduct of the border tribes. His sensitivity to any activity that influenced the internal affairs of his kingdom had a detrimental influence on British actions. Gunrunning was one such activity that drew his attention and tacit support.[51] The British approach was, reluctantly, measured and relatively uncontroversial. Like many associated closely with the challenge of preventing gunrunning, Captain H. L. Nevill formulated a personal opinion of the ensuing debate: "It is useless to expect to put a stop to the supply of arms entirely, it is better to accept the evil as inevitable, and consider how it can best be neutralized, or, at least, mitigated."[52]

Initiatives to stop the manufacture of rifles were considered.[53] However, such was the ingenuity of the tribal artisans that the effect of closing or destroying a remote rifle factory was short-lived. Factories reopened quickly with little disruption to production or relocated to more inaccessible sites, often exploiting the impregnability of the Afghan border. A more practical scheme was to impose a heavy fine and a "deposit" of rifles (but not ammunition) on those tribes that had misbehaved. The fine removed the means to acquire modern weapons, and the surrender of a predetermined number of rifles disarmed a significant element of a tribe. The punishment made a clear distinction between tribal and modern or stolen government weapons. A fine of Rs. 40,000, the capitulation of 250 tribal rifles, and the surrender of all government rifles, which was demanded of the Wana Waziris in 1920, was not uncommon.[54] But rifles were often returned after a period of good behavior. The London *Times,* reporting a significant tribal fine that included the surrender of 1,400 modern rifles in 1937, pleads with some justification: "It is to be hoped that these [rifles] will for once be retained by the authorities, who have hitherto returned them as soon as the tribesmen relapsed into temporary virtue and have been perpetually disappointed by the results of their good nature."[55]

Such fines faced a number of obstacles. Tribesmen were hesitant to surrender serviceable rifles. Instead, they yielded broken or antiquated weapons to meet British demands. There were other practical challenges. Some rifles were owned in common by several tribesmen. Moreover, a tribesman might own more than one rifle and lend them out to others.[56] In such an instance, the tribesman stood to pay an inconsistent penalty.[57] Many rifles were buried or concealed. Also, not all tribes misbehaved and this raised questions over the utility of a disarmament program in tribal territory. More significantly, once a tribe reliant on weapons for its own security was disarmed, the onus for protection became the responsibility of the government. With scarce resources, little influence over tribal territory, and a porous border this proved impractical. It was therefore impossible to disarm all of the tribes in Waziristan without the cooperation of the government of Afghanistan to disarm the tribes on their side of the border.

But if the production of rifles or their circulation could not be abated, the scarcity of ammunition could be improved upon. Denying the tribesmen spent cases from rifle ranges was a simple initiative often overlooked.[58] Empty cases, combined with cordite and lead caps smuggled across the border, provided a regular means to replenish meager ammunition holdings. But lead was also available from range butts and a number of royal artillery ranges in India. This was exploited by local villagers and transported to the frontier by traders for sale to the tribal arms factories. To counter this, the supply of ammunition became strictly controlled. Ninety percent of cases expended in training had to be returned. Failure to do so would prevent the further issue of ammunition. In addition, training areas were cleaned carefully to recover lead, and the loss of live rounds became a serious offense.[59] But despite such initiatives, the transborder tribes had amassed and hidden significant reserves of arms, ammunition, and raw materials to satisfy their needs.

Modern rifles, particularly the .303 Lee Enfield and Martini-Henri service rifles had a significant impact on tribal tactics. No longer armed with just crude *jezails,* a long-barreled matchlock, curved swords, or "missiles which nature provided,"[60] the introduction of high-quality long-range rifles posed hitherto unseen threats to the region: range, accuracy, and an increased rate of fire. "The invention of the breech-loader and magazine rifle has furnished our Frontier foes with a weapon with which they can use with only too fatal effect, as the past year has shown, against our troops," noted Major A. C. Yate.[61] Realizing the value of range, the tribesmen readily adapted to long-range harassing fire and mountain ambushes, throwing convoys into confusion or harassing retiring forces. This was supported by the introduction of smokeless powder, which no longer gave away the firer's position. Tribesmen were now capable of inflicting significant casualties and slowing the pace of operations in tribal territory. Captain H. L. Nevill, recounting his hard-won experiences of the frontier, highlights the frustrations of battle at range and inconclusive skirmishes. "The chief obstacle to decisive action encountered by regular troops in this class of campaign is the difficulty of closing with their elusive opponents, consequently any cause which tends to increase the distance at which battle is joined must aggravate that difficulty."[62] Of greater concern, the tribesmen became better armed than either the militia or frontier constabulary.

But long-range fire was only problematic if accurate and if the proficiency of the tribesmen to hit a target at distance was contentious.[63] A number of experienced soldiers considered the tribesmen dreadful shots. "This was absolutely our considered and unanimous opinion."[64] A series of factors helped shape this assessment. Tribesmen were remiss at undertaking necessary daily rifle cleaning and found the employment of the backsight, a relatively simple mechanism, difficult to utilize and master. Many chose to ignore its application with unfavorable results. Likewise, a shortage of ammunition brought into question the ability of the sniper to practice his art on a regular basis—a necessary undertaking to maintain proficiency. There were also challenges with matching available ammunition with captured rifles. But more fundamentally, casualties were light and this was the acid test for many. "While the Battalion [2nd Green Howards] was in Dakka camp sniping was a nightly occurrence and, on occasions, an afternoon one as well. However, it was annoying rather than lethal. Only one 'hit' was registered during the whole time and that was on an officer's servant bringing his afternoon tea."[65]

There may have been another plausible reason why the tribesmen's accuracy was poor when sniping at fixed locations. "It cannot be impressed too strongly on young units and young soldiers that wild firing by day or night is one of the indications whereby the tribesmen gauge the moral, physical and professional standards of our troops. It is against units with indifferent day and night fire discipline that they [the tribesmen] prepare their more elaborate surprises."[66] The tribesmen's inaccuracy, whether by design or unintentional, did not hold true in all cases. Charles Trench recounts a falling-plate competition between the South Waziristan Scouts and a tribal Mahsud team in *The Frontier Scouts*. The scouts, better shots than the majority of army battalions, were beaten by the tribesmen. Both teams used government rifles and ammunition, which would suggest that not all ignored the merits of the backsight.[67] Therefore, the London *Times* report of the death of Captain J. Agar, adjutant of the King's Own Scottish Borders, by sniper fire at "extreme range" in 1942 was not remarkable by any standards.[68] Soldiers learned never to stand in one location for too long.

Not content with modern rifles, a small number of stolen machine guns, and grenades, the tribesmen also recognized the advantages of artillery, especially against a fixed garrison location. A number of tribes demonstrated considerable resourcefulness in acquiring simple, but relatively crude and ineffective, artillery pieces. These came from Afghanistan or were manufactured in the rifle factories of Kaniguram. Despite production challenges and ammunition shortages, locally made artillery proved of some value. Guns were able to fire solid shot as well as high explosive rounds over short ranges. But such weapons often fell short of expectation. Lieutenant Colonel H. de Watteville notes that "with the greatest elation, at the close of January, 1920, the Mahsuds received the supply of artillery in the shape of two six-pounder Afghan mountain guns . . . These pieces proved but a dismal failure in action—their range was not greater than 2000 yards, whilst many of their shells were blind."[69]

A notable example was the Sadde Khan's gun. Commissioned from the Kaniguram armorers in the early 1930s, the breech-loaded gun was capable of threatening the integrity of a fortified position by firing a nine-pound solid iron shot. The weapon was highly mobile, making it difficult to interdict. The cast barrel, carriage, and wheels were all detachable and could be carried with relative ease by camels.[70] But there were also other crude examples. In 1942, a news correspondent attached to Major General R. B. Deeds, commander of the Waziristan District, wrote a short article in the London *Times* recounting his stay at the fort of Datta Khel. The report recounts the tribesmen's attempts at indirect fire: "They have come out this time with two or three guns, rustic contraptions for which positions were prepared in the mountains, especially in the Spera Ghar, which dominates Datta Khel to the north. Some shells—improved in hidden gorges—fell in and around the fort, but most did not explode."[71]

Despite the advantages of range afforded by modern rifles and artillery, the tribesmen did not abandon the close fight entirely, for which they were well known and respected. They improved on it by the skillful combination of fire and movement and covering every knife rush with long-range suppressing fire. Only when all factors appeared to be well in their favor did they press home an attack. Signaler Williams, based at a temporary camp at Biche Kashkai in 1936, recounts the chilling persistence of the tribesmen's rallying call followed by a knife rush supported by fire:

> The yell was prolonged into a long-drawn-out cry which grew steadily louder as the enemy came charging down the hill. Verey lights went up and there was a deafening crash of machine-gun fire. Someone shouted "Stand to your rifles! They're rushing the camp!" Indeed by now they sounded very close. We heard a tribesman scream out "We want the Sikhs and the British!" and somebody on our side roared back "Come and get them!" Then the Sikhs on our northern flank stood up as one man and rushed out to battle, howling and bellowing like mad animals. There was a close hand-to-hand fight of furious hacking and chopping, tribal knife against Sikh kirpan, and after that the fighting died away.[72]

Such growing tactical competence was attributable to the numerous ex-soldiers and scouts amongst their ranks who recognized the importance of suppressing fire to cover movement. It was also a result of hard-won practical experiences. The combination of both factors proved decisive. On 26 November 1936, an engagement occurred between two columns of government forces and a large number of Tori Khel Wazir tribesmen. The London *Times* reported: "The troops were not conducting any punitive or offensive measures, nor were any contemplated; the sole purpose of the two columns being sent to the Khaisora Valley was the hope that their march through the territory would stiffen the attitude of the pro-Government tribesmen."[73] But such a presence enraged the tribesmen, who resorted to violence to keep their territory free from foreign occupation. Despite the support of aircraft, the ensuing fighting resulted in the death of two British majors, a British soldier, and fourteen Indian other ranks. In addition, two British captains, nine British other ranks, and sixty-six Indian other ranks were wounded in the skirmishes. The tribesmen also suffered heavily in the encounter but disappeared from the battlefield exultant. Instead of representing strength, the operation highlighted the government's limitations. With such proven tactical ability, plans for military intervention into tribal territory had to take into account the increased fighting capability of the tribesmen.

Notwithstanding material and tactical advances, the strength of the tribesmen also resided in their guerrilla modus operandi and characteristics. This was especially true beyond 1923 when a permanent presence of regular troops was established in Waziristan. Employing strategies such as limited raids, poisoning wells, positioning crude but effective booby traps, and interfering with telephone lines proved to be a constant irritation to the government forces.[74] In the case of the latter, the area over which communications had to be provided was extensive and impossible to secure. Telephone lines, in particular, suffered persistent damage from tribal action affecting routine communications. "Many miles of route were frequently totally destroyed and had to be rebuilt."[75] Reliance, therefore, had to be made on wireless telegraphy, visual communication, and dispatch riders. Protecting the lines of communication, be they road or wire, proved to be a necessary and hazardous undertaking. Without the pressure of time, the tribesmen determined a time and place of their own accord to conduct an attack. Always looking for tactical weaknesses or careless routine, the tribesmen have been described as the best umpires in the world as they rarely allowed a tactical error to go unpunished.[76] This facet of the tribesmen was well-known to government forces but often overlooked. "Disregard of methods of security on the one hand, a too slavish routine in their enforcement on the other, miscalculations as to time and space, all of these faults have been penalised repeatedly by the Mahsud and Wazir."[77]

On occasions, the tribesmen went to unusual lengths to observe and mislead government forces. One of the tribesmen's greatest triumphs was the seizure of Kashmir Kar Post in 1901. The success of this attack was in part due to a number of tribesmen disguised as shepherds who for a number of weeks prior to the attack observed carefully the habits and weaknesses of the garrison. This success was overtaken by the capture of the Tut Narai Post in May 1917 by a group of Mahsuds who employed the ruse of sending two of their members disguised as women to attract the attention of the garrison.[78] But even after an attack, the tribesmen were adept at confusing and losing a pursuing force by rapid dispersion and deception. The tribesmen chose to exploit these inherent skills to great effect. Combining field craft with guile, the routine tactic of choice was hit-and-run raids against isolated unwired posts or picquets, avoiding potentially costly confrontations against heavily guarded outposts. The skill and tactical competence of the tribesmen helped to resist encroachments into tribal territory by the British. It was also a contributing factor in the tribal areas being largely isolated from outside influence.

There were also other more direct influences imposed upon the inhabitants of the region. As part of a wider British pacification experiment, a number of tribesmen were encouraged to leave the refuge of their mountain villages to serve in the Indian army. The 24th and 26th (Baluchistan) Regiments of Bombay Infantry each had a company of tribesmen attached. Although well-behaved and receptive to discipline, the *Allahbad Pioneer* reports, "The Mahsud recruits now and again cannot forget their old pilfering habits when in the bazaar, but this was only to be expected, for in Waziristan the immemorial custom has been for the strong to plunder the weak."[79] A key by-product of military service was to regulate and pacify the tribesmen. It was hoped that to soldier in civilized surroundings, especially in large population centers, would have a positive and enduring effect on the tribesmen. By the start of World War I there were about 5,000 tribesmen in the Indian army, of which 3,000 were Waziris.[80] Many served with distinction on the western front and in East Africa, but in other regions their performance was impulsive and erratic,[81] and due to their strong religious feelings, "many deserted rather than fight against the Turks, for the Sultan of Turkey was the Khalif of Islam, Commander of the Faithful, Shadow of God upon earth."[82]

These absconders, either unable to cope with the restrictions and hierarchy of military service or through religious compulsion, returned to their tribal areas skilled in the methods of modern warfare and schooled in the wider theory of combat. They were not alone. The locally raised scouts also faced a high wastage rate from desertion.[83] But there was another cultural reason for the high number of tribesmen with previous military experience. As the Pathan disliked expatriation, the average length of individual service was shorter than other native tribes. "The result being that a larger number of trained soldiers from Pathan squadrons and companies annually pass back to their homes than is the case with a proportionately large establishment of any other race."[84] Accordingly, each tribe contained a percentage of individuals skilled in the practice of both conventional and frontier warfare. Such tribesmen also had a wider understanding of the mind set of the administration and many of its inherent shortfalls and restrictions. Having experienced aspects of contemporary living on the flatlands below during military service, many tribesmen were content to return to village life and wished to have no further role in the administration. There were also other negatives associated with lucrative service in the Indian army. Numerous tribesmen became accustomed to increased wealth and better living conditions, attributes they were disinclined to forfeit. They were also more prone to visit centers of population to attain, either legally or dishonestly, a growing range of perceived necessities.

There was a further influence in the region that had a considerable impact on tribal politics and behavior. Political propaganda from Afghanistan was a powerful cause of unrest in Waziristan. Either instigated directly from Kabul or via forward representatives in tribal territory, an information campaign encouraged the hill tribes to rebel against British rule and maintain their independence. Collin Davies, late captain in the 2/1st K.G.O. Gurkha Rifles, posits:

> Although it is often stated that the economic factor is at the root of almost every frontier disturbance, it is my considered opinion that political propaganda, especially from 1890 onwards, has been the most potent cause of unrest. It has been Afghan intrigues, either instigated directly from Kabul with the full cognizance of the amir, or carried on by his local officials, which have from time to time incited the tribes to rebel against the British Raj.[85]

"Afghan intrigues" provided a circumlocutory source of moral support to the tribesmen. But to facilitate unrest, political propaganda was reinforced by a number of practical measures. Anti-British Mullahs and dissatisfied *maliks* were rewarded financially for their activities, and economic assistance was provided to purchase modern arms and ammunition.[86] In addition, deserters from British forces, assassins, murderers, and kidnappers were welcomed in Afghanistan.

## Centers of Population and Tribal Life

There were two principal centers of population in Waziristan in the 1930s. The largest of these was the village of Kaniguram, which consisted of about 600 stone dwellings separated by narrow cobbled passageways. Such was the uniqueness of the close proximity of the houses that the community was distinct from other tribal societies in the region. Although Kaniguram was often described as the capital of the region, Geoffrey Moore, who knew the settlement well, felt it was a "commercial capital" since it possessed the only bazaar in the area.[87] It was also renowned as a regional hub for the burgeoning iron trade and contained a number of rifle and knife factories. This unique economic center was primarily attributable to the Hindu populace. The Kanigurami, who are believed to be the indigenous people of the area, were a different breed from the tribesmen who surrounded them. They embraced trade and excelled at manufacturing. Moore posits that they were only tolerated through the centuries because of their superior engineering skills.[88] Whether this is true or not is debatable, but the Kanigurami were adroit at making weapons, particularly prized daggers, and this was a proficiency respected begrudgingly by the hill tribesmen.[89] They were also a generous people. By tradition, the Kanigurami provided free entertainment for their visiting guests. Recognizing the advantages of complimentary hospitality on neutral terrain, Kaniguram became the regular location of all important Mahsud assemblies at the expense of the inhabitants.[90]

The second major center of population in Waziristan was Makin. This was a cluster of some 200 well-built homesteads ten miles north of Kaniguram, situated on the slopes of the imposing Shuidar peak and surrounded by terraced fields and grazing areas. This smaller settlement afforded limited trade and access to a regular supply of tribal commodities. "It contained numerous smelting houses, and was the principal seat of the Mahsud iron trade. Next to Kaniguram, it was the most important and best built in the country."[91] Between these two centers of population, there were roughly forty to fifty small factories, producing agricultural tools, cooking utensils, horseshoes, and nails.

More usually, villages were a small independent huddle of fortified square-shaped houses constructed from unbaked bricks, earth, chopped straw, and rough timber surrounded by limited bands of cultivated land. These are known as *kots*. Houses tended to be grouped on available tracts of flat ground. Each dwelling typically had an impregnable high wall, up to three feet thick, surrounding it with a single point of entry. The height of the wall precluded those outside from seeing within the enclosure. These fortified enclosures were also used to protect goats, sheep, and cattle from raiding parties. Horses, camels, and buffaloes were uncommon due to the severe nature of the terrain. B. E. Hughes describes a tribal dwelling in Waziristan:

> The best we saw were houses of stone and mud, with only one room, and a roof of rough beams on which laid matting, which was covered with earth. The houses, if they may be called such, often had a small piece of ground outside enclosed by a mud and stone wall. There was nothing artistic whatever about them, they were small and dirty, and the only furniture of any sort we found in them were beds of rough wood and string on plaited straws.[92]

For early warning against attacks, larger villages often contained a series of fortified watch, or rifle, towers. They were also a sign of prestige—the more watch towers, the more important the settlement.[93] These necessary and impregnable observation posts were normally over thirty feet tall and of sturdy construction. They were carefully positioned and manned by vigilant tribesmen, each with a predetermined area to observe. Beyond the village, concealed lookouts maintained a watch from dominant hills. On raising the alarm, the villagers would recover to the relative safety of the main house, often having no option but to leave their animals outside the enclosure. The watch towers were used to snipe at the raiding party and were reinforced quickly by additional armed tribesmen. In the event of a peaceful visit by British forces, the populace were often less than welcoming. Visits often meant the introduction of a new form of taxation, conscription into the army, or the collection of bribes. Tribesmen remained deeply suspicious of the presence of outsiders in tribal territory. Recounting a visit to a village known as Dksual, F. T. C. Williams recalls that after a period of quiet, the mood changed quickly: "They [the children] then started shouting, and as if by magic a horde of villagers materialised from nowhere, complete with a pack of dogs, until that quiet village became a bedlam of shouting and screaming people and growling dogs."[94] The tribesmen were also on the lookout for the movement of government raiding parties. To provide an early indication of troop movements, the tribesmen relied on a traditional network of informants and messengers. At the first indication of an advance into tribal territory, the tribesmen would conceal their grain and send their women, children, and cattle into the upper hills.

Inside a village dwelling, conditions were basic. A house usually consisted of a single or a small number of dark interlinked rooms, many of which were used to store and dry food. Sanitation was inadequate and small black flies ubiquitous.[95] Animals lived in close contact with the inhabitants. Nonetheless, these dwellings, within a wider village structure, provided basic protection from the severe weather conditions and incessant attacks from unscrupulous raiding parties and social orientation. Permanent structures were not the only habitation on the frontier. Tents and makeshift housing from timber, cloth, and animal hides were also common and a reflection of a seminomadic culture. Caves were also numerous, both around the villages and about the region. Used principally for temporary winter accommodation, they could also house animals or provide storage for grains. Lieutenant Colonel de Watteville notes: "A peculiarity of very many of the Wazir villages is their close proximity to large caves, to which the tribesmen have recourse as dwelling-places in winter for the sake of obtaining greater warmth."[96] Colonel Sir T. Hungerford Holdich, Indian Survey Department, provides further clarity on the advantages of inhabiting caves: "A well-drained and sufficiently well-lighted cave, with room for the smoke to get out without inconvenience, is not a bad substitute for a four-walled house, and is infinitely to be preferred to a tent in winter."[97]

Women lived a restrictive life within the confines of traditional Islam and the unforgiving demands of isolated village life. The official report of operations in Waziristan 1919–1920 notes that such harsh conditions have produced in the women "a remarkable power of resisting fatigue and of nurturing their children under the most adverse conditions and circumstances."[98] But compared to other frontier tribes, many women enjoyed superior freedom, and adulterous affairs were not uncommon. Any woman found to be unfaithful was likely to be put to death or have her nose amputated as a constant reminder of her unfaithfulness.[99] In contrast, a man would have half of his right foot removed. The sanctity of marriage, at least openly, was respected. Tribesmen purchased their brides, and women possessed no legacy birthrights. After marriage, their household tasks were numerous and varied but centered principally on cooking, growing vegetables, fetching water to their fortified villages, and raising children.[100] On rare occasions they traveled with the men when fighting. At the age of ten, girls were prepared for marriage and boys handed over to the men to be trained in manly skills.

From an early age, boys were expected to regard their neighbors with extreme distrust, if not hatred, and the lesser breeds with contempt.[101] The art of marksmanship was taught at a young age and all tribesmen were required to carry a rifle wherever they went for self-protection. Sir Richard Temple notes: "They [the tribesmen] are never without weapons, when grazing their cattle, when driving beasts of burden, when tilling the soil, they are still armed."[102] On leaving their fortified enclosures, women were dressed from head to foot in traditional *burqas*, while the men wore baggy trousers and loose shirts (*shalwar kamiz*) and on their heads turbans (*pagri*) or flat squat hats (*pakol*).[103] Geoffrey Moore, an officer with firsthand experience of the Pashtun tribesman, described Waziristan as "harbouring riflemen wearing baggy trousers, grass *chaplis* [sandals] on their feet, flowing grey shirts bound round with leather ammunition belts and untidy *pagris*. There is no doubt that the Pathan was not only the smelliest and dirtiest of mortals, he also wore the last word in untidy *pagris*."[104] Such an appearance proved to be an advantage. The Pathan possessed a unique ability to blend against the rock-strewn and scrub-covered terrain to a remarkable degree. "Added to this his undoubted agility, speed of reaction to any fault made by us, and a general 'tactical sense' that was absolutely unrivalled."[105] These innate abilities placed the tribesmen amongst the most agile and feared opponents faced by the British.

# 2

# Blood for Blood: The Tribal Culture of Code

Thanks to the *Puktunwali* code, *hamsayas* ("persons sharing the same shade")—fugitives from British justice or from another tribe, Hindu merchants, Sikh mechanics, Punjabi artisans, professional entertainers—could live and carry on their business with a fair degree of safety.
—Charles C. Trench, *The Frontier Scouts,* 1985

## The Way of the Tribes

The distinctive Pashtun subtribes of the Darwesh Khel Wazirs (Wazirs), the Mahsuds, the Bhittanis, and the Dawar occupy the mountainous area of Waziristan.[1] Although united by a shared language, they lack regional cohesion due to spiritual, cultural, and political differences. These isolated and independent tribes are categorized as *nang,* or honor, tribes.[2] *Nang* tribes live in remote areas supporting only subsistence agriculture. They are free of strong centralized leadership, with individual tribesmen possessing far-reaching autonomy. By contrast, *qalang* (rent, tax) tribes reside in low-lying areas that support irrigated agriculture and produce regular surpluses used to generate income. *Qalang* tribes enjoy strong centralized leadership and greater regulation of routine activities. The psychological difference between the *nang* tribes of Waziristan and the *qalang* tribes of the flatlands was stark. These distinctions were so diverse that "when individuals from *qalang* society confront *nang* tribesmen, they show unease and uncertainty, which reflects the structural and fundamental differences in the two systems."[3]

There are also a small number of other tribal groupings living in the region. The most significant of these is a pocket of indigenous Hindus

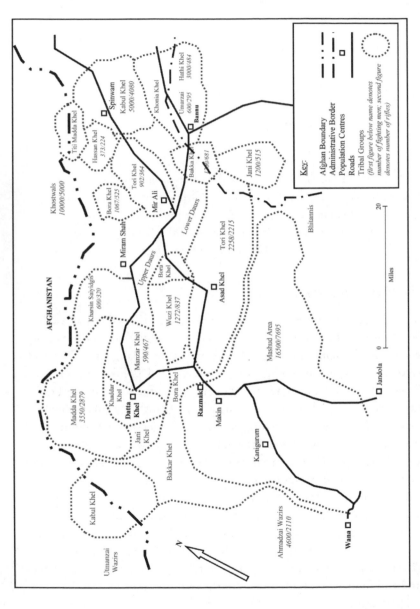

Sketch map of tribal areas, ca. 1937. (Based on the *Official History of Operations on the N. W. Frontier of India,
1936–37* [Delhi: Government of India Press, 1943])

Key:

- Afghan Boundary
- Administrative Border
- Population Centres
- Roads
- Tribal Groups
  *(first figure below name denotes
  number of fighting men; second figure
  denotes number of rifles)*

AFGHANISTAN

Khostwals
*10000/5000*

Titi Madda Khel

Hassan Khel
*373/224*

Spinwam

Kabul Khel
*5000/4080*

Khonia Khel

Hathi Khel
*3000/484*

Umarzai
*600/295*

Bannu

Bora Khel
*1067/525*

Tori Khel
*902/364*

Mir Ali

Bakka Khel
*?00/681*

Jani Khel
*1200/515*

Miram Shah

Lower Daurs

Tori Khel
*2258/2215*

Bhitannis

Kharsin Saiyidgis
*600/320*

Upper Daurs

Bora
Khel

Wuzi Khel
*1272/837*

Asad Khel

Mashud Area
*16500/7695*

Jandola

Madda Khel
*3550/2879*

Khaidar
Khel

Datta
Khel

Manzar Khel
*500/467*

Bora Khel

Razmak

Makin

Kanigurum

Jani
Khel

Bakkar Khel

Kabul Khel

Utmanzai
Wazirs

Ahmadzai Wazirs
*4600/2110*

Wana

N

0        Miles        20

that live in the town of Kaniguram. Little is known about their origin, except that they differ in customs and characteristics from their Mahsud neighbors. Various other nomadic tribes have also transited the area. The Powindahs are the most well known. Colonel Sir T. Hungerford Holdrich notes: "They are built of splendid material, and I should doubt whether in any city of Europe such magnificent specimens of humanity are to be found as you may jostle against any winter day in the bazaar at Dera Ismail Khan."[4] They journeyed through the high mountain passes and tribal areas on their way to the populated plains below to conduct trade. The Powindahs traded in Turcoman rugs, wool, horses, dried fruit, clarified butter, almonds, pistachio nuts, sugar, salt, tea as well as the products of Russian, British, and Indian factories.[5] These commodities were much sought after by the tribesmen, and raids against the Powindahs' caravans were a common occurrence.

> For generations the Wazirs carried on war to the knife with these merchant traders. To meet the opposition that awaited them at this part of the road, the Powindahs, who were heavily armed, moved in large bodies of from 5,000 to 10,000, and regular marches and encampments were observed, under an elected *Khan* or leader, exactly like an army moving through an enemy's country. They more than once attempted to come to a compromise with their enemies on payment of a fixed blackmail, but the Waziris invariably refused to listen to any compromise.[6]

But these nomadic tribesmen also proved to be a threat to the other tribes. The Powindahs were prone to kidnapping Wazir children to keep as slaves or to sell. This habit resulted in regular hostilities between the Powindahs and the tribes of the region, but particularly the Mahsud. Their presence was an additional complication to the region.

*Nang* tribes are characterized by a proud and uncooperative self-government, a partly feudal and partly democratic ethos.[7] They abide by an uncompromising, literal view of the Muslim faith and live by an austere moral concept of honor called *Pashtunwali*—the way of the Pashtun. *Pashtunwali* is believed to have originated during the pagan period and, over time, has become fused with Islamic tradition. As a general rule, the code does not apply to women, children, or mullahs.[8] This unwritten pre-Islamic belief is conveyed by the collective wisdom of the tribesmen and is the dominant force in Pashtun culture. The code is respected by all tribesmen, if not always observed strictly, and provides a degree of legal security and social orientation. "This imposes upon the individual three important compulsions which must be observed; renegades must be offered safety and protection, hospitality must be offered at all times—even to an enemy and any affront, whether it be real, imagined or by default, either to an individual, his family or his kinfolk, must be avenged no matter how long such a vengeance takes to accomplish."[9]

The code was responsible for a relentless conflict that dominated internal and intertribal Pathan society. But *Pashtunwali* permeates tribal society to a far greater extent than just the three stated compulsions. It determines decision making, social justice, self-determination, egalitarianism, cooperation, and tolerance amongst others. It is also flexible, dynamic, and open to degrees of contemporary interpretation. For example, the humble admission of guilt for a wrong committed should result in clemency from the wronged party. However, submission was not a trait admired by the hill tribesmen, and the humiliation was so great that the practice rarely occurred.

At its core, the code requires all Pashtuns to preserve *nang* (honor) and to avoid the dishonor of *sharm* (shame). Such is the severity of the code that if a man loses his *nang* he is completely ostracized: "No one would congratulate him on the birth of child. No one would marry his daughter. No one would attend his funeral. His disgrace will endure for generations. He and his family must move away."[10] In 1897, Winston Churchill, then a twenty-three-year-old journalist attached to the Malakand Field Force, noted: "Their system of ethics, which regards treachery and violence as virtues rather than vices, has produced a code of honour so strange and inconsistent that it is incomprehensible to a logical mind."[11] To provide a simple example, honor and killing are conflicting conditions by Western standards. Yet in Pashtun society they are complementary to one another. Therefore, the murder of a girl in the name of honor can actually make a tribesman honorable in the eyes of society.[12] To help understand *Pashtunwali* it is important to understand something of its components.

In *Pashtunwali* honor is to be protected at all costs. If a Pashtun's honor is tarnished or even slighted—and there are myriad ways in which this can occur—the individual is expected to conform to cultural expectations and is obliged to seek an appropriate redress at all costs. Any tribesman who fails to take up a feud where tribal custom demands it is branded for life.[13] The code dictates that *badal* (revenge) is the main means by which a tribesman's honor can be restored and is governed by the underlying imperative of relative parity: "an eye for an eye, a tooth for a tooth." Therefore, the injury inflicted in revenge must be equal to or greater than that suffered by the individual.[14] But in more extreme cases, shedding an offender's blood, or in his absence his next closest male relation, is not uncommon and is endorsed by the code. In some instances, a professional assassin is employed to deal with a murderer. In 1932, a man's life was valued at £250 amongst the Mahsuds.[15]

*Pashtunwali* does not stipulate a timeframe for reprisal, leaving the tribesman to determine a time, place, and means of his own choosing. "The Pathan may wait years for his chance, but take it he must, sooner or later, or be utterly shamed."[16] Tribesmen who are hereditary enemies may serve together peacefully for many years in the army or scouts. But once on leave, revenge will be foremost in an individual's mind. If the man dies, it is the responsibility of the man's family or tribe to carry on his pursuit. This situation is compounded by the practice of wife inheritance. This custom results in a widow being forcibly married to her dead husband's brother or cousin, thus transferring the requirement for revenge. Nothing is ever forgotten or ignored and few debts are left unpaid. "In the slang of the day, you may 'hammer' them as often as you please, but though you may cow them for a time, the men to whom a blood-feud is a cherished hereditary possession will be even with you when an opportunity exists."[17]

As even a mere taunt is regarded as an affront to a tribesmen, the requirement for justice and honor has contributed to generations of infighting in the Pashtun tribal areas. Robert Baden-Powell provides a useful illustration when he recounts an unexpected crack of rifle fire while sitting on the ramparts of Fort Jamrud. On questioning what was happening, it was explained that "it is only that the women from that village over there are going down to the stream to get water. The other village is firing at them: they do it almost every day. You see, there is a longstanding feud between them. They have been at it for years."[18] It is little wonder that government activities—including forcing entry into houses, destroying watch towers with explosives, and searching female quarters in the hunt for modern weapons and outlaws — offended the tribesmen on all accounts.

Charles Trench highlights an illustrative case of the complexities of *Pashtunwali*. The story surrounds the death of a political agent, Captain J. B. Bowring, killed by a sepoy Kabul Khan, of the Abdur Raham Khel subsection of the Bahlolzai section of Mahsuds. The sepoy had shot Bowring, who for coolness had slept on the roof of a building, as his feet faced toward Mecca. On completion of the deed, the sepoy fled to a nearby control tower for safety and periodically fired at anyone who broke cover. The sepoy's punishment was not in question, but how to effect his death was another issue. To storm the control tower would result in unnecessary loss of life; to lay siege to the tower hoping that the sepoy would capitulate would take time and was bad for morale. But there was another more pressing issue to resolve. Who should put the sepoy to his death? There was concern that the death of the sepoy would result in blood feuds as the Abdur Raham Khel sepoys took revenge on the executioner and his tribe took reprisals. To avoid this eventuality, it was decided that the sepoy must die by the hands of his brother, who lived locally. "When it was put to him the *Naik* [corporal] consented, for the honour of his family, the Abdur Rahman Khel, the Dré Mahsud, and the Militia, to execute by shooting his own brother."[19] Recognizing his destiny, sepoy Kabul Khan accepted an offer of death with dignity. At five in the afternoon, the murderer came into full view, stood proudly, cried "God is great," and was shot dead by his brother.

Linked to *badal* is *namus*. This central theme of *Pashtunwali* codifies the protection of female relatives as well as a tribesman's land and territory. As such, the wider notion of tribe and territory are merged together. The defense of both is the holy duty of a tribesman. The tenet of hospitality (*melmastia*) is also a central aspect of *Pashtunwali*. This calls upon the tribesmen to show hospitality to all visitors, whether invited or uninvited, and regardless of their ethnic or religious persuasion. Hospitality comes in the form of food, lodging in the village *hujra* (a house and hostel for men), and entertainment.[20] It also includes protection, with the host responsible for the guest's safety within the confines of the tribal boundaries. Such generosity is afforded without hope of remuneration or subsequent favor. However, in practice, those guests accorded hospitality can be called upon to return the favor to their hosts in the future. They can also be expected, if their stay becomes extended, to earn or contribute toward their keep. Stories of extreme generosity are not uncommon in Pashtun villages, despite the relative poverty of the inhabitants.

Closely linked to hospitality is sanctuary (*nanawatai*), which means literally "coming in." In principle, *nanawatai* must be offered to anyone who requests it, regardless of any crimes they have committed or if they are an enemy. Therefore, if a man were to commit murder on the Indus plain below and seek refuge in tribal territory, the tribe would be duty bound to provide it. But there is one lucrative exception to this rule. While criminals or outlaws are immediately offered *nanawatai*, sanctuary does not come free of charge. Instead, a means of regular payment has to be procured to help preserve a protected status. *Melmastia* and *nanawatai* confer many advantages exploited by outlaws and tribesmen alike. They are also tribal customs that provide the political authorities with a degree of protection. During routine liaison visits, the political agent, seen as a disinterested arbitrator, is welcomed as a guest and afforded hospitality and free passage in tribal territory. Such hospitality appears to contradict the tribesmen's inclination for raiding. But this is not the case. Guests allow the tribal headman to demonstrate his beneficence and offer the possibility of friendship, a valued commodity in Pathan social culture.[21]

Another central component of the code is the autonomy of the adult male. A Pashtun considers himself to be wholly independent and self-governing. Such self-determination is not just physical. Psychological, spiritual, and economic freedom is also engendered within the broad parameters of *Pashtunwali*. Likewise, the code also permits an individual to pursue material gains and honor. Notwithstanding such unrestricted freedom, individual parity remains an overarching tenet. No matter what his circumstances, a Pashtun has equal social status to his fellow tribesmen. Likewise, leadership is a loose and temporary concept in the eyes of the tribesmen due to the egalitarian nature of tribal politics.[22] It has to be continually created and re-created by dialogue and power-broking and is largely dependent on the character and charisma of an individual. Moreover, authority in Waziristan is subdivided and less dominant than other tribal societies, relying more on clan, sectional, and subsectional leaders than headmen. To maintain his fragile position, a tribal headman (known as a *malik*) is required to demonstrate his personal qualities and ability to procure and distribute resources from outside the tribal territory. To help him achieve this task, the *malik* relies on *nikat*, a nonnegotiable law of tribal division. This aspect of *Pashtunwali* dictates the division of each tribal clan and subsection, even of each family, in all tribal profit and loss.[23] But as Sir Olaf Caroe points out, the code goes beyond simple profit and loss: "It determines the position of the head of every family in relation to the other families. It was, and indeed remains, a tribal family tree, of which every main branch, every lateral and sub-lateral branch, is known to everyone down to the last twig and even to the last bud."[24]

Failure on any account could lead to a chief's rapid downfall. Richard Bruce recognized the individualist nature of the Pashtun in the late 1880s when he stated, "Pathans are so much more democratic [than the Baluches] and not so amenable to the authority of their chiefs."[25] Unsupported, a headman was unable to enforce authority over the tribe and was often compelled to follow in the path of the headstrong. An unpopular decision could carry the ultimate penalty. This reality contributed to years of conflict as the British found it difficult to negotiate with a tribe where *maliks* could not implement a decision. However, there were occasions in which order and control could be placed upon the tribesmen to achieve a desired effect.

> Maliks of Asad Khel were called for. Brigadier Marshall made a condition that at the first sign of sniping of Damdil Camp, Asad Khel would be shelled. The *maliks* did not approve and offered to build their own sangar [protective stone wall] and to man it in order to stop the tribesmen if they came to snipe. The Brigadier reiterated his position. The *maliks* were horrified. They protested strongly, stating their sangar was the very best they could do. The *maliks* departed shaking their heads. But the fact was that Razcol [the brigade at Razmak] spent 22 nights in Damdil and not a single shot was fired into it from the surrounding hills.[26]

*Nang* tribes reject headship beyond the control exercised by the tribal elders at an assembly or parliament, known as a *jirga*. Used as a means to resolve civil, criminal, and intertribal conflict, a *jirga* is a highly democratic and egalitarian process. Traditionally possessing neither a dominant leader nor chairman, participants sit in a circle in order to avoid a prominent position and decisions are reached through dialogue and consensus. For larger *jirgas*, *maliks* occupy the front row of the circle and dominate proceedings with their tribesmen seated behind them. A *jirga* of a larger tribal unit may consist of over a hundred *maliks* with many thousands of tribesmen in attendance. A *jirga*'s construct permits an individual or a nominated elder's voice to be heard and is a transparent means to prevent conflict through consensus and compromise. The art of the discourse is securing the most agreeable outcome while preventing an opponent gaining more than his fair share. The council remains in session until all tribesmen are convinced or until it becomes clear that consensus will not be forthcoming. Even when an influential person or commander has emerged, decisions of importance for the tribe are reached at a *jirga*; the process is rarely usurped. Once a verdict has been articulated, it is binding for every tribesman. If a tribesman defies the findings of a *jirga*, his house is summarily burned down.[27] Colonel Sir Robert Sandeman's account of a *jirga* highlights the egalitarian nature of tribal regulation.

> On that occasion the representative of tribes or sections of tribes at deadly feud with each other sat quietly side by side; each speaker rose and expressed his own views with greatest earnest, but briefly and to the point; he was answered by another, who spoke with equal earnestness and brevity, and so on to the end; there was no interruption and no disorder, and one left the meeting with the impression that assemblies in other parts of the world might well learn a lesson of business-like and orderly conduct of debate from a Pathan *jirga*.[28]

*Jirgas* were also a controlling authority used by the government. The political agent or assistant political agent held regular "allowance *jirgas*" in tribal areas. These events happened biannually. For serious occurrences, bespoke *jirgas* were instigated. These often resolved complex issues that, unless handled sensitively, could have had serious consequences. A case in point is the surrender of Bahram Khan, a notorious Mahsud rebel, and the destruction of his fortified house by fire. A positive outcome occurred as a result of a *jirga* between the commanding officer of the Wazir Division and the Makin Mahsud in June 1937. It was requested of the commanding officer, having indicated that he intended to destroy Bahram Khan's house in consequence of his hostile activities, that the Makin Mahsuds be allowed to destroy his house. In addition, the *jirga* granted authority to secure the outlaw's surrender.[29] Almost without exception, an internal tribal solution was preferable to a costly government action.

For more routine matters, *jirgas* were an informal and lighthearted affair.[30] Heckling and long diatribes, drawing on tribal proverbs and anecdotes, were customary practice. Discourteous interruptions also occurred from those who sought to interrupt proceedings or felt angered by an outsider's presence. On rare occasions intersectional bickering led to a loss of temper or bloodshed.[31] Political agents recognized that the tribesmen had to be argued into agreement and this required patience and tolerance. Issuing direct orders was poorly received and led invariably to tribesmen walking away from the *jirga*. Moreover, the democratic character of the tribes, especially the Mahsuds, meant that the *jirga* had little control over the lawless elements and therefore was not truly representative of tribal opinion. However, incessant talking, while exhausting to listen to, proved to be an excellent source of local intelligence.[32] But such events were often an unnerving experience. Tribesmen arrived heavily armed with weapons and knives that had to be deposited prior to the start of proceedings, and some, "incredibly enough," had British army medal ribbons pinned on their waistcoats in recognition for service with the scouts on the frontier and in the Great War.[33]

Despite such control measures, tribesmen were left relatively unchecked to peruse individual aims and objectives. As Geoffrey Moore summarized: "Politically, they [the tribesmen] were largely anarchists in that they paid no more than lip service to the *maliks* and reserved their more attentive ears to the *fakirs* [a holy man] when *jihad*, or holy war, was being preached."[34] But as Moore highlights, there was an exception to the rule. Despite the routine limitations of a lack of strong central leadership, the tribal chain-of-command was sufficiently mature to permit control of *lashkars* (a tribal armed force) during times of crisis. On such occasions, a headman was selected and obeyed unreservedly. Religious leaders, often playing on the feelings of the tribesmen and promising paradise to those who fell in battle, proved to be the most successful in uniting the tribes. James Lionel notes in 1898 that "wherever Islam is the creed there will be found disciples prepared to preach its cause and to fire the undercurrent of feeling which forms part of this weird belief."[35] Fanatical rhetoric, linked to Islam, proved to be a strong and cohesive rallying call. The capability of these tribal war parties implies that in certain circumstances tribesmen subordinated themselves to an agreed command structure and acted on orders. *Lashkars*, often numbering thousands of armed and fanatical tribesmen, were required to execute complex tactical maneuvers over difficult terrain. Such unity and subordination to a common cause was generally a result of an external threat or the prospect of a defensive war. The intrusion of infidels into tribal territory was a regular catalyst for tribal mobilization.

Furthermore, *Pashtunwali* requires compliance to Islam although the relationship between the two is complex and ambiguous. F. Yeats-Brown notes in *Martial India* that "the Pathan from the North-West Frontier Province is always a Moslem (although not always a good Moslem)."[36] As a rule, the tribesmen of Waziristan are predominantly Sunni Muslims. Although religious and tribal codes coexist, there are conspicuous differences between the *Sharia* (Islamic law) and *jirga* systems. To cite just one example, *Sharia* does not recognize the Pashtun habit of wife inheritance, in which a widow is forcibly married to her dead husband's brother or cousin. So while fiercely religious, Pashtuns have historically preferred their leaders and by-law to be tribal. Additionally, Pashtuns are inflexible on the issue of spiritual purity, tracing their lineage back to the origins of Islam.[37] As such, the tribesmen are assiduous in offering their daily prayers and are regarded as deeply religious. But spiritual purity does not negate the influence of superstitions on daily life. Pashtuns are inherently credulous and will often believe in implausible stories. Superstitions were not belittled or ignored by the authorities. Sir Walter Roper Lawrence notes, "I have seen so much in India of what we in England would call the supernatural, that I have an open mind . . . that in that land of enchantment there is indeed more than is dreamt of in our philosophy."[38]

Yet despite paranormal beliefs, the tribesmen paid close attention to their spiritual clerics. There are two basic types of religious leaders in Waziristan. The first is the *mullahs*. They enjoy an elevated status, operate the village mosques, lead the daily prayers, supervise religious education, and conduct rites of passage. However, should tribal territory be threatened by an outside power, *mullahs* possess sufficient influence to marshal resentment by preaching a *jihad*, or holy war. The *jihad* is a religious duty, but it was by no means a fait accompli that the *mullah*'s rallying call would unite the tribesmen in response. The tribesmen were sufficiently astute to separate personal interest from religious fervor. However, *jihad*'s call to arms was appealing to certain segments of tribal culture. It also proved to be a unifying bond that could instill cohesion on both sides of the Durand Line. Disaffected tribesmen often turned to their *mullahs* for direction, and their existence proved to be a menacing influence that countered British attempts at pacification. It was not uncommon for *mullahs* to raise a *lashkar* to besiege and burn the fortified enclosure of a headman too closely associated with the government. One such religious firebrand who gained notoriety was Mullah Powindah, a Shabi Khel Mahsud.[39] From 1898 until his death in 1913, Mullah Powindah instigated insurrection, encouraging attacks on militias and police posts, ambushes of convoys, the murder of British officers and officials, and the incitement of fellow-Mahsud sepoys in the militia.[40] Described by Lord Curzon as "a first-class scoundrel," his antigovernment stance was not unique. The official report of operations against the Zakka Khel Afridis in 1908 notes that "the mullahs dwelling in tribal territory as well as in Afghanistan are, by reason of their fanatical inclinations, ever prone to stir up strife against an alien Government."[41]

The other types of religious leaders are the *sayyids* and *mians*. They enjoy an elevated and pious standing amongst the tribesmen. Believed to be directly descended from the Prophet Muhammad, these holy men are understood to possess abnormal spiritual powers. Held in high esteem, *sayyids* and *mians* act as mediators in disputes and have a key role to play in tribal *jirgas*. Two additional hybrids are found in Waziristan: the *pir* and the *fakir*. A *pir* is a man who has studied religion under a holy man and has excelled to the point of attaining a divine status. A *fakir* is a *mullah* who has gained prominence as a spiritual leader and miracle worker.

Supposedly God-inspired, a *fakir* is also distinct, as he cares nothing for material possessions or power and endures extreme austerity. "Such men usually live off alms [donations] and often stayed within the precinct of a holy man's tomb."[42] There is no clear dividing criterion that establishes a *mullah* as a *fakir*. Charisma, a loyal following, and broad approbation all have a role to play. Unless branded by the tribesmen, a *mullah* was left to decide if he had the right attributes to claim an elevated status as a *fakir*.

One *mullah* who attained this unique distinction was a Tori Khel Wazir named Mira Ali Khan. Better known as the Fakir of Ipi, he declared a *jihad* in 1936 and for the next twelve years organized Pashtun resistance and guerrilla warfare against the British until their departure in 1947. Despite concerted efforts, the *fakir* eluded all British attempts at capture by exploiting successfully many tenets of the Pathan code of honor.

Without making reference to the code of *Pashtunwali*, Sir Richard Temple, secretary to the Punjab government, provides a valuable, if unsophisticated, summary of the general character and approach of tribesmen:

> They have nothing approaching to Government or Civil institutions; they have for the most part no education, they have nominally a religion, but Mahomedanism, as understood by them, is no better, or perhaps is actually worse, than the creeds of the wildest races on earth. In their eyes the one great commandment is blood for blood, and fire and sword for all infidels, that is, for all people not Muhammadans. They are superstitious and priest-ridden. But the priests (Mullahs) are as ignorant as they are bigoted; and use their influence simply for preaching crusades against unbelievers, and inculcate the doctrine of rapine and bloodshed against the defenceless people of the plain.[43]

For many on the frontier, such an assessment—gained from fleeting encounters and superficial newspaper reports or hearsay—seemed to portray accurately the anarchistic and brutal tribesmen. Subtlety, nuance, and a reflection of the tribesmen's advanced state of democracy was often played down or ignored. Likewise, little meaningful distinction was made between the tribes, their clans, and subclans. Far from being a disorganized and homogeneous grouping, tribal society was advanced, coherent, and diverse. To help understand the character of the region, it is important to recognize the difference between Waziristan's tribes.

## The Tribes of Waziristan

Waziristan is populated by a small number of geographically dispersed tribal groups. These tribes have fought hard to maintain their independence and to avoid centralized authority. A lack of social contact and administrative control has resulted in a populace who "remain tribal in the most profound sense."[44] The principal tribe in the region is known as the Wazirs. Frank Leeson, one of four British officers seconded to the North Waziristan *kassadars*, recollects:

> It is not easy to like the Wazir. He takes a lot of knowing. He is a complicated simplicity. If he is young he wears a flower behind his ear—though his country is a desert, and coryllium in his eyes—yet he is by no means effeminate. He loves fighting but hates to be a soldier; loves music but has a profound contempt for the professional musician. He is hot-blooded and hot-headed, poor and proud.[45]

Subdivided into four hostile clans, the Wazirs were assessed to have a combined fighting strength of 56,000 tribesmen in 1912.[46] But not all these tribesmen were armed due to a shortage of weapons. Their tribal territory stretches between the Kurram and Tochi Rivers, Wana District, and the Gomal Valley. In addition, a number of prominent groupings live across the border in Afghanistan, mainly Gurbaz Wazirs, and a small number of tribesmen migrate routinely into eastern Afghanistan during the summer months. In contrast with other tribes on the North-West Frontier, Wazirs developed an agreement whereby internal feuds or vendettas were noticeably reduced. As opposed to avenging a murder by killing a family or tribal member associated with a suspected perpetrator, Wazir practice allowed only revenge against the actual culprit. This controlling measure prevented spiraling blood feuds among the members of the tribe and assisted in maintaining a degree of tribal cohesion and order. But despite such practical measures, tribal society was dominated by fear and violence.

Hot-headed, brave, and fierce-looking, the principal clan of the Wazirs is the Darwesh Khel. Its members are seminomadic in temperament and their dwellings were often of a temporary nature. They possessed few permanent villages or settlements. "Many of them migrate annually from their native hills in the autumn to the Bannu district in British territory, and return to their homes only after the severe winter of their inhospitable upland country, softening into spring, enables them to find pasture for their flocks and herds."[47] The Darwesh Khel made their living by raising sheep, goats, and cattle. The tribesmen are generally deep-chested and compact, although some tall and well-built men are to be found amongst them. A number possess pale blue eyes. Physically, they are strong, athletic, and robust. The Darwesh Khel is a hardy, belligerent tribe that remained relatively integrated and cohesive. There are a number of further subdivisions in the Darwesh Khel. The most prominent are the Ahmedzais (or Wana Wazirs) and Utmanzais (or Tochi Wazirs). The Ahmedzais live close to the border in South Waziristan and around Wana. The majority of the tribe journey every autumn with their flocks to the grazing lands on the western borders of the Bannu District, "returning in the spring to their summer settlements in the Wana and Shakai plains."[48] The Utmanzais live primarily in the north and consist of a number of subsections; the three main ones being the Madda Khel, the Kabul Khel, and the Tori Khel.

The second most important clan in Waziristan is the Mahsuds. This grouping occupies the hills between Thal in Miranzai and the Gabar Mountain and has centers of population near Kaniguram and Makin. Their austere location is attributed to their subordinate ancestry to the Wazirs. In contrast with other tribes, the different clans (Alizai, Bahlolzai, and Shaman Khel) and subclans of the tribe often lived together in the same remote area. For centuries their inaccessibility has been a major factor in their security and a central aspect of their independent nature. It also made them one of the most hard-line tribes in Waziristan. It is therefore unsurprising that Captain H. L. Nevill describes them as "the most daring and accomplished freebooters on the whole of the North-West Frontier; their hands may, indeed, be said to be against all men, and the hands of all men against them. They are united in themselves, but are ignorant and unscrupulous at the same time."[49] It is notable that one of Lieutenant Colonel de Watteville's main lessons from the Waziristan Campaign of 1919–1920 is "the extraordinary aggressiveness of the Mahsuds."[50] However, Sir Olaf Caroe highlights a different facet of the Mahsuds' character:

And yet, outside the office, on the hillside or upon the road, there is no happier companion. Who does not remember the farewell tea-parties when men who had made your life a burden for months and years all at once crowd round with fervent hand-clasps, and, bidding you God-speed—could it be with a tear in the eye—make you half believe that after all the burden was worth carrying.[51]

The principal occupation of the Mahsuds was a combination of agriculture, trade, forestry, mining, small-scale manufacture, and incessant raiding.[52] As the Mahsuds controlled access to the Gomal Pass, raiding the nomadic Powindah caravans that passed through its narrow confines proved to be a lucrative and regular source of income. But the Mahsuds faced a number of internal disputes due to *tarburwali*, which was outlawed or mitigated in other tribes. This aspect of *Pashtunwali* makes a correlation between paternal relatives (*tarbur* is the term for a first cousin) and an enemy or rival. As a result, the Mahsuds experienced constant internal strife and disruption due to the frequency of blood feuds between individual tribesmen, close relatives, and sections. Constant domestic bickering and endemic feuding contributed to their reputation as a turbulent, fanatical, and quarrelsome tribe. Such was their repute that no border military police sepoy would shoot a Mahsud. Instead, the sepoy would fire his rifle with the purpose of deliberately missing the target. Likewise, few were arrested for fear of retribution.

Mahsuds were also renowned for taking advantage of a situation or preying on a weaker neighbor. "Inevitably the Mahsuds had taken advantage of our pre-occupation elsewhere from 1914 onwards. The entry of Turkey, as another Muslim state, had inflamed their passions and they became a thorough nuisance with raids into British India."[53] They were also adept at encouraging other tribes to join their cause. In 1919–1921, when the British government occupied Razmark, and in 1929, when Nadir Khan took Kabul, the Mahsuds, while fulfilling the lead role, were occupied by considerable *lashkars* of Wazirs.

In comparing the Wazirs and Mahsud, Charles Trench expanded on Sir Olaf Caroe's analogy when he wrote:

Wazirs and Mahsuds are related, but were seldom on good terms except when up to something which had no relish of salvation in it. Wazirs were semi-nomadic, Mahsuds more settled, but neither could make much of a success of cultivating their stony soil; they found it easier to make a living by trading, easier still by raiding. The Wazirs had been compared to a leopard, a loner, cunning and dangerous; the Mahsud to a wolf, most to be feared in a pack, with a pack-mentality, single-mindedness and persistence. Even among Pathans the Mahsud is notoriously treacherous, something that he himself will not deny.[54]

The third most populous tribe is the Bhittanis. Small in number, these rugged tribesmen inhabit the eastern and southern slopes of the hills between the Gabar Mountain and the Gomal Valley close to the flatlands. They also populate a number of small hamlets on the Marwat border. This tribe possessed many warlike attributes but was more civilized than the Mahsuds.[55] The tribe consists of three subclans: the Dannas, Tattas, and Warshpun. Owing to their limited numbers the Bhittanis were rarely able to mount large attacks alone although they contributed contingents to *lashkars* and were supportive of other tribes in times of crisis. Routinely, they served as guides or agents for their dominant neighbors. "In 1853, however, tired of their usual role of jackals, they undertook the part of the lion, and attacked and plundered two villages within British territory, in retaliation for the death of a brother of one of their chiefs, killed by the police in a plundering excursion."[56] Characteristically, Bhittanis maintained herds (often grazing their sheep and cattle in British territory) and conducted limited trade with border villages.

The final tribe of note is the Dawar. Although Pashtu is their common language, the Dawar are not seen as true Pathans and have a very poor reputation for courage.[57] This tribe is located in the Dawar Valley west of Bannu and occupies the banks of the Tochi River. Containing three clans, the Tappizad, Idak, and Uraspan, the Dawar were reported to be morally the lowest of the tribal races. "Nevertheless they are diligent, hardworking, and patient cultivators, and, though unwarlike by nature, have often resisted successfully attempts by their neighbours to oust them from their rich lands."[58] However, they were not the most hygienic of tribesmen. "To call him [the Dawar] dirty would be a compliment; his clothes, usually of black cotton to start with, are worn till they would be considered malodorous."[59] Despite an aversion to grooming, Frank Leeson recalls that they were "fanatically religious and priest-ridden."[60]

Waziristan's tribesmen and their independent culture posed a significant challenge to the administration. Ironically, British social behavior on the North-West Frontier found identifiable parallels in the tribesmen's sense of honor and courage. Life was seen and defined by the commonly accepted principles of winning fairly and losing admirably. However, Akbar Ahmed argues that such a view was one sided. "No such symbols of Frontier romance or nostalgia are visible among the tribes themselves. It is essential to underline that this is a one-way nostalgia. Pathan tribes saw the encounter as extra-ethnic, extra-religious and, in many cases, extra-savage."[61] Ultimately, the British lacked a common Islamic faith and were viewed as infidels.

## An Insoluble Problem?

Waziristan is a complex, outwardly dysfunctional, and seemingly anarchic environment. Western logic and rules of behavior do not apply to the Pathan tribesmen. Isolated by an intimidating collection of mountains and valleys, the terrain provides a natural barrier to physical incursions from the flatlands to the east. Centuries of seclusion at the periphery of civilization have helped engender in its inhabitants a fierce independence and stubbornness that balks at foreign influence or occupation and rejects many of the perceived benefits of civilization. The inaccessible terrain also provides a safe haven for criminals and fugitives who seek sanctuary within its vastness, protection from its inhabitants, and use its fortress-like qualities as a base to conduct raids. Waziristan's remoteness is reinforced by a severe and debilitating climate. Extreme summer temperatures combine with harsh winters to thwart agriculture and restrict routine movement. Raiding was the main recourse to address food shortages in a land short of fertile tracts and devoid of regular precipitation. Forays into the fertile Bannu basin below were used also for political purposes and as a means to secure modern weapons, riches, and material. These illegal activities brought the tribesmen into conflict with the villages they raided and the wider British administration. Raids were a key factor that helped aggravate the extreme poverty of the region. They were also an expression of tribal identity.

Its inhabitants, a tough and diverse array of obstinate tribes, owed allegiance to no one, rejected centralized leadership, and engaged frequently in hostilities against each other. They joined forces only occasionally to expel a threat to tribal territory or to respond to a call to arms under a religious banner or *jihad* in the name of Islam. Quick-tempered, autonomous, and courageous, the tribesman was a proficient foe and a skilled guerrilla fighter. Due to centuries of continuous fighting and biannual migration, they possessed an instinctive knowledge of the terrain and an innate tactical competence. But fighting was not the tribesmen's sole occupation. Describing the activities of the Mahsuds, Hugh Beattie posits that "[the tribesmen] divided their time between farming and robbery, while others rarely if ever took part in raids at all."[62] They were also a mobile and transient population unrestricted by the constraints or expectations of modern government. Seminomadic in nature, the legal border of the Durand Line posed no barrier to a populace who transited regularly the precipitous transborder region on ancient routes. Far from seeing themselves as primitive and archaic, the tribesmen were proud of their unique heritage and tribal groupings. They saw few benefits to an existence under British governance.

> A civilisation has no other end than to produce a fine type of man. Judged by this standard the social system in which the Mahsud has been evolved must be allowed immeasurably to surpass all others. Therefore let us keep our independence and have none of your qanun [law] and your other institutions which have wrought such havoc in British India, but stick to our own riwaj [custom] and be men like our fathers before us.[63]

The tribesmen also remained convinced of their elevated social standing, well-structured genealogical ties, and advanced democratic state. But such an insular and fragmented society was also susceptible to religious affronts, outside influences, and internal discord. *Pashtunwali*, the binding contract of the Pashtun, underwritten by the tenets of pride and honor, codified tribal expectation and contributed significantly to the volatility and impulsiveness of the region's inhabitants. In such a highly charged social environment, misplaced actions could turn swathes of the populace irrevocably against an intruder. In Waziristan, enemies were easy to make but difficult to lose.

The region's ethnic character and nonnegotiable rules of behavior frustrated British attempts at pacification. Tribal, clan, and subclan behavior was notoriously difficult to predict, and its inhabitants lived within an atmosphere of latent violence and constant uncertainty. In consequence, tribal dwellings were fortified and the carriage of arms was essential for self-protection. The cost of life in Waziristan was inexpensive and a tribesman's honor was offended easily. Any affront was defended ruthlessly and no insult went unchallenged. Blood feuds, often executed with severe brutality, were commonplace. Disagreements were also self-perpetuating and a constant threat to tribal stability. But such a culture of arms and hostility was routine to the inhabitants of Waziristan. Villages were drilled at combating raids, and tribes were proficient at mobilizing quickly to negate outside insults.

Once formed, tribal *lashkars* were capable of acting with a high degree of tactical competence and executed complex actions routinely. Those who chose to stay behind were considered cowards and ostracized by their fellow tribesmen. British authorities knew better than to underestimate the danger of a tribal *lashkar.* In a society that respected bravery, there was significant personal and tribal kudos to be gained by confronting the British administration. The possession of modern long-range rifles, a symbol of prestige, afforded the tribesmen an accurate means to execute their activities. Despite initiatives to restrict the flow of rifles into tribal territory and measures to mitigate their employment, the region was blighted by a burgeoning arms race that began with rifles and extended to crude artillery.

Waziristan also faced an array of contemporary issues that challenged tribal order. Influences from the flatlands below, due to relatively uninterrupted contact through trade, resulted in a growing economic dependence on the Bannu basin. Education, the growing availability of modern medicine, and a greater demand for material goods from the Indian Subcontinent also posed a dilemma for a society that was inherently suspicious and reluctant to embrace new ideas. Internal divergence was unavoidable and the friction between convention and the advances of modernity were often difficult to rationalize. But in a society dominated by age-old tradition, tribal lineage provided an invisible bond that helped combine dispersed clans and subclans together against an external foe. The defense of tribal society, often fueled by religious fervor, was a strong rallying call to a heavily armed people who rejected outside influences and cherished their independence. Not unexpectedly, Milan Hauner comments that "it is certainly no exaggeration to describe the Pathan tribes as the largest known potential reservoir of guerrilla fighters in the world."[64] It is unsurprising also that many rank the Pathans among the finest fighting men in the world.[65] Preventing the situation in Waziristan from reaching boiling point was the responsibility of the government and its frontier policies.

# 3

# Securing the Frontier: Politics, Policy, and Tribal Realities

> Ever since the British had come face-to-face with the problem of the Frontier tribes in 1849, it had been accepted policy that the major fighting tribes—Buners, Swaits, Yusufzais, Mohmands, Mahsuds and Wazirs—could only be administered at arm's length, by tacitly recognising their independence and by not interfering with them all the time they stayed within the limits of their territory.
>
> —Brian Robson, *Crisis on the Frontier*, 2004

## Strategic Defense and Tribal Control

The mountainous North-West Frontier was a constant concern to the political authorities. Stretching from the Sulaiman Mountains and Gomal Pass in the south to Chitral and the Pamirs in the north, this region contained approximately 2.5 million Baluchi and Pathan tribesmen. But while the defense of India remained paramount, there was another distinct problem with which to contend. Border management and the security of the frontier districts provided an equally complex challenge that shaped British policy. The immediate challenges of tribal control frequently eclipsed the threat of Russian advances, especially for those charged with controlling the trans-Indus territory. Unavoidably, Imperial defense and tribal management often competed.[1]

To help understand the dynamics of the North-West Frontier it is essential to look back to earlier times. The capture of the Sindh in 1843 and the annexation of the Punjab on 29 March 1849 advanced the British administrative boundary across the River Indus to the hills bordering Afghanistan and Kalat.[2] Ethnically, linguistically, and geographically, this new territory posed significant challenges to the administration. Major W. S. R. Hodson recalls: "You may imagine the turmoil and unrest of this eventful time; but I defy you to imagine the confusion of the process which converts a wild native kingdom into a police-ridden and civilian-governed country."[3] Despite numerous practical challenges, company advances were well received by the agricultural tribesmen of the Indus plain, who were keen to see the removal of the barbaric Sikh rule. However, this was overshadowed by a menacing reality. The British presence in the region was a constant provocation and temptation to the heavily armed hill tribesmen across the administered border. Looting forays into villages and towns on the flatlands below and attacks against trading caravans would bring the tribesmen and company into regular conflict.[4]

Establishing a presence on the frontier and understanding the means by which control was exercised under the Sikhs was important. Soldiers and political officers found the remote border regions punctuated by a string of isolated forts. Under Sikh rule, each was occupied by a chief — often referred to as a "robber chief" — whose private army collected revenues from the surrounding areas. Collin Davies notes: "Under the Sikhs, the Hindu borderers held their village lands under a ghastly system, known as the "Tenure of Blood": as yearly rent they had to hand over a hundred Pathan heads."[5] This savage approach motivated a frenzy of religious revulsion and nationalism in the local tribesmen and prohibited any chance of peaceful development.[6]

Likewise, the Sikhs attained little durable influence in the hazardous regions adjoining their territory. Their only means of collecting revenue in the mountains was to conduct annual expeditions against the hill tribesmen. Akin to their approach on the flatlands, the methods employed were barbaric and uncompromising. But unlike the plain below, resistance was fierce, fanatical, and uncompromising. In accordance with *Pashtunwali*, the hill tribesmen engaged in continuous fighting against the Sikhs in order to protect their independence. It is unsurprising, therefore, that Philip Woodruff summarizes that "the coming of the English instead of the Sikh was, then, a pleasure as positive as the end of tooth-ache."[7] However, with the arrival of the British, the hill tribesmen soon made it clear that they had no inclination to renounce their predatory habits. Moreover, as Michael Barthop suggests: "They may have welcomed the chance to pit their strength and wit against the new masters below them." Certainly border incursions became an almost everyday occurrence.[8]

The annexation of the Punjab presented additional challenges. British advances brought the administration into regular contact with the *khan* of Kalat, the ruler of Baluchistan, and the *amir* of Kabul. Each relationship demanded a bespoke policy, or treaty, to maintain regional stability. Against such a challenging backdrop, frontier strategists wrestled with identifying India's most favorable line of defense. "From the earliest days of the British connection with India there have been two opposing forces at work, a forward tendency, and a policy which sought to restrict, or to prevent, growth."[9] Supporters of a forward tendency advocated a policy of active expansion to the natural barrier of the Hindu Kush. This would result in parts of Afghanistan (including Herat) being brought under British control. Militarily, this conferred a number of advantages. However, it was also recognized that any expansion northwest would be challenging. To be coherent, any permanent advances would require the development of a strategic railway link, the delineation of an advanced Afghan-British frontier, and the subjugation of the tribes. Despite the high cost of their proposals, such moves were seen by many as essential for India's long-term security and as an investment in imperial profit.[10]

Champions of a noninterventionist or stationary policy were opposed to the occupation of any territory beyond the Indian frontier. This was attributable to a strong desire to prevent a needless recurrence of the 1842 retreat from Kabul. This incident engendered a strong sentiment against interference beyond the limits of existing British control. But there were other supporting factors to consider. The unbreakable fanaticism and indomitable spirit of the hill tribesmen remained key. Likewise, the difficulty of fighting in mountainous terrain and the expense of maintaining British garrisons in tribal territory were both valid arguments. With such a bipolar and emotive argument, any policy that would satisfy one approach would anger the other. Fierce debate centered around four so-called lines of resistance.[11]

The first line of resistance was the prominent north-south divide of the River Indus. Historically, this was the frontier between India and central Asia and was one of two natural obstacles in the region. It was also the boundary of Hinduism's influence. This was favored by the noninterventionists and was supported by Lord Lawrence, who in 1864 was appointed viceroy and governor general. He advocated meeting any invader in the Indus Valley as they left the mountain passes but was opposed to any permanent forward locations beyond the River Indus. However, using the river as a boundary was criticized by those who viewed a withdrawal to this natural feature as a loss of prestige and a betrayal to those who extended British rule at considerable cost.[12] Other commentators questioned the merits of passive defense on the wideopen plain, suggesting that the mountains were more preferable barriers in which to construct and execute a robust defense against an invading force. Similarly, some expressed concern over the "unhealthiness" of the Indus Valley and questioned its suitability as a permanent location to concentrate European troops. Lord Curzon points to another shortcoming of the River Indus: "The Indus was not a natural frontier to the Punjab, because Indian peoples, as distinct from Pathans or border men, inhabit the further as well as the nearer bank of the river."[13] Despite these realities, the proposal possessed one appealing benefit; the longer distance an invading army had to march through Afghanistan and the tribal areas, the more harassed and mauled he would be by the tribes who would be resentful of any intruder.

The second proposed line of resistance was the "old Sikh line." This matched the administrative boundary inherited from the Sikhs but left unrestrained practically the whole of the mountainous tribal areas to the west. It was recognized that adopting this line of resistance would be costly in terms of manpower and materiel if it were to be effective; it would require the permanent employment of forces west of the Indus River and demand the construction of an extensive road network linking military outposts. This proposal faced a number of concerned critics. Lord Roberts, a former commander in chief, 1885–1893, speaking on frontier defense in the House of Lords forty years later, cautioned that "a frontier more than one thousand miles in length, with a belt of huge mountains in its front, inhabited by thousands of warlike men, . . . seemed to me then, as it does now, an impossible frontier, and one on which no scheme for the defence of India could be safely based."[14]

The third proposed line of resistance was the so-called scientific frontier or perfect frontier. This sought to balance ethnological, political, and military requirements. Practically, it aimed at identifying the best line of defense against a Russian invasion. It was agreed that the most appropriate line would stretch from Kabul through Ghazni to Kandahar, the old Moghul frontier. "It was pointed out that this was shorter and could be more easily converted into a line of defence than any other frontier we had held, or that could be suggested. Neither the right nor the left flank could be turned, for the northern was protected by an almost impenetrable maze of mountains, the southern by an equally impassable desert."[15] Although the proposal was never given any serious consideration, the scientific frontier had many advocates. A strong promoter was Lord Lytton, the viceroy of India from 1876 to 1880. However, it was a title that caused a degree of confusion and was misused often.[16] By 1901, the notion of a scientific frontier was still under consideration, but its interpretation had changed significantly since its conception.

There was a great statesman, for whom I [Sir Richard Temple] have the utmost respect, who said that the frontier was unscientific. But for once he was wrong. Sir Thomas Holdich has shown us that the frontier is scientific as regards the geology, the plateaux, the plains, the natural barriers, the strategic points. Surely that is a scientific frontier, designed by nature herself the great teacher of science.[17]

The final line of resistance was an arbitrary topographical line from North Gilgit to Koh-i-Malik Siah. In 1893, nearly fifty years after annexation, this was demarcated as the Durand Line, which divided the tribal areas uniformly between Afghanistan and British India.[18] This afforded no strategic value to either side but would require a significant military effort and considerable expenditure, particularly in attempting to resolve the tribes' economic problem. Its supporters argued that this would solve the security problem once and for all. Its dissenters suggested that the area was so vast that its occupation and pacification was unrealistic with available resources.

Selecting a line of resistance was not straightforward; economics, political opinions, and strategy all pointed in different directions. However, the driving factor that fashioned frontier policy in the mid-1800s was the British approach to the region's defense. It was decided that India's protection against Russia would be achieved by diplomatic and conciliatory initiatives, not military might. Russian advances toward

Afghanistan were to be checked by establishing a strong and united Afghanistan.[19] This, it was hoped, would serve as a "buffer state" against foreign aggression. By means of an annual subsidy, together with gifts of modern weapons and ammunition, attempts were made to secure a hard-wearing and lasting alliance with the *amir* of Afghanistan. While far from faultless, this approach proved to be a pragmatic solution to an intricate problem. To complement this policy, the boundary settled upon came to be known as the "administrative border," based on the vaguely defined ethnographical divide of the old Sikh line. Theoretically, this marked the westernmost limits of British control and the beginning of Afghan authority. The policy adopted on the border became known as the close border policy.

## The Close Border Policy

The British executed a close border policy from the annexation of the Punjab in 1849 until the outbreak of the Second Anglo-Afghan War in 1878.[20] The chief advocate of the policy was Lord Lawrence, who regarded the entire frontier region as a dangerous liability that demanded discretion. In 1855, Lawrence observed to Lord Nicholson, deputy commissioner of the Dera Ismail Khan District, that "in the hearts of the Government and the Commander in Chief there is a mortal dread of going into the hills, and should any misfortune occur, a fine howl they would open on us."[21] To avoid the "mortal dread" of the mountains, the close border policy restricted activities to the "administered border" and sought no extension of the geographical areas under its control. All land to the west of the theoretical border was under Afghan rule. But the reality was far from clear-cut and no one exercised real authority over the territory.[22] The region was a no-man's-land "where knife and bullet spoke the law."[23] The policy allowed for the self-determination of the majority of hill tribesmen, on the far side of the theoretical divide.

The policy was based on two central tenets: nonaggression on tribal territory and noninterference in tribal affairs. It aimed to consolidate newly acquired territorial gains, instigate law and order, and institute tacit control over a handful of vital passes. It sought also to protect British subjects from the heavily armed and predatory tribesmen. In this respect, the administration believed that "in theory at least the innocent should not suffer from the crimes of the guilty, cruel punishments should be avoided, and officials should deal consistently with the tribes."[24] To meet these demands, it became apparent that some measure of influence would be required west of the border. With limited resources and no political will for further territorial advances, there were few options available but to manage the tribesmen by remote means.

The hands-off approach of the close border policy was reflective of an administration occupied with the daunting task of developing an effective rule of law inside the border. It was equally symbolic of an overt aversion toward the Pathans. In the mid-1800s, the tribesmen were seen as "absolute barbarians ... avaricious, thievish and predatory to the last degree."[25] Major J. Jacob uses equally stark language when recounting the tribes. He describes them as "mere vulgar, criminal, and disreputable persons with whom it is a disgrace for right-minded people to have any dealings."[26] The accepted view was that such dangerous enemies were better confined and left at arm's length. The policy recognized also that it would take time to "pacify" and "civilize" the tribesmen. The regions' poverty and traditions were seen as powerful obstacles to any form of rapid cultural and social transformation. Therefore, throughout the 1800s the contrast between the administered border and tribal areas remained pronounced. It was hoped that this disparity would close in time. But this failed to materialize.

In line with a policy of noninterference, the administration rejected local requests to intervene in intertribal fighting across the administered border, which continued largely unabated during the period. In the eyes of the British, this was a tribal or Afghan responsibility to resolve. However, intertribal fighting conferred an unexpected benefit on the frontier, highlighted in the case of the Darwesh Khel Wazirs.

> During the next few years the Darwesh Khel Wazirs gave but little trouble on our border. They were engaged in carrying on a tedious war in the independent hills, beyond the frontier, with the other great branch of the Wazirs—the Mahsuds. The feud had no injurious effect on the border administration, but rather the contrary; the occupation of these predatory tribes in internecine strife tending to withdraw their attention from plundering in British territory.[27]

In spite of the frontier's strategic significance and the challenge of the tribes, only limited resources were available to achieve policy goals.[28] A shortage of available units, limited capital, and conflicting priorities called for local and novel solutions to controlling the region.

To help maintain order, an indigenous force was established in 1849 to protect the trans-Indus areas. This was known initially as the Trans-frontier Brigade but was retitled the Punjab Irregular Force (PIF) on 15 February 1851. The force finally became known as the Punjab Frontier Force (PFF, nicknamed the "Piffers") in 1865 and was a combination of volunteers from an assortment of border tribes and remnants of the Sikh army. G. F. MacGunn notes that "it was raised on the old border plan of 'set a thief to catch a thief,' on which the original Black Watch [a Scottish infantry regiment] was raised."[29] Consisting principally of artillery, cavalry, and infantry units, the force also included the Queen's Own Corps of Guides, which guided regular units in the field and provided local intelligence. Units were complete in equipment and transport. They were also held at a high state of readiness and were able to react rapidly to tribal incursions without calling on the army.[30] In total, the force amounted to approximately 8,900 men. There were also a number of police regiments, organized by battalions, and irregular levies.[31] This security initiative provided a useful by-product. Increased opportunities for lucrative military employment reduced the region's high levels of unemployment and poverty.

To oversee the frontier the British constructed a robust chain of military strongholds along the foothills, known as frontier posts. These isolated posts were located at critical points along the administrative border dominating the main routes and passes into tribal territory. Forts were reinforced by detachments of troops at vital points who were responsible for a portion of the frontier. The aim of this fortified chain was to discourage illicit tribal activity on the plain. They also provided a means to intercept and pursue illegal raiding gangs. Large fortified posts were constructed at Kohat, Bannu, Dera Ismail Khan, Asni, and Dera Ghazi Khan. Major W. S. R. Hodson was responsible for the construction of one such post.

> In addition to the very onerous command of 876 wild men and 300 wild horses, and the charge of the civil administration of a district

almost as lawless as Tipperary, I have had to build, and superintend the building of, a fort to give cover to the said men and horses, including also within its walls three houses for English officers, a police station, and a native collectors' office.[32]

Despite the sighting of these forts, it was recognized that a militia force was incapable of performing regular duties. To conduct punitive actions in tribal territory a regular force was kept in reserve.[33]

It was acknowledged that the frontier could not be controlled by military action alone. Therefore, conciliatory measures were introduced to promote peaceful coexistence. These were designed to demonstrate the advantages of British rule. Free medical treatment was provided in frontier hospitals, and metaled roads were constructed from the passes to the bazaars to facilitate commerce. Tribal products were promoted and commercial dealings encouraged. In addition, a small number of low-echelon clerical jobs were made available. Tribesmen were permitted to cross the theoretical border for the purposes of peaceful activities, and wasteland was offered to families, free of charge, wishing to cross the border to settle.[34] These conciliatory measures fell short of convincing the tribesmen they had a tangible stake in British India. However, they did go some way to reduce the abhorrence formally prevailing between the Sikhs and the tribesmen and to reduce the number of illegal raids across the administrative border.

Trying to promote tribal trade in the frontier bazaars was far from straightforward. As one commentator notes, "Market towns were governed by fat volumes of municipal codes. Taxes were levied in accordance with a revenue act that could almost have been drawn up for England. But these burdens of complexity were mild alongside the farce of equal justice."[35] The British judicial system, with its predominantly Hindu lawyers, and the Chief Court at Lahore, was unsuited to the complexities and nuance of tribal customs. Lord Roberts recalls, "Legal technicalities and references to distant tribunals confuse and harass a population which, with comparatively few exceptions, is illiterate, credulous, and suspicious of outside influence."[36]

In 1872 various special regulations, known as the Frontier Crimes Regulations, were introduced to frontier districts to supplement the actions of the regular courts. These gave the courts the power to remove routine tribal cases from the ordinary courts and submit them for adjudication by a *jirga*. Influenced by *Sharia*, the usual punishment for crimes was the payment of financial compensation.[37] For more severe crimes, a custodial sentence of up to fourteen years imprisonment was available. The Frontier Crimes Regulations legalized the use of a number of traditional methods of tribal management and was the means by which the majority of economic and other pressure was exercised.[38] It also gave the political officer authority which could not be undermined in a court of law.

To help pacify the region, the authorities sought to settle entire villages or groups of tribesmen in British controlled territory. An illustrative case in point is the attempted relocation of twenty Bahlolzai Mahsud families on a tract of wasteland to the south of the Gomal Valley, by Major S. F. Graham, deputy commissioner of the Dera Ismail Khan District, in 1865. Despite initial reservations by the tribesmen, the proposal grew more attractive as the benefits became apparent. The land offered was rent-free for ten years, militia service for twenty-five Mahsud horsemen, under the Nawab's control, was guaranteed, and the authorities were prepared to advance Rs. 5,000 on the scheme to assist in routing water to the land.[39] Such was the enthusiasm for the offer that 120 tribesmen arrived uninvited in Tank in 1865, only to be turned away as the government officials were not prepared for their arrival. In spite of this initial setback, during the winter of 1866–1867, approximately twenty families of Mahsuds settled on the land.[40]

Such relocation schemes possessed a number of practical drawbacks. It was costly to resettle tribesmen and their families. Proposals for larger initiatives were more expensive than the authorities could afford. Moreover, hopes that fellow tribesmen would follow suit without the benefits of a financial inducement proved erroneous. Equally, relocated tribes often returned to their previous habits. In the case of the Bahlolzai Mahsud families, they were well behaved until early 1867, but toward the close of the year, "some heavy cases of plunder of camels occurred."[41] Failures in the scheme were generally attributable to two factors: the fierceness of the tribe and the distance that the tribesmen were relocated from their original habitat. The closer the distance, the easier it was for the tribesmen to return to their old habits.

The tribesmen west of the border were not left to their own devices entirely. Influence and indirect control occurred via the deputy commissioners of the settled districts. As a general rule, written agreements (often referred to as treaties) were put in place to promote security, although few of the headmen were literate in the tribal territory in the mid-1800s. To overcome language and cultural difficulties, the deputy commissioners dealt with the tribes neighboring their districts by means of Pashtun intermediaries (often referred to as middlemen or go-betweens). They also encouraged tribal *jirgas* to occur in British territory to settle disputes. *Jirgas* became the principal means to enforce tribal accountability for the outrages committed by an individual, clan, or tribe. Although the aspiration was that the innocent should not suffer for the crimes of the guilty, the reality was poles apart. Collective tribal responsibility sat at the core of the British approach to tribal management west of the border. Each tribe or clan was made responsible for any outrages committed by members of their sections.[42] However, there was nothing original or morally incorrect about this approach in the 1800s. Sir John Slessor notes, "It was universally recognised by the tribesmen themselves as a basis of tribal existence."[43] Sir William Barton reinforces this position, pointing out that "it is their own custom, not a British invention."[44]

To dissuade the tribes from raiding the plains, the authorities issued fines to secure compensation for plundered property and blood money for lives lost. In the event of nonpayment, hostages were seized and detained until damages had been paid. Hostages (known as *barampta*) were seldom punished for the errant behavior of their fellow tribesmen. However, D. S. Richards suggests that "tribesmen taken into custody on suspicion of being brigands and subsequently released for lack of evidence would sometimes meet with a fatal accident."[45] Such incidents appear exceptional. Nevertheless, the experience of captivity was far from pleasant. Privileges were often withdrawn and simply removing the tribesmen from their mountainous retreat—for example, to Lahore—proved to be punishment in itself.

The policy did, however, permit forces to cross the border for the purposes of a blockade, known as a *bandish*.[46] Correctly executed, and under the right conditions, blockades were successful at starving the tribesmen into submission. They also created less resentment and hostility in comparison to other more kinetic methods; blockades were unlikely to incite the tribesmen or lead to a desire for revenge. For example, the 1878 cordon of Mahsud territory drew considerable praise from the Indian government and resulted in the whole Mahsud tribe adhering to British terms. W. H. Padget recalls, "This blockade demonstrated what a powerful engine of coercion such a measure was against the Mahsuds for the redress of all ordinary border crime."[47]

But blockades in complex and rugged countryside were often difficult undertakings. "To be completely successful the blockading force must be in possession of the approaches to the country; they must be able to sever the arteries of trade and supplies; and must have the support or friendly co-operation of the tribes. From this it becomes apparent that the success of a blockade is largely determined by geographical conditions."[48] Such conditions rarely existed, and a number of blockades were unsuccessful, while few were without leaks. Moreover, blockades were often slow to take effect on the tribesmen. For example, one government blockade of the Mahsuds lasted three years, from 1879 to 1881. This eventually caused the Mahsuds to submit and comply with British demands in September 1881. The time taken for some blockades to become effective suggests that several tribes were self-sufficient in the bare necessities and not completely dependent on British territory.

In order to demonstrate military strength and present an appearance of prestige, reprisals, known as punitive expeditions, were sanctioned by the government. Between 1849 and 1878 the British mounted forty expeditions.[49] These were viewed as the simplest and most inexpensive method of pacifying the tribesmen. In all cases, a heavily armed force was deployed into tribal territory to exact retribution. On a case-by-case basis, artillery, cavalry, engineers, and infantry were grouped into a balanced force for a particular operation. The smallest of these expeditions could consist of a battalion size or less.[50] More usually, the force consisted of one or more brigades. Units from the Punjab Frontier Force frequently conducted expeditions without British reinforcement. For example, in 1860, Brigadier Sir N. B. Chamberlain, the commandant of the Punjab Frontier Force, commanded a force totaling 5,372 in a campaign against the Mahsuds, and his entire force was composed of native troops and tribal levies.[51] However, larger expeditions often necessitated the support of British units.

Expeditions were routinely accompanied by a political officer. He was responsible for any negotiations with the tribal headmen and had a pivotal role to play in proceedings, being directly accountable to the deputy commissioner. For example, Chamberlain's 1860 force was accompanied by the commissioner of Darajat, Lieutenant Colonel R. G. Taylor, and the deputy commissioner of Dera Ismail Khan, Captain H. W. Cox. However, the relationship between the military and politicals was not always harmonious. It was often said that the political officer stood between the soldier and his medal. Moreover, although the political officer made the decisions to conduct offensive operations in tribal territory, the commander of the military force was ultimately held responsible for its success. Friction over civil or military primacy often resulted in strained relations.

R. I. Bruce points to the core of the problem. "The trade of a soldier is soldiering, and when all are eager for active service, and to win promotion, honours, and medals, it is not always as simple a matter as it might appear for the Commander to brush these natural inclinations all aside to enter on the unpalatable and arduous labour which I have shown to be inseparable from the manipulation that would make a settlement with these tribes on peaceful lines practicable."[52] Winston Churchill, who served with the Malakand Field Force, provides additional weight to this argument: "We had with us a very brilliant political officer, a Major Deane, who was most disliked because he always stopped military operations."[53] Such authority and standing did not go unnoticed by the tribes.

Expeditions were sanctioned by the political authorities only after all other methods of border control had been exhausted. Even then, requests were refused. This was often due to the unavailability of personnel and resources. But other factors played a role. An absence of political will, the fierceness of the tribe in question, and concerns over the indiscriminate and brutal nature of military action in tribal territory constrained expeditions. There were also natural factors to consider. Severe climatic conditions or the difficulty of the mountainous terrain were also contributing aspects. These often resulted in initial proposals having to be reconsidered or amended. It often took a number of attempts to gain approval for an expedition. As a result, friction existed between the perceived necessity for an immediate reprisal versus the benefit of waiting for an opportune moment to conduct military operations. However, delays could be beneficial. There were certain times of the year when punitive expeditions could achieve the greatest effect on the hill tribesmen.

> Regarding the best time for operations, the Commissioner [of Kohat] said there were two seasons when the tribe would be peculiarly open to punishment, *viz.*, at the beginning of winter and in the spring; more real injury could be inflicted in the winter, more apparent in the spring. A force proceeding against them at the former season could carry off their winter stores, and compel them to retreat to the higher hills. In the spring the crops could be destroyed upon which the tribe is dependent in the summer.[54]

The importance of the harvest was not lost on those who served on the frontier. Tribesmen were reliant on their crops to survive the harsh winters. It was well known that raiding slowed over harvest time. W. S. Churchill notes that "by gentlemen's agreement, the energetic routine [of raids] was interrupted each year at harvest time."[55] But there were other practical reasons to support a hold-up. Many units were unprepared for frontier warfare, and a delay permitted a regular force to move to the frontier, train, and balance itself prior to an expedition.

Expeditions were often preceded by a warning to the tribe in question. This was the responsibility of the political officer and followed a regular format. Before advancing, a proclamation was addressed to the chief in question. This announced the object for which the government forces were about to enter their hills. It also told them that, within a fixed period, they were free to visit a specified camp for the purpose of hearing the demands of the government.[56] Failure to visit the camp or to agree to the terms resulted in punitive action. The main object of an expedition was the punishment of "accumulated crimes" committed by the hill tribes against the law-abiding tribesmen of the settled districts. This was well known and "the tribes calculated that they could go a long way before patience would be exhausted."[57] The standard form of chastisement resulted in the destruction of prestigious tribal watch towers by explosives or artillery fire, the cutting of crops, and the burning of villages. In addition, wells were poisoned and dams breached. The confiscation of livestock was also common.[58] When the tribe submitted, they would be expected to pay a heavy fine and surrender a quantity of modern weapons. Such activities were often violent and uncompromising affairs. Losses inflicted on the tribes were heavy. Recounting an expedition against the Dawris in March 1872, the official report notes:

> The 1st Sikh Infantry stormed the closed gates of the village and effected an entry, driving the inhabitants to the north corner, where for some time they made a stand behind some high-walled houses. The 1st and 4th Sikh Infantry having obtained entire possession of the left portion of the village set it on fire. The 1st Punjab was then brought up and sent to the right flank of the village to aid the cavalry in cutting off the retreat of the villagers. The fire and the determined bearing of the two Sikh regiments was soon too much for the defenders of the village, and, abandoning their position, they fled towards the plain, only to find themselves surrounded. The cavalry were speedily down upon them and sabred ten of their number, when the rest, seeing that all was lost, surrendered.[59]

Expeditions were also mounted to prevent incursions and to collect fines. In October 1880 an expedition occurred to collect fines and penalties totaling Rs. 13,200 from the Kabul Khel and Malik Shahi Wazirs. The fine resulted from a number of minor offenses, including the theft of property and cattle. A robust force consisting of 2 guns, 250 cavalry, and 500 infantry, under the command of Brigadier General J. J. H. Gordon and accompanied by Major T. J. C. Plowden, the political officer, departed on the night of 27 October. The aim of the expedition was to seize men and cattle of the Malik Shahi section as security for their share of the fine. Arriving with complete surprise, after making a significant detour to avoid the large Bangash village of Biland Khel, the force detained 2,000 head of cattle and 109 prisoners. The force returned to barracks on 28 October with no incidents of note. As an official account recorded, "On the 30th the Kabul Khel *jirga* attended at Thal and made their submission and by the 18th of December the whole fine of Rs. 13,200 was realized from the Kabul Khel and Malik Shabi sections; the prisoners were then released, and Rs. 6,000 taken as security for future good behaviour."[60]

Despite the fine, the conduct of the Kabul Khel Wazirs continued to be disagreeable. Drawing on support from other tribes in the Bannu region and a number of outlaws, they committed a series of raids in 1881.

In some of these they succeeded in securing large herds of Powindah camels. But in the majority of raids they were unsuccessful, the stolen cattle being recovered in pursuit.[61] In February 1882, the deputy commissioner summoned the Kabul Kels to Kohat to attend a *jirga*. At the *jirga* fines were imposed for their unlawful activities, and for a time the conduct of the section was tolerable. But this was short-lived and the Kabul Khel Wazirs, like so many of the other tribes, continued to be a regular problem for the administration.

## Mixed Results and Strong Condemnation

The practical realities of the close border policy meant that the system faced many well-informed critics. Lady Balfour summarized the crux of the issue when she wrote that while doing little in the way of putting "our relations on a better footing, we injure a whole tribe for the vicarious punishment of an individual."[62] Lieutenant Colonel C. E. Bruce noted that "the politicians in the Punjab had been sitting before those mountain ranges in Waziristan for years and did nothing but indulge in countless expeditions, which were really 'burn and scuttle' affairs which subdued the tribe or tribes concerned for a time, but were unable to prevent a return to lawlessness as before."[63] Highlighting the shortcomings of the policy, Richard Bruce suggested that the strategy was inappropriately named, the border being closed only on one side: "On our side it was in a measure closed; our officers were forbidden to go beyond the red line, our troops were forbidden to patrol beyond the mouths of the passes, and even parties in hot pursuit of robbers were cautioned against following them up into the hills."[64] In contrast, the tribesmen were uninhibited from crossing the border into the settled districts. This feature of the policy did little to prevent raids into British territory, causing grievous loss of life and damage to property. The policy was unsuccessful also in providing a practical means to obtain an adequate redress for any crimes committed. Criminals recovering to the mountains were rarely brought to justice. Moreover, the tribes had few means of realizing an imposed fine, unless secured through further looting of the flatlands below, or they found it difficult to meet imposed timelines. Large fines often remained outstanding.

Unsurprisingly, the policy had few supporters from the inhabitants of the settled districts. "They naturally disliked and despised a policy that could not effectively protect their lives and property."[65] Many blamed the government for the frequency of unrestricted violence across the region. "Tribal factions and inter-tribal feuds still went on beyond our border, leaving the wilder spirits a free hand to plunder the plains; quarrels about irrigation or sex still led to outrages in British territory; blood-feuds with British subjects were still rife on the frontier, leading to acts of vengeance."[66]

Lieutenant Colonel C. E. Bruce is particularly barbed in his disapproval of the policy: "At any rate, there is no gainsaying the fact that the history of the Frontier is a long succession of failures on the part of the Close Border Policy. Why? Surely because it failed so completely to fulfil the supreme test—the welfare of the tribes."[67] Sir George Dunbar is equally as critical of the policy in *A History of India*: "The only form of tribal responsibility attempted [in the close border policy] was the seizure of men and property of the tribe to which the offenders belonged; and the criminal code enforced on Pathans under British administration was the criminal law of England, modified to some extent, but holding murder as a capital offence." It is significant that Dunbar explores his idea further, stressing that "the Pathan, with his universal blood-feuds, takes a lenient view of murder, and his tribal law aims at redress instead of punishment. The imposition of standards looked upon as imperative in western civilization on a people who have never understood them and who might otherwise have been controlled through their own tribal law and procedure, created the outlaw who escapes from British India over the border, and has been the direct or indirect cause of numerous expeditions in reprisal for border crimes."[68] Such strong criticism was not unfounded. The semi-independent tribal hinterland constituted a perpetual menace to the tax-paying subjects of the settled districts. Likewise, the administrative border failed to provide a coherent line of resistance to protect the British subjects from the marauding tribesmen or their political discontent.

Expeditions, in particular, drew widespread condemnation. This was principally due to their brutality and viciousness. For example, the 1860 expedition against the Mahsud Wazir resulted in the death of three hundred Mahsuds, including six leading *maliks,* and many more wounded.[69] To negate such heavy losses, the tribesmen became increasingly disinclined to fight in a conventional manner and discarded systemic opposition. Instead, they turned to guerrilla tactics and became an elusive and difficult prey. As a result of superior surveillance and an effective tribal warning system, villages were often found empty by an expeditionary force. Without tribesmen to extract retribution, "[entire] villages were destroyed in a few hours. Towers were blown up here and there, and the cave strongholds were purified and disinfected with gunpowder."[70] This uncompromising approach all too often chastised the innocent, including women and children, rather than the guilty. Due to the destruction of tribal crops, villagers often faced starvation after a raid. But there were more long-term disadvantages associated with such activities. Expeditions engendered a lasting legacy of hatred and contempt against British rule.[71] They also united the tribesmen and encouraged Britain's enemies that there was considerable resistance to British rule. F. D. Cunningham notes that "it is profitable to remember that there is a certain freemasonry amongst clans of the North-West Frontier; even those who are too distant from the scene of any expedition to think of joining at once in hostilities against us begin to take some form of interest in the fate of a fellow Pathan community when they hear of the occupation of new tracts of country."[72] Likewise, no genuine attempts were made to transform the tribesmen of the hill-tribes into peaceful inhabitants or to provide them with a viable alternative to raiding. Destructive reprisals, while militarily successful, failed to produce any lasting results and a continuum of violence ensued. "The relationship between troops and tribe was one of punisher and punished; it could hardly develop into more," notes Philip Mason.[73] Similarly, the tribesmen were unwilling to bow to the superiority of the government's military strength. Instead, they used dishonesty and treachery to undermine British activities. Without permanent authority or jurisdiction in tribal areas to reinforce initial military successes, there was little hope of any lasting results. At best, many expeditions had only a temporary effect.[74] Tribesmen were only preoccupied with rebuilding villages and acquiring new rifles for a finite period of time; they returned quickly to their old predatory habits.

There were also practical concerns regarding waning British prestige resulting from a rapid extraction from tribal territory after an attack on a village. A period of consolidation could have addressed this unease.

However, it would have been costly in terms of additional expense and manpower. It was recognized that any temporary presence in tribal territory provided an appealing opportunity for other tribesmen to practice their fighting skills against a worthy opponent.[75] But there were other considerations to take into account. The frequency of expeditions also possessed an unhelpful side effect, exposing the tribesmen to British tactics, techniques, and procedures. General Skobeleff, a Russian general, observed, "By incessantly attacking them [the tribesmen], you teach them the art of war."[76] Moreover, it became clear that to disaffect the tribesmen was counterintuitive to a policy that relied increasingly on the hill tribes and frontier as a "strategic buffer." It was not in the best interests of the authorities to alienate the tribesmen's amity.

In addition, expeditions were expensive and time consuming. R. I. Bruce posits: "I have not the means to make an estimate, but Government can do so, and if they will calculate what the punitive expeditions which have taken place on the frontier since and including the Umbeyla campaign have cost the country, and strike a yearly average, the result will show a vast sum of money."[77] While expenditure was important, there was another factor to consider. Expeditions were also costly in terms of injury and loss of life. Many of these resulted from extremes in temperature and endemic diseases. Sickness was widespread among the younger and unseasoned troops. But more routinely they were a result of fierce fighting.

In 1852, an expedition against the Darwesh Khel Wazirs, led by Major J. Nicholson and consisting of 1,500 troops, resulted in 28 British casualties. Only four years later, an expedition against the Mahsuds led by Brigadier Sir N. B. Chamberlain involving 6,796 troops resulted in 361 British casualties. But not all expeditions resulted in large-scale violence with high casualty figures. Others were more passive affairs with few casualties on either side. The 1881 expedition against the Mahsuds, led by Brigadier T. G. Kennedy and comprising 8,531 troops, resulted in only 8 soldiers killed and 24 wounded.[78] Moreover, not every expedition resulted in casualties. For example, the 1880 expedition against the Kabul Khel Wazirs, led by Brigadier J. H. H. Gordon and involving 800 troops, resulted in no British casualties. But the balance sheet was not in favor of the government. Philip Woodruff summarizes that "in terms of lives, labour and goods, the punishment [expeditions] had cost the Queen's Government more than the tribe."[79]

While not always successful, expeditions did confer a number of advantages. Tribes were forced to recognize that even their secluded valleys did not protect them from reprimand; nowhere was beyond British reach. Expeditions were also used as a means of displaying British strength and had a symbolic aspect attached to them. A punitive force on the march was an intimidating sight. Moreover, it was hoped that punishing one tribe would deter the others. Likewise, attacks against rebellious tribes provided a unique training ground for ambitious British officers.[80] T. A. Heathcote notes, "As far as the military men were concerned, it was no bad thing to have a frontier where a state of virtual warfare was in existence."[81]

Expeditions also exerted a civilizing influence on some tribesmen. This was particularly true of the smaller tribes, a number of whom submitted to British demands without significant incident and turned their energies to more peaceful pursuits. Moreover, some blockaded tribes, fearful of an expedition against them, were eager for government forces to maneuver with intent in tribal territory. This provided an honorable excuse to submit to British demands.[82] But while it may have been preferable to pursue other initiatives to pacify the tribesmen, few bore fruit. It is unsurprising that some considered the hill tribesmen so intractable that there was no alternative to the use of force. Captain H. L. Nevill concludes his 1912 book, *North-West Frontier*, by stating that "the surest way of bringing the Pathan tribes to reason is the same now as it always has been, namely, by the infliction of loss in battle that the great tactical objective is still to close with the enemy as soon as possible, but that this end has a tendency to become more and more difficult of attainment."[83]

Another serious failing in the policy was that political officers, being forbidden (or certainly discouraged) to cross the border, had to depend on intermediaries or middlemen to influence the tribesmen and control trade. A number of these were ambitious individuals who gained undue influence and power. Others encouraged discontent or double-dealing that led to bloodshed between the authorities and tribesmen. Lieutenant Colonel C. E. Bruce highlights the shortcoming of the initiative: "It can, therefore, well be imagined what enormous opportunities this system gave the middlemen for intrigue and for amassing wealth."[84] Much of the money spent on allowances remained in the pocket of the middlemen. "Several families in this way have achieved unmerited opulence."[85]

Sir Robert Warburton, political agent to the Khyber from 1882 to 1896, was equally critical of the use of middlemen. He deemed middlemen a more frequent cause of trouble than even the *mullahs*.[86] None but the tribesmen chosen by the middlemen could gain access to the political officer, and then only on payment of a generous bribe. But this negative attitude was not shared by all.

R. I. Bruce acknowledged that many condemned the employment of middlemen, but he suggests that this was a mistake. He remained determined that positive results could be achieved by controlling and directing all the operations conducted by middlemen.[87] This was easier said than done. For example, the British installed Shah Nawaz Khan (the son of a former ruler and known as the Nawab of Tank after 1859) as an intermediary in the city of Tank to mediate with the tribes of Waziristan. Shah Nawaz Khan possessed many attributes that endeared him to the tribesmen; he had connections with the Mahsuds, possessing a Mahsud wife and mother, and was a respected agent with an objective and evenhanded temperament. Despite this, his overall performance was mixed during his twenty-year tenure. His rivals in the settled districts harassed him and prompted the hill tribes to conduct incursions for the purpose of undermining his reputation and discrediting his position. Shah Nawaz Khan was hamstrung also by a lack of financial and military resources to consolidate his role.[88]

It also remained uncertain if the employment of middlemen was too remote an initiative to effect positive change in the behavior of the tribes. Thomas Thornton queries the rationale of this "overcautious" constraint: "These restrictions, suitable enough at the time they were imposed, became, as time went on, not only uncalled for, but positively detrimental to our interests; they tied the hands of the district officers, and effectively checked the growth of political influence among the trans-border tribes."[89] George W. Gilbertson points to another practical shortcoming: "That we cannot address him [the tribesman] in his own language, and deal with him direct without the help of middlemen, he attributes to either of two reasons, incapacity to learn his language, or indifference to him, his people and his affairs."[90]

During 1872–1878 several important initiatives were implemented to address policy and practical shortcomings. To improve personal contact between officials and the hill tribesmen, civil officers were required to pass an oral examination in either Pashtu or Baluchi. Deputy commissioners were provided with additional staff to allow them to spend more time with the tribesmen. The Nawab of Tank, having failed to prevent the incessant raiding activities of the Mahsuds, was relieved of his duties and replaced by Major Charles Macaulay. The militia of the Darajat, a locally raised force reinforcing the Punjab Frontier Force, was recognized formally to improve its effectiveness. Members of the militia, who had become too old for arduous service, were removed from post.[91] But despite these initiatives, the fact remained that to be successful at tribal management, political officers required training, experience, and a detailed knowledge of the tribes. This was to prove challenging.

> The result is that officers possessing the essential seniority, knowledge, and experience in tribal matters prefer posts of more ease and less responsibility; so that junior men, who cannot possibly be expected to conduct complicated and delicate negotiations efficiently, have to be appointed—a cruel experiment on the tribes, on whom the brunt of our shortcomings and faulty management in the long run inevitably falls, as well as being prejudicial to our prestige and rules on the frontier.[92]

Likewise, R. I. Bruce posits that a shortage of honors and decorations handicapped frontier administration during the period. He notes that within those awards few were bestowed for peaceful tribal management alone, and the great majority were bequeathed in connection with punitive expeditions.

> In short, under the present system of frontier civil officers who for whatever cause is obliged to take over the reins of his tribal administration to the military authorities, and take his seat behind the General commanding the troops, is just as likely, if not more so, to receive honours from obtaining intelligence, collecting supplies for the forces, and such like duties, as he would be by a continuance of quiet, peaceful and successful tribal management . . . Such a system virtually affords a premium for bad management, and is, to say the least of it, demoralising.[93]

Therefore, successful tribal management could consign the officer concerned to political oblivion.

In keeping with the dynamic and unpredictable nature of the frontier, British policy was about to change. In the summer of 1878, Russia dispatched an unsolicited diplomatic mission to Kabul. Unwittingly, this set in motion a series of events that led to the Second Anglo-Afghan War (1878–1880). The British invasion of Afghanistan provoked Amir Sher Ali Khan to encourage the Mahsuds to attack Tank, which they did to great effect on New Year's Day 1879. After a brief collapse of British authority, the government instigated a blockade and demanded the payment of a fine and for the Mahsuds to hand over the instigators. The blockade was slow to take effect, and it was not until September 1881 that the tribe finally submitted to government demands. But the Second Anglo-Afghan War had far-reaching effects on the dynamics of the entire frontier. The British government signed a treaty with Amir Abdur Rahman that gave Britain control of Afghanistan's foreign policy and control of the key passes. In return, Britain would protect Afghanistan against foreign aggression. A new frontier policy was necessary.

# 4

# The Forward Policies: British Influence, Political Control, and the *Maliki* System

There can be no government without an army,
No army without money,
No money without prosperity,
And no prosperity without justice and good administration.
— Ibn Qutayba, ninth-century Islamic scholar
writing on the "Circle of Justice"

## The Forward Policy

In 1874 a new conservative government in Britain, headed by Benjamin Disraeli, determined to take a firmer stance on the border areas. Hastened by the campaigns of the Second Anglo-Afghan War, the British adopted a forward policy from 1879 to 1901. The forward policy was based on the recommendation of a strategic committee, formed after the Second Afghan War, to identify the approach to be adopted if Russia intervened in Afghanistan. The committee recommended that the Indian army should push its border as far forward toward Afghanistan as possible, meeting the Russians on militarily advantageous terms.[1] The report was embraced by the new viceroy, Lord Lansdowne, and supported by the conservative government.[2] This made the permanent presence of government forces inside tribal territory inevitable. Despite a newfound desire for active expansion, few underestimated the magnitude of the challenge during the period.

The forward policy sought to extend British influence and political control into tribal territory with a view to establishing law and order.[3]

But indirectly, it bred suspicion and British intentions appeared ambiguous. It failed also to negate the necessity for controversial punitive expeditions that continued to be a regular feature of tribal management. Sir William Barton notes, "Punitive expeditions were essentially still as they had always been—expensive, time consuming and lacking in the element of surprise."[4] But expeditions were not the only bone of contention. A direct strategy of intervention in tribal territory was also a constant catalyst for civil disobedience. Arthur Swinson posits, "[the forward policy] was to generate more heat, more controversy, more bitterness, than any other Indian policy in the nineteenth century."[5]

In the early days of the policy, government ambitions were limited. Troops garrisoned strategically valuable terrain that belonged to the tribes, and roads were built to allow rapid movement throughout the frontier to foil any potential aggression. These ran through the Khyber and Kurram valleys. Between 1890 and 1897 the policy grew in momentum. Advanced posts were built on the Samana Heights above Kohat, and in the Gomal, the Tochi, and the Kurram valleys. In addition, garrisons were established in the Malakand and Chitral.[6] These initiatives coincided with the payment of government subsidies for route security, intended to provide a lever to apply pressure to the tribes, and the establishment of levies from various tribes.[7] By the time all forward locations had been constructed and manned, approximately 10,000 British troops were situated in fortified posts beyond the administrative border. Such forward deployments were seen by the tribesmen as a preface to an enduring assault on Pashtun identity and tribal independence. They also led to deterioration in relations with Amir Abdur Rahman, who interpreted these advancements into tribal territory as a threat to his influence along the frontier. As a result, he incited the frontier tribes to rise up against the British.[8]

To placate the situation with the *amir*, Lord Lansdowne came to the conclusion that the best way to deal with the problems of the frontier was to negotiate a line that would mark the edge of British and Afghan authority, providing a clear limit to administrative responsibilities. After a number of complications, the *amir* agreed to receive a diplomatic mission headed by the secretary to the foreign department, Sir Mortimer Durand. Following prolonged negotiations, a border was agreed upon on 12 November 1893. Martin Ewans, a former head of chancery in

Kabul, notes, "The Amir was reluctant to accept the agreement, which detached many of the eastern Pushtoon tribes from his dominions, but was persuaded to agree when his annual subsidy was increased from 1.2 million to 1.8 million rupees, and he was assured that he could freely import arms and ammunition."[9] The Durand Line enclosed within British territory the lands of Chitral, Bajaur, Swat, Buner, Dir, the Khyber, Kurram, and Waziristan. In the case of the latter, the general objects of the arrangement that the government of India wished to effect in Waziristan seemed uncontroversial:

> Our desire has to carry the tribesmen with us in whatever we do, and to interfere as little as we can with their internal affairs, provided only that our obligations are discharged in protecting our posts and that the general caravan route, and in affording to those sections and leading men of the tribes who have thrown in their lot with us by co-operating in the coercion of turbulent characters and the punishment of murderers and robbers, that protection which they deserve and without which they cannot maintain their position.[10]

The Durand Line resulted in British political influence extending over an additional 26,000 square miles and an estimated 2.5 million tribesmen.[11] But many in the Afghan government failed to recognize the theoretical divide as a legal frontier and continued to view the Indus River as their eastern boundary. The line also brought into question the status of tribal territory. General Sir Kenneth Wigram notes, "I personally have no dispute in my mind that both parties, and probably the world in general, recognised that in fact the settlement constituted tribal territory as British territory and the tribes as British subjects."[12] The hill tribesmen had acquired a legal status; unwittingly, they became British protected persons.

Despite political agreement and the employment of a large force for security, the physical demarcation of the Durand Line proved problematic. It took until 1897 for the task to be finished. Even then, a number of stretches of the border remained only partially signed with pillars and cairns. Unsurprisingly, many tribesmen viewed this new boundary line as an affront to their independence and were confused by the border's necessity; physical markers were vandalized or destroyed and tempers flared. This was despite a series of *jirgas* that assembled to listen to the Indian government's intentions.[13] The Durand Delimitation Commission was attacked on numerous occasions, but most notably at Wana on the night of 2 November 1894. During this attack, the British lost twenty-one killed and thirty-four wounded. There was an additional forty-three casualties amongst the camp followers. The assault resulted in a punitive expedition in December 1894, under the command of Lieutenant General Sir William Lockhart, which smashed Mahsud villages and defenses.

There were other challenges associated with the Durand Line that affected tribal behavior. The line failed to recognize ethnographical and topographical factors on the frontier. Sir Martin Ewans suggests that tribes and even villages were divided.[14] Frank Leeson provides an equally critical view: "It is a vague sort of boundary, sometimes following watersheds and sometimes not, sometimes following ethnological divisions and sometimes not. There is the same mountainous tangle of country on both sides of it, and nowhere is there anything, artificial or natural, to tell you when you have reached it."[15] The Durand Line also put an end to any hopes of stretching Afghanistan's frontiers to the Arabian Sea and placed the main passes in British hands.

But while the Durand Line helped appease the situation with the *amir*, there were other internal border issues to address. The Second Anglo-Afghan War called into question the payment of *muwajib*, or tribal allowances.[16] These were paid direct to *maliks* for maintaining local security, refusing sanctuary to outlaws, road construction and maintenance, and as recompense for the elimination of long-established tribal tolls. Tribes also received allowances to maintain freedom of movement. For example, the Madda Khel were paid for keeping open the caravan track through their country, and the Mahsuds were subsidized for permitting the use of the Gomal Pass. Indirectly, they were used also as a means to highlight that the tribe lived under imperial government. "But now the question came to be asked: were the allowances what they pretended to be, or were they a form of disguised blackmail?"[17] The government defended the payments as realpolitik. However, the reality was that the tribesmen had become skilled in the art of extortion.

There were other serious shortcomings with the tribal allowance system. As the government wanted to pay money to the tribes in a transparent and evenhanded manner, it was necessary to do so by means of the tribal shares ratio. As a result, disobedient tribal sections were paid larger stipends than obedient sections.[18] Milan Hauner summarizes the realities of the allowance system: "As a result of their dealings with the authorities on both sides of the Indo-Afghan border, the Wazirs and other Pathan tribes had, rightly or wrongly, come to the conclusion that the shortest cut to lucrative allowances was not through loyal service, but by occasional demonstrations of their nuisance value."[19] Predictably, the troublesome Mahsuds received the greatest amount of subsidies. In contrast, the Bhittanis and Dawar, both subject to land tax, received the lowest allowances. The imbalance was stark.

## *The* Maliki *System*

In the late 1890s, a new scheme of tribal management was experimented with on the troublesome Mahsuds in Waziristan. This was known as the *maliki* system. The policy was instigated by R. I. Bruce, the commissioner of the Darajat. Bruce was influenced by the example of Sir Robert Sandeman, who, as deputy commissioner of Dera Ghazi Khan in 1866, pursued a tribal policy involving peaceful association in tribal affairs in Baluchistan. Sandeman succeeded in negotiating an agreement by which the Khan accepted the authority and ascendancy of the British government in Baluchistan, in exchange for assistance and routine security. Alfred C. A. Lyall posits that "the subordinate chiefs willingly accepted a settlement that put an end to incessant civil war, faction fighting, and misrule."[20] Sandeman's approach was based on steady and unfaltering conciliation, combined with personal interaction. It was reinforced by a range of tribal subsidies for undertaking militia duty. His objective was the "gradual civilization and betterment" of the tribes.[21] Bruce attempted to introduce into Waziristan the system that had proved successful in dealing with the transborder tribes of Baluchistan.[22] This policy exercised control through tribal chiefs and traditional organizations, allowing the government to pressure certain individuals within the tribe to influence the actions of others. The policy also permitted tribal leaders to attain the results desired by the government in their own way. But as Sir Olaf Caroe summarizes sagely, "In other words, it was the principle of indirect rule."[23]

Bruce's approach was based on three tenets. First, certain *maliks* were elected and subsidized by him, not by the tribe, and were graded according to their believed authority and influence. Second, these *maliks* were expected to produce a defined number of tribesmen for service as levies. These were paid for by the government but were regarded as tribal servants. Finally, in return for allowances, the *maliks,* supported by the levies, were expected to regulate tribal behavior and surrender offenders to justice. The *maliki* system attempted to make the tribesmen accountable for their actions. Its strength lay in trying to punish the actual culprits of crime, not the whole tribe. As such, its proponents believed that the approach was ethically superior.

But trying to transpose Sandeman's approach in Waziristan was far from straightforward, and in time the experiment proved to be a failure. Collin Davies notes:

> It seems to me that Bruce made three mistakes. In the first place, he made a fatal mistake when he attempted to introduce his system into Waziristan without first occupying some commanding central position with troops. Secondly, he entered upon his new duties with preconceived ideas that the Mahsud republic, a republic bordering on anarchy, could be controlled in the same way as the Baluch and Brahui tribesmen, who, to say the least, were far from democratic [the Mahsuds being intensely democratic]. Lastly, he completely underestimated the turbulence of the Mahsuds.[24]

There were also other serious shortcomings to the approach. The fact that Bruce had personally selected the *maliks,* and not the tribe, meant that the headmen failed to represent fully the body of the Mahsud tribe. Had the tribesmen been allowed to decide on their own representatives, the most dominant and influential men should have logically come to the fore. Moreover, in only selecting and subsidizing a small number of *maliks,* Bruce had unwittingly bypassed a number of influential men who remained unfamiliar to British authorities. The sum of these shortcomings resulted, over time, in the total collapse of traditional Mahsud governance. *Maliks,* who accepted British allowances, turned out to be ineffective and little more than middlemen or intermediaries. "Indeed, so powerless had these *maliks* become that on several occasions they had begged the local officials to persuade the Government of India to annex their country."[25]

Moreover, the *maliki* system ran aground on another facet of tribal management; the nonnegotiable law of tribal division known as *nikat*. Charles Trench notes, "Try as they would to distribute benefits according to the recipients' deserts, Bruce and his successors always came up against the *saristita* [*nikat*] system, a departure from which would cause infinite resentment. Merit often went unrewarded while iniquity prospered, and grievances arising from this were a common cause of murder and rebellion."[26]

Due to its many failings, the *maliki* system was removed and it was decided to make allowances payable to the whole tribe, an approach known as the *tuman*.[27] To implement this, the commissioner of the Darajat, W. R. H. Merk, persuaded the government "to deal with the whole tribe in mass, as it were assembled in parliament and euphoniously dubbed 'the great *jirga* of the Mahsuds.'"[28] It was hoped that this democratic process would be well-received by the tribesmen. Although a *jirga* met at Tank in 1902, Merk's replacement, P. W. Johnson, reported that the approach was unworkable.[29] It proved impractical to reach an agreement with a verbose and heavily armed crowd of thousands of Mahsuds. Instead, Johnson suggested a practical compromise between Merk's approach and Bruce's *maliki* system, known as the conglomerate scheme. This required the reestablishment of the *maliks,* who received additional allowances of their own.

But even under the conglomerate scheme, the headmen had to be assured that the government had the power and will to protect them against revenge attacks or reprisals. Likewise, the use of the headman had to be consistent. There was little long-term value in using them only when it was convenient. But this was sometimes the case. Moreover, there were other human dynamics at play that undermined the approach. Friction existed between the "intelligentsia-cum-officials" and the headmen. *Maliks* were bypassed on some occasions and politicals were deferred to as the authority. In addition, some officials were deeply suspicious of the tribesmen and wanted greater control, undermining the tribal leader from his position of influence.[30] Not content with experimenting with the *maliks,* the government also tried to use the mullahs to their advantage. Plying them with allowances and granting them land, the government hoped to undermine their influence. "Subsequently, there was yet another swing in policy, and all the Mullah's benefits were cancelled."[31] The net result was inconsistency, mistrust, and confusion.

While the administration of the Mahsuds proved pressing, there were worrying outbreaks of violence across the frontier that preoccupied the government. Within four years of the Durand Agreement, a significant number of the tribes north of Tochi rebelled. The first outbreak of violence occurred against a political officer, Mr. Herbert Gee and his escort, under the command of Lieutenant Colonel Bunny, 1st Sikhs, in the village of Maizar, on 10 June 1897.[32] From there, revolt extended to Swat, under Sahdullah Khan, the Mad Mullah, followed by an attack on Shankargarh by the Mohmand tribe. Finally, the Orakzais Afridis captured the Khyber forts and lay siege to the Samana posts. This was the most serious crisis that had confronted India since the Indian Mutiny of 1854. The uprising was suppressed by the movement of troops and the deployment of an expeditionary force into the heart of Orakzai and Afridi territory. David Dilks posits, "Some of the regions to which they [the force] penetrated had been unseen by Europeans since the days of Alexander."[33] It took two years of heavy fighting before the uprising was finally repressed. The rebellion resulted in at least 1,000 casualties and millions of pounds sterling expended. In total, 75,000 troops were engaged in pacifying the region.[34]

Collin Davies suggests that the main cause of the disturbances was the active forward policy and the influence of fanaticism, reinforced by *mullahs* calling for *jihad*.[35] This included the construction of roads in tribal areas that were deeply unpopular. But intervention in tribal affairs had troubled the *amir*, and Afghan intrigues cannot be discounted as a contributing factor. Likewise, British reverses in Sudan may have given the tribesmen renewed confidence. Although the wide scale tribal uprising in 1897 called for a reappraisal of frontier policy, change did not occur overnight. This would be left to a new viceroy to instigate. In the short term, the secretary of state reaffirmed the policy of noninterference in tribal territory.[36]

## The Modified Forward Policy

On 6 January 1899, a thirty-nine-year-old Irishman, George Nathaniel Curzon, was appointed viceroy of India. He was created a Peer of Ireland as Baron Curzon of Kedleston on his appointment. Lord Curzon was a man with an impressive political pedigree and a deep understanding of the region and its people. "I am never so happy as when on the Frontier. I know these men and how to handle them. They are brave as lions, wild as cats, docile as children. You have to be very frank, very conciliatory, very firm, very generous, very fearless," wrote Curzon to St. John Brodrick, the undersecretary of state for foreign affairs, in April 1900.[37] He was also a shrewd observer and an astute analyst of foreign policy. At a time when the government was assimilating the lessons of the 1897 Pathan revolt and trying to ascertain what went wrong, Curzon was determined to make a decision regarding the means by which the frontier should be controlled. He recognized that the Punjab government, in addition to the normal administration of a province, was unable to deal with the exacting and complex responsibilities of the North-West Frontier.[38] He also recognized that the Durand Agreement had placed upon the frontier administration responsibility for the conduct and transgressions of those living inside the line of demarcation.

His initial investigations and wider understanding of the region helped shape his perception of the problem. He found more than 10,000 British troops cantoned across the administrative border in Malakand, the Khyber, on the Samana range, and in Waziristan. These inefficient, isolated, and exposed garrisons were unconnected by lateral lines of communications. Often enduring unsatisfactory conditions, soldiers were routinely too weak from illness or too few in numbers to influence the area for which they were responsible. Due to the isolation of the posts, the physical protection of the garrison from marauding tribesmen consumed most of the available forces. Few were available for routine patrols and military activities tended to be localized through necessity. Such a posture was also unsound from a military perspective in the event of mobilization against Afghanistan or Russia. Furthermore, the mere presence of British soldiers proved to be a constant source of irritation to the tribesmen and provided a static target against which they could vent their anger. This was a hazardous situation with posts in constant danger of being overrun.

Having reviewed the situation, Curzon wished to instigate a new policy that would hopefully put a stop to the costly and unfruitful punitive expeditions that had been a feature of the frontier for many years. Curzon's policy was based on four tenets: the withdrawal of British soldiers from forward positions; the employment of tribal forces to defend tribal territory; the concentration of British forces in British territory as a cohesive reserve in a state of high readiness; and the improvement of lines of communication in the rear. Curzon's reforms only affected military dispositions. There was to be no attempt at administration up to the Durand Line except in the Wana, Tochi, and Kurram valleys. In essence, the forward policy of the 1890s was to be replaced by one of noninterference. Ironically, this consisted of a number of tenets of the close border policy.

Curzon also established the North-West Frontier Province on 9 November 1901, directly under the government of India, with a chief commissioner, Sir Harold Deane, and a judicial commissioner's court at Peshawar.[39] The province consisted of five districts: Hazara, Peshawar, Kohat, Bannu, and Dera Ismail Khan. It also included the political agencies of Dir, Swat, and Chitral, the Khyber, Kurram, Tochi, and Wana. Vincent Smith described the new province unkindly as "an irregular straggling strip of territory chiefly to the west of the Indus, made up by combining certain districts taken from the Punjab with sundry tribal territories."[40]

Local militias were built up again by turning the *kassadars* into uniformed, disciplined, and highly mobile militias. In 1899, the North and South Waziristan militias were formed and gradually replaced regular troops in Tochi and Wana. Each militia consisted of 850 Pathans, but this figure was soon increased to 1,850 tribesmen, divided into two wings of approximately battalion strength, and 150 mounted soldiers.[41] Armed with modern rifles, each corps contained six British officers, two to each wing, the commandant, and the adjutant/quartermaster who also commanded the mounted infantry. Political officers controlled these militia forces, reinforced by the frontier constabulary, which was distributed in small detachments amongst the most important villages adjacent to the foothills.

The militia possessed a major advantage over their regular counterparts. Nevill posits that "the strength of irregular forces lies not so much in their military prowess as in their freedom from the cares which clog the movements of a disciplined army. They have no lines of communication to protect, no convoys to escort through difficult country with a minimum escort, and no second line transport, consequently they are mobile to a degree which always proves an embarrassment to regular troops."[42] However, the experiment of raising militias from the local tribesmen to police their own country achieved mixed results. After the murderous activities of the Mahsud militiamen, a decision was made to disarm and disband the Mahsud contingent in February 1905.[43]

Curzon's initiative conferred a number of additional advantages. Under the old system, decisions had taken weeks, even months, to arrive. The establishment of a new province prevented hesitation and delay and negated the difficulties associated with policy execution. It helped also to reduce the level of frontier bureaucracy. Prior to the formation of the new province, Arthur Swinson recalls that "an official could not make even the smallest decision without referring to several hundred regulations, some of them vague and many of them contradictory."[44] David Dilks reinforces this position: "Slowly the work of such officers [administrating the North-West Frontier] became overlaid with that welter of reports, meetings, memoranda and dispatches endemic in every bureaucracy."[45] But reducing levels of administration could only go so far in addressing the region's problems.

Not unsurprisingly, Curzon's management of the North-West Frontier Province achieved mixed results. Although the Mahsuds returned to their intractable ways in 1898 and 1915, the province remained generally peaceful, attaining a reasonable degree of stability. While some acknowledgment must go to the Afghan leader, Amir Habibulla, who remained neutral during the period, Curzon's understanding of the frontier and measured policies deserve recognition. In summarizing his approach, Curzon recalls, "My own policy in India was to respect the internal independence of these tribes, and to find in their self-interest and employment as Frontier Militia a guarantee both for the security of our inner or administrative borders and also for the tranquillity of the border zone itself."[46] His methodology resulted in a reduction in violent crimes and marked progress in a number of areas, specifically public works, revenue, irrigation, and healthcare. Indirectly, the North-West Frontier Province also provided a focal point for Pathan identity and went some way to consolidate the frontier.

There were other areas of progress. Many commentators suggested that Curzon had made great strides in bringing the tribesmen closer to India's "socio-political-economic mainstream."[47] Likewise, his militia initiative proved effective, with limited expenditure achieving satisfactory results.[48] Much to his acclaim, there were no major expeditions during Curzon's term of office (with the exception of two short expeditions known as Wilcox's Weekend Wars in 1908), and "he took credit to himself for the fact that he had only spent £248,000 on punitive measures on the Frontier during his viceroyalty."[49] It is unsurprising, therefore, that the 1921 *Oxford Student's History of India* states that "Lord Curzon's management of the frontier has saved much money and may be fairly described as successful."[50]

Curzon's policy held until 1919, being displaced by a series of Afghan incursions into British territory and the strain of the Third Afghan War. Under the pretext of border security, the new *amir*, Amanullah, rushed troops to the region in a show of support to Indians following anti-British riots in the Punjab. Afghan occupation of Indian villages in the Khyber Pass led to a monthlong British counterinvasion known as the Third Afghan War. Despite ejecting Afghan troops from British territory, the Third Afghan War sparked the mutiny of the tribal militias that policed the North-West Frontier, the famous Khyber Rifles deserted, and the force disbanded. Other militias followed suit. In Waziristan, large numbers of Mahsuds and Wazirs deserted from the militias with their rifles and ammunition. The South Waziristan Militia mutinied,[51] as did the Afridi and Waziri elements of the North Waziristan Militia. Both turned against their British officers. A revolt by the Tochi Wazirs compounded these revolts and the British consequently lost control of Waziristan. Only the Kurran Militia remained unaffected.

During 1919 and 1920, tribesmen launched 600 raids on Peshawar, Kohat, Bannu, and Dera Ismail Khan, resulting in nearly 300 deaths, 400 wounded, and 436 kidnappings of British subjects. In Waziristan over the same period, there were 611 raids, with 293 British subjects killed, 392 wounded, 461 kidnapped, and property valued at approximately £200,000 looted.[52] Wishing to avoid a series of costly campaigns and due to the limited availability of troops due to demobilization after the Great War, the British government offered generous terms to the tribes; these were rejected outright. To reestablish order, the tribes were punished heavily "by a campaign of extreme severity," and their territory occupied in force.[53] The British took few chances, committing substantial forces to the task. It is instructive that Sir Olaf Caroe notes the following:

Unlike other wars, Afghan wars become serious only when they are over; in British times at least they were apt to produce an after-crop of tribal unrest, sedulously fostered by a Kabul government which has itself made a nominal peace but is only too willing to cause embarrassment to the former opponent by constant intrigue amongst the border tribes and by the affordance of asylum to groups of outlaws and refugees from justice on the other side.[54]

Predictably, diplomatic initiatives, such as the Anglo-Afghan Treaty of 1921, whose aim was to share the burden of managing the frontier tribes with Afghanistan, failed to achieve tangible results.

In 1923, permanent garrisons were established in Razmak and Wana, linked by a circular road with Bannu and Tank to accelerate communications.[55] The rationale behind this initiative was that tribesmen would be deterred from inappropriate behavior with the presence of government forces in tribal territory. It recognized also that control and punishment could not be achieved by economic blockade alone. Instant retaliation was possible and the garrisons remained on a high state of readiness. However, such forward locations came in for considerable criticism. Sir John Slessor posits that "if there is one lesson which stands out farther than others from the long story of operations in Waziristan, it is the expensive futility and waste of good material involved in a policy which locked up first-class troops under rather demoralizing conditions behind wire perimeters at Razmak in the midst of a waterless tangle of mountains."[56] To complement the permanent garrisons, *kassadars* were raised and became responsible for road protection. They also provided local intelligence and acted as a force to prevent minor tribal transgressions. "The *kassadars* were servants of the tribe, not the Government; they were ordered by the Government to guard a stretch of road, a pass, or an officer but they acted on behalf of the tribe. They were responsible to the tribe — and for the tribe; if the tribe misbehaved, the Government could dismiss the *kassadars* even though as individuals they were blameless."[57] But while their presence provided insurance against attack, their fighting prowess was questionable, and they were not able to deal with major disagreements or tribal disputes.[58] The uprising provoked a complete reversal of Lord Curzon's policy. After years of hesitancy, a policy of "control from within" was adopted.

## The Reintroduction of a Forward Policy

From 1923 until independence in 1947, the British adopted a forward policy. The decision to introduce a permanent presence of regular soldiers into Waziristan was poorly received by the chief commissioner, Sir John Maffey.[59] As a dyed-in-the-wool close-borderer, he was incensed by the decision for three reasons. First, it was made without his consultation. Second, he held the view that such moves would be a constant cause of offense to the hill tribesmen and that the necessary lines of communication would present a vulnerable and alluring target. He was particularly concerned that the necessity to protect the road network would restrain the garrison from dominating tribal territory. Finally, he was infuriated, as the decision was irreversible by the time he made his disagreement known.[60]

In support of heavily fortified military garrisons at Razmak and Wana, the Waziristan militias were reformed as the Tochi Scouts in North Waziristan, and the South Waziristan Scouts replaced the militia in the south. To overcome previous shortcomings, the majority of personnel were recruited from parts of the frontier outside the North and South Waziristan agencies. Although the militias were organized along different lines to meet local requirements, the army, acting as a cohesive and reliable reserve, was always close at hand. As Barthorp explains, "Over the next dozen years the quartering of the territory by columns from the new garrisons, the increasing confidence of the scouts, and the new dimension of control afforded by the air arm, all helped to damp down the lawlessness of Mahsuds and Wazirs. But it was all preventative, rather than curative, and as time went by, Maffey's forebodings would prove to be justified."[61] Likewise, the government reengaged with the allowance scheme, which provided a recognized framework for dealing with the tribes. In addition, primary schools were built alongside military posts and Western-style healthcare was introduced.

Despite these well-intentioned initiatives, many fell short of expectation. Mr. F. G. Pratt recalls: "We read of a hospital in Miran Shah, a great centre in the Tochi Valley with tribal country all round it, that there are sixteen beds and forty or fifty patients lying about in stables, sheds and rooms with no doors or windows."[62] Likewise, frontier schools were often overcrowded and underfunded. Those that were resourced adequately created additional challenges. Sir William Barton cautions: "Young tribesmen equipped with a secondary education must be given appointments; otherwise they become the prey of the political agitators from British India."[63] But the reality was that few appointments existed in either government service or commerce.

There were further shortcomings. Access to low-interest loans to buy seed and agricultural tools remained illusive, and there was little exploitation of the mountain streams to allow greater irrigation of tribal lands. Likewise, livestock and produce markets went unsupported. Many criticized the government for a lack of civilian initiatives; but the reality was that it was difficult to justify expenditure on nontaxpaying areas.[64] This was by no means a new predicament. In 1895, Auckland Calvin cautioned: "To tax the salt or the soil of the Brahman, the Mahratta, the Sikh, for the development or the benefit of the Muhammadan of Waziristan, or of Chitral, is a course which cannot be long pursued, because it is opposed to political morality; almost, it might be added, to political sanity."[65] India's figures of illiteracy and infirmity suggested a more pressing use of limited resources. Nevertheless, there were some schemes that drew considerable financial support. The British established a robust network of all-weather roads throughout the North-West Frontier, and particularly in Waziristan, as a security measure. Roads, linked to garrison forces, allowed rapid deployment of assets across the frontier, enabling reinforcements to be rushed to critical points. In turn, roads enabled the expenditure on military operations to fall and assisted in reducing casualty figures. They were also an alternative to military occupation and a much cheaper substitute. John Coatman posits:

For roads, and their modern equivalents, railroads, are the great carriers of civilisation, and if they lead into a country they also lead out. The fine highroads which have been constructed in Waziristan since 1920 and the Khyber Railway, opened at the end of 1925, are the first steps towards the accomplishment of a new frontier policy—a forward policy in the highest and truest sense of the word. Civilising influences can now penetrate, and are penetrating, the wild highlands whose name has hitherto been a synonym for terror and bloodshed and degradation.[66]

Roads were constructed to pacify new areas, provide tribal employment, and extend political control. Although time consuming and expensive to build, they provided the means for tribesmen to help themselves. Tribal goods, such as timber, hides, wool, potatoes, and fruit, made their way to the markets of India. But they were not an end in themselves, and this led to varying degrees of resentment. Roads often failed to provide a visible advancement in the tribal areas in which they passed. Instead of trade and opportunities, the primary users of the roads were the military, "and this was not well received."[67] Troop movements became routine, which caused resentment among the tribes. Captain M. C. T. Gompertz, Indian army, notes that roads were built as a means of assisting military operations, "not of promoting the peaceful penetration of a country."[68] Moreover, tribesmen viewed their construction as a form of deception, a means by which to contain the tribes and restrict their liberty.

Roads became an easy target to vent tribal frustrations, and road protection became a major headache.[69] Likewise, units were tied to advancing along predictable routes. These enabled the tribesmen to anticipate and intercept an approaching force. Despite these realities, the British continued a program of road building and often combined punitive expeditions with basic road construction. "It is now generally agreed that if and when we find ourselves compelled to send a military force into tribal territory, that force will not withdraw without leaving a road behind it."[70] Such roads allowed forces to be supplied in the mountains with greater ease. They also made the recourse to future military actions easier. However, when troops withdrew from an area, roads often fell into disuse. Within a decade most were inoperative due to landslides and erosion.

Conciliatory measures also continued and included limited gifts of seeds, fruit trees, and agricultural implements. In addition, hill tribesmen were given preference for all contracts and supplies in tribal territory. The reality was that skilled labor was often required from down-country or even Hindu contractors, but the majority of unskilled labour was given to the tribesmen. C. E. Bruce, describing the construction of a road from Sarwekai to Wana, which required a mail contract from Jandola to Sarwekai, provides a useful case in point:

A Bannu Hindu contractor, who had run "mail" contracts for many years, applied for the contract. He was a good business man with plenty of experience. He also had "capital" behind him to carry out the work successfully. The tribal headman, without assistance, had none of these qualifications. So, the headmen, through whose limits the road passed, were called in and a case put to them. Then they and the contractor got together and, with assistance from us [the political authorities], a working agreement was arrived at. The contractor agreed to open a school for tribal motor drivers at Sarwekai, who were to be ready to take over as soon as the mail contract came into force. In short, the Hindu contractor was to run the business part of the transaction, the labour was to be tribal, and the benefits to be shared to the mutual satisfaction of all concerned. In this manner the work would be satisfactorily done and our pledge to the tribes carried out.[71]

But not all ventures were so straightforward. Costs continued to rise and many of the Hindu down-country contractors were driven by self-interest, at the expense of pacification. Ironically, it was the greed of the tribesmen demanding exorbitant rates that resulted in the Hindu contractors becoming the cheaper option.

There were also new influences to contend with. Nationalist emotion reverberated throughout India in the 1920s. The India Act of 1919, which sought to associate Indians with all branches of the Indian administration, was not, on the advice of Sir George Roos-Keppel, extended to the North-West Frontier Province. He considered the Pathans insufficiently advanced to take on the responsibilities of self-government. This was a position not shared by Abdul Ghaffar Khan, who had been politically active since 1919. In protest, he began to incite Pathans outside of the tribal areas to demonstrate against this discrimination. After a brief acquaintance with the Congress Party, Abdul Ghaffar Khan formed a semimilitary nonviolent organization known as the Khudai Khidmatgaran (Servants of God), more commonly known as the "Red Shirts."[72] Their message was simple: drive the British out of India.

Unchecked by the authorities, the Red Shirts grew in strength, working in close cooperation with the local Congress agitators in spreading disaffection.[73] In 1930, a Red Shirt rally in Peshawar led to severe rioting and eight days of anarchy. It also stimulated tribal resentment, particularly in the Afridis. After much indecision, the British finally declared the Red Shirts an illegal organization and arrested Abdul Ghaffar Khan. Despite the arrest of the movement's leader, the activities of the Red Shirts continued to influence government policy.[74] In 1932, the status of the province was raised from a chief commissionership to that of a governorship, with a Pathan, Sahibzada Abdul Qayyum, as chief minister. But there were other developments that may have had a profound effect on the tribesmen. Lieutenant Colonel C. E. Bruce points to an interesting development on the death of Abdul Qayyum: "Try, then, and put yourself into the minds of the tribesmen—the tribesmen with their mentality and outlook—and think with what amazement they heard of the Red Shirts Leader's brother [Dr. Khan Sahib, an ex-officer of the Indian Medical Service] being called on to form a Ministry!"[75] In a culture where compromise and benevolence were nonexistent, the government was sending a mixed message. "And Pathans, who are nothing if not realists, naturally failed to see why a strong Government should deliberately handicap itself by a kid-glove policy if it genuinely desired peace. For too long the British trumpet had been sounding an uncertain note; and no ear is quicker than the Pathan's to detect the change with its probable implications."[76]

The reason for the frontier igniting again was not just as a result of the Red Shirts movement. C. E. Bruce argues that the root cause of the problem was that other events in India had weakened irrevocably the tribesmen's belief in British power.[77] Likewise, a strong motive for insurrection was a feeling that Islam was in danger and that the Muslims in India must restrict the encroachments of a possible Hindu *raj*. Sir William Barton posits, "To the explosive Islam of the Pathan tribesmen the predominance of Hinduism is repellent; the Pathan would fight to the bitter end rather than submit to the rule of the Hindu majority."[78] But there may have been another reason resulting from British policy. Philip Woodruff suggests that in the 1930s the frontier tribes "were still treated like tigers in a national park; they risked a bullet if they came outside and took the village cattle."[79] But this was not strictly true. Tribesmen were given increasing freedom of action, and military activity faced growing restrictions. Although advances in technology from the Great War had improved the armory of the government's forces, political considerations aimed at limiting casualties hamstrung military actions. "Political Officers restricted the movement of troops to certain 'proscribed areas' in which they were not allowed to fire at any group of less than ten men unless the men were armed and not using a path or track."[80] But such restrictions were short lived, and the frontier, after seven years of relative peace, was about to flare up again.

In 1936, Mirza Ali Khan, a religious firebrand known as the Fakir of Ipi, declared a *jihad* against the government after the trial case of the so-called Islam Bibi. The crux of the discontent was the marriage of a fifteen-year-old Hindu girl, Ram Kori, to a Pathan student named Sayyid Amir Noor Ali Shah. Claims that she had been abducted against her will and forcibly converted to Islam followed and both sides claimed custody. British mishandling of the situation, including two years' imprisonment for Sayyid Amir Noor, enraged many tribesmen and proved to be the catalyst for an insurgency. For eleven years, the charismatic and courageous Fakir managed to unite and organize Pashtun resistance, including various sections of the Tori Khel Wazirs, the Mahsuds, and the Bhittanis. From 25 November 1936 to 9 June 1937, 163 British and Indian troops were killed, with 440 wounded during disturbances. Successfully opposing the establishment of effective colonial control over the region, the Fakir's enduring objective, an independent Pashtunistan, proved to be an astute and enduring rallying call. The British departed India in 1947 without capturing or killing the Fakir.

## The Unattainable Circle of Justice

The troublesome North-West Frontier, linking central, west, and south Asia, was one of the most complex and challenging territories of the British Empire. Afghanistan, Imperial Russia, and the troublesome tribes of the region all conspired, to a lesser or greater degree, to undermine the peace and stability of the region. Against this multifaceted backdrop, the government adopted a number of basing strategies and employed a series of negative and positive incentives. The army was used as a stick with which to threaten or strike the tribesmen. The carrot came in the form of conciliatory measures for good behavior. Both sought to influence and control tribal behavior as a means of pacifying the area. However, as the tribes behaved in an impulsive way, these measures achieved only mixed results, and the region oscillated between relative peace and periods of open conflict. No amount of knowledge of the behavior of the parts would allow the government to predict future activities of the whole. Local events were dealt with as they arose, often without reference to a fixed central policy. Similarly, the heavily armed tribesmen, influenced by *Pashtunwali*, were by no means susceptible to domestic change and remained apathetic to the opportunities it had to offer. They viewed the presence of foreign troops on their territory as an affront to their independence and continued to carry on their centuries-old struggle for independence by forcefully keeping foreigners out of the hills.

British policy failed to address the practical realities of the region. Instead, British control moved back and forth between close border (1849–1878), forward (1879–1901 and 1923–1947), and modified forward (1901–1923) policies, due to resource limitations, political constraints, and individual objectives. This resulted in a lack of fixed policy or principles, creating political confusion and tribal mistrust. Lieutenant Colonel C. E. Bruce recalls:

> We never knew what the next Government at home was going to do or the next Viceroy who came out. One Viceroy comes out from a Government who cry "Forward." The next comes out from a Government who cry "Back to the Indus," and other people come out perhaps who allowed a great deal too much freedom to go on among people who ought to have been kept in order, like those Red Shirts.[81]

Such uncertainty maintained the tribesmen in a state of latent unrest and frustration. The problem was particularly acute in Waziristan, which represented the greatest challenge to the British along the North-West Frontier from 1919 onward.

The British had mixed successes in influencing the tribes of Waziristan. Conciliatory measures, including medical treatment, resettlement programs, monetary benefits, and membership into paid militias routinely fell short of expectations. In a culture that failed to recognize compromise and kindness, the tribesmen reviled the government for their perceived conciliatory weakness rather than admiring them for their benevolence. Similarly, the use of *jirgas* to settle disputes was far from clear-cut. Even when the government effectively negotiated agreements with the hill tribes, individual tribesmen disobeyed its conditions. When appeasing activities failed, fines, blockades, and expeditions did little to transform the martial ethos of the tribesmen into peaceful law-abiding citizens, and offensive actions were rarely conclusive. Instead, such activities engendered a durable culture of hate and contempt toward British rule.

Due to the diverse nature of the region, no single policy or course of action offered a higher probability of success. Each tribe or clan was so distinctive that making generalizations or implementing a standard approach across the region was perilous. A bespoke policy, using negative and positive incentives, was necessary for each localized problem. Past successes offered few clues to address contemporary challenges. The tribal experiment of implementing the *maliki* system, so successful in Baluchistan—where a tribal chief, known as a *tomandar,* had some control over his tribesmen—on the troublesome Mahsuds in the late 1890s is a telling case in point. The initiative was a failure. There were other factors that helped undermined British attempts at controlling the region. An increasing torrent of ethnic, nationalistic, and religious fervor helped to ignite the region. Likewise, there was a growing feeling that Britain was about to leave India and that the might and invincibility of the British Empire was weakening. The success of the Red Shirts movement in the early twentieth century must have been an unmistakable example of waning British influence to the tribesmen. In the 1930s, justice and good administration were slipping through the hands of the government. In the eyes of the tribesmen, the downfall of the British Raj was imminent and conditions were ripe for insurrection. Preventing this and overcoming the deteriorating circumstances was the responsibility of the political and military structures employed to govern and control the region.

# 5

## 1930s Waziristan: The British Administrative Apparatus

We are in truth always striving to attain two ideals, which are apt to be mutually destructive—the ideal of good government, which connotes the continuance of our supremacy, and the ideal of self-government, which connotes the whole or partial abdication of our supreme position.
— Lord Cromer, quoted in C. E. Bruce, *Waziristan, 1936–1937*, 1938

### Frontier Politicals

The British recognized the need to delegate accountability within the North-West Frontier to achieve security while still maintaining political primacy. Strong central control alone, which the British enjoyed, could not address the unique challenges of diffuse tribal management. Responsibility for the day-to-day administration of the North-West Frontier fell to the Indian Political Service. L. S. S. O'Malley notes, "The work connoted by the word Political is entirely unlike that which would be inferred from its English sense, for it is chiefly diplomatic and includes political work (in the Indian sense)."[1] J. W. Spain summarizes the role simply as "half-ambassador and half-governor."[2] The Indian Political Service was drawn mainly from the Indian Civil Service and Indian Army in the proportion of 30:70. On rare occasions, officers from the Indian Police and Provincial Services, keen to experience frontier service, were seconded to the service for special reasons. Charles Trench recalls one such individual known as "Lotus" Lewis: "[He was] one of the few who came into the Political Service from the Frontier

Constabulary, a real Frontier expert, fluent in the Mahsud and Wazir dialects of Pushtu."[3]

Civil and military applicants for the Indian Political Service were interviewed by the Foreign and Political Secretaries for suitability,[4] during which candidates expressed a preference for the self-governing states, the frontier, or the foreign consulates.[5] The duties of the political officer in each area were distinct. As Sir Malcolm C. C. Seton, deputy undersecretary of state in the India office, explained in 1926: "they are employed as Residents or Political Agents in the Indian States, as administrative officers in the North-West Frontier Province and certain other frontier tracts, and as Consular officers beyond the borders of India."[6] Most served in two areas and a small number in all three.

Applicants for the Indian Political Service always exceeded vacancies. Volunteers were drawn by the prospect of a varied and demanding career. This was particularly true for the unbureaucratic frontier, which promised excitement, danger, and a break from the routine of long hours at an office desk. Akbar S. Ahmed, who joined the Civil Service of Pakistan in 1966 and was posted as the political agent, Orakzai Agency, posits that "the Frontier was the French leave, the excitement involving an out-of-bounds adventure, the forbidden drink; the innocently exciting infringement of school laws and social taboos, that the 'likable rogue' at school attempted without being caught."[7] Others had family connections in the service. Some, like Peter Nicholson, joined the service after an injury prevented an active military career on the frontier.[8] A small number were encouraged by the prospect of monetary gains. Understandably, commanding officers and provincial governments were averse to releasing their better officers to the service.

For those applicants who were successful, a "political's" first posting was generally as a personal assistant to a resident.[9] To provide a case in point, Sir Basil Gould's initial political appointment was as the assistant secretary to the agent to the governor general for the states of central India. But this was not always the case. A. J. Dring, who joined the service in 1927, was sent first to North Waziristan as the assistant political agent. Such demanding initial appointments drew criticism. Likewise, some cautioned that there were too many junior posts on a frontier region that required officers with maturity, experience, and a proven track record. More typically, a political new to the frontier was sent to one of the quieter districts in Baluchistan or to a settled district to become skilled at his employment and to prepare for his professional examinations. After enrollment, "the Indian Civil Service officer, who had passed his departmental examinations, faced only a simple examination, after six months, on the *Political Department Manual* and one or two historical books. The military Political had to spend eighteen months on civil (largely magisterial) training in the Punjab or the United Provinces and to pass the Indian Civil Service departmental examination as well."[10] This was a well-tried arrangement provided the political served under a mentor who had the time and the enthusiasm to oversee his training. This was not always the case. As a general rule, more was learned by the exercise of responsibility than in the library.[11]

In addition, those posted to the frontier had to pass the Higher Standard Pushtu examination. Speaking the language was essential, and the mastery of tribal dialects was a matter of pride.[12] It was the political's job "to understand whatever might be said in a variety of dialects and to catch nuances implied but not expressed; to be able to put things clearly; and to know how to reason with *maliks* or perhaps with a large *jirga* of a whole tribe."[13] A significant amount of training occurred on the job, but it was often left to a political's personal motivation to study local customs, religion, proverbs, and tribal relationships during the course of his duties. Dedicated service produced officers who possessed a broad and progressive understanding of the land and its people.

In addition to the politicals, the service was also supported by a small number of Royal Army Medical Corps personnel. These were appointed to the most important medical posts on the frontier. As the tribal areas lacked infrastructure to meet the population's basic health-care needs, doctors and trained medics filled an important role in Waziristan, treating government forces, tribesmen, and their families. Unsurprisingly, gunshot and knife wounds were a universal complaint.[14] Likewise, malaria and other fevers, as well as pneumonia and jaundice, were frequent ailments. An important aspect of a doctor's responsibilities was to examine all the recruits that the scouts' recruiting, or leave parties, acquired. "Plenty were brought in as, in addition to paying their travelling and subsistence expenses, the scouts paid a few rupees for each accepted recruit to the man who brought him in."[15] Each agency in Waziristan possessed only a handful of trained medics, whereas the tribesmen of the settled districts across the administrative border had access to a wider suite of medical facilities. The contrast between the two was indicative of the government's approach to their administration.

Each of the six settled districts in the North-West Frontier was run by a deputy commissioner supported by an assistant commissioner. These districts were modeled on other districts of India where the legal system was run under the Indian Penal Code, with regular court procedures, and where security was provided by the police. The districts possessed two police forces: the civil police force, about 6,000 strong, which was organized and trained to prevent or punish crime (i.e., "traditional" policing), and the armed frontier constabulary, 4,600 strong, skilled, and structured to deal with looters from across the administrative border (i.e., a paramilitary police force). Both forces worked in close cooperation under the deputy commissioner.[16] Tribal territory, the *real* frontier, contained five political agencies. These agencies were unadministered. Normal Indian law did not apply and there were no "traditional" courts or police. "Pax Britannica" only extended to government property (army cantonments and scouts' posts), the principle lines of communication, and 100 yards either side of them. As a result, few genuine attempts were made to enforce law and order.

Waziristan was divided administratively into two agencies: North Waziristan, with its headquarters at Miranshah, and South Waziristan, with a summer headquarters at Wana and a winter head office at Tank. Each agency was controlled by a political agent who acted as an umpire or arbitrator between the tribes.[17] Beneath the political agents were assistant political agents. These were established in 1928 to oversee the tribal *kassadars*. Charles Trench recalls, "Most of them knew the ABC of soldiering, and many had distinguished military records in the First World War."[18] Political agents were also supported by assistant political officers. These were mostly Pathans, but from a different part of the frontier to that in which they served. These loyal, hardworking, knowledgeable, and effective individuals proved invaluable to the service. T. C. Cohen, a former member of the Indian Political Service, recalls, "The Political Agents, too often frequently transferred, would have been as blind leaders of a blind and distant Government without the skilled advice of their . . . assistants."[19] Despite such high praise, a small number were reputed to be corrupt and motivated by self-interest. "Many are the stories told of how they pulled the wool over the eyes of the not always wise Deputy Commissioners and Political Agent."[20]

As a general rule, it was the political agents' responsibility to discourage tribes from raiding, to arrest offenders and outlaws, round up raiding gangs, and settle tribal disputes. These responsibilities were achieved, wherever possible, by mediation and the employment of a comprehensive scheme of allowances. Only in severe or exceptional circumstances would a political agent punish a tribe when their activities destabilized the region. Tribes were routinely controlled and disciplined by a sliding scale of violence: first enticement, rewards, and threats, next tribal *kassadars,* then the lightly armed scouts; only in extremis, when outbreaks were too excessive to be contained by the scouts, would the political agent call on the heavily armed army brigades at Bannu, Razmak, and Wana or the Royal Air Force. At this stage, control of the operation, including political control and oversight of the civil armed forces, passed to the military commander.[21]

When called on by the civil authorities to assist with small-scale disturbances, military commanders were obliged to use force, although the method of employing the force and the extent to which it was used remained the responsibility of the military commander. Political agents also advised on the class of troops to be employed, on account of their special knowledge of the characteristics of the tribesmen to be punished.[22] However, the final decision as to the type of troops to be employed rested with the military authority.[23] As a general rule, the political agent's local knowledge remained paramount throughout, allowing institutional responses to adapt to suit different circumstances. Only in times of crisis would a political agent be placed under army orders. Commanders accepted that actual circumstances were the compelling factor in any response and that inflexible solutions were often inappropriate.

Political agents exercised influence rather than authority, and whether the tribes remained peaceful or agitated often depended on their proficiency. To help transform the tribesmen's martial predisposition, politicals were charged with improving the economic life of the tribesmen and often introduced European methods to assist efficiency. These limited measures—such as improved irrigation techniques, well-digging, enhanced beekeeping, and small-scale silk production—were well received by the tribesmen of the settled districts but were viewed with suspicion in tribal territory. Politicals also oversaw a number of contracts to supply such commodities as firewood, grass, meat, and other local produce as well as the construction of roads and buildings. Despite many pan-district initiatives, each of the agencies possessed a unique challenge that was the focus of activity.[24] In the case of North Waziristan, the routine duties of the political agent were to maintain uninterrupted passage of military traffic to and from the military garrison at Razmak. This was achieved with the help of subsidies and the establishment of a string of fortified encampments.[25] In South Waziristan, the political agent had to contend with and placate the troublesome Mahsuds. This was particularly important as the roads leading to the military garrison at Wana dissected Mahsud territory.

By devoting time and patience to these unique problems, political agents were afforded an elevated position of respect by the tribesmen and assumed a traditional role of mediator and referee. Without the tacit agreement and respect of the local *malik*, their presence would have been untenable. Politicals found that tribesmen best responded to a man-to-man approach based on stature. Recounting a *jirga* conducted by Lieutenant Colonel Sir Benjamin Bromhead, Frank Leeson recounts that "they filed in quietly and after bowing towards the PA [political agent] or saluting clumsily, squatted down in a wide semicircle round his table."[26] Such deference was not uncommon. Those who effectively balanced government policy and tribal aspirations became a respected component of the tribal structure.[27] To be effective, political agents relied on fair judgment and personal contacts: "allegiance was given, if at all, not to a Government but to a man."[28] Lieutenant Colonel C. E. Bruce posits that "security rests not on the number of battalions, but upon the individual character of the men we choose."[29] Therefore, it was essential that the tribesmen valued the acumen of the political agent and followed his advice. This was not always the case.[30]

As a result of frequent personal contact, it was not uncommon for "friendships" to develop between a political and his *maliks*. Far from being savage brigands, many *maliks* were well educated and well disposed to the government.[31] The majority of tribal leaders approved of an approach to ethnic management that formally recognized their role and influence in tribal society. Even those who were uneducated or hostile to the authorities possessed many appealing features. However, "friendships" could be hazardous and several "loyal" or "sympathetic" *maliks* were murdered as a clear warning to others. This was not the sole problem associated with tribal relationships. Politicals were prone "to be biased in favour of their Mahsuds and their Wazirs, against the brutal and licentious soldiery, if only because the entry of the Army on to the scene implied that the situation had gone beyond the Political Agent's control."[32] They were also guilty of being too involved in intertribal discord, thereby undermining the *malik* from his position of authority. Similarly, they were condemned for unnecessarily constraining troop movements.[33] There were other conflicts up the chain of command. For example, ministers sometimes felt that a political agent was not exerting sufficient pressure on the tribes under his control. As a result, the Indian army always alleged that politicals had divided loyalties.[34] Colonel H. R. C. Pettigrew recalls, "I have even heard some Army officers, albeit rather narrow-minded and ill-informed ones, state that they often wondered whose side the Political was on. On the other hand, in extreme cases, a P. A. [political agent] has been known to refer tactlessly to the hostile tribal sniper as 'my chaps'!"[35] Nevertheless, "friendships" were routinely put to the test. According to Charles Trench, "It was his [the political agent's] job to settle troubles of all kinds—inter-tribal fights, raiding into settled districts, highway robbery, kidnapping, murder and mayhem—before it blew up into a situation which required the intervention of a brigade of regular troops."[36] The political agent's role often put him at variance with his *malik,* who viewed his responsibilities as developing government interference in tribal matters. This was further complicated by the nuances of the allowance scheme. As the initiative paid *maliks* to control troublemakers, ruthless headmen had cause to encourage and direct such tribesmen to destabilize the local area. Much to the political agent's irritation, this double-dealing allowed *maliks* to profit from their proficiency at instigating and managing trouble. Mediation, central to resolving such complex issues, required politicals to possess a persuasive manner, a matter-of-fact approach, and a thorough knowledge of tribal customs. It also called for individuals who were patient, evenhanded, and first-rate listeners; a political agent would spend a considerable amount of time taking note of tribal grievances. Charles Trench recalls "twenty or thirty Maliks would be waiting after each

*Jirga,* every one of whom felt himself entitled to a long, cosy chat with the Political Agent. Such petitioners, liable to turn up at any time, generally the most inopportune, were known as *malaqatis* (mole-cats), and diaries are full of such entries as 'sixteen mole-cats waiting at Boya.'"[37]

During routine discussions, the challenge for the political agent was in deciding who was lying and who was not. "Or, more accurately, who was lying the most," as Pettigrew put it.[38] Failure to manage a situation appropriately could lead to a blood feud, resulting in a rapid transfer to another political appointment.[39] This was particularly true of tribal *jirgas,* as the political agent was responsible for both the ruling and sentence. Not only had he the authority to arrest and jail offenders, but in extreme cases he could instigate a blockade or even order the destruction of an entire village. Such responsibility was exhausting and imposed a heavy strain on the individual. Even routine responsibilities could be strenuous. "Only one who has spent a long day listening to the arguments of Mahsud visitors will understand the exhaustion which comes from resistance to his importunings, the effort required to meet his plausibility, even the struggle to cap his wit," recalls Sir Olaf Caroe.[40]

Moreover, it was an established custom that each allowance holder in the tribe would interview the political agent. "This was quite an arduous matter, as each man had his own particular favour to ask, and it was necessary to humour as many as possible and to offend as few, otherwise there might be trouble."[41] Exhaustion was a major factor of frontier service. According to Charles Trench, "It meant that only a very exceptional Political Agent, such as Robert Warburton, half Afghan, could remain in one posting for more than three years, which was hardly long enough to get to know the tribes."[42] Unless a political agent decided to remain on the frontier in a different guise, his tenure would last no more than a few years. Those who chose to stay were often criticized for "going native."[43] Akbar S. Ahmed cautioned that extended service amongst the tribes "produced Frontier officers like Howell, Cunningham and Caroe—often more Pathan than the Pathans themselves."[44] Philip Mason, an experienced frontier hand, posits in *A Matter of Honour* that "frontier officers were a rather special breed of the British and they were sometimes almost converted to the Pathan's sense of honour and usually to his sense of humour; it did not often happen the other way around."[45]

Each political agent had at his disposal a private militia composed of tribesmen commanded by British and Indian officers seconded from the Indian army. These units, trained and equipped for mountain warfare, were not part of the army and only rarely came under military command. As a demonstration of confidence, but tempered by an understanding of *Pashtunwali,* political agents often chose to travel in tribal territory without a militia escort. Instead, they relied on *kassadars* or tribal "gunmen" provided by the local *malik* for protection. It was hoped that as a guest of the tribes the political agent would be relatively safe in times of peace. However, he could never be certain that, should he be attacked, his escort would defend him for fear of provoking a blood feud with their fellow tribesmen. In times of peace, a political agent's escort was small and consisted routinely of an orderly and a couple of escorts. However, in times of trouble, such as the 1930s, a political agent was accompanied by a "whole lorry-load of *Kassadars.*"[46] This placed a significant mental and moral strain on the individual.[47] Physical danger was ubiquitous on the frontier, and the political agent lived in constant fear of his life. To help mitigate this threat, *kassadars* were charged with providing escorts, road protection, and preventing minor tribal disobedience.

## Kassadars— "Spit and No Polish"

*Kassadars* were rarely very busy and spent most of their time on leave, lolling around the various posts they occupied (like Chagmalai, Splitoi, and Kotkai), or squatting like vultures on a cluster of rocks above the road they were "protecting."

—H. R. C. Pettigrew, *Frontier Scouts,* 1964

*Kassadars* were reestablished in Waziristan in 1921 to help remove the burden of general police work from the army and to enable the tribes to discharge their obligations. Based on the Indian tradition of employing locally recruited tribesmen to guard property, the force consisted initially of 4,600 tribesmen but was increased in size to approximately 5,400 by 1935. In order to attract the best men to the service, *kassadars* received higher rates of pay than the police or frontier constabulary.[48] To prevent the loss of equipment, particularly rifles, *kassadars* were not armed or equipped by the government. These responsibilities, like those of training and administration, fell to the tribes. Under the jurisdiction of the assistant political agent, each tribe or section was salaried to supply a notional number of *kassadars,* including noncommissioned officers and officers.[49] As servants of the tribe, *kassadars* were ordered by the government to undertake a number of routine security and revenue responsibilities but acted on behalf of the tribe.[50] The opportunity of a regular income, without any prospect of leaving tribal territory, was welcomed by the tribesmen. As a result, competition was fierce for the available positions. However, instead of being seen as a legitimate attempt to broaden the government's economic and political base, the system was often perceived as another means to help "divide and rule" the tribesmen of the region, while inflated incomes were often viewed as a form of blackmail.[51]

An average company was comprised of "forty privates (*Khassadaris*), five corporals (*naiks*), three sergeants (*havildors*), one second lieutenant (*jemadar*) and a commanding lieutenant (*subedar*)."[52] These loosely formed companies were employed to regulate their respective tribal areas. In addition, they were tasked to provide road and site protection by occupying picquets and by providing escorts for officers.[53] They were also used as an opening into the tribes, an important source of local intelligence, and as a thread that joined the political authorities with the tribesmen. On rare occasions, *kassadars* accompanied patrols in order to identify property owned by insurgents.[54] The initiative worked reasonably well in peaceful times for routine matters. Even so, many, like Sir Evelyn Howell, questioned the cost-effectiveness of the venture. "The Government spends a good deal on them—between 25 and 30 *lakhs* or rupees a year—and, some people think, gets poor value for its money."[55] Opinion was equally divided on their contribution to the stability of the region. Sir Arthur Parsons, the officiating head of the External Affairs Department, suggested that the *kassadars* could be "credited with the abstention, or partial abstention, of many tribes, especially the Mahsuds," during the height of the 1936–1937 troubles.[56] Others disagreed. As Sir Basil Gould summarizes, "They had their critics, but they were useful."[57] Interestingly, Colonel H. R. C. Pettigrew points to a more basic failing of the initiative: "Where it failed was that though it removed some of the poverty of the tribes, and gave them something to lose and thereby some incentive to keep out of trouble, and to keep trouble out of their areas, it did nothing to give them something to do."[58]

There were other challenges associated with their employment. *Kassadars* were not always able to deal with major disagreements or with differences with the government. Likewise, *kassadars* were not well liked or trusted by the army. The hierarchy knew little about them and few could talk to them in their own language. Moreover, to most ordinary soldiers, a *kassadar* looked indistinguishable from the enemy they were fighting.[59] Even as late as 1942, a London *Times* report recalls *kassadars* as "wild-looking men, with their loose garments, bandoliers, and rifles."[60] The army frequently asked for the withdrawal of all *kassadars* from an area prior to the start of a military operation. "We don't like the *kassadars,* of course . . . They're a nuisance to us because we're supposed to trust them but can't. After all, they're local tribesmen, and their own interests naturally come before ours."[61] To address these concerns, *kassadars* were never made aware of plans in advance of an operation or initiative. They were also unreliable, "more often than not keeping out of the way of the raiding gangs they are supposed to deal with."[62] John Masters points to another failing: "*Kassadars* were permanently irritated about pay or promotion, and a significant proportion of stray shots fired at the army in Waziristan were fired by peevish *kassadars."*[63] Moreover, they had few scruples in abandoning their responsibilities for the call of a religious war, only to return to their duties on completion of hostilities.

To combat these shortcomings, formed companies were regularly disbanded or suspended in punishment for disloyalty.[64] For example, all Tori Khel *kassadars* were discharged in April 1937. Heavy fines were also commonplace. Although an individual *kassadar* was notionally paid directly by the government, in practice each tribesman's pay was divided and subdivided by the *malik,* and the whole tribe felt the effect when recompense was withheld. Similarly, pay was often withheld in order to settle a fine imposed on their tribe. Despite the threat of punishment, it was also well known that *kassadars* would not fire to kill when their own tribesmen attacked, as they were fearful of starting a blood feud.[65] However, the reverse was also true, with fellow tribesmen being equally reluctant to open fire against them. On rare occasions this was put to good use. Charles Trench recalls a case in point:

There was some chance, now that a long day was drawing to a close, that the Mahsuds would not fire on *Khassadars* of their own tribe; but if these were seen to be led by a *Faranghi* [foreigner], they were certain to shoot him. So [Lotus] Lowis, after discussing the matter with them, sent in the *Khassadars* marching in columns of four straight down the middle of the road. Not a shot was fired on them, and they occupied the caves, sangars and culverts from which the tribesmen had been firing. It was the Mahsud *Khassadars'* finest hour.[66]

Fortunately, *kassadars* had few qualms about fighting raiding parties from another tribe.

Despite the best efforts of the assistant political agents, control of the *kassadars* was invariably problematic. Few turned up for duty and many regarded their allowance as a reward for inactivity rather than as recompense for services rendered; some tribesmen even paid others to undertake their limited duties. Many were young boys or older men selected by their local *maliks.* Over time, a significant number became hereditary *kassadars,* with positions passed down from father to son or brother, regardless of age or competence. This applied to both noncommissioned officers and officers, so that if a man was a noncommissioned officer, then his successor became a noncommissioned officer on his death. Put simply, no man could be promoted for commendable or loyal service.[67] Such a method of enlistment, which disconnected any accountability or judgment from the tribes, had the tacit agreement of the government. The result, over time, was a tangible decline in the efficiency and capability of the force. This was compounded by another contributing factor: neglect. According to Sir Ambrose Dundas, "They [the *kassadars*] were neglected rather than disaffected, poor things—neglected and bewildered, attacked from all sides and befriended by none during all those bad years, not even by their own [political] officers. From 1936 to 1940 they were just kicked and messed about by everybody."

## Frontier Scouts

The *kassadars* required constant supervision, which fell routinely to the scouts. The post-1919 scouts were a political force, maintained almost entirely for transborder police duties, and comprised principally of tribesmen from the administered areas. They proved invaluable in relieving regular troops of the expensive work of garrisoning frontier outposts. Reformed after the Third Afghan War to serve as the private militias of the political agents, the scouts sat midway between the *kassadars* and Army of India. Service in the scouts provided the tribesmen with a viable alternative to road-building, subsistence agriculture, or raiding. It also assisted with political integration and was viewed as an honorable occupation.[68] Likewise, service in the scouts went some way to reduce the numbers of unemployed tribesmen between the wars, a constant source of instability. It also reinforced the principle expressed succinctly in a report of the chief commissioner that "to live honestly the young men of the tribes must be given Government employment."[69] Clothed, fed, and armed by the government, there were approximately 5,000 scouts in Waziristan in the 1930s, and they cost over Rs. 30 *lakhs* a year.[70] The financial contribution to tribal income, provided by service in the scouts, was considerable.

The scouts were commanded by officers of the Army of India, which included a number of "keen and active" British officers seconded for three years.[71] Volunteers had to have a strong liking for Pathans and a desire to serve on the frontier. When a vacancy existed, the scouts helped choose who they wanted seconded to their unit. "Acceptance or rejection was carried out in an unusual manner. You went to live with the Corps at its headquarters at Miranshah, so that you were judged by your might-be future brother officers. It was a little like the Pack Meeting at the Council Rock in Kipling's Jungle Book. The verdict was not based at all on academic qualification."[72] Suitable individuals would be asked for by name, and it was then the responsibility of army command to approve the attachment. Charles Trench notes that British officers seconded to the scouts were not, as was widely believed, "the insolvent and the destitute, on the run from moneylenders and irate husbands (at least, not all of them)."[73] Like the politicals, officers joined for a variety of reasons, although it was recognized that officers who were in debt, or saving to get married, were drawn to the scouts for financial motives.

The scouts sat underneath the control of the inspecting officer of the Frontier Corps, not the Army of India command; the inspecting officer, in turn, was answerable to the chief commissioner (subsequently upgraded to governor in 1932) of the North-West Frontier Province. Routinely, the scouts were employed in close cooperation with the political agent, the support of whose authority was "the main reason for their existence."[74] The political agent told the scouts the effect he wanted to achieve but not how to achieve it. As a general rule, the level of direction largely depended on individual personalities.

Deployed in small isolated forts, the primary duties of the scouts included mediation between tribes; discouraging raids and the assembly of hostile *lashkars*; updating topographical records; giving moral support to friendly tribes; keeping the road network open; escorting Powindah convoys; collecting fines; guarding prisoners; demonstrating government forces' unrestricted access to the Durand Line; enforcing blockades; and punishing offenses. Typically, the scouts enforced collective justice, holding an entire village or section responsible for the crimes committed by an individual. But this was no easy undertaking, especially as the effectiveness of the scouts was increasingly debatable. "Mauser" notes candidly that "To-day [1931], they are no longer a terror to the Tribes. Their tactics, their traditions, their very name, have become a dwindling memory. The Wardens of the Marches are gone."[75]

Scouts often employed indirect methods to achieve their objective, demonstrating an intelligent understanding of tribal culture. On one occasion in Waziristan, the political agent, Major Baines, as Jack "Lotus" Lowis recorded, decided to use the scouts to "bring to order" an important tribe of Wazirs, the Zilli Khel, by restricting the autumn movement of their flocks from grazing in British India. "From the air he spotted the trespassers, and then directed the SWS [South Waziristan Scouts] onto them."[76] The scouts succeeded in capturing nearly one thousand sheep, eight shepherds, and two rifles. "The sheep round-up was wholly successful in its purpose," Lowis noted, although he himself was criticized by an officer from the brigade at Wana for cruelty to sheep. "But there had been no shooting, no casualties and no sheep died."[77] Only in extremis were the scouts subordinated to the army. However, small detachments, acting as guides or a screening force, often deployed with regular formations under the direction of the military commander.[78] Over time, the custom of irregular forces working closely with the army became commonplace in Waziristan. Both benefited from a close professional relationship that had developed since the formation of the scouts.

In 1922 the dependable elements of the North and South Waziristan Militias and the Mohmand Militias were formed into the Tochi Scouts, named after the Tochi River, and the South Waziristan Scouts. Scouts enlisted for a fixed period, which was extended on promotion. The Tochi Scouts had a headquarters company of specialists, two troops of mounted infantry (each fifty-nine strong), and two infantry wings. Its combined strength was 12 British officers and 2,278 tribesmen. Correspondingly, the South Waziristan Scouts had a total of 14 British officers and 2,774 tribesmen.[79]

> The South Waziristan Scouts were made up of three wings [each wing was made up of class companies consisting of one tribe only], and their location and responsibilities were changed from time to time, but most often one Wing was based on Jandola, with detachments at Tanai (beyond Sarwakai) and at Chagmalai, Splitoi and Kotkai when it was thought necessary to occupy them. Another Wing was at Sarwakai with detachments at Wana and Tiarzha, and the third Wing would be at Sararogha with a detachment at Ladha—holding the Jandola-Razmak line in other words. The mounted infantry [two troops] was split between Jandola, Wana, and Tanai.[80]

However, class companies were rarely used as a formed body. Instead, post garrisons always contained a mixture of platoons from various companies, with transborder tribes always in the minority.

By 1933 the South Waziristan Scouts had forty-eight infantry platoons and two mounted infantry troops to draw upon. Within this, a varied tribal composition enhanced reliability and ensured that a unit could not be infected at the same time with the same complaint. This was reinforced by strict discipline and harsh punishment. As a result, wastage from desertion was low.[81] Conversely, a mixed structure, which included few Wazirs and no Mahsuds, often lacked a detailed understanding of the region's tribesmen and terrain. Such men "could not know it [tribal territory] as well as men who had been herding goats there as little boys, familiar not only with every *nullah* [ravine] and patch of thorn-scrub, but every house and fortified tower—who owned it, how many sons he had, whether he was to be deemed a friend or enemy."[82] However, their knowledge of Pushtu and Pathan customs, gained through regular contact, proved invaluable and was in stark contrast with the Army of India serving in Waziristan. A 1932 article titled "Mobility" highlights a practical reality: "In searching Pathan villages, British troops and Sikhs, Dorgas and Gurkhas are greatly handicapped by their ignorance of the language, and their inability to tell friend from foe when both are so similar."[83]

Despite some misgivings, Pathan officers were permitted to command platoons in the scouts, but the *subedars* (company commanders) were changed around routinely and were always drawn from different tribes to the men of their platoons. Each rank in the scouts carried greater responsibility than in the regular army, and Pathan officers were men of considerable authority and sway. Having gained their commission after not less than twelve years' service in the ranks, they knew thoroughly the duties of each scout and the standards expected. Pathan officers were also central to maintaining the scouts at a high state of readiness in their outposts. Sir Basil Gould recalls, "A Scout or Political officer might drop in suddenly at a Scouts post. If he whispered the word *chigha*, which meant 'pursuit party,' a platoon would be fallen in within a minute. If, in addition to his equipment and rifle and ammunition, any man had not on him some food to keep him going for a day or two and a full water bottle, he was likely to be degraded or discharged."[84]

Patrolling, known as *gashting* or "showing the flag," was the regular activity of the scouts. This generally occurred twice a week, at irregular intervals and at varying times. *Gashts* were conducted mainly by company-strong foot patrols of 100 "rifles" or more, although mounted units were also used. Distances of twenty-five to thirty miles a day were common.[85] In contrast to regular army patrols, which traveled approximately six to ten miles a day,[86] scout *gashts* achieved on average four to five miles an hour.[87] The objectives of the *gashts* were threefold: to demonstrate freedom of movement; to provide moral support to friendly tribes; and to act as a physical deterrent to the tribesmen—it was better to deter than to punish. *Gashts* relied on secrecy, surprise, and the choice of an unpredictable route, thus "the route for the next day's *gasht* was never divulged until the fort gates were closed for the night."[88] Such patrols, which could last for two days without resupply, were well liked by the scouts in clement weather. They afforded a feeling of autonomy, often provided excitement, and proved to be excellent training. In contrast, winter *gashts* were less popular. Debilitating winds, mud, snow, and ice all hampered movement. However, despite seasonal conditions, scouts moved faster over the hills than any other troops. Such rapid mobility was attributable to their robust fitness and knowledge of the local topography. It was also helped by their light equipment load.

Scouts, unlike regular troops, only carried a small haversack divided into compartments to "hold a bag of flour, lumps of un-purified brown sugar, a pinch of tea, an onion or two, needle and thread and spare nails for the soles of the sandals [for gripping on steep slopes]."[89] To prevent dehydration, scouts were issued a lightweight aluminum water bottle that was larger than the regular issue water bottle. Such was their efficiency that "the Regulars can learn a great deal from them as regards mobility, from their sensible equipment, and how to move rapidly and effectively over the Frontier hills."[90] According to Sir Evelyn Howell, "Anyone who has accompanied a Scouts' patrol or even watched a body of Scouts move over the hillsides has some idea of what the prophet of old meant when he exclaimed, 'How beautiful upon the mountains are the feet of them that serve the Lord.'"[91]

In addition to lightweight equipment, troops wore practical clothing for operating in the region, which "was purposely allowed to be rather sloppy and untidy."[92] The men wore loose khaki shirts outside baggy Muslim trousers and on their heads a small, tight turban wound round a skull cap. In order not to stand out from their men, "the Scout officers . . . were dressed in the same manner as their men, even to the turbans, though they carried automatics, commando knives and walking-sticks instead of rifles and bayonets."[93] Such measures did not fool the tribesmen. It was often said that a vigilant tribesman could pick out a British officer with little difficulty simply by the gait of his walk.[94] However, it was not uncommon for inexperienced soldiers to mistake the scouts in their loose khaki clothing for hostile tribesmen. The color of their clothing blended in with the surroundings, and their style of dress was similar to that worn by the tribesmen. As a political force, the scouts were robust, dependable, and respected by the local tribesmen.[95] They were also proficient marksmen of a far higher standard than the regular army soldiers. This was attributable to their reliance on single-shot accuracy, due to a deficiency of light machine guns and the fact that scouts carried lighter loads of ammunition.

When not on patrol, there were plenty of other activities to keep the scouts busy. Colonel H. R. C. Pettigrew recalls that "there were drill and musketry parades to keep the men smart and accurate with their rifles, especially for the recruits who were pretty rough when they came in from their villages with the recruiting parties."[96] More routinely, scouts had to undertake guard and garden duties.[97] Likewise, livestock had to be looked after daily. Despite concerted attempts to provide fresh fruit and vegetables to help counter scurvy and dysentery, a steady trickle of scouts ended up in hospital with frontier ailments. Malaria also took its toll, as mosquito nets could not be used on *gashts* and provided no protection against sand flies. Therefore, malaria, sandfly fever, and diarrhea were dangers that had to be tolerated and "helped by doses of quinine, aspirin and chlorodyne, and applications of citronella oil."[98] There were other natural hazards, including venomous scorpions and spiders. Boils and sores were an equally common complaint of the scouts.

A comparable organization of armed police, known as the frontier constabulary, supported by local police and village watches, conducted equivalent duties on the British side of the administrative border in the "settled districts." Armed with modern rifles and organized on a platoon basis, the force consisted mostly of Pathans but also included a number of British officers seconded from the Indian police. Sir Percival Griffiths provides a useful assessment: "The Constabulary's personnel were not highly trained in the military sense, but were tough men, natural guerrilla fighters and accustomed to a hard life."[99] Located in fortified posts and picquets along the border and held at high readiness, the constabularies' main purpose was dealing with raids from tribal territory, but they were not allowed to operate in the tribal territories, except in actual pursuit of raiders. As a general rule, they were not involved in the ordinary police work of the settled districts of the North-West Frontier, which was the responsibility of the regular police.[100] But the reality was that on frequent occasions the frontier constabulary supported the civil police and cooperated loyally with the scouts and Army of India. As with the irregulars, British officers commanded the frontier constabulary. "As proof of their devotion to duty can be cited the fact that from the year of its inception [1913] to the present day [1953], there has not been a single desertion with arms and ammunition and that nowhere have they disobeyed orders and shirked from fighting against their own kith and kin."[101] Like the scouts, the frontier constabulary was overseen by the Army of India.

# The Mailed Fist in the Velvet Glove: The Army of India and the Royal Air Force

> Major trouble was the Army's responsibility. That is what the Bannu, Razmak, and Wana Brigades were for—to send out strong columns when needed.
>
> —H. R. C. Pettigrew, *Frontier Scouts,* 1964

## *Army of India*

In the event of a situation escalating out of control, the Army of India was the fallback force on the frontier. Consisting of both the British and Indian armies, this sizable standing force of "covering troops" was capable of guarding India from invasion or suppressing the tribes in the event of war on or beyond the international boundary.[1] Located at key sites on the frontier (which proved to be a constant temptation and irritation to the tribesmen) and other garrison locations throughout India, the Army of India was generically organized and trained to carry out any duty the Empire required of it, in any part of the world.[2] The breadth of possible contingencies extended from traditional combat to internal security. Such a span of responsibility was subject to considerable professional controversy.

> There appears to be a feeling that the Army in India, for its special role, has become too regularised and encumbered, and is too much trained to fight a European foe, provided with masses of artillery and mechanical aids, which it will never, it is contended, have to do. Is this theory correct? Probably not. Surely no one wants an

army trained on North-West Frontier mountain lines only ... Any tendency towards specialization for mountain warfare operations on the North-West Frontier must be resisted. These are a very small part of the Army's possible commitments, and specialization means a waste of part of our already very small army.[3]

The two armies shared a common command structure under the commander in chief. The British army maintained a moderately small force on the North-West Frontier, which served more as a cohesive and dependable reserve than a force of first choice. British battalions possessed up to thirty officers, including many long-service noncommissioned officers. The majority of soldiers were young and inexperienced, and many came from the inner cities. The minimum time period of enlistment for a private soldier was five years. Despite a small core of experienced "frontier hands" and progressive training prior to deployment, based on the *Manual of Operations on the North-West Frontier of India,* some units arrived on the frontier ill-prepared for the nuances of mountain warfare.[4] Many relied on a lengthy handover and on-the-job training. This often failed to have the desired effect. Recalling one such battalion in Waziristan, a commentator notes: "They [2nd Battalion, Argyll and Sutherland Highlanders] really are hopeless and all their casualties have been due to their own incompetence."[5] Incongruously, the battalion sent to replace the Argylls at short notice, the 2nd Battalion, Green Howards, had little opportunity to train in mountainous conditions and arrived undermanned.[6] Due to tactical shortcomings, personnel rotations, and professional overconfidence, British regiments were often easy targets for the tribesmen.[7] A sign of an efficient regiment on the frontier was that it was rarely attacked. "The Wazirs and Mahsuds knew when a new regiment, British, Indian, or Gurkha arrived, and they would watch it, try it out, and soon decide whether it was easy meat or not."[8] In general, the performance of units on the frontier relied upon their readiness and capacity to adapt.

The majority of regular forces were from the long-service professional Indian army. These were cheaper than British regiments but no less complex and unpredictable than the frontier tribes.[9] With the exception of the Gurkhas, widely regarded as the "finest and bravest soldiers in the world," most Indian battalions encompassed a blend of different

Indian races and religions.[10] These were recruited from certain classes of India's population. Peasant farmers, pastoralists, and tribesmen from the frontiers filled its ranks. An Indian battalion had three rifle companies, each of four platoons with a Vickers-Berthier light machine gun per platoon. In addition, each battalion had eight Vickers machine guns, which formed the nucleus of Support Company.[11] While inadequately equipped for modern warfare (they lacked heavy weapons and modern logistic assets), the Indian army was redoubtable in terms of unit cohesion and basic skills. Qualities such as discipline, stamina, marksmanship, and courage were highly prized. The army was also well trained and could easily adapt to frontier operations and a supporting role as an imperial constabulary. Many soldiers possessed firsthand knowledge of tribal warfare due to the regular rotation of units through the frontier stations. Experience in low-intensity conflict exerted an important influence on the organization, equipment, and training of the force. Allen Warren provides a useful summary of the Indian army's military competence: "By the mid 1930s, after a long period of peace, the officers and men of the Indian Army were both experienced and confident. *Esprit de corps,* built up in part by an endless round of regimental sport, was excellent, and, within the constraints of existing army tactical doctrine, all ranks could be counted upon to fight well."[12]

Under routine conditions, there was only one British regiment in Waziristan garrisoned at Razmak. To avoid this becoming localized, and to give every unit the opportunity of service on the frontier, regiments only served a one-year tour of duty.[13] In contrast, all Indian and Gurkha regiments spent two years out of every six on the frontier. As a consequence, such regiments had a significant proportion of their ranks who had experience in the complexities of frontier warfare and the ways of the Pashtun.[14] But despite familiarity, frontier service was often unpopular. Based on his own experiences, Collin Davies was of the view that "both Indian and British troops . . . strongly object to any prolonged service on the frontier . . . In fact, all ranks regard frontier service as an exile."[15] But this was not always the case. During an interview in 2001, Colonel H. A. Styles recalled, "You have no idea of the excitement felt when the Battalion heard that they were to be posted to the North-West Frontier to join the forces in the campaign against the *Fakir of Ipi* and his tribesmen in September 1937."[16] This was said despite the knowledge of the death of over 250 Indian and British soldiers since the start of hostilities in November 1936. A small number of soldiers would even request to transfer to a relieving regiment in order to stay and fight on the frontier.

The main duties of the Army of India in Waziristan were to protect the inhabitants living peaceably within the "settled districts"; to undertake road construction and protection patrols;[17] site protection; and, when called on, to impose the will of the government upon the frontier tribes. The army would, if required, undertake a show of force, repel raids by tribesmen from across the border, or conduct punitive operations in support of the scouts. If required, existing formations could be reinforced quickly by road or air. The infantry, supported by machine guns,[18] a small number of light tanks, and mountain artillery,[19] undertook the lion's share of the duties. Unlike the scouts, units from the Army of India operating in tribal territory were constrained by protecting long and vulnerable lines of communication. Any column (the term used for the Razmak, Wana, or Bannu Brigades when moving through tribal territory) mounted beyond a road head was accompanied by an extended train of slow-moving camels, horses, and mules provided by the Indian Army Service Corps, carrying machine guns, rations, water, ammunition, medical supplies, tents, and barbed wire. Armored vehicles and mountain artillery were generally too heavy and rarely mobile enough to accompany a frontier column. Patrols were confined to the easier ground in the valley floors and became undemanding prey for mobile tribesmen.

To help mitigate the threat, no column moved without first having deployed mobile troops into adjacent open country or any hill within range of the axis of advance.[20] This could often mean first having to dislodge an enemy from a strongly held position. Once established, outlying picquets on either side of the route of advance were responsible for protecting exposed columns as they transited an area. These were marked with orange panels to enable them to be seen by the column below and were mutually supportive. Known as "crowning the heights," picquets were withdrawn to the main body only when a column had successfully passed through an area.[21] Picquets were often in situ for a considerable period of time, as the total length of a column from vanguard to rear party could often exceed two miles. However, the recovery of the picquet to the main body was always hazardous and required great skill and coordination.[22] During major operations, aircraft frequently supported such withdrawals.[23] The deliberate positioning and recovery of picquets restricted movement to a deliberate and cautious pace.

There were greater dangers during the hours of darkness. To provide protection, a fortified camp would be constructed each evening, complete with a breast-high wall of rocks, barbed wire, and surrounding picquets. This further removed valuable hours from the day's march. It was desirable to reach an overnight site by mid-afternoon. Such predictability and caution was deemed necessary. Standardized tactics ensured that each component of a column understood their function despite the challenges of terrain and irregular communications.

The Army of India's additional duties included aid to the civil power in suppressing riots and putting down internal subversive movements. But as "Mouse" notes, training was rarely specific to the complexities and nuance of frontier warfare, the principal focus of most units in the 1930s.

> At the moment the sepoy is being taught to fight anybody from the French General Staff down to Ayab Gul, Malikdin Khel. He is given instruction by his omniscient young officers on how to defend himself against anything from Trynocthecene gas ejected by electric generators to boulders shoved over the edge of a khud. He is taught how to advance steadily in tidy formation under a barrage of bullets, shells and smoke, —and, a week later when he comes off guard duties, he learns how to evacuate a picquet like a scalded cat.[24]

"Mouse" summarizes the crux of the issue: "Our present day training is still based on what somebody called 'the meticulous formula for massed attacks,' which owes its birth to France, its adolescence to the aftermath, and its maturity to post-war training. Personally I would like to strangle the darned thing. It is all right for continental armies; it is heinous for the small formations that have to operate on the frontier."[25] While many avoided direct comparisons between the scouts and regulars, the reality was, at least for those serving on the frontier, that their duties were closely interlocked and, on occasion, mutually supportive.[26]

However, despite the evolving complexities of frontier warfare, many tactics, techniques, and procedures remained stagnant in the army; best practice from the scouts did not transfer easily on the frontier. As Lieutenant Colonel O. D. Bennett questions, "Why should the art, simple as it is, of applying elementary tactics correctly to suit the peculiarities of frontier fighting have remained at a stand-still when so great a proportion of the Army in India is stationed in surroundings which are ideal for the purpose?"[27] E. W. Langlands, serving with 2/3 Gurkhas, provides a persuasive overview as to the difficulties of serving in Waziristan:

> During this period as a Company Commander in 2/3 Gurkhas I had some training in Frontier warfare. I soon came to the conclusion that commanding a Company in Waziristan was far more difficult than commanding a Battalion in France (during 1915–18 I had served in France and Macedonia with the Royal Scots Fusiliers, and in 1919 I took part with 7 Gurkha Rifles in the attack on the Fort of Spin Baldak in the Afghan War). So far on active service I had always been near other troops and could usually see the enemy. In this wild mountainous country of Waziristan a Company Commander was often completely on his own, and he never knew from which direction the tribesmen would attack.[28]

Such realities were well known to applicants. However, for many Englishmen, the Indian army was more attractive than the British army. It offered better pay—which permitted those without a private income to enjoy a comparable existence with British army officers—earlier promotion, greater responsibility, and regular active duty. Before joining an Indian regiment, aspirants had to first serve an apprenticeship with the British army for twelve months. Such an attachment was aimed at cross-fertilizing evolving doctrine. However, John Prendergast was less than enthusiastic with the arrangement. "As was the custom for all officers, I was to be attached to a British unit for a year, presumably in order to advance along orthodox lines, though the value of the arrangement utterly escapes me. How much better it would have been to have joined my ultimate Indian unit immediately, where I would have found the learning of the obligatory language . . . so much easier."[29] On completion of his attachment, a British officer soon found himself in the minority in an Indian battalion:

> The small number of British officers—only about twelve to a bat-talion—was augmented by a system of officers created from the Indian rank and file who formed a good solid background for the regiment and were an invaluable source of advice for the junior officers. An able Indian sepoy could work his way up from lance naik to naik, to havildor, to havildor-major, the equivalents of lance corporal, corporal, sergeant-major. After this came a change. He could be created a jemadar, or commissioned platoon com-mander, and then if he merited it, a subadar, or company second-in-command. The plum appointment was subadar-major, akin to but more than the regimental sergeant-major of a British regiment. These commissioned ranks were something superior to the war-rant officers of British service.[30]

A recognized strength of the Indian army was the viceroy's commis-sioned officers (VCOs). These able individuals, approximately seventeen per battalion, were promoted from the ranks. To achieve this position of authority, which included such trappings as membership of a mess and the allocation of a batman, an individual had to be a first-class soldier and pass a series of exams, a significant achievement for those without prior schooling. VCOs acted as the vital connection between the British officer and his men and were treated with respect. They also provided much needed continuity and esprit de corps due to the regular rotation of British officers.[31] It was foolhardy for a decision to be made without having first discussed it with a VCO.

VCOs also assisted with the important task of recruiting. Recount-ing the strength of the Indian army, John Prendergast reveals the role of VCOs in this important undertaking.

> Wherein did our [the Indian army's] particular magic lie? This is hard to say, but I think the truth lies in the following: nepotism and love of intrigue are an essential part of Indian life. Even the best of VCOs would command men of his own village, knowing that the village elders would approve and that a fellow villager

would not let him down in a jam. The elders would take it out of the youth if he did.[32]

Despite the proficiency of the Army of India, the expense of large ground formations to maintain order in Waziristan was increasingly burdensome. In 1930, the Army of India cost Rs. 166.9 *lakh* (a hundred thousand), compared with Rs. 60.33 *lakh* attributed to the scouts, *kassadars*, and the frontier constabulary.[33] Airpower offered an inexpensive means to deter rebellion, and if it did occur it presented an evolving capability for coercing the tribes with a minimum of bloodshed on both sides.

## The Royal Air Force (RAF)

Airpower made its first appearance on the frontier in 1916. A year later, a small number of slow-moving BE2c Bristol Fighter biplanes, working from Tank, cooperated with ground troops during the Waziristan campaign of 1917. Aircraft were used again during the Third Afghan War; notably, a single twin-engine Handly-Page V-1500, piloted by Captain "Jock" Halley, bombed Kabul on 24 May 1919, which was credited with playing a key role in the *amir*'s decision to sue for peace.[34] It was not until the 1919–1920 campaign in Waziristan that airpower emerged as an indispensable component of all future operations. Such was the physical and psychological impact of aircraft on the frontier in the early days that ground operations were postponed when weather conditions prohibited aerial support. With the advent of better aircraft and improved relations between the air staff and general staff, airpower was seen as an inexpensive and effective means to observe and punish rebellious tribal behavior.[35] It also permitted an almost instantaneous response to tribal transgressions, laying aside the slow method of persuasion and negating the laborious preliminary measures necessary for a military expedition.[36]

In contrast with traditional expeditions, the employment of airpower made government forces relatively inaccessible to the tribesmen.[37] Sir Edgar Ludlow-Hewitt posits: "The effect on the tribesman of depriving him of all the happy possibilities offered by an invading column of troops must be something similar to the feeling of the matadors in a bull-fight if the bull were removed from the arena—no sport, no honour, no prizes, nothing to do but go home."[38] Airpower also afforded additional benefits. Even the most isolated tribes could now be reached with relative ease. Likewise, aerial actions were also out of reach of war correspondents; throughout the period public opinion became increasingly cognizant of military escalations in Waziristan.

By the 1930s, airpower was employed on the frontier in two ways: in cooperation with other arms and services and as a "new" weapon. In the case of the former, aircraft undertook reconnaissance, artillery observation, offensive action (bombing and machine gun raids) sanctioned by the political agent, resupply of ammunition and supplies, delivery, demonstrations to deter rebellion, convoy protection, casualty evacuation, protection, and messaging duties.[39] They also conducted daily "reassurance" visits to isolated scouts' posts.[40] Although offensive action, like punitive expeditions, was criticized by some senior British officials in India as being brutal and indiscriminate, Sir John Slessor, marshal of the Royal Air Force, argued that its routine employment was carefully controlled and more restricted than other forms of punishment. "It was considered perfectly legitimate to *shell* [with mountain artillery] a tribal village without warning, but even in an area when troops were in actual contact with a tribal enemy, villages were not allowed by the regulations to be bombed without special permission and the usual [twenty-four-hour] period of warning."[41] Therefore, despite poor levels of literacy, tribes were warned of an impending operation by a colored leaflet, written in Pushtu.[42] White leaflets were dropped a number of days prior to the bombing, followed by red leaflets twenty-four hours before the attack. Both set out the reason and nature of the action. They also articulated the government terms and directed the tribe to evacuate their village or a prescribed zone by a specified time.[43]

Whereas *lashkars* have collected to attack Gandab and are to this end concentrated in your villages and lands, you are hereby warned that the area lying between Khapak-Nahakki line and the line Mullah Killi-Sam Chakai will be bombed on the morning of [date] beginning at 7 A.M. and daily until further notice.

You are hereby warned to remove all persons from all the villages named and from the area lying between them and the Khapak

and Nahakki Passes and not return till further written notice is
sent to you. Any person who returns before receiving such further
written notice will do so at his own risk.

    Signed Griffith-Governor, dated 4th September 1933.[44]

These advanced notices allowed the tribesmen to relocate their families and much of their movables, valuables, and livestock to a place of
safety in order to avoid casualties.[45] Regrettably, leaflets were not always dropped on the correct villages in time. Moreover, a number of
tribesmen remained to protect their property for fear of being robbed
by their fellow countrymen.

    Tribes generally took shelter in surrounding caves, which "were flea-
infested and extremely uncomfortable" or became unwelcome guests in
neighboring villages.[46] *Pashtunwali* ensured that requests for food and
shelter were approved, but should any fighting occur with government
forces, receiving villagers ran a considerable risk of being mistaken for
the errant tribesmen. Colonel F. S. Keen in his "1922–23 Gold Medal
Prize Essay" cautions: "By driving the inhabitants of the bombarded
area from their homes in a state of exasperation, dispersing them among
neighbouring clans and tribes with hatred in their hearts at what they
consider 'unfair' methods of warfare, bring about the exact political results which it is so important in our own interests to avoid, viz., the permanent embitterment and alienation of the frontier tribes."[47] Moreover,
in providing a detailed warning, the element of surprise was lost and
many tribesmen chose to join their families in refuge rather than endure
an aerial bombardment, many of which lasted both day and night for a
number of consecutive days. While the physical impact of aerial attack
was far from decisive, the morale effect of an aerial assault could be considerable. However, the net result was that attacks against villages soon
began to have little or no long-term effect on the tribesmen. Continuous operations against a nomadic enemy, with limited possessions, at
best achieved a transitory effect. To counter this, many called for raids
to occur without prior warning. Although the proposal was rejected,
British aircraft, on rare occasions, bombed tribes on the frontier without notice.[48]

    Of particular significance, the bombing of villages (often viewed as
the stronghold and headquarters of the tribal forces), which lay at the
heart of airpower doctrine, was rarely politically practical or justifiable.

"The *ultima ratio* of reprisals on a raiding *lashkar,* that of bombing to pieces the village whence it set out, is, in theory, our trump card. In practice, it is not only difficult but—as we are beginning to realize—inadvisable."[49] Referring to the use of airpower on the frontier in 1930, Major General Sir Charles W. Gwynn highlights the challenges associated with its use: "During these operations it was seldom either politically expedient or justifiable to adopt the usual tactics of bombing villages from which the hostile elements came. Under the prevailing conditions, the hostile bodies were often made up of men drawn from wide areas and from villages which contained many opposed to their conduct."[50] To avoid these complexities, aerial raids were frequently diverted from village communities to strafing attacks against large herds of sheep and cattle or small groups of personnel. In response, the tribesmen divided their animals into small groupings in order to reduce the size of a potential target.[51] In reply, standing crops were often set alight with "jerry can" petrol bombs.

In the RAF's defense, Slessor is quick to point out that "in point of fact bombing was never indiscriminate; even with the relatively primitive equipment of the nineteen twenties and early thirties it was surprisingly accurate."[52] Thanks to vertical and oblique aerial photography, it was theoretically possible for pilots to identify not only each village and hamlet but also an individual dwelling for attack. This was achieved by combining aerial photographs into a large montage on which almost every group of houses was identifiable by grid references and named with the help of informers. To cite a case in point, during an operation in March 1932, the political agent deemed it necessary to destroy the house of the Haji of Turangzai, a religious firebrand. Slessor recalls:

> It was a particularly difficult target, lying as it did at the foot of a very steep hill, and it was essential not to damage the tomb of a specially holy Mullah situated in the same small village. Selected crews dived down the hill-side and bombed from about a hundred feet, the gunners firing the while to keep down the heads of enemy sharp-shooters. Eighteen 230-lb. bombs were dropped scoring ten direct hits on the Haji's house, and no other damage was done.[53]

Such an example was an exception. An experienced aircrew in perfect conditions could hit a point target with a relative degree of accuracy. However, such a crew and conditions rarely existed.[54] More usually, bombs fell wide of their target, causing collateral damage. Even routine air supply, out of contact, was challenging. Recounting an aerial resupply of rations by parachute in 1937, M. F. Kemmis Betty recalls: "Great accuracy had not been achieved and loads dropped everywhere, but luckily no one was hurt."[55]

Inexperienced pilots, overeager to take action and often under considerable pressure, were to blame for some inaccuracies. As the tactics of air-to-ground attack were still in their infancy, aircraft effectiveness left much to be desired. David Omissi notes that of the 182 bombs dropped on frontier tribesmen in November 1928, 102 completely missed the target villages.[56] Only low-level attacks increased accuracy. Moreover, many attacks missed their targets altogether. Despite improved mapping, aerial navigation on the frontier was difficult, and it was often awkward to distinguish between villages at seven thousand feet. It is unsurprising, therefore, that a number of villages were bombed in error. The tribesmen knew through experience they had little to fear from a retaliatory air attack. However, the use of airpower in conjunction with ground forces was a different matter. Combined action often forced a strong-willed tribe to submit to government terms.[57] Air Chief Marshal Sir Glen Torpy posits: "Success was most effectively delivered by an integrated use of air and land forces, with the lead in individual operations going to whichever Service was best placed to do so, depending on the circumstances particular to an individual operation."[58] Air cover was also vital in suppressing tribesmen and negating their movement by daylight. Even aircraft that had run out of ammunition and bombs could repress hostile tribesmen by conducting mock attacks.[59]

Despite the challenges associated with bombing villages, airpower was particularly useful when employed in support of a force or post engaged with hostile tribesmen, although "levels of support" were often driven by personalities. The *London Gazette* of 29 October 1937 notes:

The close and cordial relations which were maintained between the Royal Air Force and the Land Forces [during operations in Waziristan from 25 November 1936 to 16 January 1937] were a marked feature of these operations. This satisfactory result was due, in great measure, to the high example and ready co-operation of Group Captain N. R. Bottomley, C.I.E., A.F.C., under whose direction the units of the Royal Air Force played a prominent part in bringing the operations to a successful conclusion.[60]

Airpower was also effective in helping to disperse hostile *lashkars* by bombing raids, ground strafing, and the dropping of flares. Air Commodore H. le Brock recounts that while attacking *lashkars* around Sararogha and in the Tank Zam, one bomb was reported to have killed twenty tribesmen and wounded nineteen.[61] But this was not always the case. "Mauser" points out that "as a matter of cold fact, six thousand pounds of air bombs have utterly failed, in recent days, to prevent or even seriously to delay the advance on Peshawar of the Afridis, who have shown their contempt for modern mechanical inventions by practically besieging our cantonments at short range. The power of our air-arm against the only target that matters—the armed man himself—is, frankly, derisory."[62] The dispersion of hostile tribesmen by airpower added to the difficulties of the ground troops and made less effective the assistance aircraft could provide in locating and fixing the enemy.[63] Moreover, some observers criticized its employment in the attack as "a misuse of aircraft" and turning "valuable reconnaissance aeroplanes into mobile machine-guns."[64] However, the value of aerial reconnaissance was not lost on the British. Scouting sorties were used to locate and monitor hostile *lashkars*. Information from these patrols enabled column commanders to site protective picquets and to direct long-range artillery fire. It also assisted in recognizing forming-up places and lines of departure for an attack.

Airpower was also used as a "new weapon" to compel submission and enforce discipline via an air blockade. The term referred to depriving an aberrant tribe of their customary means of livelihood to such an extent that a continuance of hostilities became unendurable. This approach included preventing the watering of livestock; thwarting the plowing or harvesting of cultivatable crops; and denying the tribesmen any form of compensation that other forms of punishment might offer.[65] Air Commodore H. le M. Brock notes: "We are not aiming at infliction of casualties, but to cause intolerable inconvenience for an indefinite time by excluding the tribesmen from their villages [including their fields], and, of course, to punish them by causing material damage."[66] Sir Stuart

Pears, chief commissioner of the North-West Frontier 1930–1931, confirms Brock's position. He suggests the object of such operations is "to make the normal life of offending sections so disorganised that they are compelled to comply with our just and lenient demands."[67]

However, the employment of airpower in cooperation with other arms and services and "as a new weapon" had its limitations, challenges, and dangers. To be effective, airpower relied on accurate intelligence and speed of employment; any delays in action were increasingly viewed by the tribes as weakness.[68] The main source of intelligence came via the political chain and various informers who were keen to sell their information. The former depended mainly on personal contacts and tribal knowledge, supported by the *kassadars,* scouts, and tribal structures. This hierarchy provided a regular supply of actionable intelligence. But informers were prone to informing both ways and were adept at misleading government forces.[69] Likewise, it was not easy to gain timely information in such a xenophobic environment.[70] The RAF also possessed its own intelligence officers who linked into the regional intelligence networks. In contrast, British and Indian battalions often failed to develop effective intelligence structures. The same was also true at brigade level. Geoffrey Moore recalls, "I was soon to find that my grandiose title of Brigade Intelligence Officer masked the old-fashioned role of Brigadier's Orderly Officer. As my platoon wag remarked later when someone asked the meaning of my B.I.O. armband, 'Brigade Ignorance Officer, I expect.' He really had hit the nail on the head."[71]

Once a report had been verified, triggering aircraft in a timely manner was vital. The aim was to isolate any outbreak of violence before it could spread. According to Air Commodore H. le M. Brock, "It is as with a fire brigade—one engine can deal with a small outbreak, but if there is much delay in attending to it the fire becomes a big conflagration."[72] As the mere threat of airpower could cause a tribe to reappraise its position, the speed of response was essential. Field Marshal Sir Philip Chetwode explains that "in many cases, by taking swift action in a few hours instead of the weeks that it might have taken ground troops, aeroplanes have crushed our incipient trouble which, had it spread, would have involved a serious campaign."[73] This kind of response relied on the efficient working of the administrative machinery to obtain political and government decisions. It also called for effective communications and a duty pilot at a high state of readiness to support a *gasht* in trouble.

Despite the remoteness of the region, both line and wireless communications networks were becoming increasingly mature. According to an official report of the 1936–1937 operations, "Communications continued to be very good throughout the year, a great deal of the efficiency obtained was, no doubt, due to the fact that for the first time all L. of C. [lines of communication] in Waziristan were linked up by L/T [line telegraphy]."[74] To guard against tribal damage, consideration was given to procuring a "few converters capable of giving one ampere at 4000 to 5000 volts when run off the normal power supply."[75] Such a voltage would prove lethal to anyone touching the wires and, it was suggested, would act as a strong deterrent to sabotage. In the event of the tribesmen cutting the line, wireless telegraphy was the alternative means of communication. This proved relatively satisfactory despite the age of the equipment and mountain atmospherics. It allowed deployed politicals to remain in contact with the air staff headquarters and political authorities. It also facilitated discourse that cleared up any misunderstanding. However, range remained a limiting factor, and the technology could work effectively only if operated from the summit of a local hill, as high ridges often interfered with radio transmissions. Communication from air to ground was either by pack radio telegraphy or by dropping messages by hand.

Mule-pack sets accompanying deployed columns formed the basis of routine communications, but experience proved that for close support duties the quickest and most effective means of communication were message dropping and the employment of Popham panels and ground strip codes.[76] Should wireless telegraphy fail, the country was well suited to the use of visual signaling (both semaphore and heliograph), although this had significant restrictions. While signalers were trained to send messages by colored flags, shutter lamps, and heliograph, all three required visual contact between sender and receiver. This was not always possible to achieve. Equally, a flag was unable to be interpreted over long distances and it was difficult to establish a heliograph link. Moreover, once contact was established, the heliograph tripod could not be moved by "so much as a quarter inch until the message has been sent and acknowledged."[77] Flag, lamp, and heliograph all took time and could be unreliable. To compensate, carrier pigeons were also employed on the frontier and were viewed as the only sure link in trouble. Every scout patrol carried with it a basket of four. These were always sent off in pairs, each with the same message, due to the threat of falcons or a lucky shot. Charles Trench recalls, "So efficient were communications—a carrier pigeon from *gasht* to fort, thence by telephone or radio to Miranshah—that within half an hour of calling for help a *gasht* could expect a plane overhead."[78] When ground forces were in tribal territory, aircraft were always armed and fueled, ready for action.

> We had been very busy in Miranshah and had been given a Sunday off. We were all on the tennis court when a call came from the South Waziristan Scouts. A political had been ambushed and cut off . . . We were airborne quite quickly, three aircraft in this particular sortie. We found the Scouts on a hilltop with signs out indicating hostile fire from three sides.[79]

Limited funding also posed a constraint on close air support. The government was averse to allocating sufficient capital to the RAF to assist with routine maintenance. As a result, aircraft serviceability proved to be difficult.[80] This enabled the army to question the availability of close air support. Moreover, once deployed, aircraft were "cribbed, cabin'd and confined" by a range of out-of-date instructions on the height aircraft must fly, when, how, and against what target a pilot might use his weapons.[81] The region's extreme weather also posed significant problems. High temperatures, resulting in strong convectional air currents, made flying conditions hazardous. On several days in the year, aircraft were prevented from operating in the mountains by heavy clouds, mists, or sandstorms. Few pilots possessed experience of such an unforgiving environment, especially as flying over tribal territory was strictly controlled by the political agents. Likewise, flying in narrow steep-sided valleys was also dangerous. A moment's lapse in concentration could result in catastrophic damage to a wing tip.

There were other risks associated with flying in the mountains. Although the tribesmen possessed no recognizable anti-aircraft defense, low-flying aircraft conducting close approaches were not immune from ground fire.[82] "It may be said, in fact, that the Pathan will make good shooting against aeroplanes flying as high as 2,500 feet above his head."[83] Even at higher altitudes aircraft were not immune from tribal fire. Lieutenant Colonel C. H. T. MacFetridge notes that during large-scale operations in 1935 a Mahsud tribesman shot down, "with a brilliant shot," a RAF reconnaissance aircraft flying over Makin: "It plummeted in sickening fashion to the ground."[84] Despite the dangers, pilots had no option but to drop to lower altitudes during an attack. To mitigate tribal fire on these occasions, the air gunner fired his Lewis gun to dissuade tribesmen who routinely engaged aircraft.[85] This proved effective, but bullet holes were found repeatedly in aircraft returning from low-flying missions. During operations against the Fakir of Ipi in 1939, the London *Times* reported that "a Hart aircraft of No. 11 (Bomber) Squadron was fired at near Chaprai and the air gunner was wounded in the leg. This is the first time during the past two years of operations in Waziristan that any member of the crew of an aircraft has been wounded by rifle fire. Operational flying times during the period under review totalled about 27,000 hours."[86] Should a pilot get into difficulty through enemy fire or engine failure, there were few suitable forward landing sites for aircraft carrying ordnance. If available, pilots tried to land on the straightest section of road nearby.[87] A small number of aircrews were killed during crash landings in rugged terrain. On rare occasions, aircraft were disabled and crash landed in tribal territory. To help aid his release, each pilot carried a document promising a reward for the safe return of the bearer, known as a "blood chit." The exact amount varied according to the condition in which they returned. Although routinely held for ransom, there are only a small number of reports of pilots being killed or gravely tortured. Roger Chapman recalls a more usual outcome: "One of the RAF men, Lieutenant Howe had previously served with the battalion [Green Howards] and had to make a forced landing in enemy territory. He was returned to Landi-Kotal after two weeks; probably in exchange for a 10,000 rupee award."[88]

Furthermore, tribesmen became adept at camouflaging themselves from the air behind large boulders and in deep ravines, reducing the value of air reconnaissance. Visual reconnaissance proved less effective than expected due to challenging flying conditions and broken terrain and often turned out to be a matter of luck.[89] Lieutenant Colonel H. de Watteville suggested that "the enemy's force, moreover, are numerically insignificant, they adopt no very definite formation; they are composed of individual combatants who are, one and all, experts in taking cover both from sight and against bullet, and, consequently, are never exceedingly visible."[90] This included the employment of rudimentary slit trenches for shelter and concealment.

It was also extremely difficult to distinguish between hostile and peaceful villagers as well as government forces. "Their targets are tribesmen, who, clothed to assimilate to the exact colour of their background, and scattered in shapeless groups which have no clear outline either when halted or on the move, are all but indistinguishable at ground-level and quite invisible from a height," recalls "Mauser."[91] Reciting an incident while fighting in the village of Bui Khel, Frank Leeson highlights the realities of a mistaken identity: "This time, diving steeply over us, the Tempest [aircraft] strafed the road just as our last section was crossing it. The pilot had evidently mistaken the Scouts for pursuing tribesmen."[92] Fortunately, there were no casualties on this occasion.

More often than not, pilots had to rely on the ground commander, who was often being shot at, to tell him roughly where the enemy was. Despite the limited employment of ground-to-air radios, Popham panels, or improvised visual target indication were the primary means of communication. In the case of the latter, a number of linen strips, forming an arrowhead visible from the air, pointed in the direction of the attack. A system of linen bars across the tail of the arrow provided an approximation of distance. This provided only the most basic information and was slow to erect. This method was replaced by the "X V T Close Support Code" in 1936. Like the Popham panels, the Close Support Code relied on a number of strips of white material weighted down by stones. These were used to create an $X$, a $V$, or a $T$ to inform the pilot of friendly and enemy positions.[93] The advantage of this method was its speed and simplicity.

But even this method faced practical challenges. It was not always possible to display a character to the circling aircraft above. Moreover, letters were often masked by shadows and bushes. A common mistake was pointing the $V$ in the wrong direction. Such a rudimentary system was incapable of dealing with dynamic situations or of expressing a commander's intent.[94] Pilots could drop written messages during an overflight, but these were often lost, misunderstood, or placed the retriever in unnecessary danger. On rare occasions, political agents guided bombing raids. Such was the importance of striking the right target that during operations in 1919–1920 "Parsons [Major "Buch" Parsons],

Political Agent, South Waziristan, guided, navigated and identified targets for the bombers."[95] Parsons was subsequently awarded the Distinguished Service Order for his actions. More routinely, scout officers flew as observers.

Despite its contribution to frontier management, airpower faced considerable criticism because its effects were transitory, failing to put a lasting stop to the activities of the tribesmen. Punishment alone could not control the tribesmen. The ability to manage and pacify tribal territory, "to get into close personal touch with the people, to make roads and to develop the country," could only be achieved with the aid of ground troops.[96] This was a position echoed by Captain M. C. T. Gompertz, Indian army, when he wrote the following: "Our enemy lives on the earth, not in the air, and his mode of life offers few objectives; he lives in difficult country for warfare, and though the machine, in its multiple forms, may give us the power of swift motion and heavy fire effect, yet it is man who must finally bring him to book."[97] This commonly held opinion proved to be a misconception over the wider utility of air assets.

## Administrative Competence?

Although fully developed by the 1930s, a negligibly small British administrative and military apparatus routinely controlled Waziristan. Centuries of development produced organizations, within constraints, that were relatively optimal to the demands of the region and sympathetic to local conditions. As a rule, the rights and customs of the tribesmen were respected; nothing was ever done to interfere with their religious beliefs and customs. Managing this complex and volatile region was a central core of dedicated and knowledgeable British officials and officers. Few in number, these hand-picked rulers were like-minded individuals dedicated to a common and shared purpose. They possessed a deep sense of duty, a strong national identity, and were culturally astute. Years of experience produced individuals who were well versed in the region's traditions and people. They were equally adept at combining cultural realities with political necessity. All required a great depth of administrative competence and judgment to wield successfully the extensive powers that lay at their disposal. These frontier officials and officers worked together efficiently, benefiting from a single, political chain of command. It is telling that Colonel Khushwaqt Ulmulk, a former commanding officer of the South Waziristan Scouts, concludes from his experience that "the real issues on the frontier were political, not military. With the power of the Political Agents and the efficiency of the scouts in handling situations . . . I have no doubt that this team could have tackled most situations without resorting to the Army for help."[98]

The political agent was the central player around whom the entire local administration revolved. Highly respected and well informed, he was invaluable in navigating the intricacies of tribal politics. Supported by a small but effective staff, the political agent exercised wide-ranging powers, whether on tour or from a fixed headquarters. Due to the nuances of tribal behavior and evolving local conditions, a bespoke political approach to each agency was customary. Political agents had to bargain continually and use varying political and economic levers to achieve a desired outcome. This localized approach, based on decentralized governance founded in tribal realities, proved relatively effective and contributed significantly to the region's stability. However, isolated service amongst the tribesmen presented its own challenges. Danger, anxiety, and exhaustion were constant bedfellows for the political agent. To help alleviate these factors, tours of service in Waziristan often lasted no more than a few years. Additionally, the political agent had at his disposal an indigenous security force consisting of *kassadars* and scouts. These forces had no connection to the local military commander in peace. Similarly, the political agent was under no compulsion to consult him about their activities, although routine liaison occurred, dependent upon personalities. On a daily basis, *kassadars,* recruited from the local tribes, escorted the political agent and visiting government officials, protected roads, and assisted the *maliks* in implementing government orders. Although incapable of dealing with major disputes and disliked by the Army of India, the administration was tolerant of their many shortfalls in order to allow the initiative to work. Their removal would have created a vacuum of tribal lawlessness and confusion.

The scouts—a resident political force that provided day-to-day security in the agencies—formed the second component of regional security. Comprised principally of tribesmen from the frontier districts and commanded by British officers, the scouts were a loyal, inexpensive, and efficient force. Decades of experience in tribal management led them to develop a distinctive style of frontier policing that held the region under reasonable control. Despite their numerous qualities, the scouts were incapable of dealing with widespread outbreaks of violence due to their inadequate numbers. In such circumstances, the Army of India, held at a high state of readiness, was called upon. Consisting mainly of Indian battalions, the force possessed considerable experience of frontier operations and was highly proficient. However, notwithstanding the effectiveness of the security forces at the political agent's disposal, there was an explicit understanding that the employment of force represented only a partial solution to Waziristan. Concurrent social and economic development and political reform had to accompany the security forces' stabilizing effect. Such an all-inclusive approach, coordinated by the political agent, had a profound effect on the region.[99]

Despite regional progress, the constant threat of tribal unrest ensured that the military was quick to embrace the tactical advantages offered by technological innovations. Wireless telegraphy, machine guns, armored cars, and light tanks all had a positive impact on operations in Waziristan. However, it was the introduction of aircraft to the frontier that had the greatest impact on tribal control. Airpower permitted an almost immediate response to tribal transgressions and proved to be a worthy deterrent. Employed in collaboration with other arms and services and as a new weapon, a small number of air advocates proposed the scheme of controlling the tribesmen by airpower alone. However, the primacy of the Army of India in frontier operations and the political dependency on civilizing influences, requiring security through physical presence, prevented the theory becoming practice. Likewise, the tribesmen became air-minded and increasingly conscious of the devastating effect of close air support. Despite this, the physical and psychological impact of aircraft continued to be an important feature of tribal control. This was particularly true from 1936 onward, when the Fakir of Ipi, a compelling leader and frontier personality, began a political career that would test the British administrative and military apparatus to the full.

A typical village with multiple watchtowers; the more watchtowers, the more important the village.

A mountainous village with bordered strips of well-tended land in the foreground.

A typical tribal dwelling with fortified watchtower.

A lone tribal watchtower. Note the perforations for coolness and the holes for rifle fire.

Pathan tribesmen.

Fearless, daring, and determined, a tribesman takes aim in Waziristan.

A tribal *jirga* addressed by political officers.

Frontier scouts.

Typically dressed *kassadars* pose for a picture.

The 2nd Battalion, the Green Howards, on column of march in Waziristan, 1938.

Infantry soldiers manning a stone picquet, October 1937.

British troops marching through tribal territory to conduct a punitive expedition.

Road construction in Waziristan.

A marching column passing through a dry *nullah* in Waziristan.

Men and mules marching in Waziristan.

The imposing entrance to Razmak Camp.

A logistics resupply convoy halted in a *nullah*.

Hawker Harts of 39 Squadron at Marim Shah, 1938. Courtesy of Air Historical Branch, Royal Air Force.

A Bristol Fighter of 20 Squadron over the Khyber Pass, 1925. Courtesy of Air Historical Branch, Royal Air Force.

The Fakir of Ipi.

# 7

# A Cause Célèbre, the Fakir of Ipi, and the British Response: The Trial Case of Islam Bibi and the 1936–1937 Campaign

> Ah, Sanjak, your name that was yesterday's glory,
> Today is the veriest flash in the pan.
> Salute to the paragon! Hail your successor!
> The *Fakir of Ipi* in Waziristan.
> —Maurice Sagoff, *The Saturday Evening Post,* 18 December 1937

In 1936, after years of relative peace in Waziristan, a fifteen-year-old Hindu heiress called Ram Kori, from the settled district of Bannu, eloped to tribal territory with a Pathan student named Sayyid Amir Noor Ali Shah.[1] The teenager converted to Islam and changed her name to Noor Jehan, but was known provocatively as "Islam Bibi"—meaning "Muslim Woman"—and married the young tribesman. The girl's influential father, allegedly a "wicked Hindu *baniya* [shopkeeper]," appealed strongly to the British authorities and had the student and Islam Bibi, still a minor, taken into custody, and charges of an alleged abduction and forcible conversion to Islam were brought against Noor Ali Shah.[2] At the same time, the girl's parents brought a civil suit for her restoration to their guardianship.[3]

In April 1936 Islam Bibi's parents took the case to a British Indian court in Bannu City amid considerable publicity. With mutual Hindu-Muslim resentment growing, the proceedings took on an increasingly religious character. As the case was now in the hands of the official legal system, there was little chance for a private resolution. With no evidence to suggest that Islam Bibi was forcibly abducted, the case hinged on the fact that the girl was still a minor. Pending proceedings, Islam Bibi was put in the care of an Indian Christian woman.[4] However, due to the presence of 2,000 angry Bannu Muslims picketing the law courts, stirred by agitators, and others demonstrating outside the deputy commissioner's house on 7 April, the trial was delayed by nine days until 16 April.

Lieutenant Colonel E. H. Cobb, Order of the British Empire, the deputy commissioner of Bannu who tried the Islam Bibi case, recalls the spark that led unexpectedly to a major tribal rebellion:

> The Islam Bibi case was a simple case of the kidnapping of a minor Hindu girl—common in Bannu. One Muslim (political) party took up the case as an election stunt. Naturally the girl had to be entrusted to a neutral pending decision of her age, which was *sub judice*. The Muslim Premier, Sir Abdul Qayum, ordered that her statement be taken—I did so under objection, as I had evidence that she was a minor. I handed her over to a Muslim magistrate on [her] saying that her name was "Islam Bibi," but I continued to try and sentence the accused for kidnapping her from her Hindu parents.[5]

During the ensuing trial Noor Ali Shah's claim to Islam Bibi's custody was dismissed, as he possessed no evidence to prove legal marriage. In punishment for the crime he received two years' imprisonment for abduction. In a display of neutrality, the magistrate ordered Islam Bibi to live with a respectable Muslim family in Bannu until she came of age, at which point she could decide on her own future. In the meantime, the government looked on uneasily as tribal behavior became progressively more restless. The first tribe to protest during the trial was the Dawars, "a fanatical, priest-ridden tribe, not particularly renowned for their valour," located in the Lower Tochi Valley.[6] Allan Warren notes: "On 11 April a meeting of Dawar mullahs at Idak decided to ask that Islam Bibi be placed in Muslim hands. On 15 April the North Waziristan political agent, Major Gerald Crichton, saw the Dawar *jirga* and explained to them the government's viewpoint. In a bid to placate the tribesmen, certain Dawar mullahs were offered the chance to attend the Bannu hearings."[7] Not content with the suggestion, a *lashkar* of angry Dawar tribesmen formed. This left the Tochi Valley on 16 April and headed south to incite the neighboring tribes of the Tori Khel Wazirs and Mahsuds to join them on a march on Bannu.[8]

At the head of the *lashkar* was a "very holy" Muslim priest, Mirza Ali Khan, known as the Fakir of Ipi. Mirza Ali Khan was born sometime between 1892 and 1901 in a small village near the Khajuri Post at the western end of the Shinki Defile.[9] A member of the Bangal Khel clan of the Madda Khel section of the Tori Khel Wazirs, which belong to the greater Utmanzai branch, his father, Arsala Khan, and grandfather, Muhammad Ayaz Khan, were both spiritual leaders in North Waziristan. Although his father died when Mirza Ali Khan was around twelve, sufficient financial support was available to allow him to pursue independent religious studies. Initially he studied on the British side of the border, but he subsequently traveled to Afghanistan, to a place near Jalalabad, where he became a pupil of the Naqib of Chaharbagh, a prominent Qadariyya sufi and influential religious leader. Returning to British India in the early 1920s, Mirza Ali Khan and his brother Sher Zaman, a former teacher, sold their father's estate and bought land in the Sham and Spalga area. In 1923 Mirza Ali Khan performed the *Haj* to Mecca. On his return he settled in the village of Ipi, located close to the British military road connecting Bannu and Razmak, and lived a peaceful life, visiting shrines and religious leaders.[10] It was in the village of Ipi that Mirza Ali Khan obtained the standing of saintliness amongst the Dawars, "but not attracting as yet the attention of the authorities as a potential agitator."[11] This may have been an oversight, as the Fakir had been an important *mullah* with the *lashkar* that traveled to Khost in 1933 to join a revolt against the Afghan King.

Transiting the lower Khaisora, the Fakir—now the chief agitator—and his supporters continued south into the Shaktu Valley to drum up support from the Shabi Khel Mahsuds, promising invulnerability from bullets, shells, and bombs for those who joined his cause. The Fakir's first port of call was Fazal Din, the son of influential Mullah Powindah and the most important and influential of all Mahsuds living at the time, in the village of Latakka. However, the Fakir's pleas appear to have fallen on deaf ears, and physical support was not forthcoming. There was a similar outcome when he appealed to the wider Mahsud population of the Shaktu Valley. Disappointed, but perhaps not totally surprised, as relations between the Mahsuds and the Tori Khel, of which he was a member, were strained, the Fakir returned to the main *lashkar* in the Khaisora on 22 April.[12] Ironically, the political authorities had ordered the Shabi Khel *maliks* to expel the Fakir, but, as Allan Warren proposes, he more than likely left of his own accord.[13] In tandem, the government also sent a small number of Dawar *maliks* to the Khaisora to encourage the tribesmen to return to their tribal lands. Their efforts were not in vain, and on 22 April a number of Dawars started to disperse. This was hastened by a RAF demonstration flight over the river valley.

On the following day a contingent of Tochi Scouts destroyed three houses of the leading Dawar *maliks*, including that of the Fakir's.[14] Despite a visit by a number of Dawar and Tori Khel *maliks* to help placate the situation, the Fakir appeared defiant and the remaining members of the *lashkar* cohesive. An intelligence report of 26 April 1936, drawing on the *maliks'* findings, notes that the Fakir had three demands: the return of Islam Bibi to tribal territory; the return of the Shahidganj Mosque (an old and partially demolished mosque situated on Sikh land) in Lahore to the Muslims; and an assurance that the government would not meddle in religious questions in the future.[15] To further tighten the screw on the Fakir and his tribesmen, the Tochi Scouts and 2/19th Hyderabad were ordered to block the routes between the lower Khaisora and the lower Tochi. In addition, villages in the Tochi Valley were surrounded to prevent movement. As a result, the remaining Dawar tribesmen chose to return home on 26 April, and the following day the blockade was lifted and the Dawars surrendered abjectly. As was customary, the offending tribes were punished: supporting *maliks* lost their allowance for a defined period; the Dawars were fined Rs. 12,000 in total; and eleven tribesmen were taken into custody. Having avoided direct conflict by the deft employment of political pressure, the political authorities thought that the incident was closed and had no plans to arrest the principal instigator. Outwardly, the situation seemed calm.[16] However, the Fakir had other ideas.

Fleeing in disgust, the Fakir, accompanied by a small number of supporters, traveled south to Biche Kashkai in the lower Khaisora Valley, amongst his native Tori Khel subsection, to take refuge. Here he built a house and mosque, and after convincing his brother, Sher Zaman, to join him as his right-hand man, set out an ambitious agenda to provoke, actively trouble, and unite the tribes against the government.[17] Making friends with leaders of the local tribes and settling tribal feuds to raise his prestige, the Fakir continued his antigovernment propaganda among the Wazirs and Mahsuds, although with the latter he had limited success. However, the Fakir's misinformation began to bear fruit on certain excitable elements of the Tori Khel Wazirs. His accusation of government interference in religious affairs, principally based on the case of Islam Bibi, but also regarding the Shahidganj Mosque, resonated with many of the more youthful and turbulent elements in the tribe, many of whom found the prolonged period of peace in Waziristan irritating. "He thus collected a following of Tori Khel irresponsibles and a few Mahsud malcontents, and by November 1936 there was evidence of his influence spreading."[18]

The Fakir's activities gained momentum in August 1936 when an appellate order was passed by the judicial commissioner in Peshawar, the highest judicial authority in the North-West Frontier, consigning Islam Bibi to the custody of her Hindu parents on the grounds that the girl was under sixteen. Predictably, the decision to take away Islam Bibi from the "arms of Islam" was a major affront to the Pathan tribesmen, and it was feared that the girl's conversion might be reversed under duress. On receipt of the news, the Fakir intensified his efforts to arouse religious malcontent amongst the local tribes, which did not go unnoticed by the government.[19] Later, the court of appeal was to return Islam Bibi to the respectable Muslim family, but the damage was done, and in September mother and daughter journeyed to Bannu, never to be heard of again.[20]

Efforts to persuade the Tori Khel *maliks* to expel the Fakir from their territory or to put an end to his antigovernment activities were pursued through consultation. The political authorities were quick to remind the tribe that in March 1935 they had come to a formal agreement not to shelter persons hostile to the government in their territory and had approved the right to move troops through the Lower Khaisora Valley. Moreover, the Wazirs, who benefited considerably from numerous government incentives, had much to lose. Their annual *kassadar* pay totaled Rs. 175,260 and the *maliks'* allowance totaled Rs. 28,000. In addition, rent for the Razmak cantonment site was in excess of Rs. 20,000, and government supply and maintenance contracts, mainly for wood, meat, and milk at Razmak, came to almost Rs. 400,000.[21] It is unsurprising, therefore, that Charles Trench recalls that, "ironically, they [the Tori Khel Wazirs] were the 'fat cats' of Waziristan—none had benefited more from contracts, allowances, irrigation schemes and all the goodies of British rule."[22] However, despite the stakes and concerted efforts, the tribal *maliks,* while admitting their responsibility, professed themselves to be unable to control the activities of the Fakir and his supporters. The Tori Khel *maliks* were powerless in the face of a charismatic leader with a religious mission.

To counter the growing tide of malcontent, the resident, Sir James Acheson, decided to send a routine demonstration march through the Lower Khaisora Valley in the hope that this would put an end to the Fakir's activities.[23] This plan was poorly received by the governor, Sir Ralph Griffith, who was unconvinced of the necessity of a military patrol, especially as the timing of the request coincided with Ramadan, which would make conditions for Muslim troops and the tribesmen difficult during daylight hours. On further reflection, Griffith authorized the column on 17 November 1936. It was agreed that no punitive or offensive measures would occur, not even against the Fakir, unless troops were attacked: "the sole purpose of the two columns being sent to the Khaisora Valley was the hope that their march through the territory would stiffen the attitude of the pro-Government tribesmen and put an end to the *Fakir's* activities."[24] On 19 November the decision was made known to the *maliks,* who outwardly expressed no objections to the columns, but explained that they were unable to guarantee peaceful passage. Forewarned, the military column entered the valley on 25 November.[25]

The plan was that two independent brigade columns—the Razmak column (Razcol) and the Tochi column (Tocol)—should concentrate at camps in Damdil and Mir Ali, respectively, by the evening of 24 November. The following morning both columns marched into the Khaisora.

Razcol, consisting of four battalions and three mountain batteries, was to move via Asad Khel and thence east into the Khaisora valley; Tocol, consisting of two battalions and one squadron of cavalry [but no artillery], was to move South-West along the track from Mir Ali; the rendezvous of the two columns was Biche Kashkai. The Tochi Scouts were to cooperate in the advance, and both columns were to withdraw by the same routes on the 27th November.[26]

Up until the evening of 24 November, information from political sources suggested that opposition would be light, though long-range sniping remained a strong possibility. However, reports received that evening suggested that tribal *lashkars* were forming, although political and military opinion envisaged no serious opposition.[27] In order to negate any potential threat, Major General Donald Robertson, commander of the Waziristan District, requested additional RAF support, in the form of a second flight. This arrived at Miranshah on the morning of 25 November and was available to support the columns during their march. With the benefit of additional aerial support, the Razcol and Tocol columns advanced from Damdil and Mir Ali according to plan.[28]

Razcol's progress was unobstructed for the first five miles, but at approximately 10:00 hours, in the region of the village of Zerpezani, advanced elements of the column, including picquets, met growing Tori Khel Wazir opposition.[29] In addition, aerial reconnaissance reported the movement of small parties of tribesmen in the hills surrounding the village. Employing artillery and leapfrogging units forward against stiff resistance, the rearguard of the column reached Biche Kashkai at roughly 20:15 hours, but not before Major J. B. P. Seccombe, of the 6th Battalion, 13th Frontier Force Rifles, and two sepoys had been cut off and killed in the growing darkness.[30] The cost of the advance was fourteen killed and forty-three wounded. The enemy strength was assessed to be about 300 tribesmen. Razcol arrived at Biche Kashkai with no sign of the Tocol column.[31]

Tocol left Mir Ali with one squadron of cavalry and one battalion as the advanced guard, four platoons of Tochi Scouts operating on the right flank, and two mounted infantry troops of the Tochi Scouts screening the left. The column encountered no opposition until it crossed the Katira River at approximately 10:00 hours. Here the column attracted heavy and accurate sniping from hills on both sides of the line of advance. Pressing forward slowly against determined resistance, the column reached the south bank of the Jaler Algad by 18:30

hours, despite undertaking a complex attack by the 3rd Battalion (Duke of Connaught's Own), 7th Rajput Regiment, against a strong enemy position, including a spirited cavalry charge by a squadron of Probyn's Horse, resulting in two casualties. Despite growing casualties and discarding a golden frontier rule of establishing a secure perimeter before nightfall,[32] for which he was heavily criticized, the Tocol commander, Brigadier Francis Maynard, considered it essential to reach the rendezvous that day, a further distance of five miles, and decided to continue the march in the dark.[33]

At 19:30 hours the column advanced once again. Unsurprisingly, the head and the rear of the column were attacked at close range by fanatical tribesmen. According to Charles Trench,

> They were ambushed, many of their horses (including the Brigadier's) stampeded and were lost, and they eventually had to stop because they could go no further. At one time the Assistant Political Agent for North Waziristan, Captain Roy Beatty, who thought it his duty to move at the head of the column with the vanguard of Tochi Scouts, was crawling round a bush, revolver in hand, in pitch darkness, stalking the Scouts' commander who was crawling round it, stalking him.[34]

With further casualties and reassuring news of Razcol's progress, it was decided to halt for the night, approximately two miles short of Biche Kashkai. Tocol's casualties for the day were eleven killed, including Major J. W. B. Tindall, 3rd Battalion, 7th Rajputs, and forty-one wounded.[35] The following day, two battalions and one mountain battery from Razcol assisted Tocol in reaching Biche Kashkai. Fortunately, this operation occurred without casualties. The following day, due to materiel shortages and numerous casualties requiring evacuation to Bannu, both columns recovered to Mir Ali at the cost of ten more wounded.[36] The withdrawal was closely pursued by the enemy.

Instead of demonstrating a show of force, the operation surrendered the initiative to the enemy and many saw the planned withdrawal as a clear manifestation of the Fakir's mystical powers. Surprised by the level of resistance, the leadership displayed by the Fakir, and the arrival of additional tribesmen to join the cause, the political authorities were concerned that disaffection could spread easily to the Mahsuds and the

Madda Khel Wazirs and to other parts of Waziristan.[37] To address this situation the government decided to conduct further military operations in the region. These had three objectives: the punishment and submission of the tribal sections that had opposed the columns in November 1936; the construction of a road from Mir Ali to the Khaisora Valley — which became known as Bond Street after the Commander Royal Engineers Lieutenant Colonel Bond;[38] and the prevention of disaffection spreading to other parts of Waziristan. On 29 November political control of North and South Waziristan was handed over to the military, with the resident being nominated as the chief political officer.[39]

On 2 December, a Tori Khel *jirga*, in which representatives of all sections were present, was informed by the political agent that the government would conduct a punitive expedition and that a road was to be built into the lower Khaisora Valley. The political authorities also instigated *jirgas* among the Madda Khel and Shaktu Wazirs. The former returned to the Khaisora to retrieve their tribesmen,[40] and the latter, promising to prevent armed gangs moving through the valley, produced twenty-two British rifles as a guarantee.[41]

With significant reinforcements and the reorganization of the Waziristan District into "Wazirforce" and the "Waziristan Area," the former comprising all troops in the defined area of operations and the latter comprising all remaining troops in the Waziristan District, the advance of Wazirforce commenced on 5 December. Against negligible opposition, but hindered by heavy rain 9–12 December, the column advanced at a pace matching the speed of road construction: approximately one mile a day. "During this period [5–18 December] very few hostile tribesmen were seen by the troops or aircraft, but the destruction was carried out of certain selected fortified buildings belonging to tribesmen proved to have been actively hostile during the period 25th to 27th November."[42] This included the Fakir's townhouse in the village of Zarinai. Sir John Slessor recalls that "it [15 December] was a lovely morning and from where I sat on my boulder among some gunners about five hundred yards away across the valley I could watch through my field-glasses the sappers busying themselves about the *Fakir's* house, which stood among fruit trees on the edge of the village . . . At that very moment a sapper leant on the key, the Boom! of the explosion rolled across the valley and the tower collapsed."[43]

By 19 December it was decided that the road from Mir Ali to the Khaisora Valley should be extended, through the Sein Gorge to Dreghundari on the main Bannu-Razmak road.[44] Therefore, 19–30 December was characterized by road improvements and construction, although there was also a successful operation by the 2nd Infantry Brigade on 22 December to flush out a growing concentration of tribesmen in the western end of the valley. This action resulted in sixteen killed and wounded, while enemy losses were estimated at twenty killed and twenty-one seriously wounded.

It was during this period that the Fakir, who had moved to Arsal Kot and set up a food kitchen (*langer*), allegedly feeding between 200 to 300 tribesmen per day, pronounced that tribesmen from outside the area were rallying to his calls and that a Mahsud *lashkar* was forming on his behalf.[45] Although there was no *lashkar*, additional tribesmen gathered. Afghan tribesmen from Birmal, the only part of Waziristan on the Afghan side of the border, continued to flow into the area, becoming the principal component of the Fakir's force. This cross-border reinforcement was not unusual, but their arrival challenged the rudimentary supply system, which was already overstretched.[46] To assist the situation, "long-hidden village grain caches were opened, and occasional camel-loads of rice and flour [were] smuggled in from Bannu via the Shaktu Valley."[47] Further supplies were received from the local tribes. However, despite the logistical challenges, the arrival of Afghan tribesmen encouraged the local tribesmen to continue their cause. Due to the presence of the Fakir and his supporters at Arsal Kot, No. 60 (Bomber) Squadron of the RAF, after customary warning from both messengers and leaflet drops, attacked the village on 31 December 1936 and 1 January 1937 using high explosive incendiary and antipersonnel bombs. The Fakir and his followers, warned of an impending attack, moved to some nearby caves and remained under the protection of Said Rakhnan Kikarai.[48] The hamlet of Arsal Kot was completely destroyed.

Prior to this, a Tori Khel *jirga* held on 28 December was ordered to give up one hundred rifles and the same number of hostages "as an earnest of good faith, and to expel the intruding tribesmen from their limits."[49] However, the tribesmen explained that they were powerless to eject the tribal reinforcements. A subsequent *jirga* took place on 5 January, during which the participants surrendered the required number of rifles and hostages to the authorities. Nevertheless, the Tori Khel were informed that until the "intruding" tribesmen had been evicted from their territory, they were forbidden to return home. Although the number of tribesmen shrank noticeably, it was decided to eject the remaining intruders by force on 7 January.

> A combined air and land operation was, therefore, carried out on the 8th January by Razcol, Tocol and the Royal Air Force. Razcol advanced eastwards from Damdil, and Tocol westwards from Jaler, along the high ground north of the Khaisora stream. In conjunction with these movements, the Royal Air Force carried out offensive action in the valley and the hills to the South, and a section of 6-inch Howitzers stationed at Damdil Camp registered targets in the valley, with the help of air observation.[50]

Despite a concerted attack by Afghan Kabul Khel Wazirs on 9 January against an isolated picquet, resulting in four dead and eight wounded, the reentry of troops into the Khaisora was relatively unopposed.[51] Thereafter, tribal opposition waned and subsequent operations were undertaken without major incident. The supplement to the *London Gazette* suggests two reasons for the temporary cooperation of the Tori Khel and their supporters: the destruction of the Fakir's headquarters at Arsal Kot by the RAF and the employment of harassing fire on registered targets, principally on 8–9 January, causing panic amongst the hostile tribesmen.[52] However, the shortage of loot, dwindling supplies, growing casualties, and a lack of tactical success also played a part.

On 15 January, with resistance almost at an end and conditions in Waziristan returning to normal, all Tori Khel allowance holders were summoned to a *jirga* at Mir Ali. In an atmosphere of compliance, the terms announced to the tribesmen were the forfeit of a year's allowance and rent from the government; the return of all government property looted or captured; the acceptance of responsibility for good behavior of hostile elements of their own tribe and of strangers within their tribal limits; the dismissal of one hundred and twenty *kassadars* who had failed in their duties; and the adoption of unspecified measures to ensure the good behavior of the Fakir if he remained in Tori Khel territory. With the tribesmen in agreement, normal district administration through the political authorities resumed on 1 February, the ban on movement was lifted, and the Tori Khel were allowed to return to their homes. With the withdrawal of all military reinforcements by early February, the campaign came to a close.[53]

Encouraged, yet again, by the withdrawal of troops from the region, the Fakir renewed his hostilities. On 6 February, Captain John Keogh, 1/12th Frontier Force Regiment, who was attached to the South Waziristan Scouts, was mortally wounded by a fanatical tribesman eight miles south of Razmak on the road near Ladha. On the following day Captain Roy Beatty, Hudson's Horse, attached to the Tochi Scouts and acting as the assistant political agent, North Waziristan, was murdered by a Madda Khel tribesman, named Zawel, in the Upper Tochi Valley, near Boya.[54] Fanaticism was behind both murders, but in the case of the latter, loot was a driving factor. These attacks acted as a catalyst, and numerous raids and kidnappings followed, many across the administrative border. With unrest growing and the Fakir receiving increasing support, including fresh reinforcements from southern Afghanistan, Waziristan District was reinforced by the 1st Abbottabad Brigade. Concurrently, political pressure, reinforced by air action, was brought to bear on the tribesmen. *Jirgas* were also held with the Mahsuds and Madda Khel. Despite a concerted effort by the government to placate the situation, the Fakir announced a decree calling on all *kassadars* and *maliks* to leave government service or be denied Muslim funeral services. This was met with only limited support.[55]

Conditions continued to deteriorate despite an announcement on 9 March by Sir George Cunningham, the newly appointed governor, encouraging the tribes to restore the status quo.[56] As a result, additional forces, including the Headquarters of the 1st (Indian) Division, under Major General E. de Burgh, and the 3rd Infantry Brigade, were ordered to the region. Political negotiations continued, but, instead of improving the situation, discussions were used by the Fakir to buy time.[57] A London *Times* article dated 15 April 1937 reported, "Whatever the nature of the propaganda he [the Fakir] is disseminating, it is having a violent effect on the tribesmen, who are reputed to be fighting with fanatical fury whenever engagements occur."[58] To help control the situation, the Arsal Kot area of the Shaktu was placed under an aerial blockade and *kassadars* of the Haibatai Tori Khel section were dismissed. Despite these measures, outrages continued, and on 21 March a camp picquet of the

1st Infantry Brigade was attacked. This was followed by a concerted attack by approximately 1,000 Tori Khel Wazirs against troops of the 1st Infantry (Abbottabad) Brigade, who were conducting "Road Opening Day" duties near Damdil on 29 March. The attack was a surprise and included the daring ambush of a machine gun section. Despite government forces regaining the initiative, fighting continued throughout the day with considerable casualties on both sides.[59]

With little improvement in the general situation and no sign of a settlement, an array of measures was brought to bear against the Tori Khel tribe to calm the situation in early April. They included the stoppage of allowances; exclusion of the tribe from certain settled districts; the evacuation of villages located within a three-mile radius of the Bannu-Razmak road; and the evacuation of inhabitants within a defined geographic region around Arsal Kot and a belt of country in the Lower Khaisora. In the case of the latter, failure to evacuate was punishable by air action. Despite these measures, the situation showed little sign of improvement. Without tribal order, raids into the settled districts continued, and sniping, ambushing, bridge-blowing, and wire-cutting were commonplace.[60] To further discourage attacks, tribesmen were warned that any hostile action within a two-mile radius of troops or posts would be liable to an aerial or ground attack. In the case of the former, a time lapse would allow nonhostiles to leave an area before a retaliatory attack occurred.

Although the situation in South Waziristan appeared relatively stable, conditions in North Waziristan had a far-reaching impact on the tribesmen of the region. Despite a warning of an imminent attack, at 07:45 hours on 9 April a motorized convoy of forty-five military and hired civilian lorries and two or three private cars, including four armored cars and an infantry escort, traveling from Manzai to Wana was attacked in the Shahur Tangi by a party of Mahsuds and Bhittanis led by Khonia Khan, a Jalal Khel Mahsud.[61] Nearly all the vehicle commanders, sitting in the passenger seats of the lorries and private cars, were killed in the initial attack, and the majority of lorries were immobilized on the road.[62] A gallant defense by the infantry escort, supported by armored cars, prevented the column from being overrun. Receiving news of the attack, detachments of infantry and South Waziristan Scouts hurried to the scene to repel the tribesmen. This was followed by an infantry battalion from Bannu and a "busload" of loyal Mahsud *maliks*. After a tense but relatively uneventful night, the raiding party vanished and the convoy was extricated.[63] Government casualties totaled forty-seven dead and approximately fifty wounded. In addition, one aircraft was shot down while providing close air support to the stranded convoy. In contrast, tribal losses were assessed to be sixteen killed and twenty-six wounded.[64]

The success of the attack and punitive reprisals proved to be a spur to further violence amongst the Mahsuds. This materialized in the form of attacks on mail and passenger lorries and an assault against the Tiar-zha Scouts' post near Wana. Fortunately for those in the post, aerial attacks against the village responsible for the attack caused the *lashkar* to disperse. To apply further pressure against the Jalal Khel, who under the leadership of Khonia Khan were the main perpetrators of the attack on 9 April, the tribe was ordered to vacate their grazing grounds from 28 April to 30 May.[65] The attack had a profound effect on routine resupply.

> The organization of the lines of communication and the arrangements for supply of Razmak and Wana at this stage are of interest. After the attack on the convoy in the Shahur Tangi on the 9th of April the movement of Government convoys ceased, except on roads which were protected by posts and piquets held by regular troops. Arrangements were made for supplies to be delivered to Razmak and Wana in privately owned lorries with tribal drivers [Mahsuds], running under their own tribal protection, while full use was made of bomber transport aircraft . . . The protection of the forty-six miles of road from Bannu to Damdil was carried out by the 1st Division, and the permanent piquets thereon were supplemented by the daily patrolling of the road by infantry and armoured cars, supported by artillery and aircraft. The system worked smoothly and efficiently but reduced the number of troops available for active operations.[66]

With tribal attacks on civilians and government forces rising and the Fakir undeterred, further reinforcements were sent to the area. By 12 April, the 3rd (Jhelum) Infantry Brigade was positioned at Mir Ali.

Three days later, the 2nd (Rawalpindi) Infantry Brigade arrived in Waziristan. As a further insurance, the 9th (Jhansi) Infantry Brigade was held at a high state of readiness in its home station. With little sign of improving conditions, and large numbers of tribesmen assembling in the Khaisora and Shaktu Valley on 22 April,[67] political control, including control of air operations, was handed to General Sir John Coleridge, who was tasked with pacifying the area.[68] Allan Warren correctly notes that while the government had been reluctant to conduct major reprisals up to this point, principally due to negative experiences the previous November, this approach had inadvertently allowed the situation to deteriorate to a dangerous extent.[69] With the governor keen to restore order, and many *maliks* still providing resolute support to the government, Coleridge was given a relatively free hand.[70] His plan was simple: bring the tribesmen to battle on grounds favorable to government forces and then inflict heavy losses on them.

With large concentrations of hostile tribesmen in the Lower Khaisora and the political dismissal of a request from the Fakir to reopen negotiations, a column, consisting of the 2nd and 3rd Infantry Brigades, advanced southwards from Mir Ali on 23 April. The column encountered little opposition as it reached the Khaisora River on 25 April, and it became evident that the tribesmen would not concentrate for battle.[71] A further advance was necessary. On 27 April, the 2nd Infantry Brigade moved westward up the Khaisora Valley and camped at Bishe Kashkai, on the north bank of the Khaisora River. After dark, the camp came under intermittent sniper fire followed by a concerted attack by several hundred tribesmen on the camp's perimeter and picquets, using Mills grenades and homemade bombs.[72] At one point tribesmen came within fifty yards of the perimeter. With fighting over in the early hours of the morning and casualties light, the advance resumed on 29 April toward Dakai Algad, where the enemy were concentrating.[73] Accompanied by close artillery support and air cover throughout, the column was able to inflict significant casualties on the tribesmen in the surrounding hills. After a series of actions, the enemy remained elusive, and sniping practically ceased as the force withdrew on 3 May. Although the enemy had received heavy punishment, somewhere in the region of 200 killed and 150 wounded, the operation was far from decisive. The Fakir was still at large in Arsal Kot in the Shaktu Valley, claiming the government was too frightened to linger in the area. Moreover, his composite force, also located in the valley, continued to grow in strength.

It was now necessary to strike a decisive blow against the Fakir and his supporters, who had gathered in the Upper Shaktu Valley in the area of the Sham plateau, the summer grazing grounds of the Tori Khel. Despite the recent tribal losses in the Khaisora, additional reinforcements from Afghanistan and a small number of Mahsuds had helped swell the Fakir's force to approximately 3,000 tribesmen. Under the command of General A. F. Hartley, a veteran of the Boer War, government forces were repositioned from Mir Ali to the mud fort of Dosalli, a scouts' post twenty miles northeast from Razmak, prior to the start of the operation.[74] The opening moves began on the night of 11–12 May, when the Bannu Brigade, supported by eight platoons of Tochi Scouts, who had some familiarity with the route, conducted a silent night advance over the Iblanke Pass.[75] Frank Leeson notes: "The physical difficulties of the route turned out to be much greater than expected, and owing to the need for absolute quiet nothing could be done to improve the path for the transport animals, which were heavily loaded with guns, equipment and supplies."[76] John Prendergast, who took part in the operation, recalls, "Slowly we mounted the spine [over the Iblanke ridge] and as dawn broke we were over the lion's shoulders. We could hear the army behind us and the occasional crash of a loaded mule as its burden touched the steep side of the track to throw it off balance and send it hurtling to the valley below."[77] Despite the challenges, the force, assisted by a simple deception plan, surprised the tribesmen, and the Bannu Brigade, after light fighting, was able to establish a foothold on the Sham plateau with few casualties. Outflanked and having taken heavy casualties, the tribesmen were driven from their positions and their numbers fell rapidly to less than 50 percent. This was exacerbated by regular aerial attacks and supply shortages.

Advancing by a different route, a second brigade, supported by light tanks, joined the Bannu Brigade on 12 May. Six days later the Bannu Brigade set out to establish a new camp at Ghariom and, despite stiff opposition, achieved its objective with few casualties. The brigade was subsequently reinforced by the 1st Brigade and Wazir Division headquarters on 24 May, and a road was built between Kach and Ghariom camp. "The next stage of the operations," as reported in the *London*

*Gazette,* "was an advance from Ghariom to Arsal Kot, in the Shaktu Valley, in order to engage the Fakir's immediate following, evict him from his headquarters, and, if possible, apprehend him."[78] The column consisted of 37 British troops, 3,358 Indian troops, and 926 animals. Though progress was frequently held up by opposition, Arsal Kot, a small hamlet consisting of eight to ten houses and a tower, was surrounded in the early hours of 28 May. Although the Fakir had escaped the closing net, his headquarters, a cave complex extending thirty feet below ground, was penetrated by government forces.[79] An eye-witness recalls, "that which appears to have belonged to the *Fakir,* and which showed signs of very recent habitation, consisted of two large rooms each capable of accommodating 20 to 30 men [and] a small alcove probably used for the *Fakir* himself."[80] Despite suggestions that the Fakir had fled as government forces arrived, it is more likely that his personal bodyguard, comprising of about eighty trusted Wazirs and Mahsuds, anticipating the advance, had extracted him from the area secretly on 19–20 May.[81] The official history notes that the Fakir had moved to Bhawana Manza, six miles southeast of Arap Kot, with *malik* Khonia Khel.[82]

Despite its failure to achieve its primary goal, the operation had broken the resistance of the Tori Khel, who, tired of having a war fought on their territory, sued for peace at a *jirga* at Miram Shah.[83] At the same time, certain restrictions previously imposed on the tribe were relaxed, and air actions over evacuated areas wound up. There were also wider benefits from the operations: many Afghans, demoralized by the government action, had chosen to return home; raids into the settled districts were reduced; and, temporarily, the Fakir was out of business, having suffered a severe blow to his reputation.[84] John Masters recalls in *Bugles and a Tiger* that the Fakir's cave complex was destroyed "unceremoniously" by detonating three unexploded RAF bombs found near the entrance to his hideaway.[85]

But there was still more to be achieved, and government activity now turned against the Mahsuds. As a tribe, the Mahsuds had not declared their participation in hostilities against the government, although many of its tribesmen had taken part in *lashkars* in tribal territory or raids into the settled districts.[86] With the *maliks* professing their inability to control the hotheaded members of their tribe, the government deemed it necessary to carry out a punitive action in Mahsud territory, despite their relatively satisfactory behavior.[87] The first advance, in extreme temperatures of 110 degrees Fahrenheit, occurred from Ghariom, via Sararogha, to Razmak. Mahsud *kassadars* picqueted the camps to prevent sniping, and, throughout, the column was accompanied by large numbers of Mahsuds, giving the impression that the force was there by request. However, in the meantime, the situation between Razmak and the Shaktu deteriorated. With a *lashkar* of between 150 and 200 strong gathering in the upper regions of the valley, operations were conducted from 15 to 17 June to disperse the tribesmen. This was followed by a surreptitious raid conducted by eight platoons each of the Tochi and South Waziristan Scouts, supported by the 1st Division, on 20 June in the Shaktu Valley against the Fakir.[88]

The Fakir was reliably reported to be in a tower at Gul Zamir Kot, the largest village in the Shaktu Valley, approximately five miles southeast of his former headquarters in Arsal Kot on the Wazir-Mahsud boundary.[89] Here he received support from both sides of the border and kept in close touch with many of his supporters, notably Sher Zaman, Azal Mir, *malik* Khonia Khel, and the Din Fakir Bhittani. The village was surrounded at dawn on 21 June by sixteen platoons of scouts, but after an extensive search, it was discovered that the Fakir had flown the nest. With news of an impending raid, the Fakir had apparently slipped through the net of advancing scouts. However, the raid was not a total waste of effort. Ten Mahsuds, a Tori Khel tribesman, and Arsal Khan, the owner of Arsal Kot and a rebel government *malik*, were taken prisoner. In addition, two Hindu hostages were released from captivity. They had spent nearly four months in prison and were in a terrible condition.[90]

A number of operations were subsequently undertaken to disperse hostile gangs in South Waziristan. Independent action by the Bannu, Wana, and Razmak brigades against Mullah Sher Ali, the leader of the Mahsud contingent, and a number of hostile *lashkar* totaling 250 mostly Afghan tribesmen occurred 22 June to 1 July. Despite determined resistance and the failure to capture Sher Ali, the main hostile gatherings were dispersed, and by 1 July the government announced that there were no formed bodies of tribesmen left in the region.[91] With their mission complete, the Bannu Brigade returned to Razmak and the Wana

Brigade to Wana. However, the Razmak Brigade remained in Asman Manza.

Despite a series of government successes and improvements in some areas, conditions in Waziristan remained volatile, and routine intimidation and violence continued.[92] Tribal *maliks* had still not regained control of the hotheaded elements, and the Fakir, after fleeing Gul Zamir Kot following repeated attacks by aircraft of No. 1 (Indian) Wing, RAF, had settled in an inaccessible natural cave complex on the northwestern slopes of Prekari Sar, astride the Wazir, Mahsud, and Bhittanis tribal interface. This location was chosen with great care. "Four passes had to be crossed to reach the stronghold from the nearest valley, and the last pass was so steep and narrow that only one man could cross at a time. As an additional precaution picquets were posted night and day."[93] From here, the Fakir reopened his communal kitchen, received visitors from Bannu, and continued his hostile propaganda, inciting the tribes to rebel under the banner of his *jihad*.[94]

With large-scale opposition at an end, road construction, in both Wazir and Mahsud territory, was started as a means to help pacify the tribesmen and assist with their economic development.[95] Four roads were constructed through the Shaktu Valley: from Dosalli in the north; the lower Khaisora Valley in the east; Ahmedwan on the south; and Razmak in the west. They totaled ninety miles. The roads were built by a combination of government troops, contract laborers, and four specially enlisted construction battalions.[96] These efforts were not well received by the tribesmen, who opposed any penetration into their territory. Exploiting growing government opposition, the Fakir encouraged sniping against camps, picquets, and those working on the new roads.[97] He also sent his brother, Sher Zaman, on an ambassadorial mission to the Tirah, south of the Khyber Pass, to encourage the Orakzai tribe to join the Fakir's cause.[98] Other attempts to gain support included communications with the Fakir of Shewa, an influential religious leader in North Waziristan, who, fortunately for the British, remained unresponsive to the Fakir's calls for help.

With government forces homing in on the Fakir's new lair, including a targeted aerial bombardment 1–9 August, Mirza Ali Khan was left with little option but to move to safety. Departing Madda Khel territory, the Fakir moved westward to Mandech, a Mahsud village, five miles southwest of Razmak. Here he participated in a number of tribal *jirgas* instigated by Firqa Mishar Mohammed Khan, the Afghan government's representative in Urgan. These gatherings, attended by many of the leading outlaws, were opportunities to encourage tribesmen to continue their struggle against the government.[99] Such was the Fakir's popularity that on 16 August he attracted approximately 4,000 tribesmen from within Waziristan and the Khost Province; 2,000 of the tribesmen present were Mahsuds, who were in favor of resuming hostilities. The gathering dispersed the following day, possibly owing to the effects of heavy rainfall and a lack of food supplies.[100] With his popularity on the rise, the Fakir addressed a letter to the Afghan government seeking their assistance. This complete, the Fakir addressed a "great throng from horseback," announcing that if the Afghan government's reply to his correspondence was unfavorable he would renew hostilities on his own initiative.[101]

With unrest spreading, including the routing of small garrisons at Sharawangi, Tara Jowar, and Sholam and renewed activity by Mullah Sher Ali, the political authorities endeavored to restore order by instigating a number of complementary measures.[102] Tori Khel *kassadars* were reinstated, specified areas were placed under government control, and road construction advanced, with Wazirs and Mahsuds hired as laborers. The government also constructed scouts' posts and continued punitive attacks against selected villages. In addition, tribal fines were issued to the Mahsuds on 24–26 August, amounting to 1,020 rifles and a fine of Rs. 40,000. Likewise, the Tori Khels were fined 420 rifles and Rs. 20,000; the Bhittanis, 350 rifles and Rs. 5,000; and the Dawars, 150 rifles and Rs. 3,000. The combined effect resulted in the Tori Khel agreeing to government terms on 10 September, but the fines had little impact on the insurgency's core of irreconcilable tribesmen. Moreover, the Fakir continued to rally some support from the local area and to encourage *kassadars* to desert.[103]

Due to the threat of punishment against those who sheltered the Fakir and the aerial bombardment of his temporary hideout in the Gumbakai caves, Mirza Ali Khan dispensed with a permanent headquarters and remained relatively mobile.[104] He now returned to an old tactic: the employment of hit-and-run attacks, sniping at camps, and poisoning

military water supplies with picric acid crystals. This was comple-
mented by an increase in petty offenses in the Datta Khel area. In the
*Green Howards' Gazette* of December 1937, the 2nd Battalion mused
that "the maddening thing about this so-called 'War' is that one rarely
ever encounters any organised resistance—fighting for the most part
consisting only of the odd sniper, who will wait, apparently for days
and months, for the opportunity of shooting the 'Infidel' with comparative immunity."[105] Despite Musa Khan Mahsud and the Mullah of
Karbogha encouraging peace, others under the Fakir's influence tried to
force the government presence from the region by more conventional
means. Mullah Sher Ali, who had established a headquarters and communal kitchen at Laswandai, formed a *lashkar* of approximately 300
Mahsud tribesmen from the Baddar and Main Toi valleys and used it
to good effect in September, damaging the Razmak water supply and
blockading the brigade. The Bannu Brigade countered this with two
full-scale attacks on the *lashkar* on the night of 26 September, as well
as the bombing of Sher Ali's headquarters. Likewise, the Bhittanis, who
under the leadership of Din Fakir, the Fakir's commander in chief, supported raiding gangs in August and September, were also subject to an
attack. Government forces also penetrated the Bhittanis' stronghold of
Kot, freeing Hindu prisoners kidnapped by the tribe. They also started
constructing a road, joining the village with the Bannu District, which
was complete on 3 December. During the expedition, and much to the
government's surprise, Din Fakir sued for peace, despite the protests of
Sher Ali.

The Fakir next based himself in some inaccessible caves in the mountain cliff at Kaurai, near Barman Sar, only a few miles inside the international border in Madda Khel country. Allan Warren notes, "As the
*Fakir* was so close to the Durand Line, the Government was reluctant
to pursue him for fear of arousing both the local [Ghilzais] Afghan
tribesmen and the Afghan Government."[106] In relative safety and with
little possibility of the Fakir's presence causing a considerable influx of
transborder tribesmen into Waziristan, he was "left sitting on the mountain top."[107] Naturally, the Fakir continued his antigovernment propaganda and started to agitate the tribesmen in the local Spinwam area.
Here he was supported by a *malik* called Gulla Jan, who undertook
recruiting on the Fakir's behalf. On 1 November, with tension rising

and conditions deteriorating, the government ordered a Madda Khel *jirga* to expel the Fakir from its territory or face punishment. But, with prior warning and the tribe relatively powerless to control his actions, the Fakir slipped effortlessly across the border into Afghan territory and safety.[108] By 10 November the Fakir reached Pasta Mela, a Madda Khel village in Zadran territory. In late November, he crossed back into India, and the Madda Khel reluctantly sheltered him in Maizar despite government reprisals.

With weather conditions deteriorating and the tribes battle weary, the government decided to undertake a final "mopping-up" operation that started on 13 November. The operations concentrated principally on the Khaisora and Shaktu Valleys, areas known to have harbored hostile forces throughout the year. The troublesome Lower Shaktu Valley fell to the 1st (Abbottabad) Infantry Brigade under the command of Brigadier R. D. Inskip.[109] It was here that Sher Ali and a number of hostile leaders gathered a *lashkar* of irreconcilables and professional criminals. Despite a relatively easy advance, conditions became difficult when a covering camp picquet, established by the 3rd/15th Punjab Regiment, came under fire. On the night of 16 November, six enemy tribesmen hidden among the hills wounded two soldiers.[110] This was followed on 17 November by further difficulties when the 1st Battalion, the South Wales Borderers, advanced through a narrow *tangi* (gorge). Major T. H. Angus recalls:

> A platoon of the vanguard had moved forward into the *tangi,* another platoon was on its way to piquet the eastern ridge on the right bank and another to the eastern ridge of the left bank when the enemy opened fire. A few seconds before fire was opened the intelligence officer of the South Wales Borderers had reported enemy. No enemy had been seen, but he had spotted a loophole through which he could see daylight. Suddenly the daylight was blotted out and he reported enemy. The first burst of fire caused casualties in the vanguard platoon and the piquet moving out to the right.[111]

Seemingly caught unaware, the enemy had allowed the lead troops to move into the *tangi* before opening fire. In a position of some danger, a platoon of machine guns returned fire immediately on the enemy positions. The officer commanding the lead company brought a number of guns of the 13th Mountain Battery forward into action in the direct fire role. This prompt and effective action, supported by close air support, dislodged the enemy, who were concealed behind rock faces with narrow fissures that had been filled with stones to create firing positions. The remainder of the advance proved uneventful, and events drew to a successful conclusion.[112] With conditions returning to normal and the presence of so many troops deemed counterproductive, Coleridge transferred political control to General Sir Allan Hartley on 15 December, and the 1st Division Headquarters and the 1st, 2nd, and 9th Brigades returned to their peacetime locations in India, closing major operations for the year. A temporary state of peace endured throughout the worst of the 1937–1938 winter. The official report notes warily:

> The *Fakir of Ipi*, who had been the focus of all the trouble from the beginning, was still at large, as were four or five of his most ardent lieutenants, but his and their power and prestige had been very considerably diminished, and they were finding it very difficult to obtain supporters.[113]

# Keeping the Flame of Insurrection Alight, 1938–1947

Don't you know! Why, it's Ipi's cannon!
—Frank Baines, *Officer Boy*, 1971

Abandoning his ambitious plans for regional supremacy, the Fakir resided in the inaccessible hills of the upper Tochi Valley for the remainder of the winter. Despite all the leading tribes of Waziristan supporting his activities in various guises throughout 1936–1937, the Fakir had failed to unite the tribes' substantial fighting power and support under a unified banner. Moreover, he was equally unsuccessful in providing a single point of command or even a unified chain of command. As a result, major tribal *lashkars* amounted routinely to no more than 700 to 800 tribesmen at best and were uncoordinated in their activities. Despite this, the rebellion had inflicted nearly 1,000 casualties on government forces and cost the Treasury approximately £1.5 million. Predictably, the Fakir continued to incite trouble against the infidel British while preserving his own existence, and in January 1938 tribesmen attacked government property near Spinwam.[1]

Annoyed by an upsurge in violence, the government announced to a Madda Khel *jirga* on 8 February that they must give security to the Fakir or expel him from their land. The *jirga* denied the presence of the Fakir in their territory but were told that the government did not accept their denial and that the onus was on them to prove he was not with them and to explain where he had gone.[2] Adjourning for a short time, the *jirga* reassembled, stating that given extra time they would make every effort to encourage the Fakir to live among them at peace or, failing that, would evict him. Accordingly, an extra ten days' grace was granted to the tribe. However, the tribe proved incapable of meeting the government's demands and were attacked by aircraft as punishment. With conditions slowly deteriorating across North Waziristan, the Madda Khel were subject to a land blockade by early April as relations with the tribe continued to deteriorate.

With tensions high in North Waziristan, Mullah Sher Ali, a constant irritant to the authorities and a more prominent field commander than the Fakir, renewed his antigovernment activities. Forming a *lashkar* of 150 tribesmen near the intersection of the Tank Zam and Shahur rivers, the tribesmen thwarted a two-pronged attack by scouts, leaving 150 South Waziristan Scouts encircled on a nearby mountain all night. Help arrived in the form of four successive loads of ammunition and one of Very Lights dropped from a circling aircraft, piloted by Lieutenant Jackson, which enabled the force to survive the night.[3] Flying at a low altitude and encountering heavy rifle fire, Jackson was subsequently awarded the Distinguished Flying Cross.[4] Vanishing at dawn, the *lashkar* was responsible for the death of four scouts and ten additional casualties. A concerted air attack followed, but by July Mullah Sher Ali and his followers were once again in action in Splitoi, Sararogha, and in the hills near Ladha, surprising a road *gasht* on 18 July. There were also wider outbreaks of violence. The London *Times* reported on 21 May:

> During April offences throughout Waziristan and in the settled districts continued. A police sentry in Bannu City was shot, and a *munshi* [language teacher] of the Military Engineering Service was murdered near a post in the Shahur Tangi. Over 50 home-made bombs were laid on roads and railway lines, and even on parade grounds as far apart as Miranshah, Kohat, Frohal, and Bannu.[5]

Motivated by the successful exploits of Mullah Sher Ali, the Madda Khel formed a *lashkar* and attacked the Tochi Scouts' post at Datta Khel, some twenty miles west of Miram Shah and about 170 miles southwest of Peshawar. This was the most remote of the scout posts in North Waziristan and not very far from the Afghan border. Cutting many of the roads through the upper Tochi Valley, the tribesmen isolated the post and subjected its inhabitants to a thirty-day siege, which included the limited employment of tribal cannon against the fort. The blockade ended on 9 June when a small relief column reached the post, but it was not until August that the road to Datta Khel was repaired and opened to routine traffic.[6] This incident was followed by an attack on Mami Rogha camp by approximately 500 tribesmen with two tribal cannon on the night of 13 June. After some fierce fighting, the *lashkar* was dispersed on 16 June.[7]

The region's affairs became more complicated with the arrival of Muhammad Saadi al Kailani, better known as the "Shami Pir," who claimed direct descent from the Prophet and was a member of the Gilani clan. He was also the first cousin of ex-Queen Souriya, Amir Amanullah's wife, who had abdicated in 1929. Kailani, the son of a chief judge and leader of the Syrian branch of the Islamic Qadiriyin, was born in Damascus on 15 May 1905. Educated in Beirut, Kailani completed his studies in Germany at the agricultural Royal Gymnasium College, Potsdam, and in 1929 he married Ingeberg Knuht, the daughter of a senior German police official. Returning to Syria in late 1929, Kailani found himself in genuine financial difficulty. By 1936 his debts amounted to 15,000 gold sovereigns and, despite a number of measures to build up capital, including the sale of his residence at El Ghouta, Kailani decided to travel to India, a country he had visited before, with the objective of collecting money from his followers, a customary practice among religious leaders.[8] He left Damascus in December 1937 and arrived in Bombay on 1 January 1938, accompanied by an "orderly" believed to be a Turkish citizen.[9]

From Bombay Kailani traveled to Tank, where he was entertained by the Nawab of Tank before entering South Waziristan in March. Preaching on religious matters and acting as an arbitrator and intermediary, Kailani quickly gained a substantial following.[10] Suggesting that he possessed ample supplies of cash, Caroe recalls that "he [Kailani] wore a Sayyid's robes, a beard and a sanctimonious air" while in tribal territory.[11] Understandably, both the Afghan and British governments were suspicious of his activities, but Major Barns, the political agent for South Waziristan who interviewed Kailani at Kaniguram on 12 June, was unable to substantiate any doubts.[12] Moreover, his activities from March to June were not objectionable. However, the following day, Kailani, persuading the tribes to accept him as their leader, raised a *lashkar* of 3,000 tribesmen in Kaniguram. As an incentive, he offered forty Afghan rupees a month to any volunteer who would join his cause. Denouncing the ruling of Afghan King Zahir Shah as a charlatan, he espoused

Anglophobe Amanullah as the lawful king of Afghanistan. The *lashkar* advanced toward Afghanistan on 23 June.

A diplomatic flurry ensued, with the Afghan ambassador in London calling for immediate action. On the third day of the march Barns got a message to Kailani stating that he must disperse his following within twenty-four hours and leave Waziristan or the *lashkar* would be bombed. Since there was no compliance, the *lashkar* was bombed repeatedly and attacked by military forces from the Ghazni District. Following a number of actions, Kailani sought a peaceful outcome. Meeting Barnes on 26 June, Kailani was offered £25,000 on the condition that he depart India immediately, under government arrangements, having first recalled and dispersed his *lashkar*. Agreeing to the bribe on all accounts, Kailani left India on 4 July in an Imperial Airways flying boat, bringing to a close an interesting crisis that, luckily, remained confined to South Waziristan.[13]

Meanwhile, in North Waziristan the Madda Khel, who had been harboring the Fakir, attended a *jirga* at Miranshah in mid-June, during which they declared that Mirza Ali Khan was no longer among them and surrendered a number of rifles as security for their good behavior. The Fakir now based himself in the isolated Kharre Mountains north of Datta Khel. With strong intelligence regarding his whereabouts, the government decided to attack the Fakir with ground forces. On 13 July a force left Degan to evict the Fakir from his new hideaway while concurrently dispersing his following of hostile tribesmen and destroying his supply dumps. However, a number of factors, including the difficulty of the terrain, resulted in a less than successful operation. Despite scattering Mirza Ali Khan's followers deeper into the mountains, the raid failed to achieve surprise and the Fakir slipped across the border into Afghanistan. Unfazed by government activities a number of tribal outlaws continued to exploit the lawlessness of Waziristan, and raids into the settled districts, encouraged by opportunism and bitterness, continued to increase. One of these was a well-planned raid on 23 July on Bannu City. It was instigated by an ex-Tochi Scout called Mehr Dil and involved upward of 300 tribesmen.[14]

Returning to Waziristan once government forces had departed, the Fakir continued his antigovernment activities, despite the offer of a free pardon announced in October 1938.[15] To counter his influence, the government bombed any tribe or village known to be harboring him. This proved to be a relatively successful tactic, with the Fakir being kept on the move. "By the end of May, 1939, he [the Fakir] had been exiled by both the Tori Khel and the Madda Khel, and the former were thus able to make peace officially with [the] Government on June 15th."[16] However, this was the third settlement with the Madda Khel in as many years and, with the Fakir still at large in the local area, few were prepared to forecast an end to hostilities with the tribe.[17] Moreover, the Fakir continued to have power over a dedicated core of followers and routinely received visitors keen to listen to his counsel, despite efforts to weaken his authority. The *Evening Standard* of 31 May noted: "Mountain artillery have shelled him, regiments have gone into action against him, but he has wriggled out of every hole until then. If they want him, they need to dig [for] him like a badger."[18] But, not for the first time, events on the world stage started to call into question the effectiveness of the existing frontier policy.

In 1938 a committee chaired by Admiral of the Fleet Lord Chatfield was the first to call for a review of frontier policy. However, it was the Russo-German nonaggression pact of 1939, which renewed concern over India's external security, and the declaration of war against Germany in September 1939, which led the government to review the defense of India's mountain passes. Nevertheless, with no plans to deploy an expeditionary force from India and no end in sight to tribal raiding, change would have to wait. Indeed, despite the anxiety of the cabinet, who feared committing large numbers of troops and the RAF at a time when relations with Russia were so uncertain, by February 1940 it was business as usual, as government columns departed for the Ahmedzai Salient to remove a troublesome *lashkar* that had terrorized the inhabitants of the region.[19] A newspaper report concluded optimistically: "The operation will mark a definite military effort to end the pinpricking episodes which have interrupted normal life in North Waziristan during recent months."[20] While not conducting a wholesale review of frontier policy, the government made a number of revisions to existing force dispositions and defenses.

By early 1940 the garrisons in the Khyber, Kurram and Tochi Valleys had been considerably reinforced, while in Chitral equipment and ammunition supplies were moved up to Mastuj in order to be readily available in an emergency for the northern companies of the Chitral Scouts. Reinforced concrete pill-boxes, gun-emplacements and "dragons" teeth sprang up in the defiles of the Khyber, in the lower Kurram and in the Shinki and Shabur gorges of Waziristan.[21]

Likewise, steps were taken to help preserve order in the settled districts by reinforcing the frontier constabulary and strengthening the hands of the civil authorities.

In late 1940 a *lashkar* led by the influential Mahsud Hayat Khan attacked the Tiarzha Narai and Ladha posts with cannon fire. Their field gun was allegedly on short-term loan from the Fakir, who remained relatively quiet throughout the year.[22] As was customary, Hayat's village was attacked by the RAF, followed by the dispatch of a Razmak column into the area. However, all did not go according to plan during the ground operation. A company of the 5/8th Punjab, conducting picqueting duties, lost contact with the main body during the withdrawal phase on the night of 6–7 December. From the valley below, a mêlée could be seen unfolding, and as darkness fell on the valley, it was clear to all that a tragedy had occurred. Casualties for the entire operation amounted to sixty-six dead and sixty-five wounded; almost all losses and casualties occurred on the night of 6–7 December among the 5/8th Punjab.[23] As Alan Warren notes poignantly, "The fate of the December 1940 Razmak column was an example of the misfortune that could befall any troops who failed to meet the exacting requirements of mountain warfare."[24]

No doubt heartened by the success of Hayat's *lashkar,* the Fakir was keen to sustain the momentum of rebellion in 1941, despite the reality that the Tori Khel and the Madda Khel had become increasingly war weary. Instigating trouble in the village of Barzai, the Fakir preached insurrection to a crowd of 2,000 tribesmen in early May. Although the gathering was dispersed by the RAF, the weakly garrisoned fort at Boya nearby was attacked by repeated cannon fire while, concurrently, a number of roads were blocked by tribesmen. To restore order, troops were sent to the upper Tochi, and the Bannu Brigade was made responsible for the security of the road network. In addition, Boya village was destroyed as a punishment.[25]

Despite isolated outbreaks of violence, which were relatively straight-forward to control, there was a more troubling development that vexed the government. Notwithstanding sensational newspaper articles in 1937, stating that the Italians were behind the revolt in Waziristan, reliable information, including a number of decoded messages, now suggested that the German and Italian Legations in Kabul were in contact with the Fakir through a chain of agents and that arms and money were being supplied to him. According to one report, "Very recently it was reported from a well-informed source that a sum of sixty-thousand rupees was received by the Fakir of Ipi from the German Minister at Kabul, on July 14th, and that on the same date twenty-five .303 rifles, bought with Italian money, were also delivered to him."[26] It was also suspected that European agents had at various times been in contact with the Fakir and that a German named Hans T. von Bassewitz, traveling incognito as a newspaper correspondent in Kabul, was in contact with the religious leader. An extract from an intelligence summary from the Military Attaché in Kabul notes that "he [von Bassewitz] is reported to know English, Persian, Arabic and Pashtu well and to be able to read and recite the Koran by memory. He is dressed as a Pathan *fakir* or *malang* and wears an artificial beard."[27] Unsurprisingly, the government concluded that Germany was putting into action a plan to stir up trouble for Britain on the North-West Frontier, thereby tying down units of the Indian army.[28]

There was further evidence to support this assessment. In a 1941 intelligence summary it was reported that two Germans, Professor Manfred Oberdöffer, an entomologist, and Doctor Fred Brant, a leprosy expert, had left Meshed for Kabul with the intention of making their way to India. Allegedly part of a wider initiative to establish contact with the Fakir and incite violence, the two specially trained agents fell into a trap set up by the authorities.[29] The report notes the following:

They duly arrived in Kabul and, on the night of July 19th, were fired upon by an Afghan interception party, which encountered them on the Logar road on their way towards the Southern Province accompanied by a party of *Jajis,* armed and carrying a large sum of money apparently destined for the *Fakir of Ipi.* Oberdöffer was killed and Brant was wounded. In addition to the money, which is reported from one unconfirmed source to have been about one lakh Indian currency and two thousand gold coins, they carried a number of maps and two light automatic guns.[30]

Moreover, it was known that Enrico Anzilotti, the secretary of the Italian Legation, visited the Fakir at the Gorwekht caves in 1941 disguised as a Pathan tribesman. He reported that the Fakir was keen to continue to incite the frontier tribes but required money, weapons, and ammunition.[31] Despite the disappointment of Oberdöffer and Brant's attempts to gain entry into Waziristan, the German Legation was reported to be sending regular payments to the Fakir. Their task was made more difficult when the British government persuaded Afghanistan to repatriate all Axis nationals, excepting those in the Legations. By the end of October 1941, just over 200 Axis nationals had left India. Fortunately for the British, German funding, combined with "protection-money" subscriptions, appeared to have little impact on the scale of violence in Waziristan. Likewise, the Fakir appeared reluctant to support the Germans and was equally opposed to any anti-British scheme not of his own making—a somewhat naive and not self-indulgent appreciation of his own unique position.[32]

The year 1942 saw an incessant level of lawlessness, with hit-and-run attacks being a regular feature of frontier life for government forces. Predictably, the Datta Khel fort was again the target of the Fakir and his followers. In May, with the joining roads cut, the scouts' garrison was surrounded by a *lashkar* of over 500 tribesmen. "By day there was desultory sniping and at night the fires of the tribesmen's picquets shone on the hilltops; occasionally the post was shelled and on a few occasions there were concerted attacks which were beaten back by the defenders."[33] After a prolonged siege of nearly three months, which included a brief visit from a scouts' column from Miranshah, a brigade column, under Major General R. B. Deeds, was sent from Gardai to free the post. After successfully achieving their objective, the brigades joined other government forces in a series of punitive actions in the local area. However, the operation was not without casualties on both sides. Tribal casualties were assessed to be approximately 60 dead and 100 wounded. Government casualties were recorded as seven killed and forty-five wounded.[34] However, there were other challenges vexing the government. Further to the south in the Sind, a zealous sect of Hurs under Pir Pagaro conducted a sequence of sporadic guerrilla attacks against railway lines. Although not politically motivated, such was their success at "train-wrecking" that martial law was introduced. Attacks continued until the capture of Pir Pagaro in early 1943.[35]

Nevertheless, such large scale attacks as those experienced at Datta Khel were increasingly rare. Tribal attrition and the volume of recruits keen to join the ranks of the Indian army and scouts weakened the ability of the tribesmen to form a critical mass in tribal territory. Moreover, a less visible profile, improved targeting, and surgical strikes by aircraft also helped to dissuade large-scale violence. Despite such procedural advances, background guerrilla activity continued in 1943. However, a poorly considered decision to train 4/2nd Gurkhas on a mountain close to Makin proved too much for the local tribesmen to stomach. Pettigrew recalls the events that resulted in a major outbreak of violence:

> In [December] 1943 a wartime Gurkha battalion asked for trouble by moving up one of the spurs of Pre Gul on a training scheme. They presently reached a height of nearly eight thousand five hundred feet, to a hill looking down over Makin. That was asking too much of the Abdullais. As soon as they realised that the Gurkhas (good soldiers but Hindus, remember) were virtually in position overlooking their back-yards in Makin, the tribesmen took to the hills all round and the fight was on. Quite soon the Gurkhas were so hard pressed that another Gurkha unit [4/3rd Gurkhas] had to come out from Razmak in support. By dusk it was chaotic. There was even fighting on the hockey ground just outside the Razmak perimeter wire. Fifty rifles were lost and many men were missing. Most of them, dead of course, were brought in by the *maliks* the next day and retribution was swift.[36]

In early 1944 the Fakir reappeared in the Shaktu Valley, living among the Shabi Khel Mahsuds. Wishing to maintain a low profile and not wanting to further incite the tribes, the government chose to counter his presence by airpower alone. Throughout the first quarter of 1944, the RAF bombed the Fakir's headquarters and strafed *lashkars,* which totaled on occasions close to 1,000 tribesmen.[37] Undeterred, the Fakir and his followers shelled the Tochi Scouts' post at Ghariom and the Iblanke picquet. These attacks led the political agent of North Waziristan, Captain Lotus Lowis, to address the problem indirectly. Wishing to eliminate the Fakir once and for all, Lowis gave a Wazir spy an incendiary device made by the RAF to plant in his cave. "When no news was received of the explosion, Lowis sent for the informer who swore that he had planted the bomb correctly. To prove his point the [spy] went back to the cave and brought the unexploded bomb back to Miranshah, where he dropped it on the PA's desk. Lowis noticed with some relief that the spy had merely forgotten to pull out the safety-pin."³⁸ Unaware of the attempt on his life, the Fakir returned to the sanctuary of his caves in the Gorwekht Mountains in late October.³⁹

With victory for the Allies in World War II almost certain, it was timely for a review of frontier policy. In 1945 a Frontier Defence Committee, established under Major General Francis Tucker, concluded that the frontier had consistently tied up large numbers of allied servicemen and that the tribesmen, while uncoordinated, had persistently dictated the tempo of military operations. In simple terms, the tribesmen maintained the initiative; government forces were largely reactive, not proactive. However, the committee's answer to the problem was hardly novel. Their recommendation was a reduction in regular army numbers, with a compensatory increase in scouts and irregular forces.⁴⁰ Unsurprisingly, the review's findings were regarded with skepticism.

In 1946, with the Fakir and many of his most determined followers still at large, periodic sniping, outbreaks of violence, and kidnappings continued. The abduction of Hindus from the settled districts, in particular, had become a favored tactic of the troublesome Shabi Khel Mahsuds. Frank Leeson recalls: "Some of these kidnapees were bought back by payments of Mahsud allowances to the Dre-Mahsud *Jirga,* who in turn paid a portion to the Shabi Khel, at the same time bringing tribal pressure to bear on them for the release of the Hindus."⁴¹ The Shabi Khel tribesmen, disgruntled with their share of the allowances, planned to rectify a perceived imbalance by kidnapping Major John ("Jos") G. S. Donald, the political agent of South Waziristan.

Summoned to attend a meeting with the Shabi Khel to discuss allowances, Donald was ambushed on 21 June while transiting from Razmak to Tank. Despite putting up a spirited fight against his abductors, Donald and two of his agency staff were extracted forcibly from their vehicle and moved quickly into the cover of the surrounding mountains. With political negotiations under way and Donald demanding his immediate release, his captors agreed on a ransom of Rs. 110,000. On receipt of the first installment of Rs. 10,000 on 2 July, Donald and his agency staff were released unharmed in Razmak, having promised first to do their best to mitigate any government reprimand. Punishment, as the tribe refused to return the ransom money, was handed over to the RAF.[42] Despite the untold psychological pressures of his time in captivity, a short period of rest at Nathiagali concluded with Donald keen to return to his old post. However, Donald's return to duty coincided with the decision to bomb the tribesmen in seven villages.[43]

> As an honest and sensitive person he [Donald] found himself in an unenviable and awkward position and, after wrestling with a series of indignant Mahsud *jirgas* he wrote to the Governor asking to be relieved of his post and stating that he felt altogether incapable of carrying out his duty. Soon afterwards he found the strain so intolerable that he took his own life [on 25 September 1946].[44]

Aerial attacks against the Shabi Khel began on 1 August.[45] With prior warning, few casualties were reported. However, there were three fatalities during the accidental bombing of a neighboring village, which encouraged a number of letters to the editor of the London *Times*.[46] Keen to exploit the situation, Abdul Ghaffar Khan, the Redshirt leader and "frontier Gandhi," condemned the attacks in a number of provocative speeches. However, despite increased press interest, local events were overshadowed by the growing reality that the British presence in India was drawing to a close. In October, Pandit Nehru, the Congress president, conducted an ill-advised visit to Waziristan amid a blaze of publicity. Conducting a series of staged events, the Hindu politician received a lukewarm reception. Verbal abuse was commonplace, and at one stage, during a *jirga* on the residency lawn at Razmak, all tribesmen attending the hearing rose to their feet in unison and walked out of the event.

The final year of British rule was 1947. With uncertainty, confusion, and anarchy commonplace throughout India, the Mahsud and Bhittani tribesmen attacked and pillaged a Hindu bazaar on the outskirts of

Tank. It took three days of concerted effort before order was restored. Under the false assumption that Bannu was equally open to plunder, the tribesmen recalibrated their sights and crossed into North Waziristan. However, the loosely formed *lashkar* was intercepted as it traversed the administrative border in lorries, and it never reached its final destination.[47] Allan Warren provides a summary: "The tribesmen had been drawn to the settled districts by news of the communal riots that had reached fever pitch by mid-April. From 15 to 25 April 121 people were killed in D. I. Khan City, and almost the entire minority population was displaced. However, after the partition plan to create Pakistan was made public on 4 June, Muslim fear of Hindu rule, in both the settled districts and the tribal agencies, subsided dramatically."[48] Perhaps prudently, the Indian National Congress decided to discard the North-West Frontier Province, with local voters in favor of joining the new state of Pakistan and most Hindus having already departed the province.

Despite heavy losses to key tribal personnel, June and July saw the Fakir's guns shell Miranshah and the fort at Datta Khel without significant damage. In addition, the Fakir openly denounced the notion of a partitioned British Indian empire, encouraging visitors to abstain from voting for Pakistan in the approaching referendum. Despite widespread propaganda, Viscount Louis Mountbatten, the last British governor general of India, announced the partition of India on 3 June, and responsibility for the North-West Frontier Province was transferred to the new Pakistan government on the fifteenth of the month.[49] In a public attempt to forge improved tribal-state relations, the government decided to withdraw the regular garrison from Waziristan to be replaced by scouts and *kassadars*. However, the practical reality was that troops were needed elsewhere in Pakistan and during a phased withdrawal a series of ambushes occurred, resulting in numerous casualties. However, with the departure of the British and the regular garrisons, the Fakir's rationale for resistance was weakened. Having previously declared his hand, the Fakir now called for an independent Pashtunistan, transferring his old hatred of the British to the new Pakistan government.[50] Although his new cause failed to arouse the passions of his most ardent supporters, the Fakir continued his antigovernment activities until his death in 1960.

The Afghan press have, as would be expected, made quite a splash of the death some days ago of that redoubtable divine whom they call Haji Mirza Ali Khan and whom we know as the *Fakir of Ipi*.

It is doubtful whether Gorwekh, the *Fakir of Ipi's* mountain retreat is actually in Afghanistan or Pakistan, but it is certain that he was often brought to Gardez and other places in Afghanistan for rest, treatment and discussions with the Afghan authorities.

Although the *Fakir* was in many ways the titular head of the Pashtunistan movement and held the title of President of the Nationalist Government of Central Pashtunistan since 1950, there is reason to think that he was not all the Afghans desired in the way of a Pashtunistan leader since he was so notoriously "independent minded." And for the last few years of course he had been very old and very ill. Nevertheless the Afghan press expressed much sorrow at his death and praised his life, achievements and deeds of daring.

His passing brings to an end one of the great acts of the drama of the Frontier.[51]

Despite concerted efforts to apprehend or neutralize the Fakir of Ipi in Waziristan, Mirza Ali Khan evaded capture and directed resistance against the British from 1936 to 1947, successfully undermining all attempts at colonial control and capitalizing on constitutional changes in India. For the Fakir, the case of Islam Bibi was little more than a catalyst to unite the well-armed and martial tribesmen of the region against non-Muslim interference; it was not the raison d'être for his *jihad*. Claiming divine support and encouraging tribesmen from both sides of the border to rally to his cause, the Fakir caught the government flatfooted in the initial stages of the 1936–1937 campaign. With rich pickings among the impetuous and hotheaded elements of the region's tribesmen, who were angered by government interference in Islamic laws, the Fakir, erudite and charismatic, directed rebellion to oust government forces from tribal territory. Such was his success at rallying support amongst a divided tribal society while simultaneously avoiding capture that the region experienced levels of violence and direct contact unseen since the

Third Afghan War. Fortunately for the government, this intensity was short lived.

In spite of lacking a coherent design for operations and experiencing, on occasion, campaign inertia, the numerical and technical superiority of government forces, supported by political initiatives, helped transform the Fakir's campaign away from traditional battle. Heavy attrition among the younger elements of the tribes, extensive material destruction, fear amongst some *maliks* of losing highly prized tribal allowances, and an increasingly war-weary population left the Fakir with little option but to revert to hit-and-run style guerrilla attacks, kidnappings, and criminal activity. Having lost the ability to conduct prolonged operations, such tactics played into the hands of the Fakir's most ardent supporters, creating a determined, dangerous, and elusive enemy. However, in changing his approach, the Fakir encountered reduced cooperation among some *maliks* as the government endeavored to placate the region by exploiting the benefits of allowances and building roads. To counter this, the Fakir relied on ideological persuasion, propaganda akin to an election campaign, and a number of trusted and unscrupulous lieutenants to help carry on his cause judiciously. He also exploited government policy on dealing with tribes. Charles Miller notes: "Instead of making it plain that government terms had to be accepted on a tribal-wide basis, the British dealt piecemeal with individual sections or clans. The result of this was that even if two or three or four groups submitted, other large Pathan forces would still remain in the field, and thus assure shelter for the *Fakir of Ipi* . . . while they continued to hound and harass and mutilate and simply drag the war on."[52]

Pressuring the tribes to expel the Fakir from their territory or face government retribution, Mirza Ali Khan was pursued from one hideout to another. Exploiting the proximity of the Durand Line, *Pashtunwali*, and his religious status, the Fakir enjoyed refuge amongst the tribesmen on both sides of the border and proved to be an elusive prey. Despite garnering moral and financial support, the government chose not to irritate the Afghan government by large-scale operations against his lairs close to the border. Instead, they decided to counter the Fakir's presence by airpower and indirect means while continually encouraging the Afghan government not to cooperate with him. This proved to be an exasperating state of affairs. Colonel Khushwaqt Ulmulk recalls: "At that time the impression we had was that Government of India was not making enough effort to capture him. It was quite puzzling."[53] But there were also other worrying complications in Waziristan that required careful handling. The arrival of the Shami Pir proved again that a charismatic religious leader, even one from outside tribal territory, could unite the tribesmen in fanatical enthusiasm.[54] For a short period in the late 1930s, the demise of the Kabul government seemed feasible as a *lashkar* marched on the capital.

With the outbreak of World War II, many of the Fakir's supporters joined the British army. With a reduced pool from which to draw support, the Fakir appeared to be an acquiescent recipient of Axis support. However, his naivety, indifference to his inimitable position, and reluctance to support any anti-British scheme not of his own creation, resulted in the Fakir remaining aloof from major Axis initiatives. With no external assistance, the full potential of his movement was never realized and the Fakir became more concerned with his own survival as his freedom became increasingly constrained. Despite this, his activities, and those of his closest supporters, successfully kept government forces fully mobilized on the frontier until independence, rendering them unavailable for other tasks outside India. Indeed, in the 1930s there were more troops stationed in Waziristan than in the remainder of the Indian subcontinent. Likewise, he employed the full gamut of tactics available to him in order to stall, undermine, and belittle the mechanisms of government. At all times he appeared to know the psychology of his adversary. With hindsight, the Fakir exposed the vulnerability and physical constraints of British policy on the frontier and, in so doing, has helped shed light on a number of useful insights regarding current and future political and military challenges.

# 9

# The Hard-Earned Lessons and Realities of the British Experience in Waziristan, Part 1

Speak to an old soldier, just mention the North-West Frontier of India, then watch his face—his eyes will sparkle, practically lighting up his features. Then a tremor will come into his voice. He will say, "Yes, I was there," emphasising that, as a soldier in India, they were the best days of his life.

—T. S. Donnelly, "Afghanistan and the North-West Frontier," 2002

## Introduction

Waziristan's independent Pashtun population and mountainous terrain posed a significant challenge to the political authorities charged with controlling the region. Without central authority, tribal law and governance proved to be an imperfect substitute, but the only one available, and forces operating in tribal territory had to adjust to this reality if they wanted to be effective. The best results were achieved when the tribal structure was co-opted to a degree (with bribes and threats) but many of the decisions were left in the hands of the locals—with mixed results. Despite a varied record of success, the British approach to tribal control was adopted by the Pakistan state at independence. Such was the credibility of the British method of controlling the frontier that in 1947 Sir George Cunningham, who had been retired for a year, was invited by the governor general, Mohammed Ali Jinnah, to return as governor of the North-West Frontier Province, "being the man everyone trusted."[1]

Despite the absence of a framework of British officers and officials in key appointments, the well-developed model of a political agency, overseen by a political agent and regulated by indigenous *kassadars* and militias, remained largely intact following partition. However, in contrast with the British approach, the Pakistani government agreed not to base regular troops in the tribal agencies beyond September 1947; this was seen as key to securing the loyalty of the frontier tribes and discouraged the formation of an independent Pashtunistan. Recognizing that the factors that helped shape British policy on the frontier remained largely unchanged beyond independence, the Pakistani government continued to embrace the British techniques of tribal control until late 2001, when the Pakistani president, Pervez Musharraf, implemented a significant change in policy following his decision to support U.S. efforts in Afghanistan in the wake of the September 11 terror attack on the United States.[2] Therefore, despite the passage of time, the British experience of the forward policy in Waziristan remains pertinent.

## The Importance of Grounding Policy in Reality

Unlike its predecessors, the forward policy, which lasted from 1923 until independence, was a pragmatic and cost-effective compromise adapted to the realities of the frontier. The policy did not place a regular government presence throughout the breadth of Waziristan, nor did it disarm the independent tribes on the Indian side of the border or impose taxation; all would have been impractical and might have resulted in a long-term legacy of hatred. Instead, the government only maintained pockets of indigenous and regular forces, held at high-readiness at strategic locations, and assumed only tacit responsibility for the welfare of the tribesmen. The majority of tribal territory was left largely untouched. Full-scale Western administration, as in the Indian States, was not deemed necessary or practical. Routine control occurred through the political authorities by means of the Frontier Crimes Regulations.[3] Unaffected by everyday government interference, the tribesmen were left alone to govern themselves according to their customs and religion. This occurred within the existing tribal framework and structures. However, far from being anarchistic, traditional methods resulted in a practical, if fragile, balance based on tribal society. Blood feuds, for example, acted as a brake on violence and adultery. The expectation that revenge would occur made a tribesman think twice before committing a brutal crime or eloping with his neighbor's wife.[4] Other customs provided a similar stabilizing influence. Trench recognized this important dynamic, writing, "In Tribal Territory there is not what is generally understood as law and order, nor is there sheer chaos and anarchy—although there would be were it not for the *Pashtunwali* code which sets a standard of behaviour to which the Pathan at least aspires."[5] However, the balance between *Pashtunwali* contributing to stability and acting as a catalyst for violence was often upset.

There was limited government intrusion as long as the tribesmen abstained from raiding. Instead, the government relied on heavily subsidized tribal *maliks* to maintain order. However, these headmen, despite being loyal, had insufficient authority to bring the more hotheaded tribesmen to account. Moreover, it was not in their best interests to do so, as there were financial benefits from orchestrating limited violence; each situation presented unique opportunities for financial reward or concession if handled deftly.[6] There were also other more profound challenges. The tribesmen appeared incapable of existing physically or psychologically without episodic pillaging. Nurtured in an atmosphere of raiding and blood feuds, such activities "constituted life, liberty and the pursuit of happiness" for the tribesmen.[7] This was linked to another interesting facet of tribal culture: a readiness to both fight and deal with government forces simultaneously. Despite large annual allowances combined with limited initiatives designed to transform the martial ethos of the tribes, the tribesmen preferred to maintain their warrior traditions while concurrently dealing with the political authorities. This was rarely seen as paradoxical or a conflict of interests. When incentives failed to pacify the tribesmen, punishment for tribal transgressions was rapid and overwhelming but rarely decisive.

Philip Woodruff likened the tribesmen of the frontier to tigers in a national park: "They could kill what deer they liked in the park; they risked a bullet if they came outside and took the village cattle."[8] This strategy of containment, reinforced by a "glint of steel tactfully hidden behind the glitter of gold," resulted in a predictable pattern of conflict and a unique approach to controlling the frontier.[9] Tribal transgressions were countered initially by political mediation and financial initiatives. If unsuccessful, these were followed by punitive strikes, which generally took their objectives with comparative ease, although forces often suffered during the withdrawal. Consequently, the government hit back even harder, with the tribe finally agreeing to terms during a tribal *jirga*. These terms were seldom fully met, however.[10] Therefore, instead of retaining the initiative and constantly seizing opportunities, military forces relied heavily on deliberate disrupt, interdict, or defeat operations, which had a profound effect on the perceptions of the local populace and were, effectively, irreparable actions. Little importance was placed on a meaningful long-term strategy that sought to clear, hold, and build on initial military successes. Understandably, this reactive approach came in for repeated criticism. A *Times* article notes, "Indian politicians cannot be expected to give their uncomplaining support to expensive frontier operations if each costly 'pacification' of Wazirs, Mahsuds, or Mohmands is to be followed by their equally costly repacification at regular and almost predictable intervals."[11]

Moreover, any advantage gained in the initial phase of an operation was lost during the retreat. As government forces withdrew, tribesmen regained the initiative psychologically and harried army columns from their territory, undermining government prestige and bolstering tribal confidence. In a society where resolve and firmness were essential, frontier tactics did little to send an unambiguous message to the tribesmen. With episodic outbreaks of violence and no prospect of an end to the tribal problem, it is hardly surprising that Air Commodore N. H. Bottomley, commander of the RAF group in Peshawar 1934–1937, described the frontier dilemma as a "perennially interesting, fascinating and apparently insolvable problem."[12]

However, from 1923 onward there were never any genuine attempts to solve the frontier problem, nor was there a desire for a "decisive victory" or a conclusive political result. The very essence of the tribal problem was containment, and benchmarks of "good enough" and "maintaining the system in check" sufficed. Initiatives designed to pacify the tribesmen served mainly to make the military problem less difficult to handle. Therefore, tolerating shortfalls and inconsistencies was fundamental to making the policy work. Defending the settled areas and guarding the frontier with limited resources required the acceptance of a dynamic, ambiguous, and volatile environment while tailoring the reaction and method to the threat. Compromise and accepting a suboptimal solution were routine. This approach relied on suppressing the symptoms of the frontier dilemma and not effectively tackling the root causes. However, to help encourage long-term transformation, the government planted the seeds of control via indirect means and encouraged local political arrangements.[13] It was hoped that time and regular contact would change the psychology of the Pathan.

But why did the government not attempt to export Western ideals of governance into tribal territory? Undeniably, resource limitations had an important role to play in the decision.[14] The government did not possess the force numbers or finances necessary to secure and administer the frontier on an indefinite basis. The reality was that it would take vast sums of money to construct dams to make the region profitable. With only a limited works budget available and negligible income from tax, there was little appetite for investment. The government was careful also not to overextend its reach, especially with other outposts needing reinforcement.[15] Likewise, the hard-won lessons of the close border (1849–1878), forward (1879–1901), and modified forward (1901–1923) policies had an important role to play. Experience questioned the utility of trying to dominate an area that had challenged all previous attempts at governance, but there were other equally important factors that helped shape government strategy. Hardheaded pragmatism was one. There was little cultivatable land that could be exploited for crops and fruit trees, and the region's natural resources were few and insignificant. Economically, this was the least important province in India.[16] The only profit gained from Waziristan in 1935–1936 was land revenue from the Tochi Valley. This amounted to a pitiful Rs. 32,887.[17]

The region's physical characteristics also shaped government policy. The mountainous terrain and severe climate were both in part responsible for the strong tribal culture and inability of successive regimes to impose any form of central control. Moreover, for those serving in tribal territory, conditions were unforgiving, objectionable, and dangerous. The mountainous terrain along the border reduced government forces to a level where the tribesmen almost achieved tactical parity. Unsurprisingly, there were no opportunities for accompanied service. A posting on the frontier was a lonely and socially isolated experience demanding a unique breed of volunteer.[18] Furthermore, the region's inhabitants, particularly the Wazirs and Mahsuds, possessed a determined and seemingly irreversible spirit of independence that revolved around violence.

Sir William Barton notes, "There is no hope of weaning the tribesmen from his wild independence; therefore, the best policy to adopt is to leave him to stew in his own juice in the hills."[19] The tribesmen were also regarded as menacing, backward, and dishonest. Therefore, rather than trying to understand the tribesmen, it was often safer and easier to consider them as hostile. Perceived to be at a far lower level of development than the Hindus across the administrative border, there was very little impetus to make the tribesmen into Imperial and loyal subjects—a source of strength to the Empire—instead of an ever-present danger. Therefore, cultural transformation was also not a realistic goal.

There were other compounding factors that helped determine the government approach to the region. The introduction of well-intentioned economic and educational initiatives often resulted in a traditionalist reaction, especially among the more isolated communities. Instead of encouraging development and rational thinking, government initiatives were viewed as clandestine means designed to transform tribal customs away from traditional society. One tribesman stated in 1936: "All that your education has done is to make my son look down on his father, and the tribe and his father to look down on my son. You have unfitted him for any other work except a Government appointment, and that you seem either unable, or unwilling to give him. What, then, is the use of your much-valued education?"[20] Many went as far as viewing educational "inroads" as a physical breach of Islamic values. Unsurprisingly, the opening of the first Mahsud school in 1922 resulted in a *mullah*-led uprising.[21]

Therefore, throughout the period of British involvement in Waziristan, the tribesmen remained doubtful of government motives and rejected attempts to introduce schools and other facilities into their villages. Experience led the government to recognize that interfering with tribal customs and beliefs, even unintentionally or indirectly, would result in resentment and hostility. To complicate the situation further, any form of dependence on outside assistance was viewed as evidence of weakness. Tribal norms expected that a man would meet the needs of his family alone and unaided. What motivated the tribesmen was not a lack of economic development or educational opportunities but resentment at occupation and outside interference. Therefore, while the British recognized that military operations alone could not effectively stabilize Waziristan, simultaneous social and economic development was difficult to implement. This reality often turned government focus away from consent and support-winning initiatives and placed a greater focus on the enemy.

Against a backdrop of resentment and with few opportunities for long-term meaningful employment, the government relied almost exclusively on road construction and the employment of *kassadars* as a means to pacify the region and prevent raiding.[22] While far from ideal, both made practical inroads into helping to address the economic problems of the frontier. However, the limitation of available options was well known to the government. The official report of the 1936–1937 campaign notes the following:

> The economic problem of Waziristan still remained to be solved. The military occupation and development of roads had brought money into the country and led to an improvement in conditions. But the chief need appeared to be that of finding employment for the young men, now deprived of their traditional occupation of raiding, if they were to develop into useful and peaceable members of society. A few Mahsuds were enlisted in the army and a considerable number of tribesmen found part-time employment as *kassadars*, but the possibilities of economic development were limited and it is doubtful whether much more was possible in this direction than was being done.[23]

This reality was to remain largely unchanged throughout the final period of British involvement in Waziristan. It was also complicated by another factor: economic development could not take hold until suitable control had been established. Without the rule of law and free passage in tribal territory, few entrepreneurs showed interest in investing in a region that would require economic cooperation on both sides of the border. Those investors who did visit the frontier often remained under strong scout or military protection for the duration of their stay for fear of their safety.[24] Similarly, those contractors who supported the outposts had to pay a high stipend to the tribesmen for their continued safety. Geoffrey Moore notes: "The principal contractor, Begai, who kept Razmak supplied, was able to do so more or less without let or hindrance. His rates, we were told, were exorbitant, dictated so we understand by the need to pay the tribesmen heavily in protection money."[25] Likewise, there were few government incentives or stimuli to encourage outside investment to boost the region's economy. With rich pickings elsewhere in India, the frontier remained an impractical and risky investment option.

## The Requirement for Cultural Understanding

The political authorities recognized the need for an in-depth understanding of the tribesmen, their customs, politics, language, and ways. Only a deep knowledge of the social foundations and dynamics of the region, gained through regular contact and longtime experience, could help point to the conditions necessary to help maintain control, especially as local opinions and loyalties changed on a frequent basis. This required the constant mapping of political, economic, and social information to gain a temporal insight into the views, motivations, and differences among the tribes and subclans.[26] The deft employment of this information was indispensable in settling intertribal disputes and provided insights necessary to gain tactical advantages. It was also vital for manipulating and marginalizing troublesome tribal members. Even with such a relatively comprehensive understanding, political officers constantly had to negotiate and adopt varying ploys to accomplish their goals, since subclans of the same tribe often viewed the same situation in different ways. Furthermore, the political authorities recognized that each situation was so distinctive that doctrinal solutions or past approaches presented few clues to solving future problems. Success or failure was often determined by personal relationships, interpretation, and political agility. As the stakes were high, any mistakes of judgment or approach had far-reaching effects.

The political authorities, working within a single chain of command and benefiting from decentralized governance, formulated and guided frontier policy.[27] This occurred within an open-ended mandate and with minimum oversight. Although few in number the political officers were highly effective and their influence was broad. Despite a cultural gap between the British officers and the tribesmen, such was their familiarity with the tribes they controlled that they excelled at understanding the nuances and complexity of tribal society.

Furthermore, an experienced political officer was able to think like a tribesman and was capable of assimilating Pathan ideas. This inimitable understanding of the region led to a unique and highly prized set of competencies. It also allowed politicals to interpret and reflect the feelings and desires of the tribes to the government. This was a particular talent of the predominantly Pathan assistant political officers who implicitly understood the behavior, needs, and difficulties of the tribesmen. These largely loyal and hardworking individuals were central to success on the frontier and provided much needed cultural balance and legitimacy. Sir Olaf Caroe points to the importance of indigenous support: "A Mahsud is seldom strictly orthodox in his creed, but at least his mental processes, his attractions and his repulsions, will be clearer and more comprehensible to a fellow-Muslim than ever they were to us."[28]

The scouts were subordinate to the political authorities. These locally raised regiments, commanded by British officers, were well versed in the region's culture, politics, and idiosyncrasies. They also proved to be an excellent source of local intelligence. In contrast, military activities were undertaken without local language skills or a broad understanding of the tribal mind-set and nuances of *Pashtunwali*.[29] This lack of cultural knowledge was understandable, as the army was only used in extremis and in a traditional military role. However, there were dangers in a superficial understanding of tribal culture and assuming that the tenets of *Pashtunwali* were universal. This was not the case, and much depended on convention and the practical application of a given tribe in a geographical area. It was also a flexible code and open to degrees of interpretation. Ignorance of tribal customs could lead to misunderstanding and long-term alienation. Nevertheless, knowledge of the cultural standards and practices of the tribesmen remained elementary at best for those filling the ranks of the military columns. Due to regular rotations and compressed handovers, few possessed an intricate understanding of the land and its people. Moreover, many found it difficult to conceive of a people who despised the benefits of Imperial control and who considered killing an infidel soldier as a shortcut to Paradise. Unsurprisingly, the army failed to consider the tribesmen first in everything they did, and this had far-reaching consequences.

Nevertheless, tribal codes and traditions were often puzzling and incoherent even to those familiar with tribal society. For example, although many viewed revenge simply as shedding an offender's blood, "revenge," notes Major Richard Strickland, "is improperly viewed if one conceives of it as retribution; rather it is the re-establishment of the norms of behaviour and interactions betweens groups within the tribe."[30] Likewise, a tribesman's value as a man was shaped by his bravery on the battlefield. Therefore, tribal prominence was gained not through peaceful activities but by the display of courage under fire. Many went to extreme lengths to demonstrate their worth and position in the tribe by attacking outposts or isolated columns, or ambushing convoys. However, this was not true in all cases. For example, since bravery increased the reputation of a tribesman, it is surprising that some chose to attack telephone cables, water supplies, and bridges.[31] These were hardly laudable targets that elevated a tribesman's manliness. Moreover, the influence gained from such activities was minimal.[32] This perhaps helps to explain why support for the Fakir's activities waned after 1937. However, there were also other perplexing dynamics at play. *Maliks,* who enabled and encouraged fighting to take place within tribal territory, also secured respect by merit of their hierarchical position relative to those who conducted antigovernment activities. To further add to the perplexity, in Pathan society "a man may respect and even admire another man who has betrayed him, just as he will betray a man he likes if it appears advantageous."[33] Therefore, deceit and disloyalty were to be expected.

However, *Pashtunwali* also provided predictability. For example, despite government attempts to encourage the tribes to dispel the Fakir from tribal territory, the twin tenets of hospitality and asylum, combined with the complex terrain of the region, thwarted all initiatives to capture him. Therefore, in spite of the threat of tribal retribution, the Fakir was granted food, shelter, and protection on request, making Waziristan a perfect place to seek sanctuary. However, in providing assistance, and if fighting occurred, the tribesmen ran considerable risk of being mistaken for disobedient tribesmen and would be dealt with accordingly by the authorities. Furthermore, despite the dangers, a tribal *malik*'s honor and status were reinforced by meeting this obligation. There were other complications. While the arrival of large numbers of tribesmen from Afghanistan posed a significant administrative and logistic burden to the region's tribes, *Pashtunwali* demanded that hospitality be given to all strangers "under the belief that one cannot know the face of God, and by being gracious to strangers, we [the tribesmen] are being gracious to God."[34] For those unwilling to learn the customs and politics of tribal society, a posting to the frontier was a confusing and unnerving experience.

## The Unique Challenges of the International Border

The close proximity of the highly permeable and disputed Afghan border posed an interesting dynamic for the political authorities in Waziristan. The Durand Line, imposed in 1893 to suit British needs, bisected tribal territory, with tribesmen from Birmal, the only part of Waziristan on the Afghan side of the border, receiving influence from the two governments. It also presented a unique impediment to military operations. Not only was military encirclement or pursuit across the border impossible, but many operations were constrained for fear of agitating the Afghan authorities. British aircraft, for example, were not permitted to fly within three miles of the border, restricting operations significantly. Moreover, the permeable nature of the border permitted rapid reinforcement from Afghanistan. Pettigrew notes: "To fog up the whole situation in these troubles, whenever a *lashkar* formed, it would be joined for the fun of it by the Zadrans and the Tunnis from Khost, that inaccessible area of southern Afghanistan just over the frontier. This remote territory was hard for the Afghan government to control and it was probably only too glad if these tribes looked for excitement beyond their own border."[35] This is a view shared by Alan Warren, for whom "Afghan officials along the Frontier often turned a blind eye to tribal movement across the Durand Line; and Afghan allowance-holders in Waziristan provided a whole network of contacts for tribesmen travelling to join the insurgency."[36]

Despite concerted political activities, including the public cooperation of the Afghan prime minister, resulting from improved relations in the 1930s, tribesmen continued to cross the Durand Line into Indian tribal territory to commit acts of violence. However, while unhindered in its verbal support, the Afghan government was restrained in its physical cooperation as it risked incurring unrest in its own territory. In a telegram dated 3 November 1937, the Afghan prime minister clarified that he was unable to cooperate physically with the British government due to political and religious reasons.[37] Moreover, any treachery against the Fakir, who was widely regarded as the "champion of Islam," had the potential to ignite a major outbreak of tribal violence. But there were a number of other practical reasons for this lack of assistance. The Afghan central government was particularly weak, with authority divided amongst ministers based on tribal allegiances. Moreover, the Afghan army, mal-located in Kabul and the major provincial cities, was not in a position to control frontier tribesmen on the Afghan side of the border. There was also another important reason. In trying to remain neutral, there was also a necessity to maintain passable relations with the Axis powers. The Afghan government could not be seen to be siding with the British in India. This resulted in an interesting and challenging dynamic.

## Maximizing Medical Assistance

Notwithstanding a reluctance to accept economic and educational initiatives, tribesmen made regular use of the limited medical facilities in Waziristan. Treating a tribesman or a member of his family provided a welcome opportunity to exhibit compassion and build goodwill. It also pointed to the benefits to be had in cooperating with the government. Pettigrew recalls: "There is no doubt that the best way to get round a savage enemy is to give him medical aid . . . That is why I think it was a pity there was only one British medical officer in the whole of South Waziristan, excepting of course those with the army in Wana."[38] Pettigrew adds, "Of course, if properly trained Moslem, or better still Pashtu-speaking Moslem, medical people had been available, then they would probably have been able to do even more than British doctors."[39]

The same frustrations were applicable equally in the settled districts. Dr. T. L. Pennell recalls:

Patients flock to us from far and near: we are surrounded by them from morn till eve; we cannot send them away empty, for "drivers of them come from afar." Yet our staff is absolutely inadequate, our hospitals are bare, our dispensaries often lack the most necessary drugs, and our purses are so empty that we have nothing wherewith to replenish our stores. Last year, in the Bannu hospital alone, we dealt with 34,000 individual cases, and admitted 1,655 of them to our wards. There were 86,000 visits paid to our out-patient department, and we performed nearly 3,000 operations; yet for this and the work at our three out-stations we had only four qualified medical men (two English and two Indian) and one qualified medical woman. We had, moreover, not a single trained nurse.[40]

However, Brigadier C. A. L. Graham notes that dispensaries were used often by the tribes, but "evoked little practical gratitude."[41]

Despite Graham's balancing position, there were concerted attempts to increase access to medical facilities. For example, in North Waziristan in 1923 medical services reached approximately 8,000 patients. Only nine years later, Western-style healthcare was accessible to roughly 133,000 tribesmen and their families in both North and South Waziristan.[42] Lieutenant Colonel C. E. Bruce recalls: "As regards hospitals, we were doing our best to increase the medical facilities for the tribesmen. At first none of the tribal women would go near them, but gradually this prejudice was dying away, and I remember well Miss Sherbourne, a very well-known missionary lady doctor, asking whether it would be possible for her to visit Kanigurani, in the centre of the Mahsud country." Bruce promised her that he would do his best to help but was far from optimistic. However, he need not have worried, as the offer was received positively by the tribesmen. "Indeed, the headmen went so far as to say that not only were they ready that she should do so, but were quite willing to give her a hut in which she could work. Moreover, they naively remarked that she need not bring either instruments or drugs, as they could hand over to her those which they had stolen from us in 1919!"[43]

The employment of female missionaries, like Miss Sherbourne, overcame another important aspect of tribal culture known as *purdah*, or gender separation. This prevented male doctors from treating female members of a tribe. Trench highlights the difficulty: "There were problems in treating the tribal ladies, since any husband would far rather his wife died than her body should be seen, let alone touched, by another man. In cases where modesty was at risk, the patient's husband would describe the symptoms while the doctor, on the other side of a screen, asked questions and prescribed treatment."[44] But this compromise approach was not always workable. Pettigrew recalls an incident where a tribesman threw some gun-cotton or gelignite on the fire in his hut, resulting in his wife and daughter suffering terrible burns. Having treated the tribesman for minor burns, the doctor then demonstrated to the tribesman how to treat the burns of his wife and daughter. Before leaving, the doctor gave the tribesman the necessary bandages. "When he [the doctor] went back the next day the village women told him that the victims were in great pain and very ill, but still the husband would not let him treat his wife and daughter." With the arrival of the agency surgeon from Jabdola, he too tried to treat the wife and daughter but was denied access. "And from the description of the extent of the burns their condition, he knew, must be very serious. As indeed it was. Within three days they were dead, but still in strict *purdah*."[45]

More routinely, malaria, fevers, pneumonia, typhus, eye infections, and infected wounds were treated by the medical services. However, advances in medical science also permitted more sophisticated treatment.[46] No longer was a serious injury synonymous with death on the frontier. "As far as surgery went the greatest number of cases was certainly the treatment of gunshot wounds, of Scouts' wounds in skirmishes . . . , of tribesmen themselves who had been hurt in a feud shooting, and sometimes of hostiles who had actually been wounded in action against the Scouts."[47] The major anxiety of those admitted to hospital was of being put under general anesthetic for fear of losing a limb or being castrated. However, amputation was often the only answer, especially for those suffering from gangrene or multiple fractures. Nonetheless, such was the fear of general anesthetic and amputation that a tribesman would often prefer to return to his village to die rather than undergo surgery. For those tribesmen who agreed to amputation reluctantly, life was undoubtedly difficult. Commenting on the future of a tribal amputee to Frank Leeson, the agency surgeon at Miranshah recalls: "Bad thing in this country. He'll be useless for life and'll probably become a mullah, crawling from place to place and leading prayers, living on the charity of the tribesmen. A good many of these crippled *Fakirs* you see about have been lads in their day."[48]

Due to resource limitations, the government was unable or unwilling to maximize the effects of medical support to the tribesmen. As tribal territory lacked the infrastructure to meet the basic health care needs of the tribesmen, the political authorities missed a valuable opportunity to influence the uncommitted "middle ground." Moreover, the political and military structures were poor at using their integral resources imaginatively. With 10,000 horses and 800 camels employed in Waziristan in 1937, the authorities could have done more with their veterinary assets.[49] For example, the mounted infantry veterinarian, attached to the scouts, could have performed a much needed preventative veterinary service in tribal territory. However, the reality was that the authorities were indifferent to this approach and reluctant to put a long-term strategy into effect that would see female doctors and large animal veterinarians administering treatment to the tribesmen and their animals.

## Perception Is Reality

Tribal society was influenced heavily by superstition, paranormal beliefs, and myth. In a culture that was largely illiterate, history was routinely recounted in the form of fable and folklore. This approach transcended rational Western thinking and influenced every aspect of tribal existence. For example, in describing a traditional "conviction cure," Pettigrew highlights a tribesman's belief in a traditional method of healing:

> I once watched an older British doctor try one out for a scorpion bite, although he gave the victim the usual injection as well. The man was bitten in the upper arm and the doctor obtained a large rusty nail from somewhere and set to work. Starting high up near the bite he scored the man's arm in short downward strokes. The rusty nail gave enough friction to scratch, but not often to draw blood, and the patient could certainly feel it. Little by little the downward strokes worked down the arm until they reached the wrist, then across the back of the hand, along all the fingers and away! The poison had been drawn out, in theory anyway. Whatever, if anything, had actually happened the bitten man was much more cheerful and confident and said that he felt much better.[50]

Such was the credulity of the tribesmen that implausible promises, mixed with religious fervor, regularly received wide credence in tribal areas. This was not lost on those calling for a *jihad*. For example, the Fakir promised that:

> Firearms would not harm his followers, provided they were true *ghazis*, i.e. followers of Islam, and not mere plunderers and adventurers in search of private gain. The *ghazis* would be helped by divine power, and the troops would be assailed by showers of stone and sand from the skies. A few loaves of bread in a basket covered by a cloth would suffice to feed a multitude. Any person who gave information concerning the *lashkars* would be visited with everlasting disgrace and shame. . . . Divine power would turn bombs dropped from aircraft into paper.[51]

The Fakir also assured his supporters that those who died in support of his activities were assured a martyr's reward in Paradise. Such promises continued to encourage tribesmen from both sides of the border to join his cause. Other propaganda sought to mask his movements. The Bannu superintendent of police recalls: "It was commonly believed that anyone who gives information about him [the Fakir], or about those who go to see him will be instantly struck blind."[52]

However, while somewhat implausible to outsiders, the reality was that truth and false notion often intermixed, and the dividing line between the two was often finely drawn. For example, the dropping of white warning leaflets from an aircraft a number of days prior to a show of aggression, followed by red leaflets twenty-four hours before an attack, was viewed by the tribesmen as physical evidence of the Fakir's mystical powers of being able to turn bombs into paper. Likewise, the Fakir's declaration that the visible withdrawal of government forces from the Khaisora Valley in May 1937 was a clear example of government policy to give up Waziristan was believed to the extent that some tribesmen arrived at Wana bringing camels to remove the loot.[53] Moreover, the tribesmen perceived the withdrawal of government forces from the Khaisora Valley as a sign of weakness and defeat, further reinforcing the Fakir's elevated position and religious appeal.

Such half-truths were reinforced by further examples of the Fakir's power and reliability. Frank Baines notes: "With his famous gun probing sensitive places deep into the soft underbelly of the British, the *Fakir of Ipi* quickly began to assume lineaments recognisably similar to the *Rani of Jhansi*."⁵⁴ The perception that the Fakir could hit the British was out of all proportion to the reality of the striking power of the gun, although its continued use against the Razmak cantonment affected the morale of the Indian troops significantly.⁵⁵ Moreover, the possession of such a powerful weapon was significant from a moral point of view; only occupying powers had benefited from the possession of artillery in the past.

The Fakir was equally skilled at employing misinformation to his advantage. The *Green Howards' Gazette* of October 1938 notes that "*Ipi* himself appears to be ill, no doubt a convenient way of explaining to his henchmen his inability to raise another *lashkar*."⁵⁶ However, whether the Fakir could or could not generate a strong *lashkar* was not the issue. The decrease in large-scale activities beyond 1937 could now be attributed to the Fakir's health, a common complaint on the frontier, and this made sense to the tribesmen. Moreover, his alleged ill health also went some way to explain his change in tactics. Interestingly, the government never challenged the Fakir's propaganda. Even the most skilled information campaign would have had little impact on a population that remained deeply suspicious of government motives. Messages were only effective when *maliks* cooperated and spoke directly to the tribesmen.

However, it was not just the Fakir who relied on manipulating reality. The government also relied on degrees of false impression and influence. Walter Lawrence notes:

> Our life in India, our very work more or less, rests on illusion. I had the illusion, wherever I was, that I was infallible and invulnerable in my dealings . . . How else could I have dealt with angry mobs, with cholera-stricken masses, and with processions of religious fanatics? It was not conceit, Heaven knows: it was not the prestige of the British Raj, but it was the illusion which is in the very air of India.⁵⁷

This "air of illusion" was exploited by Sir Louis Dane, a settlement officer, on the frontier in the early 1900s. Recounting one visit, he recalls:

"I let it be known that I would have no guard on my camp and would be the guest of the *khans* [tribal heads], but that if anything happened to me or mine my successor would see to it that they lost their frontier allowances and that their land revenue for the next thirty years would be full and even grievous."[58]

## Allowances as a Peacemaker

Tribal control occurred primarily through the payment of allowances through sympathetic and loyal *maliks*. These were intended to tilt the political balance in favor of the government. Despite the challenges of *nikat*, the nonnegotiable law of tribal division, allowances proved to be relatively effective, even though few of the *maliks* possessed the authority to control the more youthful and turbulent elements of the tribes. Although focusing on the headman was intended to give the initiative "an air of traditional legitimacy," pecuniary benefits, notes Alan Warren, transformed consenting tribal *maliks* into a "government funded elite."[59] Despite this reality, allowances were accepted freely by the *maliks*, even though many recognized them as a deliberate attempt at bribery. At the core of the initiative, allowances were intended to help pacify the region and provide a practical lever to control a tribe when it misbehaved. They also acted as a strong deterrent against tribal transgressions. For example, due to the large sums of money available to *maliks* and *kassadars* for maintaining tribal order, the majority chose not to cooperate with the Fakir after 1937 for fear of losing a major source of tribal income. Due to such successes, the payment of allowances was seen as a rational investment of government funds and a far cheaper alternative to the deployment of large numbers of government forces.

To provide a comparison, in 1936 the army employed in Waziristan cost the government Rs. 166.9 *lakh*, with expenditure on scouts and *kassadars* totaling Rs. 60.33 *lakh*. In the same year, only Rs. 5.8 *lakh* was spent on allowances and political staffs in Waziristan. Of note, the Rs. 5.8 *lakh* "political expenditure" was only a small element of the Rs. 179 *lakh* budget attributed to political expenditure throughout India.[60] Likewise, the figures prove that the *kassadars* initiative was also value for money. Bruce posits: "Provided they carry out their duties—and most onerous ones they are, if done properly—and there is peace both in Waziristan and in the neighbouring districts, they are cheap at the price."[61]

There were other benefits to the distribution of allowances. Payments allowed a headman to develop his personal power. This was significant for two reasons. First, it contributed to strengthening an ambiguous tribal hierarchy that was challenged by the self-determination of the adult male. Second, such were the monetary benefits of the allowance scheme that *maliks* had to think carefully if they wanted to risk losing their government stipend and elevated position. However, there were also challenges with this approach. If allowances were withdrawn it was often equivalent to the removal of a treasured bone from a savage dog. Sir Evelyn Howell notes: "We should get our bone, but we should also almost certainly get our hands severely bitten. The tribes themselves regard these allowances as payment for services rendered, as indeed in the main they are."[62] Moreover, the most troublesome areas received the highest allowance. Therefore, if handled deftly, it was profitable for the tribesmen to misbehave as long as they were careful not to cross the political threshold.

Unfortunately, the initiative did nothing to help address the wider issue of unemployment in tribal territory. Pettigrew points to the heart of the problem: "Where it failed was that though it removed some of the poverty of the tribes, and gave them something to lose and thereby some incentive to keep out of trouble, and to keep trouble out of their areas, it did nothing like enough to give them something to do."[63] However, despite this reality, Pettigrew provides a more positive summary of the approach:

> In many ways the collectively large sums paid out in allowances to the tribes and *maliks,* and in pay to the *kassadars,* were bribes. Bribes to keep the peace themselves and to try to make the others in their area or village keep it too. Up to a point it worked very well. If an army column was heavily sniped for example the Political Agent would call in the local *maliks* and almost certainly fine them; either by deductions from their allowances or, for serious trouble, by an indefinite stoppage of their allowances altogether, or by a fine in kind of so many rifles.[64]

## The Value of a Mixed Political and Military Force Structure

The British approach to Waziristan benefited from a flexible and responsive administrative and military machinery, defined by a clear-cut hierarchy and common objective. This was sufficiently agile to permit a rapid escalation in political and military activity in times of crisis and an equally swift decrease when tactical conditions permitted; transition to major operations was, therefore, simply a change in scale rather than a start from square one.[65] It also allowed the swift transfer of authority from political to military control and vice versa. Political and military agility benefited from decentralized control, which proved to be more flexible to changing events. This dexterity was underpinned by a robust political chain of command that only reverted to military primacy in extremis. Reliant on a dedicated core of like-minded British officials and officers, control depended routinely on an individual's character, wisdom, and sense of duty. These hand-picked individuals contributed significantly to the region's security and stability. They also endeavored to improve the economic life of the people they controlled. Therefore, selecting and training the right individual was imperative.

At the heart of this well-established structure were the political agents and their supporting staffs. Exercising personal influence rather than authority, the political agents adopted a paternal approach to the tribesmen, treating them as equals and men of honor. Supported by dedicated Pathan assistant political officers, they were invaluable in plotting a course through the intricacies of tribal culture and politics. As their intentions were transparent and not driven by greed, political agents were regarded as unprejudiced and fair-minded neutrals. Bruce notes that, with few exceptions, political officers "set a brilliant example of selfless devotion to duty."[66] But there were inherent dangers in this decentralized and isolated approach. Politicals were prone to being biased in favor of "their" tribesmen. They were also guilty of being too involved in intertribal discord. Equally, there was a danger of them "going native" and attempting to convert to a Pathan's sense of honor.[67]

However, political activities placed a heavy physical, psychological, and moral strain on the incumbent.[68] Such a burden of responsibility was unsuited to many, even amongst a specially selected corps. Of those who were suitable for the demands of frontier life, few could carry the burden for an extended period of time. For some the pressures became intolerable.[69] The stress of even routine duties was considerable. Trench notes:

> The job of a Political in Waziristan was as dangerous as that of a Scouts officer. Since he must not seem to fear or distance himself from his tribes, he seldom went about his work with Scouts or military escort. Normally he was escorted only by *kassadars* or tribal *badraggas* [tribal escorts] and he could never be certain that they would provoke a blood-feud by defending him against their fellow-tribesmen.[70]

It is unsurprising, therefore, that a political agent's tenure would last no more than a few years on the frontier.

Subordinate to the political authorities were the *kassadars* and scouts. Despite a number of shortcomings, the *kassadars* were central to control on the frontier. Tasked to regulate their respective tribal areas, *kassadars* were relatively successful for routine matters. They were also cost-effective and an excellent source of local intelligence. The British experience demonstrated that the overarching benefits of tribal police significantly outweighed the shortfalls. Overseeing the *kassadars* were the lightly armed scouts, the resident political force. They were more agreeable to the tribesmen than the army but still unpopular. Pettigrew provides a useful synopsis of their role:

> The main role of the Scouts was not to look for trouble with the tribes but to do all that was possible to keep the peace. Not only to avoid having to do battle with Mahsud and Wazir but to try to prevent them from fighting amongst themselves. Of course little could be done about small private quarrels and feuds, although the Political Agents were often called in by the *maliks* to arbitrate in these too, but something could be done about quarrels which threatened to involve whole communities, village or tribal, on each side.[71]

However, such were the scouts' flexibility, speed, fitness, and understanding of local conditions that in times of crisis they were employed in a traditional manner in support of the army. The scouts' mobility was in contrast to military columns, which were slow and at a constant disadvantage against the highly mobile tribesmen. The official report of the 1936–1937 campaign posits:

> Why they [the scouts] are particularly suitable for these tasks [advance guard troops, flank protection, and exploitation] is because they are very mobile, being much more lightly clad and equipped than the regular forces, and they have continuous practice in long and rapid marches over the hills, and from their normal employment they have an intimate knowledge of the country. Their organization and equipment are not such as to enable them to overcome serious opposition without the support of regular troops and by using them in these roles, economy of the better equipped regulars for tasks more suited to them is ensured.[72]

Only when outbreaks of violence were too excessive for the scouts to address would the political authorities turn to the military to help restore order. This always occurred as a last resort and in a limited manner, as the presence of troops often led to increasing numbers of hostile tribesmen. Consequently, it was routine practice to withdraw a force as soon as it had completed its mission, in the hope that this would have a pacifying effect.

Therefore, the roles and limitations of the various structures resulted in an intricate dynamic. John Masters provides a useful précis: "Here were the actors: on one side the ponderous army, the handcuffed air force, the racing Scouts; on the other, anonymous thousands of tribesmen; in the middle, the Political agent; on both sides, as the whim of the moment dictated, the *kassadar.*"[73] Although the combined political and military apparatus on the frontier was comparatively small, those serving in isolated outposts never lost sight of the volatility of the tribesmen and the necessity to reinforce rapidly. "In fact, these border tribes are an ever-present military liability which would tax the resources of a far greater army than India can boast of: a constant thorn in the side of the military organiser, who cannot fail to allow for the tribal outbursts at a time when all the limited forces at his disposal are urgently required elsewhere."[74]

# The Hard-Earned Lessons and Realities of the British Experience in Waziristan, Part 2

> That brings us to the most remarkable aspect of the whole paradoxical situation. Except for the very small number of British officers, the scouts were all Pathans. They enlisted for a fixed period, which was extended if they were promoted, but in any case they went back to live among the tribes from whom they had come. They fought against Pathans—yet they went back and lived among them in honored retirement.
>
> —Philip Mason, *Frontier Scouts*, 1985

## Learn and Adapt

Waziristan was a complex and unpredictable region. Coercion, intimidation, and violence were commonplace. Similarly, the political goals at stake, the stakeholders involved, and the impulsive nature of the tribesmen often presented dynamic and fast-moving challenges. It was an environment in which the link between cause and effect were ambiguous. In such a highly charged atmosphere, doctrinal solutions offered few guarantees for success, as the differences between even similar situations were significant. Against an imaginative and dynamic enemy, bespoke solutions were the only hope of achieving an acceptable outcome. The complexity of the region made it essential for all institutions to learn, adapt, and constantly reassess while operating in tribal territory.

The importance of a "learning approach" to tribal control was clear to the political authorities, whose longer tours of duty and thirst for knowledge meant that officers had time to learn and adapt. It was also understood by a number of senior military commanders.[1] Major

General Sir Charles Gwynn, a seasoned British colonial officer, notes poignantly in *Imperial Policing*: "In small wars the habits, the customs, and the mode of action on the battlefield of the enemy should be studied in advance . . . . This is not the imperative only on the commander and his staff—all officers should know the nature of opposition they must expect, and should understand how to best overcome it."[2] However, this was not always the case for those in the military conducting punitive expeditions in tribal territory. The extreme requirements of the army often demanded a direct tactic that left little room for adaptation or understanding. Few recognized the benefits of a more dynamic and learning-based approach to their duties. Unsurprisingly, many in the army were frustrated by their predictable role and took away negative experiences from their experience on the frontier. Colonel Harry Styles, who served in Waziristan in the 1930s, recalls: "Frontier operations were both backbreaking and, at times, heartbreaking, and to my mind, a waste of any intelligent soldier's time and effort against an enemy who was seldom seen."[3] Moreover, military experience away from the frontier offered few pointers or new clues as to how to deal with the tribesmen. Fortunately, a number of more junior critics understood the importance of a learning-based approach. "Mauser" points to the heart of the issue: "To take on the tribesman and defeat him in his own hills is a game demanding a lifetime of specialized study."[4]

Despite this realization, the army's ability to learn was often too repressed by a sense of anti-intellectualism, conceit, and conservatism in its approach to adapt to the unique challenges of the frontier. Moreover, with the principle of security often more dominant than surprise or mobility, written orders, procedures, coordination, and regulations hamstrung creativity on the battlefield and stifled initiative. But there was good reason for this. Due to the threat in Waziristan, nothing short of a brigade-sized formation could transit tribal territory without major incident. As "Mouse" notes, "This means that battalion commanders are tied to the red-tape strings of the brigade commander's apron. It means also that company commanders have to be wrapped in binders, with comforters stuffed in their mouths, and only allowed to perambulate under the direct supervision of their Commanding Officers. It means finally that the *sepoy* gets an inferiority complex."[5] There were other contributing factors that hampered learning the lessons of the frontier.

According to John Masters, "Many Aldershot-type officers maintained that we learned only bad habits in this tribal warfare against what they called 'ragged-arsed barnshoots.' It was not true. From the Frontier itself we learned un-winking, unsleeping alertness. From the Pathans we learned more about the tactical value of ground than any of our competitors or future enemies knew."[6] Such skills were to prove invaluable during World War II. But there was also a practical requirement to approaching the frontier with the right attitude. Pettigrew notes:

> How good or bad these regiments were on the frontier depended on just one thing, and that was how ready they were to learn. . . . If a British regiment arrived at Razmak, or better still at Bannu prior to its march up to Razmak, and said: "We are new to this. You are not. Please teach us!" then it would soon be a regiment well able to look after itself and take its share of responsibility in the mobile columns, piquetting and so on. But let a regiment think it knew, that it was too famous to have to learn, to think that the Highlands of Scotland bore any real resemblance to the mountains of Waziristan, and that regiment would have trouble.[7]

In principle, frontier lessons were captured in training manuals and standing orders, as well as in the *Manual of Operations on the North-West Frontier* and *Frontier Warfare (Army and Royal Air Force) 1939*.[8] However, lessons were quickly overtaken by changing enemy tactics, and there remained a deficiency of printed best practice.[9] Gwynn notes that "in the absence of literature on the subject tradition becomes the only means of broadcasting experience, and tradition is apt to be based on experience limited to a small number of cases."[10] To help overcome this shortfall and to address tactical deficits, the military turned to technological innovations and new weaponry. Despite being condemned as "unfair" by the tribesmen, fighter aircraft, machine guns, enhanced communications, and armored cars made an impact on the North-West Frontier but were not decisive.[11] In 1919 the general staff even considered using poison gas against the troublesome Mahsuds. Further requests occurred throughout the 1930s for the use of tear gas to help quell civilian disturbances. These were rejected outright.[12]

Unsurprisingly, there were calls for the Indian army to become increasingly irregular and more akin to the scouts. One exponent notes:

If battalions could be sent out alone through the country with a battery of guns (to train), and permitted to wander about as they liked; if companies could be pushed off into the blue; if company commanders could be allowed out at night with their men to *"gasht"* about the hills, mixing with the inhabitants, shooting with them and eating with them; if Captain Snooks could be encouraged to emulate Nicholson in a quiet way; if the forward policy would look backwards for one hundred years and in doing so ignore what has occurred in the interim; if we could have an enormous bonfire . . . The result would be that officers and men would develop individuality, initiative, a lasting knowledge of the country and its inhabitants, and eventually the frontier problem would cease to exist.[13]

However, for organizational and practical reasons this aspiration was undesirable and unworkable. Callwell notes: "To hope that the average soldier could be trained to attain so high a state of perfection at such difficult work without the requisite terrain being available for practising over in peace time, would be delusive. It would seem wisest to accept the inevitable, to consider special scouts for hill warfare as a necessary consequence of a mountain frontier, and to leave nothing undone likely to add to their efficiency in future campaigns."[14]

Despite tactical advancements, little evidence exists of the Army of India transforming itself to meet the unique demands of the frontier.[15] Conventional military operations remained the main effort, and the frontier presented the only combat experience of the army between the world wars.[16] Although not totally lacking in the experience and training necessary for frontier warfare, regular forces often fell short of the irregulars. Therefore, instead of a major doctrinal, cultural, and structural reorganization of the army to meet the distinctive challenges of tribal territory, the government relied heavily on the irregular political structures to deal with routine problems. The scouts, in particular, proved to be an organization better suited to adjusting to the ever-changing demands of the frontier. They were able to adapt and implement measures that allowed them to best take advantage of the force levels and structure at their disposal. This was perhaps because the scouts were unconstrained by conventional thinking and adept at employing imaginative solutions to complex problems.

This policy allowed the army to concentrate on fighting the tribesmen using conventional frontier tactics. It is telling that, despite the introduction of technological innovations and new weaponry conceived for European battlegrounds, frontier warfare, for both British and Indian units, changed little throughout the period of colonial control.[17] However, it would be unfair to imply that some of the lessons and hard-won experiences of frontier warfare were not converted into doctrine. Even if not captured in official documents, they were passed on during "on the job training" or by word of mouth and unofficial writings.[18] However, not all lessons were easily transferable, especially in organizations bound by strict rules, harsh discipline, and the steadfast employment of the principles of frontier warfare. Moreover, as John Nagl posits in *Learning to Eat Soup with a Knife*: "Changing an army is an extraordinarily challenging undertaking."[19] Fortunately for the army, this was not necessary. Instead, the British employed the advantages of an indigenous political force to address the challenges of the tribesmen.

## *The Realities of Unified Action*

Waziristan benefited from the full integration of all political and military resources under a unified chain of command. Such authority vested in the civil powers demonstrated the unique command relationships within the North-West Frontier and the flexibility of British methods of control. Local knowledge remained paramount, allowing institutional responses to adapt to suit different circumstances. Commanders accepted that actual circumstances were the compelling factor in any response, and that doctrinal solutions were often inappropriate and personal discretion was essential.[20] Likewise, as political and military leaders were frequently collocated, there was often an improved physical and psychological understanding of the problem. This allowed greater agility and speed in decision making when dealing with complex and fast-moving situations. However, while collocation often resulted in a shared understanding, it did not always result in conformity or a uniformity of approach. Cultural differences remained prevalent on the frontier. John Masters, who experienced these challenges firsthand, provides a straightforward summary of the differences between the political and military approach to the frontier:

> The two [approaches] conflicted violently and we, girding for war, heard ourselves being advised by contrapuntal voices. The first voice, that of military experience in all the wars of recorded history, was hard, unequivocal, and merciless. The second voice, that of the civil government, was oleaginous, ambiguous—and merciless. The chant went like this, and I sang it gloomily to myself to a psalm tune:
>
> *Get there fastest with the mostest men.*
>
> Do not get there at all until we have referred the matter to the Governor-General-in-Council, which will take months.
>
> *Shoot first, shoot fastest, shoot last, and shoot to kill.*
>
> Do not shoot unless you have been shot at, and then try not to hurt anyone, there's a good chap.
>
> *Mystify, mislead, and surprise the enemy, then never leave him a moment to gather himself again, but fall on him like a thunderclap and pursue him to his utter destruction, regardless of fatigue, casualties, or cost.*
>
> Announce your intentions to the enemy, in order that he may have time to remove his women and children to a place of safety—and time to counter your plan. At all events, stop what you are doing as soon as he pretends to have had enough, so that he may gather again somewhere else.[21]

The frequent use of terms such as "pursue him to his utter destruction" meant that there was always a mistrust and fear of the ruthlessness of military tactics on the frontier. However, such a reality was the result of decades of campaigning and hard-won experiences. Lieutenant Colonel O. D. Bennett points to the rationale for the "military approach" to frontier operations: "A vigorous offensive, strategical as well as practical, is always the safest method of conducting operations, and no one will deny that to do any good against the Trans-Border man, one has to go after him and hit him as hard and often as possible."[22] However, this hard-nosed approach had a serious shortcoming. The political authorities remained reluctant to turn to the army for assistance in a timely manner. Gwynn suggests that this often resulted in the army being withheld until a situation had developed which called for the employment of force "on a scale greater than timely intervention would have required."[23] This proved to be a frustrating situation for the army. However, as the political authorities had primacy over military jurisdiction, the army had little opportunity for protest. In essence, this was a clash of approaches and a reality of the clear demarcation of responsibilities. There were other fundamental differences: whereas the political authorities relied on transparency and accountability, the military relied on secrecy, protection, and overwhelming force. These two differences in approach were often poor bedfellows.

Despite these practical realities, many senior officers eulogized interservice cooperation on the frontier. Air Commodore N. H. Bottomley notes: "I think I represent the general view of Political Officers, Soldiers, Scouts and Airmen alike when I say that there is great mutual understanding, most friendly cooperation and the greatest confidence in inter-Service relations on the North-West Frontier itself."[24] General Sir Sydney F. Muspratt, also an experienced frontier hand, adds: "The best results are only obtained when, as is the case now, we are working in close, constant and happy cooperation. I would say that nowhere else in the British Empire, except possibly in Palestine at the moment, is the ordinary day-to-day work in the two Services so closely and harmoniously interconnected. In referring to the two Services, we must also associate the political officers. Our work presents many difficult problems and awkward situations. If it is to be successful, the more closely the Royal Air Force, the political officers, and the Army can get together the better off we shall be."[25]

However, jealousy and competition were not uncommon. This extended well beyond political-military relations. Trench recalls: "There was a degree of rivalry between politicals from the Army and ICS [Indian Civil Service]. The latter felt that the former had arrived via the back door, without going to Oxford, Cambridge or Trinity College, Dublin.

Army Politicals resented the fact that civilians got a higher pension and also many of the better appointments."[26] There was also competition between the Pathan intelligentsia-cum-official tasked with helping oversee a tribe and the tribal *malik*. Likewise, while many in the military recognized that it was not the "colour of the commander's coat" that decided what method was to be adopted, but what you wanted to achieve, a handful of high ranking officers continued to reinforce service agendas. For example, some in the RAF proposed that airpower alone could manage the frontier.[27] Charles Trench recalls: "A very senior R.A.F. officer held out at tedious length on how he would run the Frontier, until Packie [K. C. Packman], exasperated, said, 'Listen, chum, your job is to drive the f — g aeroplane.'"[28] Such individuals were not alone. Recounting the Khaisora operation of 1936, Sir John Slessor posits: "Actually I think the necessary punitive action could perfectly well have been done by the RAF without incurring all the cost in lives and money of what eventually grew into quite a handy-sized campaign on the ground."[29]

However, the practical reality was that interservice cooperation was essential for success on the frontier; the sum of the whole was always greater than the parts. Columns were accompanied by close air support, and aircraft were employed routinely in key roles in support of the army as flank guards or aerial picquets. For example, on 15 December 1936, during the demolition of the Fakir's village in Zarinai, there was an area of mountainous country to the northwest of the village that the column commander wished to avoid picquetting. Fearing a substantial delay and the dispersion of his available combat power, the area was allotted to the RAF to "deal with." Aircraft remained overhead throughout the operation and only recovered once demolitions were complete and the column had left the area.[30] Likewise, a squadron of aircraft would fly over an area when an important decision was announced in a *jirga,* in order to provide visible evidence of the force which lay behind the government's disposal.[31]

The experience and personality of an individual also played an important role in overcoming interservice frictions. Previous frontier experience helped provide a broader understanding of the realities of political-military cooperation. It also afforded an understanding of the capabilities, restrictions, and workings of the indigenous forces. Likewise, the personality of certain individuals had an impact on the success of operations. Air Commodore N. R. Bottomley, then a Group Captain, received high praise in the official report of operations in Waziristan over the period 25 November 1936 to 16 January 1937 for his personal example. The same was true also of Major A. Felix Williams, Military Cross, who also warranted special mention for his command of the South Waziristan Scouts.[32] Personalities added a further unpredictable dynamic to the complexities of interservice cooperation.

## The Difficulty of Surprise

Surprise remained a potent weapon against the tribesmen, its effect often quite out of proportion to force ratios employed.[33] It acted as a force multiplier, increased the probability of success, and helped reduce casualties. However, to achieve surprise required effective, accurate, and timely intelligence.[34] This was rarely available and military responses to tribal transgressions occurred usually after a significant time delay. Consequently, the ability to strike the tribesmen at a time or place of the government's choosing was difficult. Government forces relied on a combination of political information, instinct, or news obtained from sympathetic tribesmen and informers. This was reinforced frequently by "intelligent forecasting" based on previous tribal actions. This proved to be a useful technique. Captain H. L. Davies, Military Cross notes, "In Waziristan the Ahnai Tangi and Barari Tangi, have been the scenes of numerous actions during the campaigns of the past hundred years in that country, while the Mahsud tactics, and the positions they occupied, during the destruction of Makin in 1920 and in 1923 were practically identical."[35] However, despite information regarding the terrain, the inhabitants, the political situation, and previous campaigns in the area concerned, operations were often conducted with unsatisfactory or partial intelligence; fusing and interpreting multiple sources of intelligence was a complicated undertaking.[36]

Moreover, it was often difficult to achieve physical surprise. Almost every tribesman was an information gatherer and an early warning system. Even with the advent of a road network and motorized transport, it was almost impossible for a government force to pass through tribal territory without the tribesmen knowing almost every detail of the force composition and direction of travel. Callwell notes:

News spreads in a most mysterious fashion. The people are far more observant than the dwellers in civilised lands. By a kind of instinct they interpret military portents even when totally deficient of courage or fighting capacity. Camp gossip is heard by those who are attracted by the ready payment which supplies brought to a civilized army always meet with, and it flies from mouth to mouth till it reaches the ears of the hostile leaders.[37]

Prendergast provides a telling insight into the realities of operating on the frontier: "On one occasion we synchronised a swift-moving patrol with a similar force from the redoubtable South Waziristan Scouts, planning to capture the *Fakir of Ipi.* We found the ashes of his fire still warm in a cave, but he had flown. Our informer, as usual, had informed both ways."[38] As a result of informers, superior surveillance, and an effective tribal warning system, villages were often found vacated by an advancing force. *Lashkars* were also rarely caught unawares.

However, it was well known that there were "informers" within the existing force structure. Some even filled key appointments. Frank Lesson notes in *Frontier Legion* that the leader of the senior *kassadar* officer's personal bodyguard in North Waziristan was a tribesman nicknamed Sitti. Providing an instructive assessment of Sitti's character, Jock Mathieson cautioned: "Oh, he's not so bad for his job. In fact, it's his habit of having a finger in every pie that makes him so useful. He's even said to be a friend of Ipi's. No one dare bump off Daffedar Said Payo, to give him his full title . . . As I was saying, he's an influential man, so no one is going to upset him by sniping at his responsibility."[39]

To try to overcome these realities, written orders and instructions were not issued until the last possible moment. Likewise, the minimum number of responsible officers were informed of future intentions and soldiers were not told about impending operations until after "night arrangements" were in place or before the start of a planned march. "Plans which were either misleading and consequently cancelled before the commencement of the operation or were so framed that with very slight alterations they could apply to the intended operation were made public. False reports were spread about as to the destination of the movement."[40] Such practical measures, designed to maintain security and surprise, were implemented routinely.

Very thorough arrangements were made to ensure the secrecy on which success depended, and to deceive the tribesmen. Written orders and instructions were not issued by Headquarters, Waziristan Division until 12–10 hours on the 11th of May [1937]. Brigade Commanders were told of the proposed operation on the 9th. Other officers were given verbal instructions in sufficient time, only, to enable adequate preparations to be made, and the smallest possible number of individuals were informed of the real objective. Thus, in the Bannu Brigade, Commanding Officers of units were not taken into the confidence of their Brigade Commander until the afternoon of the 10th of May, and the troops in general were not told their true destination until after night arrangements were in force on the 11th. Meanwhile, reports were spread about that the Division was to move to Razani to put the water supply there in order and to repair the road to Razmak. Colour was lent to this report by a reconnaissance of the Razani water supply on the 10th of May and by the issue of orders to the Razmak Brigade to move there on the 12th, these orders not being cancelled until 23.00 hours on the 11th, when there was no possibility of the truth leaking out before the operation began.[41]

Despite these elaborate measures, political restrictions often prohibited surprise. Any shock action that aircraft might have been able to bring to frontier operations was heavily constrained by rules and regulations. Not only was high-level authority a prerequisite for offensive action, but tribesmen also had to be warned of an impending attack.[42] Moreover, any offensive action taken by aircraft against hostile tribesmen was confined to those tribesmen actually engaged in hostilities with government forces. In simple terms, a surprise attack from the air could not take place against tribesmen approaching a column with obvious hostile intent, nor could a pilot engage a concentration of tribesmen patently preparing to ambush a government force. In contrast, a column commander was perfectly at liberty to use his artillery to shell a village from which an enemy was opposing his advance. Recounting the "absurdity" of the rules restricting the use of airpower, Sir John Slessor notes: "However, there they were, and I am afraid I derived some satisfaction from being extra meticulous in observing them, in the hope that as a result their absurdity would become patent even on high."[43] Political policy applied a powerful influence on military tactics employed on the frontier.

The most common method of attempting to achieve surprise was the use of darkness to cover troop moments. A good example of this was the raid made by detachments of the Tochi and South Waziristan Scouts, supported by the 1st Infantry Brigade, to capture the Fakir on 21 June 1937. The official history notes: "An advance by day would certainly have resulted in the flight of the Fakir if he was actually there. The detachments of Scouts moved to their positions successfully, during the night of the 20th/21st of June."[44] Other useful illustrations include the march of the Bannu Brigade up the Sirdar Algad on 27 September and the 9th Infantry Brigade advance to Sinwam on 20 October 1937. In addition to surprising the enemy, night marches also saved precious time. The requirement for all round protection, so necessary and time consuming in daylight operations, was reduced, permitting a faster rate of advance. However, night advances presented practical command and control difficulties, especially when supported by pack animals and large numbers of attendants, as well as the risk of troops becoming lost or confused in complex terrain.

Night marches, despite a number of advantages, were considered a dangerous undertaking, especially for inexperienced troops or those unfamiliar with the terrain. Previous reconnaissance of the route and knowledge of the terrain were often determining factors if a march should go ahead. However, if executed correctly, the element of surprise could be achieved, as the tribesmen rarely maintained adequate protection or any early warning system at night. Prendergast recalls, "Superstitious fears of fairies and devils kept the tribesmen low in the hours of darkness."[45] This was equally true in inclement weather and at certain times of the year.[46] However, in summer the tribesmen were often found sleeping in the open or in preprepared battle positions, which could lead to a different encounter for an advancing force. Moreover, the tribesmen quickly became familiar with a repeated tactic. Therefore, night attacks had to occur in a random manner, interspersed with daylight assaults. The force best suited to achieve surprise during the light of day was the scouts, due to their speed, local knowledge, and freedom of movement. For example, the scouts were used to great effect in the attempt to capture the Fakir of Ipi on 21 June 1937, and the maneuver to destroy the Fakir's supplies at Karkanwam the following month.

In contrast, the tribesmen continued to conduct hit-and-run operations that consistently achieved total surprise. Combining local intelligence, a detailed knowledge of the terrain, and benefiting from unconstrained movement, the tribesmen possessed all the factors that allowed them to undertake operations at a time and place of their choosing.

## Roads—A Means to an End and Not an End in Themselves

The government constructed a network of roads throughout Waziristan in the early twentieth century for a variety of well-intentioned political and military reasons. Viewed as productive expenditure, it was hoped that roads would provide a means for the tribesmen to help themselves.[47] Moreover, it was expected that roads would also allow the "infiltration of more civilised ideas" into tribal territory and contribute to the economy of the country by opening up trading facilities.[48] Their construction and upkeep also gave lucrative and much-needed employment to the tribesmen. However, road construction faced a number of practical challenges. Jealousy occurred over the distribution of work among the sections, which could lead to dissonance or violence. Moreover, those involved in road construction were particularly susceptible to intimidation, and protection for the laborers was an unwelcome government commitment. This reality was not lost on the Fakir. According to a 1937 London *Times* article, "The Fakir of Ipi and his lieutenants have been trying to prevent tribesmen from working on the new roads, and work on the section between Bahadur Camp and the Shaktu River was suspended until arrangements to protect the labourers were completed."[49]

Despite these realities, road construction offered a wealth of military advantages. It helped increased prestige, strengthened control over the region, reduced transportation costs, and eased the problems of supply.[50] It also improved the mobility of units and enhanced the use of armored cars and tanks (which had limited cross-country capability) and allowed rapid movement of artillery. Roads also enabled the army to support the scouts in a timelier manner and proved to be "a definite rung on the ladder for future campaigns to mount."[51] Moreover, troops transported in vehicles arrived at a drop-off point rested and relatively fresh. Frontier mobility was aided by the employment of reliable motorized vehicles, improved road-making skills, and enhanced wearing surfaces developed during the Great War.

To support an increasing flow of traffic, bridges capable of supporting constant motorized traffic were required. These were both time-consuming and expensive to construct. Likewise, due to the difficulties of construction in a barren and mountainous terrain, the cost of the roads themselves was high. The cost per mile of a "first-class" frontier road, 16 feet wide and 9 inches deep, was approximately two *lakhs* in the 1920s. A third-class road, 9 feet wide and 4 1/2 inches deep, was only marginally cheaper at just over one *lakh*. However, the practical benefits were considerable. "It must be borne in mind that 1,000 animals eat 10 tons daily as against 1½ tons required for 1,000 Indian troops. The weight of this grain and fodder, coupled with the low carrying power of the camel (5½ to the ton) and the mule (14 to the ton), and their small radius of action, have made frontier campaigns largely a matter of supplying camels to feed camels."[52] Moreover, in fiscal terms, the camel worked out to be roughly nine times more expensive than motor transport.

> Is it [the camel] cheap? No, its cost is nine times that of a motor lorry. Does it affect supply dumps? Yes, because its use accounts for five times the weight of the food stuffs needed. Is it reliable? No, by reason of its 13 to 65 percent sick rate. Does it use road space? Yes, it congests roads so much that separate routes have actually to be used. Does its radius of action affect the L. of C.? Yes, owing to the formation of sub-posts and the necessity for extra man-handling. Does it prevent secrecy? Yes, any long, slow-moving column must do so. On every ground, therefore, the camel on the L. of C. is a costly way of securing inefficiency.[53]

Even with the construction of new roads, which often occurred simultaneously with major operations, the limited road network still left large areas of the country inaccessible to vehicles, and pack transportation remained essential to all operations in the mountains.[54]

Road construction also provided strategic advantages to government forces. In the event of being forced to undertake operations in

Afghanistan, new lines of communication through tribal territory presented greater options. However, they also absorbed large numbers
of *kassadars,* scouts, and troops to protect them.[55] For example, it required four brigades and a number of detachments of scouts to keep
the seventy-four-mile road between Bannu and Razmak open in the
1930s. This was further compounded by the number of isolated military
outposts, each of which had to be resupplied on a regular basis. Frank
Leeson points to a major shortcoming of the growing network of roads
linked to Razmak:

> Razmak represented the high-water mark of the Government
> of India's Forward Policy. With its satellites and system of mili-
> tary roads, it was intended to pacify Waziristan once and for all.
> For a variety of reasons, some military and some political, all it
> succeeded in doing was to tie up between 5,000 and 9,000 alien
> troops in a permanently beleaguered fortress. It was described as
> "India's whitest elephant" and to maintain it . . . several thousand
> road-protection troops, the mere transport of whom cost £750 per
> ROD (Road Opening Day), had to picquet the hills and establish
> report centres at intervals along the 70-mile road to Bannu so that
> convoys of supplies and reinforcements might pass unmolested.[56]

Picquetting the heights on Road Opening Days was a necessary undertaking, but it was also a thankless and dangerous task. "It was on one
of these occasions when we were opening the road which runs from
Ghariom to Biche Kaskai, that we had three casualties: Sergeant Smith,
who came out with the draft last January, Private Tuffs, due to go home
this trooping season, and Sergeant Horne of the Band, who was slightly
wounded and remained at duty."[57] Casualties were a predictable outcome of a routine static requirement.

Notwithstanding stated government intentions, many tribesmen regarded roads simply as an overt means to deprive them of their freedom
and independence and treated their construction with great hostility.[58]
To further compound the problem, the road network failed to deliver
visible progress in the welfare of the tribes: there was little noticeable
increase in cultivable land; vegetation continued to diminish; outside trade remained scarce; and the tribesmen experienced a decrease in
available water. The region's forests were also decreasing rapidly with

few benefits in return. Despite anticipated difficulties, the government failed to complement road construction with tangible social and economic benefits. They were also remiss in not making it patently obvious that roads were for the tribesmen's benefit and not just for the military's. Moreover, there was perhaps too great a focus on the roads and not enough investment in other areas of the territory to help pacify the region.

## Take Your Enemy Seriously

The tribesmen were natural fighters and highly sensitive to the presence of infidel troops in tribal territory. They were resilient, hard-hitting, and daring and possessed an intimate knowledge of the local terrain. Many had a working knowledge of government tactics, techniques, and procedures gained from former service in the ranks of the Indian army. They were also an enemy that welcomed hand-to-hand combat, and they constantly sought excitement and personal glory from their exploits. Often high on opium and *charas,* their preference was the hasty ambush and pursuit. However, although well armed and endowed with a martial ethos, there were many military shortcomings when they formed an ad hoc war party. *Lashkars* lacked mobility, control, and discipline. Supporters were volunteers, and there was no contract or moral obligation for them to remain under arms ad infinitum. Tribesmen would often leave a *lashkar* and return to their villages without warning, especially in inclement weather conditions or at harvest time.

However, *lashkars* could form quickly, disband, and then re-form. A volatile combination of ennui, anger, and lack of purpose amongst tribesmen meant that tribal territory was fertile ground for raising a *lashkar.* Moreover, there was no requirement for major recruiting, organizing, or training activities. Because the tribes continued to provide the warring tribesmen with the basic necessities of life, those engaged in unlawful activities were able to rely on the local population and moved about unencumbered by the logistical problems faced by the Army of India. However, trying to sustain a large force for an extended period of time presented its own challenges. As the tribesmen possessed little capacity to transport the necessary supplies and lived off the local population, it was difficult for a village or group of villages to support a *lashkar* for an extended period, despite religious compulsion. Moreover, in massing tribal power for an extended period of time, *lashkars* became attractive targets for attack.

The tribesmen were also a wily and patient enemy. Davies notes: "The tribesman will seldom commit himself to any operation until he has had an opportunity to study the dispositions of his adversary. This is the reason why an advance is seldom disputed with vigour, whereas a withdrawal is ferociously harassed."[59] Moreover, the tribesmen were masters at waiting to see who would win out; time presented no boundaries on their activities or approach. Bruce notes poignantly: "He loves the winning side! That is the lesson of the frontier."[60] To identify the victor, the tribesmen were prepared for a long struggle; their attachment to Islam and their code of honor proved to be a constant motivational force. They also remained extremely sensitive to the presence of government troops in tribal territory. Therefore, after 1937 their goal was to hit and disrupt government forces while surviving to fight another day. They also became adept at attacking softer and more lucrative targets. The danger after 1937 was underestimating the tribesmen whose aim it was to liberate their way of life from an alien occupier and to be a constant menace to the Hindu of the plains.

The army was often guilty of not taking the enemy seriously.[61] Colonel Khushwaqt Ulmulk recalls:

> I remember an incident when we were under shelling from the *Fakir* in the post of Tiarza near Wana. The *Fakir* was using solid shell from his cannons which were falling on our fort. Our post commander was Major French and I was his Wing Officer. The shells frightened Major French's fox terrier named Geoffrey who suddenly went missing which in turn created a lot of commotion and excitement among our men. Every one got busy looking for Geoffrey and almost forgot that we were under artillery fire. The whole excitement of this episode died down only after we found Geoffrey. This shows just how non-seriously we took frontier warfare.[62]

There are many other examples of the army not taking the enemy seriously.[63] Prendergast recalls: "One day I noticed a bright patch of pink. It was a British soldier propped up against his Vickers machine gun, reading the 'Pink Un'[64] with no look-out set and oblivious of danger, or snipers. The British soldier simply would not take things seriously and got into unnecessary scrapes."[65] Colonel Wally Pryke recalls a most unusual example of complacency:

> Even before we reached the Frontier, we had heard tales about the Afghans' and Pathans' proclivity for homosexuality. We never had much proof of this as we met few . . . But one day, on a long march, a solitary Pathan approached the column. He was a good-looking, tall, young man, with an open silk shirt, a rose behind his ear and a swaying walk. Over one shoulder he carried a rifle. There were cat-calls and whistles amongst the ranks as he passed by with a wide grin on his tanned face. This continued until he passed the rear guard at the end of the column. Suddenly, the rear guard came under rapid and very accurate rifle fire from the same man.[66]

However, the tribesmen had a minor chink in their armor. Despite accepting an unevenness of casualties in encounters with government forces, the tribesmen were susceptible to becoming disenchanted by a long sequence of expeditions and wars. Losses inflicted on the tribesmen were often heavy, taking months, if not years, from which to recover. During the period 25 November 1936 to 16 January 1937 it was estimated that tribal casualties amounted to 119 killed and 186 severely wounded in Waziristan. The *London Gazette* notes: "It is impossible accurately to state the number of less seriously wounded casualties but they undoubtedly outnumbered the severely wounded cases."[67] From 16 January 1937 to September 1937 casualties increased significantly. "The enemy casualties are reliably estimated at nearly 700 killed and over 350 seriously (as distinct from slightly) wounded."[68] In comparison, Alan Warren suggests that total losses in Waziristan from 25 November 1936 to 15 December 1937 were 898 dead and 856 seriously wounded. Over the same period, the government lost 250 soldiers to enemy action and sustained 687 casualties.[69] It is unsurprising, therefore, that with significant tribal casualties sustained during the 1936–1937 campaign the Fakir's revolt had little option but to turn to more indirect actions.

However, any approach that relied on perseverance and attrition faced major challenges. There was a genuine fear that concerted efforts against the Fakir and his followers would have a "backlash on the many

Hindus that used to then live in the tribal areas."[70] There was also a concern about igniting the tribesmen on the Afghan side of the border. Therefore, any crushing military response to the tribesmen was fraught with difficulties. Despite this, there appeared to be little bad feeling between the army and the tribesmen.

> There appeared to be no great enmity between the British and the tribesmen. I have often talked to them about our skirmishes since then. Rather was there mutual respect. We liked their hail-fellow-well-met, open manners and manliness and they were given to much reminiscence about the fighting, almost as if talking about some hard-fought cricket match. Certainly it provided them with the excitement they craved.[71]

## The Importance of Leadership

Leadership was essential to the effectiveness and longevity of the tribal insurrection in Waziristan. Without a figurehead and supporting lieutenants, actions would have lacked focus and inertia, and fatigue may have taken hold. Unfortunately for the government, the Fakir provided a charismatic and enduring leader of the rebellion. He was also a brutal and treacherous man. Despite having no formal military training, he maintained his position through dogged determination, strength of personality, and an elevated religious position. Such was his belief in his cause that he possessed the nerve and courage to face considerable danger and privation. Moreover, he convinced his supporters that God was on their side and that his prayers could restore to health those wounded in battle. Tribal society placed great importance on supernatural gifts, believing that those who reached an elevated level of holiness were blessed with spiritual powers. The more the Fakir eluded government forces and guided the insurrection, the more his divine status was confirmed. This was further strengthened by external support and encouragement.[72]

However, the Fakir provided more than just a spiritual head to the rebellion. Not only did he lead a number of *lashkars* in 1936; he also canvassed *maliks* for manpower and support. If his appeals failed, the Fakir, undeterred, appealed personally to the tribesmen to join his cause.

Moreover, he generated funding and supplies and provided sanctuary to those who requested his assistance; the mountainous border region was a recognized safe haven for outlaws.[73] Despite the Fakir's best efforts, his ability to provide this service waned after the 1937 campaign. Nevertheless, he continued to recognize the need to deliver tangible benefits to his followers. Likewise, the Fakir was only too aware that his presence in tribal territory would result in government retribution and declining tribal support unless managed carefully. Religious conviction only went so far.

Fortunately for the Fakir, his insurrection was based on a highly decentralized and geographically limited arrangement that enabled the tribesmen to be resilient in the face of overwhelming power. In the place of central coordination, the Fakir delegated responsibility to a changing structure of lieutenants that continued the rebellion forward in their territory, allowing Mirza Ali Khan "to preach and pray for victory behind the fighting line."[74] These loyal and dependable individuals had a profound interest in the continuation of hostile activities because their stature and raison d'être often depended on their militant activities. A number were particularly active. At various times Sher Ali was a more prominent field commander than the Fakir.[75] Others, such as Sher Zaman, Azal Mir, Malik Khonia Khel, Din Fakir Bhittani, Mehn Dil, Fakir Mohammed,[76] and Gul Nawaz also played leading roles at various stages.[77] These lieutenants led *lashkars* that ranged in size from half a dozen to several hundred tribesmen. Most fought with groups of kith and kin. Likewise, the arrival of the Shami Pir highlighted the reality that a compelling religious leader, even from another country, could unite the tribesmen in fanatical enthusiasm. Decapitating any one of these influential leaders would have had little impact on the rebellion in the long term. There were always many in the ranks waiting to carry the torch of independence forward. Nevertheless, the government frequently attempted to kill or capture the Fakir and many of his leading lieutenants, but these attempts mostly came to naught.

## Summary

Waziristan remained the Achilles' heel of the frontier. Despite limited government ambitions, technological advances, and the sheer weight of the Army of India in reserve, the region remained largely untamed and unpredictable. It was, however, controllable, and the forward policy, underpinned by mature political and military structures, provided a well-tested framework to manage and contain the tribesmen with limited resources. It came as no surprise that, when the nascent Pakistani government inherited responsibility for the frontier in 1947, it maintained, with few exceptions, the agile machinery of British control. This endured until 2001, when President Musharraf abandoned support for the Taliban in Afghanistan, resulting in a fundamental change in frontier policy. Consequently, the lessons of the British involvement in Waziristan continue to have contemporary relevance. However, it is the parallels between the British experience of the region and the current challenges faced by the Coalition and North Atlantic Treaty Organization (NATO) in southern Afghanistan that offer the most constructive insights. Although twenty-first-century issues are rarely identical to old ones and despite the dangers of placing too much stock in historical analysis, the hard-earned lessons of the British involvement in Waziristan appear transferable and can help shed light on a number of practical dilemmas currently faced by the coalition.

## Analysis of the Effectiveness of the British Empire's Control of the Region

Winston Churchill, writing as a soldier and politician, posits that the historian of great events is always oppressed by the difficulty of tracing the silent, subtle influences that in all communities precede and prepare the way for violent outbursts and uprisings. By examining the complex relationship between frontier policy, tribal realities, and British methods of control in the most troublesome agency, Waziristan, and over a timeframe that experienced some volatile periods, particularly 1936–1947, this book has attempted to uncover the understated causes of British success and failure against an unpredictable, persistent, and dynamic enemy. In addition, by analyzing the hard-earned lessons of the British experience in Waziristan, it is possible to discern a number of overarching themes and practical measures that are relevant to settling tribal unrest along the Afghan-Pakistani border today.

The fact that there is a deficiency of contemporary analysis into the colonial British methods of controlling Waziristan means that many modern political and military commanders employed in Afghanistan remain largely ignorant of the benefits of this approach to managing the troublesome frontier.[78] Indeed, a number of senior British commanders still turn to the staple works of Sir Robert Thompson and General Sir Frank Kitson for insights into countering the insurgency in Afghanistan.[79] This is despite their findings being based on the responses to insurgencies in Kenya, Malaya, Muscat, Oman, and Vietnam. The insightful works of Sir William Barton, Charles Bruce, Sir Olaf Caroe, and Charles Trench, among many others, based on similar challenges against a familiar enemy in the same geographical area, appear forgotten or old hat. This is a mistake.[80] In order to help address this imbalance, the preceding chapters have attempted to offer a detailed synopsis of the British political and military apparatus of control and how they fared against a charismatic and elusive troublemaker, the infamous Fakir of Ipi.

By analyzing the dynamic nature of the frontier and the British response, this book has shown that to have any hope of successfully controlling and pacifying the Pashtun tribesmen requires a lifetime of specialist study. Such is the structural and interactive complexity of tribal politics that there are very few individuals or organizations who truly understand how tribal alliances shift, or how the pre-Islamic code of *Pashtunwali* and *Sharia* combine to shape everyday life. Only a deep-seated knowledge of the region, gained through regular contact and an enduring desire to learn, can help point to the conditions necessary to help maintain control. To function in tribal territory without this vital foundation is to operate deaf and blind. Seeing events through the cultural prism of the indigenous population is fundamental to success.

As the first five chapters show, trying to unravel and comprehend this complexity is difficult and dangerous, even for a handpicked organization like the Indian Political Service. However, reductionism is not always helpful, and political authorities must be skilled at looking at local problems in a holistic manner. Even so, ignoring or downplaying the primacy of cultural values will adversely affect regional stability. It may also result in politicians and military commanders relying on instinct and their own values and standards, which will often be mistaken, unsuitable, or inappropriate.

Moreover, as local opinions and loyalties change, localized solutions, as the British recognized, have to be the norm. But to exploit this reality, regional policy makers have to have an intimate knowledge of the terrain, the tribesmen, and their daily way of life. Only a detailed understanding of these components will lead to an intuitive understanding of tribal atmospherics and provide the insights necessary to gain local advantages.

Thus, regular military rotations or political upheavals will continue to challenge and frustrate an in-depth understanding of the behavior, needs, and motivations of the frontier tribesmen. This will be particularly acute for policy makers in distant capitals who rely on "bottom-up" feedback from trusted representatives to help translate cultural considerations into effective policy.

Yet, in reality, success or failure will often depend on the skill of empowered individuals and their personal relationships with the tribesmen. Cultural and linguistic affinities are essential for creating the right conditions for a successful and enduring alliance. As the preceding chapters have shown, the ability to control an area will not necessarily be determined by the number of battalions employed in ground holding roles, but by the dexterity, diplomacy, and language skills of selected individuals charged with tribal management. While much can and should be taught, intuition and moral fiber also have important roles to play and must not be underestimated.

As the British discovered, frontier policy must be born of pragmatism and reality. It must also be culturally sustainable and realistic in its long-term ambitions. Similarly, it must address the practical challenges faced by the tribesmen and rigorously contest negative propaganda; incongruously, these were two key tenets that colonial policy consistently failed to take in hand. Moreover, in a region where continuity and firmness are essential, unexpected advances, ill-timed retreats, and changes in policy will result in confusion, mistrust, and violence. Summarizing the numerous policy changes in Waziristan between 1849–1947, Sir Olaf Caroe notes: "It is not surprising that amid all this opportunism no fixed point could be found, and confidence in authority tended to be slow and uncertain."[81] Hence, frontier policy will only be successful if consistent, evenhanded, and transparent.

Equally, terms like "containment," "good enough," and "maintaining the system in check" should be commonplace in frontier parlance and better reflect the "art of the possible." Accordingly, tolerating ambiguity, shortfalls, and inconsistencies must be central to any sustainable policy. Changing the culture of the region is probably impossible, at least in the short to medium term. Moreover, the notions of a free market economy, human rights, and Western democratic standards remain alien to the tribesmen of the region. Protestant European logic and rules of behavior do not apply to the tribal belt. As the British recognized, full-scale administration may not be practical or even necessary. Employing and, where necessary, reinforcing the existing tribal framework and structures offers the best opportunity for success.

Moreover, due to the diverse nature of the frontier, no single approach or course of action offers a higher probability of success. Each tribe is so distinctive and each situation so unique that making generalizations or implementing a standard approach across the region is hazardous. Customized solutions are key. Therefore, frontier policy also has to be sufficiently agile and malleable to meet a wide variety of localized needs. However, each bespoke approach carries an implicit message and a raft of potential second- and third-order effects that must be considered in advance. Hence, it is unlikely that any confined initiative will deliver a conclusive political result in the short term.

Frontier policy is best implemented by flexible and responsive administrative and military machinery. This must be defined by a clearcut hierarchy, based on political primacy but shaped by common and agreed objectives. This will allow transitions to major operations, in times of crisis, to become a change in scale rather than a start from nothing. The transfer of authority from political to military control, and vice versa, must also be agile and responsive. Such an approach, which sat at the heart of British successes in the period under consideration, will only succeed if accompanied by decentralized control. Central government is ill-equipped to deal with the exacting and complex responsibilities of diffuse tribal rule, as regional challenges require the delegation of responsibility. Likewise, frontier policy will only succeed if led by home-grown politicians and controlled by indigenous forces. Imagination and political agility, grounded in tribal realities and encompassed in an all-inclusive strategy, are fundamental to meeting the evolving needs of the tribesmen.

By investigating the British historical experience of Waziristan this book has also shown the value of establishing and maintaining control through the payment of allowances. Although conservative Western policy makers might balk at their contemporary employment, the ability to influence and "pay off" a population or tribe must not be underestimated in its contemporary utility. Paradoxically, the payment of a regular stipend may be a more cost-effective method of ensuring security than the employment of regular or indigenous forces. Likewise, allowances, if targeted correctly, can accomplish an almost instantaneous effect, whereas reconstruction and development takes time for the benefits to be felt. The modern-day benefits of paying allowances to buy consent should not be underestimated.

The martial spirit of the tribesmen means that a worthwhile cause, or external catalyst, will quickly unite the tribesmen in anger or religious fervor. This is especially true of non-Muslim interference in tribal territory. However, without a figurehead, the effectiveness of any uprising will be temporary. To maintain coherence and longevity, militant leaders have to rely on a combination of persuasion, religious fervor, propaganda, terror, and the tenets of *Pashtunwali*.[82] Those who deftly exploit these elements can achieve considerable success, frustrating security forces and posing a significant physical and ideological threat. Recent history suggests that it is unlikely that they will be captured or neutralized. However, even someone from outside tribal territory can unite the tribesmen in fanatical enthusiasm. The case of the Shami Pir points to the dangers of ignoring a relatively unknown outsider with a hidden agenda.

The dynamic complexity of Waziristan made it essential for all institutions to learn, adapt, and constantly reassess while operating in tribal territory. However, the importance of a "learning approach" to tribal control was only truly prevalent in the political authorities and scouts. This was rarely the case for those in the military, who were constrained by conservatism, rigid doctrine, and unbending rules.[83] To help overcome these shortfalls, the military turned to technological advances and new weaponry. These failed to have a decisive effect and the tribesmen always adopted new tactics that offset any advantage in military capability. Instead, the British relied on the irregular political structures to deal with routine problems, harnessing their cultural advantages, intelligence-gathering skills, and tactical agility to achieve regional control. Employment of the army was therefore for conventional military operations.

The preceding chapter highlights the merits of considering a hybrid British colonial model to meet contemporary challenges along both sides of the Afghan-Pakistani border. Despite many changes in the makeup of the tribal belt, sufficient similarities exist to warrant employment of a hybrid model in full or part. Centuries of evolution produced structures and organizations, within constraints, that were suitable to the demands of the region and sympathetic to local conditions. By the 1930s, a small but well-developed British administrative and military apparatus routinely controlled Waziristan. This was cost effective and accomplished at working in concert with local customs and beliefs. Recognizing that the factors that helped shape British policy remained largely unchanged after 1947, the Pakistani government continued to embrace the British techniques and structures of tribal control until 2001. Despite the current deviation in policy, at the behest of the United States, a return to an "enhanced" historical model, under a recognized ethnic framework, has many potential benefits for the tribal belt and is worthy of careful consideration. As an adapted well-known proverb cautions, whereas a fool learns by his experience, a wise man learns by the experience of others.

# Contemporary Parallels and Prognostications

> The world is very old; we must profit by its experience. It teaches that
> old practices are often worth more than new theories.
> —Quoted in C. E. Bruce, *Waziristan, 1936–1937,* 1938

## Overview

The Fakir of Ipi's influence over the region waned notably after independence in 1947. No longer polarized by a foreign power, the ultraconservative tribesmen appeared satisfied with the nascent Punjabi-dominated government and its indirect approach to the frontier. However, the Fakir failed to share this pragmatic viewpoint. Instead, he remained determined to maintain his spiritual standing among the tribes. Looking for a new cause célèbre to unite the tribesmen, the Fakir condemned the government's rule, suggesting it was un-Islamic. To reinforce his standpoint, the Fakir became an advocate of a self-governing Pashtunistan and, in 1950, became the first president of the Waziristan branch of the Pakhtunistan National Assembly.[1] This political group, headed by Abdul Ghaffar Khan, sought to establish a Pashtun homeland independent of Afghan and Pakistani authority. However, this nationalistic cause failed to appeal to the tribesmen, and the baton of internal rebellion passed from Waziristan to the predominantly Muslim state of Kashmir.[2] The Fakir's role on the frontier had come to an inauspicious end, and he died of natural causes in 1960, though the remnants of a Pashtun separatist movement remained in his wake.[3]

With no major plans for tribal integration and the absence of *feranghi,*

Hindu, or Sikh troops to antagonize the tribesmen, the region was left largely untouched by the new Pakistani government. Proven methods of control, including the employment of allowances, indigenous scouts, and *kassadars,* continued to help control and pacify the region.[4] After an initial rebalancing of forces and sporadic outbreaks of violence, during which the tribesmen were as "wild as ever," a period of relative calm ensued, resulting in little government interference.[5] Usman Ansari recalls, "Some areas never saw any form of Government presence, except perhaps for the occasional 'political agent.'"[6] However, the Christmas Eve 1979 Soviet invasion of Afghanistan fundamentally changed the dynamic along the frontier.

From 1980 to 1991 the United States and other countries provided the *mujahadeen* guerrilla fighters in Afghanistan with financial support and arms through Pakistan's intelligence agency, the Inter Service Intelligence.[7] Additional recruits willing to fight the Soviets came from Pakistan and the Muslim Middle East. However, this policy of using proxy forces, which relied on external funding and transnational networks ignoring the integrity of the international border, resulted in the government losing control over much of the frontier. Due to the large influx of foreign fighters and refugees in the 1980s, the frontier became increasingly remote and isolated. Hamstrung by financial and political problems, and without any means to regulate the cross-border trade of drugs and arms, government control collapsed. The resulting void was filled by separate fiefdoms under tribal law.

After the Soviet withdrawal in 1989 the *mujahadeen* continued to fight the Marxist government in Afghanistan.[8] During the late 1990s the Taliban or "religious students" (most of its members had been recruited from the *madrassa,* or Islamic religious schools) grew in importance and radical Islam flourished. The Taliban embodied both traditional religious values and the Pashtun concept of honor, a recipe that gave the movement an extremely forceful dynamic and enabled it to prevail not only against the secular tendencies in Afghan society "but also against the adherents of an Islamist ideology."[9] Their goal was the establishment of a strict Islamic state under *Sharia,* dominated by the Pashtuns. With extensive aid from Pakistan, the Taliban came to dominate most of the country, but the Northern Alliance (a loose grouping of Tajik, Uzbek, Hazara, and Pashtun opponents of the Taliban, assisted predominantly by Russia, but with Iran and India also being major contributors) maintained control over a number of provinces.[10] Afghanistan, under Taliban rule, became a safe haven for international terrorists like al-Qaeda, who were able to live, train, and plan operations with no interference.[11]

Despite the Pakistani government's concern over a lack of frontier control, the situation remained largely unchanged until the Allied intervention in Afghanistan in 2001. With the U.S. systematically destroying al-Qaeda's main training camps through a mix of fixed-wing air strikes, Tomahawk cruise missile attacks, and special forces raids, thousands of militants withdrew south over the Afghan-Pakistani border into the relative safety of the Pashtun-dominated tribal areas along the frontier.[12] This included almost the entire Taliban leadership, together with al-Qaeda leader Osama bin Laden. There they reorganized as an insurgent organization.[13] Those who sought sanctuary in the tribal areas were a volatile combination of Taliban supporters and foreign fighters attempting to establish bases and hidden training camps from which to launch attacks against coalition forces in Afghanistan and the pro-U.S. government in Pakistan.[14] As Usman Ansari notes:

> Those taking up arms against the [Pakistani] government largely comprised three groups—tribal fighters indigenous to the region who sometimes signed peace deals with the government; "guns for hire" (basically smugglers or other criminals whose income had lessened because of the increased presence of government forces to restrict movement across the border); and ideologically-driven militants, both domestic and foreign.[15]

President Musharraf's carefully considered 2001 decision to abandon ties with the Mullah Omar-led Taliban regime and back the United States resulted in a violent reaction.[16] This was exacerbated by the establishment of military bases on the frontier and the use of regular forces alongside the lightly equipped Frontier Corps to search for al-Qaeda and Taliban militants. Coordinated military advances, at the behest of the U.S. government, were also conducted to secure parts of the Afghan-Pakistani border and to deny sanctuary to al-Qaeda and the Taliban. The first of these occurred in the Khyber, Karamu, and North Waziristan agencies in December 2001 and June 2002.[17] Both were preceded by long negotiations to gain access to the tribal areas. Development projects, including schools, hospitals, and an improved road network, were offered to the *maliks* to promote good behavior. Predictably, punitive actions were threatened against those who resisted the deployment of Pakistani troops.[18]

However, despite these peace-making initiatives, Pakistani forces operating in tribal territory were ambushed and isolated bases came under regular attack. With local support waning and casualties growing, regular Pakistani forces withdrew to several large military cantonments. Significantly, outposts were abandoned and border crossing points returned to the control of the local tribes and the Taliban. Despite renewed government activities and new proposals, including ambitious "peace deals" with "reconcilable" militants, North and South Waziristan, the poorest and most isolated agencies, have emerged as al-Qaeda's principal centers of operations and a magnet for foreign fighters. Efforts to broker a lasting peace deal with the local tribesmen and the Taliban in the region have proved futile so far. Not for the first time the tribesmen have refused to negotiate from a position of strength. Behroz Khan, the regional bureau chief for a Pakistani daily newspaper, points to the reality of decades of isolation: "The strength of the militants in Waziristan has built up over a generation; it will take a generation to pacify and integrate this region."[19]

Notwithstanding renewed efforts to achieve the goal of pacification, the Pashtun tribal areas continue to provide Afghan, Arab, Uzbek, and Western *jihadists* with a strong base for military operations and terrorist attacks. This is unlikely to change in the short term unless countered by a comprehensive political strategy that combines force, persuasion, and economic development. If this does not occur, and if politicians continue to downplay the cultural dynamics and importance of the region, the notoriously difficult terrain along the border will remain a dangerous and unpredictable security concern for the foreseeable future. This has the potential to unhinge President Hamid Karzai's fragile regime in Afghanistan, threaten the Pakistani government, and pose a major challenge to regional stability. It might also develop into a credible global threat. Drawing on the British experience of Waziristan in the period covered by this book, there are a number of pertinent contemporary parallels that are relevant to today's political and military strategists charged with pacifying "the badlands on both sides of the Afghan-

Pakistani border where the resurgent Taliban, Al Qaeda and their allies have built up a formidable power."[20]

## Thoughts and Prognostications

The first time that the author visited the region for an extended period of time was in Afghanistan in the spring of 2004. He was carrying a weapon, like every other male, and wearing a desert-colored British army battle uniform. He looked across the mountain border (such as it is) at the land once part of the British Empire. Thus began a period of intense study and a fascination with this region "where the wild things are." He subsequently did two separate master's theses plus a doctoral thesis on the area. He has undertaken language training and drunk hundreds of cups of tea in *chaikahanas* and *caravanserais*. He is still a student of the area, but a more informed one. When this book goes to press, he will be back in Afghanistan in battle uniform, drinking teas and looking for the next version of the Faqir of Ipi and his wily lieutenants.

## Waziristan Has Changed Little in the Past Fifty Years

There are many aspects of the frontier that remain the same. Predictably, the topography has altered little since the British departed in 1947, and the mountainous terrain still influences tribal culture and linkages.[21] Likewise, the region is inhabited by a complex mixture of independent tribes that have changed little over the years. For the majority of tribesmen, life is still tedious and opportunities for excitement and travel are rare.[22] Moreover, the inaccessible terrain continues to make the region an impregnable base in which to hide, train, and launch attacks. Insurgent and fugitive forces have little difficulty in finding long-term sanctuary in the region; it is almost impossible to distinguish militants from peaceful tribesmen. Equally, the terrain helps to mitigate technological advances and frustrates regular forces. Accurate intelligence is rarely available. The climate remains extreme and the region still suffers from elevated levels of poverty and underdevelopment.[23] Unemployment, illiteracy, and infant mortality remain high. Access to medical facilities in many remote regions is almost nonexistent. It remains an area in desperate need of social and economic development. Likewise, the tribes remain particularly susceptible to blood feuds and religious extremists. As with their ancestors, the tribesmen continue to resist outside influence or control, regardless of its legitimacy, and regard any foreign presence as a personal affront to their independence. The Hindu and the Westerner are equally foreign to the tribesmen. *Pashtunwali* still usurps Islamic *Sharia,* and internal politics still govern tribal behavior.

Despite these similarities, there are also a number of notable differences that have occurred over recent years. Perhaps the most disturbing is the number of *maliks* who have been intimidated or killed by the local Taliban in Waziristan. Seen as evidence of creeping "Talibanization" across the region, the militants have employed a reign of terror against *maliks* and alleged government sympathizers.[24] Such targeted violence has generated new tensions that have further added to the region's volatility and unpredictability. This is not without precedent. As one tribesman warned Mountstuart Elphinstone in 1809: "We are content with discord, we are content with alarms, we are content with blood . . . we will never be content with a master."[25] Nonetheless, many local leaders have been replaced by radicalized Taliban substitutes. Some, like Baitullah Mehsud, have established tacit control throughout South Waziristan, imposing a strict interpretation of Islam. Such leaders provide a recognized chain of command and a clear hierarchy. They also provide basic, if limited, training and engender tribal discipline. However, in overriding the traditional tribal hierarchy, the Taliban have unconsciously damaged long-established Pashtun civil society and reinforced ethnic suspicion. Fortunately, the damage is repairable and the foundations of society remain strong. It is unsurprising, therefore, that Chris Tripodi cautions that the difficulties experienced by Pakistan's political and military initiatives to control the Federally Administered Tribal Areas indicate that the tribes are just as complex to handle today as they ever were in colonial times, "even for those sharing the same religious and cultural affiliation."[26]

## Similarities between Mirza Ali Khan and Osama bin Laden

Significant parallels exist between the pursuit of the Fakir of Ipi and Osama bin Laden in Waziristan. These have not gone unnoticed, and the Fakir's celebrated exploits have experienced a superficial renaissance in recent years. Several newspaper articles suggest that Bin Laden can draw lessons from the Fakir's actions and the inability of the British to kill or capture him.[27] Others point to the practical frustrations of trying to capture a high profile outlaw in tribal territory. Or as one 2007 article cautions:

> For nearly a decade, the British army chased him [the Fakir of Ipi] and his followers through the remote reaches of Waziristan and the North-West Frontier Province—the same ground where allied troops have spent the past five years searching fruitlessly for bin Laden, and where the remnants of Afghanistan's Taliban fled to lick their wounds and recover their strength. The region was then, as it is today, a powder keg of fractious tribes and fundamentalist firebrands, and Britain's experience with trying to capture Khan mirrors the frustrating hunt for bin Laden.[28]

Despite well-developed political and military machinery, the British government consistently failed to kill or capture the Fakir or fully negate his influence. Bombing raids by the RAF and several division-strength operations proved futile. The Fakir's superior local intelligence, mobility, and ability to blend in with the local tribesmen routinely thwarted British efforts. Similarly, as of the time of writing, coalition forces, despite employing advanced technology, have failed to kill or capture Bin Laden or eradicate al-Qaeda from the Pashtun tribal areas astride the border.[29] However, far from being frustrated by this similarity, coalition forces can draw some comfort from one aspect of this important parallel. Both leaders experienced a high point in their popularity, followed by a gradual decrease in their influence. In the case of the *Fakir*, he lost most of his influence with independence and became little more than an irritant to the Pakistani government. Likewise, Bin Laden's authority has diminished considerably in recent years. No longer the driving force behind al-Qaeda, Bin Laden remains the notional or spiritual head but has largely become sidelined. In his place, Ayman Al Zawahiri has emerged as the organization's strategist and driving force.

However, as with the Fakir's lieutenants, Bin Laden has also encouraged a network of independent leaders, like Baitullah Mehsud, to continue the insurgency. At only thirty-four years of age, Mehsud carries significant political credibility and is regarded as a natural leader who is both physically and mentally tough.[30] Despite a lack of religious credentials, Mehsud, a traditional tribal man, has cleverly reinforced his own position while maintaining a degree of law and order in South Waziristan. His following is largely comprised of a new legion of radicalized militants. These tribesmen, including criminal elements and foreign fighters, have little loyalty to local tribal and religious leaders. Instead, they draw strength from the Taliban's deep-seated ideology, which the Pakistani government seems incapable of countering. Unsurprisingly, Mehsud and his militant tribesmen have become a major target for the coalition.[31]

Mehsud proves, yet again, that a charismatic leader with an ideological vision and wider political agenda can unite the tribesmen of Waziristan. Moreover, the hydralike insurgency, based on a highly decentralized and geographically localized approach, also highlights the difficulties of countering a distributed insurgency under local control. Decapitating any of the current leadership will do little more than buy time. As recent history proves, there are always plenty of ambitious individuals in the wings ready to take on the challenge of leadership. Therefore, tackling the cause of the violence and not the symptoms is the key to lasting success.

## The Significance of Cultural Acuity

Failure to understand cultural norms and practices or to dismiss their significance can lead to extreme danger and adversely affect campaign authority. In March 2006 Canadian soldiers conducting a routine meeting with tribal leaders in the Shah Wali Kot District in southern Afghanistan were assaulted by an ax-wielding tribesman. The unexpected attack resulted in one soldier, Lieutenant Trevor Greene, receiving severe injuries to his neck. Members of the patrol had assumed that they would be relatively safe from assault while conducting the meeting, "primarily because of the supposed protection and application of *Pushtunwali*."[32] Immediately following the event, the resident Canadian unit, the 2nd Battalion, Princess Patricia's Canadian Light Infantry, undertook a highly focused information operations campaign, exploiting the *Pashtunwali* tenet of hospitality (*melmastia*), to discredit both the attacker and village in which the meeting occurred. At the tactical level this approach experienced some success, with the village losing honor with many of the tribesmen in the region. However, the incident exposes two important aspects of the tribal code:

> First, the question must be asked as to whether or not the villagers saw the soldiers as legitimate guests, or as unwanted visitors? . . . If guests, then the provision of *pushtunwali* should have applied and our [the Canadian army's] resultant actions can be seen as appropriate. If the soldiers and their leaders were not invited, then there is certainly scope to view the attack as justifiable in the mind of the attacker and his fellow insurgents.
>
> Second, in using the principles and practices of *pushtunwali* to bring discredit to the village involved, one has to ask whether or not our actions reinforced the legitimate government of Afghanistan or eroded its authority in that particular district? Certainly there was nothing wrong with a response to the attack that would be understood by local villagers, as well as demonstrating that we understood elements of their cultural makeup. However, in reinforcing the legitimacy of the *jirga* and the code itself, we were not reinforcing the short-term perspective with regard to the authority of President Karzai in that one particular region of Kandahar province.[33]

However, as the British experienced in the colonial period, cultural acuity must extend beyond those engaged in everyday contact with the tribesmen. As policy is often determined by those in distant capitals, politicians and senior military commanders must also understand regional culture, customs, ethnicity, and religion. This is equally true of nongovernmental organizations, such as private military companies and aid organizations. Failure to understand these complex dynamics can have a damaging effect on campaign consent.[34] Likewise, policy makers must be tolerant of indigenous assumptions, methods of behavior, and everyday life choices. These will undoubtedly pose moral dilemmas for foreign and regional governments. Unsurprisingly, Western values and standards of government are often alien to indigenous populations. Expecting either a strong centrist or Western-style administration to take hold in a conservative tribal region with no recent history of strong central government is unreasonable.

Cultural understanding between governmental and nongovernmental organizations is just as important and will help to reduce friction. It will also assist in building effective working relationships and negate procedural barriers. Linked to cultural understanding is the ability to communicate. As one commentator on the frontier noted: "The gain in personal influence, besides other advantages, which an ability to converse directly with the people gives an Englishman among Pathans is so obvious that I need not dilate on it."[35] The same is equally true today. However, due to the difficulty of learning Pashtu, few Western politicians or military commanders possess the ability to converse with the tribesmen without the use of an interpreter.

Cultural acuity remains an important but underresourced goal. Regular rotations of military commanders and political reshuffles continue to thwart an in-depth understanding of cultural norms and standards on the frontier. Unsurprisingly, this has resulted in some Western policymakers disregarding or downplaying the primacy of cultural values in their efforts to shape policy along the Afghan-Pakistani border. In contrast, the Taliban and al-Qaeda cleverly exploit them for "recruitment, shelter, and social mobilisation."[36] The key to success is translating cultural understanding into effective frontier policy. However, to do this effectively requires a lifetime of specialized study and long periods of unbroken service. Creating an organization similar to the Civil Service of Pakistan in southern Afghanistan may be one initiative to help address the deficiency of cultural awareness and regional knowledge along the border.

## The Importance of Border Control

The Afghan-Pakistani border is 1,640 miles in length. It follows arbitrary geographical features and represents the historical limits of British authority in 1893. With little consideration for tribal or ethnic boundaries, the border divided the Pathan tribes between Afghanistan and Pakistan. Since its establishment, the artificial border has been viewed with disdain and is largely ignored by politicians and tribesmen on both sides of the divide. In practical terms, the border is unenforced and, arguably, unenforceable. In countless places the line of demarcation remains contested.

In others, it dissects villages and even individual homes between two opposing governments.[37] Unsurprisingly, tribesmen from both sides of the border continue to cross freely, often using hidden mountain tracks. A significant number of tribesmen have family ties on both sides.

The Soviets, like the British, tried to exert greater control along the border in the 1980s. However, their efforts proved futile. Due to growing frustrations, they resorted to Draconian measures, including mining trade routes throughout the area.[38] This failed to bring an end to cross-border movement and the supply of vital aid. After the Soviet withdrawal, the security of the border was largely ignored and both sides only saw fit to hold key entry and exit points. However, as a result of growing coalition pressure, this policy has changed. Increasing efforts are now being made to secure the border through a combination of manned crossing points, improved surveillance, and focused patrolling. Pakistani projects are also under way to "fence off" sections of the border and to restrict movement in and out of Pakistan, primarily through the use of antipersonnel mines. In the long-term, this initiative aims to contain the Taliban and al-Qaeda in Afghanistan, although in the short to medium term it is expected to fuel more fighting on Pakistani soil.[39]

However, restricted access and antipersonnel mines will only go so far. Robert Kaplan points to one reason why: "Only Pathans could make walking through a minefield a test of manhood."[40] To overcome such realities, both governments should formally recognize the international border and place historical bitterness and mistrust behind them. They should also view the border as a joint problem, requiring joint solutions. Likewise, both armies must patrol their side of the border effectively and work together to monitor militant activity and provide early warning of cross-border movement. They should also combine the use of information operations to influence the local tribesmen.

Indigenous forces, like the paramilitary Frontier Corps, are best placed to undertake the difficult task of controlling the frontier.[41] However, should regular forces be required, these must consist of Pashtun units; mixed battalions, as the British experienced, will have little success. Outsiders will not be tolerated in tribal territory. This will prove particularly challenging for the Pakistanis. Ethnic Punjabis dominate the army, and their presence in tribal territory will be a constant affront to the tribesmen. Moreover, efforts to control the border must not challenge the autonomy and freedom of the tribesmen. Communication, economic development, and cultural ties must not be severed. Achieving an effective balance will be difficult. In 1975, Wali Khan, the National Awami Party leader, was asked if he was "a Muslim, a Pakistani or a Pashtun first." His reply highlights the complexity of the border problem. Khan responded by saying that he was "a six-thousand-year-old Pashtun, a thousand-year-old Muslim and a twenty-seven year old Pakistani."[42]

## A Major Western Power Sits Adjacent to Waziristan

The coalition presence in Afghanistan continues to provide a visible target and rallying point for the extremists. As the British experience proved, the presence of Western forces in tribal territory is a constant affront to the tribesmen and provides a welcome opportunity to test their manhood and courage against a recognized foe. To overcome this, the coalition should give thought to reducing its footprint in the provinces along the Afghan-Pakistani border and make better use of locally recruited forces.[43] Despite ethnic tensions and desertions, the Afghan National Army has the skill and weaponry to maintain stability along its side of the border. However, it lacks specialist technology, and intelligence, surveillance, reconnaissance, and communication assistance will be required in the short term. It should also conduct operations on terms that the tribesmen accept and understand. This will undoubtedly require compromise. The same shortfalls are equally true of the Pakistani army, which, in addition, can also rely on the highly skilled militias of the Frontier Corps.[44] Should Western coalition forces be required in tribal territory on the Afghan side of the border, they should only deploy for a finite period of time against a recognized target. Only in extremis should coalition forces cross the border into Pakistan. Advanced technology and long-range weapons should be used where possible to negate the need for inserting troops on the ground.

## The Past as Prologue

History may not repeat itself exactly, but the past provides a useful blueprint for adaptation, and Waziristan provides good proof of this. Certain combined measures worked to settle, suppress, and pacify the region during the colonial period. For example, the establishment of a robust network of roads, medical missions, the payment of allowances, and the employment of political officers, indigenous scouts, and tribal police all helped to control the region within recognized limitations. Predictably, this was not lost on the Pakistanis, and the established methods of British tribal control remained largely in place until late 2001. However, growing U.S. political pressure resulted in Musharraf resorting to greater military action, including the use of helicopter gunships and artillery, to quash the upsurge of violence emanating from tribal territory. Unfortunately, the Pakistani army was an organization structured and trained for a conventional fight against India, Pakistan's arch rival, and ill-prepared for guerrilla warfare on the frontier. The army's ham-fisted approach to the unique problems of the frontier irritated and alienated the indigenous tribesmen. The ensuing breakdown in relations was entirely predictable.

A return to the British approach to tribal management has merit for the entire Pashtun tribal belt. Inevitably, a small number of politicians and military commanders have drawn valuable lessons from the British historical experience. General Sir David Richards, commander of the International Security Assistance Force in Afghanistan from May 2006 to February 2007, for example, points to the contemporary utility of establishing influence through the "lavish use of money":

> Our modern scruples might not permit it, but I think you could buy off ninety percent of the opposition tomorrow in the way our grandfathers would have done. Instead, today we seek influence through reconstruction and development—but that is in danger of not keeping pace with people's expectations. Nor does such an approach chime with the feudal nature of a society . . . Our colonial forebears understood the way feudal societies worked; for the most part, we don't.[45]

Richards goes on to highlight another important historical parallel: "And so we always worked very hard on achieving and maintaining consent: countless hours were spent talking to tribal elders and other influential people. We had to justify ourselves to them, explain what we were trying to achieve and work to retain their support. That is an abiding lesson from our own historical experience, which we relearned and applied pretty aggressively."[46]

However, at the psychological level, the notion of a colonial model of control will be unacceptable to the tribesmen unless rebranded within a recognized ethnic framework.[47] This is best achieved by electing empowered provincial governors and providing them with clear jurisdiction. Selected individuals could be tasked with overseeing regional security and reconstruction. However, proficiency will be based on education, experience, and personality; selecting the right individual will be key. Moreover, in addition to decentralized control, multiple lines of economic and social development will be central to controlling the region in the long term. These need to be approved by tribal leaders and have the consent of the tribesmen and their families. They must also reflect population densities. For example, the lines of development in sparsely populated rural areas must be different from those in the densely populated urban areas. One size will not fit all.

Moreover, panregional initiatives should focus on strengthening traditional tribal structures and on bringing rapid improvements to the lives of the tribesmen. Health programs and food aid are also essential and would go some way to addressing allegations of regional discrimination. Even a small amount of the U.S. $80 million a month "coalition support fund," paid to reimburse Pakistan's military for the cost of their counterinsurgency operations, would help to redress the perceived imbalance.[48] But the reality is that social and economic development will take a long time and patience is essential. Moreover, aid must be administered by the tribesmen themselves, no matter how haphazardly they do it. Outsiders operating in tribal territory would polarize the tribesmen and further add to the volatility of the region.

## A Pressing Necessity for a Wider Regional Solution

The disturbing growth of al-Qaeda and the Taliban in the isolated Pashtun tribal belt astride the Afghan-Pakistani border is a major cause for concern. A growing alignment of the Pashtun nationalist movement and radical militant leadership could lead to the unification of approximately 40 million tribesmen on both sides of the Durand Line.[49] In theory, this could result in the breakup of Afghanistan and Pakistan, both fragile multiethnic states, and allow the emergence of a new radicalized state: Pashtunistan.[50] Fortunately, two prominent fault lines exist in this hypothesis. First, many of the tribesmen dislike the extremists and would not throw in their lot with fanatics and suicide bombers. The growing friction between the Taliban and the tribal leadership (both *malik* and *mullah*) is evidence of this growing rift. Second, the notion of a unified Pashtunistan has always been predominantly symbolic. Trying to unite the fiercely independent and autonomous tribes into a cohesive whole would be difficult. This could only occur under extreme duress or under the inspiration of a charismatic leader. However, the signs are increasingly clear that this might be possible. As Pakistani Ambassador Major General (Retired) Mahmud Ali Durrani cautioned in March 2007, "I hope the Taliban and Pashtun nationalism don't merge. If that happens, we've had it, and we're on the verge of that."[51]

Unlike the challenges faced by the British in the first half of the twentieth century, this is no longer simply a regional dilemma. Instead, the tribal complexities demand an international approach based on shared security objectives. Political efforts must be made to succeed in driving an irreparable wedge between the moderate (reconcilable) Taliban and extremist (irreconcilable) Taliban associated with al-Qaeda. Provincial autonomy should also be considered. It worked well for the British and could help reinforce the long-term survival of Pakistan in its current form. Likewise, both governments must address the long-standing conflicts over the frontier region. In short, the border tribesmen must be a key part of the solution and not just the target audience.

## Can We Reuse the Lessons of History?

The *Official History of Operations on the North-West Frontier* in 1945 notes:

> Wars between 1st class modern powers come and go. Armaments and battlegrounds change with each upheaval. The tribes of the North-West Frontier of India, however, remain as heretofore an unsolved problem. The Indian Army of the future will still have

to deal with Mohmands and Afridis, Mahsuds and Wazirs. The *Tangis* and *Kandaos* of the past will again be contested. History repeats itself. Let it be read profitably.[52]

If the past is prologue, the British experience of Waziristan points to a difficult and frustrating road ahead. A violence-truce-violence cycle can be expected along the border, with ceasefires both fragile and short lived. For the most part, government forces will not encounter direct military confrontation. Fighting will consist of sniping, ambushing, and the use of mines and improvised explosive devices. Militant tribesmen will display remarkable levels of ingenuity and tenacity; opportunities for decisive effect will be fleeting and unconventional. Initiative will be required at all levels. Government reprisals will struggle to achieve surprise, and tribesmen will regularly withdraw to isolated caves to seek sanctuary. The danger is that military operations will run at a tempo and a momentum that misleads commanders into thinking that they are succeeding. Only a holistic, joint, and measured approach, employing all the elements of national power, will offer the greatest opportunity for pacifying the region and gaining consent. This must be consistent, sensitive, and coherent.

In the short term perhaps the best that can be achieved is containment; a safe, democratic, and prosperous area may be too much to hope for. Political objectives must be realistic and born of pragmatism. However, failure to address the long-term challenges of the region with a firm and consistent policy could be disastrous for both Afghanistan and Pakistan. The stakes are high and it would be wise to heed Lord Curzon's maxim: "No man who has ever read the pages of Indian history will ever prophesy about the Frontier."[53] True as this is, when governments are short of ideas and the "Talibanization" of the frontier is gaining in momentum, the historical British approach to Waziristan offers a number of valuable insights and practical measures worthy of consideration.

NOTES

For archival citations, please refer to the bibliography for manuscript collection name, depository, and location.

INTRODUCTION

1. J. R. Rodd, *Social and Diplomatic Memories* (London: Edwards Arnold & Co., 1925), 3:393–394.
2. J. Coatman, *Years of Destiny* (London: Jonathan Cape, 1932), 48; R. C. Majumdar, *An Advanced History of India* (London: Macmillan & Co., 1951), pt. 3, 1007.
3. A British expression, attributed to Arthur Conolly, for strategic competition between the British and Russian empires for domination in central Asia.
4. British involvement in India dates back to the founding of the East India Company on 31 December 1600, when Queen Elizabeth I granted a charter to the company providing exclusive rights to trade with the East. As trade improved, the company protected its interests, which were threatened by the instability surrounding the declining Mongol Empire, the varying fortunes of local rulers, and the interference of ruthless chieftains. In 1757 the company's fortunes rose, and it transformed from a trading venture to a ruling enterprise when one of its military officials, Robert Clive, defeated the forces of the Nawab of Bengal, Siraj-ud-daulah, at the Battle of Plassey. Thereafter, the company conducted many of the functions of governance and administration, generating considerable revenue. The resulting structure was a functioning government, owned by businessmen. Such an accomplishment had not gone unnoticed by the British government, and company activities fell increasingly under London's control. In 1813 London broke the company's commercial monopoly, and from 1834 on it served as the managing agency for the British government of India. The company lost this function after the Indian Mutiny (1857) and ceased to exist as a legal entity in 1873.
5. P. Woodruff, *The Men Who Ruled India: The Guardians* (London: Jonathan Cape, 1954), 69; F. S. R. Roberts, *Forty-One Years in India* (London: Richard Bentley & Son, 1897), 2:103–108.
6. *Frontier and Overseas Expeditions from India*, vol. 3, *Baluchistan and the First Afghan War* (Calcutta: Superintendent Government Printing, 1910), 4.
7. A. Lyall, *British Domination in India* (London: John Murray, 1920), 371.
8. Quoted in D. Dilks, *Curzon in India* (London: Rupert Hart-Davis, 1969), 40.
9. See J. A. Norris, *The First Afghan War, 1838–1842* (Cambridge: Cambridge University Press, 1967); B. Robson, *The Road to Kabul: The Second Afghan War, 1978–1881* (London: Spellmount, 1975).
10. T. H. Holdich, *The Indian Borderland, 1880–1900* (London: Methuen & Co., 1901), 372.
11. W. Barton, "Waziristan and Frontier Policy," *Fortnightly Review* 142 (1937): 194.
12. M. Evans, *Afghanistan: A Short History of Its People and Politics* (London:

HarperCollins Publishers, 2002), 108–109; P. Skyes, The *Right Honourable Sir Mortimer Durand—A Biography* (London: Cassell & Co., 1926).

13. K. Wigram, "Defence in the North-West Frontier Province," *Journal of the Royal Central Asian Society* 24 (1937): 73.

14. J. W. Spain, *The Pathan Borderland* (The Hague: Mouton & Co., 1963), 151.

15. Close Border (1849–1878), Forward (1879–1901, 1923–1947), and Modified Forward (1901–1923).

16. For example, post 1901 the single dominant factor influencing frontier policy was the requirement to reduce costs (L/PS/12/3171 PZ2435, Report of Tribal Defence and Control Committee Meeting, June 1931).

17. See V. Gregorian, *The Emergence of Modern Afghanistan: Politics of Reform and Modernization, 1880–1946* (Stanford, CA: Stanford University Press, 1969); G. Molesworth, *Afghanistan, 1919* (London: Asia Publishing House, 1962); L. Poullada, *Reform and Rebellion in Afghanistan, 1919–1929* (Ithaca, NY: Cornell University Press, 1973); W. Vogelsang, *The Afghans* (Oxford: Blackwell Publishers, 2002); and *The Third Afghan War, 1919: Official Account* (Calcutta: Government of India Central Publishing Branch, 1926).

18. See A. Warren, *Waziristan, the Faqir of Ipi, and the Indian Army* (Oxford: Oxford University Press, 2000).

19. Sir Olaf Caroe, a former governor of the North-West Frontier, notes: "The record of that century [the colonial period] shows that, of all the Pathan tribes up and down the North-West Frontier, the Mahsuds were without question the most intransient" (O. Caroe, *The Pathans, 550 B.C.–A.D. 1957* [London: Macmillan, 1965], 397).

20. Brian Robson, vice president of the Society for Army Historical Records and a founding member of the Army Records Society, notes, "But, with two honourable exceptions—Tim Moreman and Alan Warren—the younger generations of military historians has largely ignored the Frontier as a field for study, for reasons which it would be interesting but unrewarding to explore" (B. Robson, *Crisis on the Frontier* [London: Spellmount, 2004], x).

21. M. Crawshaw, "Running a Country: The British Colonial Experience and Its Relevance to Present Day Concerns," *Shrivenham Papers*, no. 3 (April 2007).

22. Warren, *Waziristan*, xxviii.

23. For example, H. Hussain, "Letters," *Military Review* 86 (March–April 2006): 119; R. Stewart and S. Cowper-Coles, "Are We Failing in Afghanistan?" *British Army Review* 144 (Spring 2008): 10.

24. The Pakistan government has released little archive material beyond independence.

25. J. Shaw, "Don't Fight the Soil," speech on cultural understanding delivered to the Defence Academy, Shrivenham, 11 June 2008.

26. T. R. Moreman, *The Army in India and the Development of Frontier Warfare, 1849–1947* (London: Macmillan, 1998), xviii.

27. Ibid.

28. The UK army field manual *Counter Insurgency Operations* defines counterinsurgency operations as "those military, paramilitary, political, economic, psychological, and civil actions taken by the government to defeat insurgency" (Ministry of Defense, *Army Field Manual*, vol. 1, *Combined Operations*,

pt. 10: *Counter Insurgency Operations* [London: Ministry of Defense, 2001], A-1-1).

29. The draft document was released for comment in March 2008.

30. For example, D. Galula, *Counterinsurgency Warfare: Theory and Practice* (Westport, CT: Praeger, 1966); F. Kitson, *Low Intensity Operations: Subversion, Insurgency, Peace-Keeping* (London: Faber & Faber, 1971); F. Kitson, *Bunch of Five* (London: Faber & Faber, 1977); and R. Thompson, *Defeating Communist Insurgency: The Lessons of Malaya and Vietnam* (New York: Praeger, 1966).

31. This is in contrast to Allan Warren's position. In the introduction to his book on the 1936–1937 revolt, he states, "The British Indian experience in Waziristan can be considered, in some respects, as a case-study in the 'failure' of imperial policing" (Warren, *Waziristan*, xxvi).

32. Brigadier John Prendergast died on 9 February 2008 (Obituaries, *The Daily Telegraph*, 3 March 2008).

33. Moreman, *The Army in India and the Development of Frontier Warfare, 1849–1947*, 185.

34. A. Gordon, *The Rules of the Game* (London: John Murray, 1966), 2.

CHAPTER 1. THE LAY OF THE LAND: WAZIRISTAN'S
PEOPLE, HISTORY, AND TERRAIN

1. L. Adamec, *Historical Dictionary of Afghanistan* (Metuchen, NJ: Scarecrow Press, 1991), 66–67.

2. H. de Watteville, *Waziristan, 1919–1920* (London: Constable & Co., 1925), 19.

3. Ibid.

4. H. L. Nevill, *North-West Frontier: British and Indian Army Campaigns on the North-West Frontier, 1849–1908* (1912; reprint, London: Tom Donovan Publishing, 1992), 2.

5. A. G. Jacob, "Waziristan," *Journal of the Royal Central Asian Society* 14 (1927): 239.

6. R. I. Bruce, *The Forward Policy and Its Results* (London: Longmans, Green, & Co., 1900), 32.

7. *Encyclopedia Britannica* 28 (1911): 436.

8. T. H. Thornton, *Colonel Sir Robert Sandeman—His Life and Work on Our Indian Frontier* (London: John Murray, 1895), 194.

9. Bruce, *The Forward Policy and Its Results*, 32.

10. *Operations in Waziristan, 1919–1920*, compiled by the General Staff, Army Headquarters, India (Calcutta, 1921), 43.

11. H. R. C. Pettigrew, *Frontier Scouts* (Selsey, Sussex: privately printed, 1964), 2.

12. de Watteville, *Waziristan, 1919–1920*, 17.

13. D. S. Richards, *The Savage Frontier* (London: Pan Books, 1990), 184.

14. F. C. Simpson, "Review of N. W. Frontier Policy from 1849–1939," *Journal of the United Services Institution of India* 74, no. 16 (1944): 52.

15. C. H. T. MacFetridge and J. P. Warren, eds., *Tales of the Mountain Gunners* (Edinburgh: William Blackwood, 1973), 119.

16. G. Moore, *Just as Good as the Rest* (Bedford, UK: Jaycopy, 1979), 39.

17. A. Warren, *Waziristan, the Faqir of Ipi, and the Indian Army* (Oxford: Oxford University Press, 2000), 14.
18. Nevill, *North-West Frontier*, 10.
19. A common tribal saying for wishing a child success in life was, "May God make thee a good thief" (B. J. Gould, *The Jewel in the Lotus* [London: Chatto & Windus, 1957], 133).
20. C. E. Bruce, *Waziristan, 1936–1937* (Aldershot, UK: Gale & Polden, 1938), 13.
21. *Frontier and Overseas Expeditions from India*, vol. 2, *North-West Frontier Tribes between the Kabul and Gumal Rivers* (Simla, India: Government Monotype Press, 1908), 332.
22. C. C. Trench, *The Frontier Scouts* (London: Jonathan Cape, 1985), 79.
23. "India's Southern Front," *Times* (London), 5 November 1942, 5.
24. J. Masters, *Bugles and a Tiger* (London: Cassell & Co., 1956), 73.
25. Bruce, *The Forward Policy and Its Results*, 32.
26. MacFetridge and Warren, eds., *Tales of the Mountain Gunners*, 114.
27. Richards, *The Savage Frontier*, 182.
28. G. A. Brett, *History of the South Wales Borderers and the Monmouthshire Regiment, 1937–52*, pt. 1 (Pontypool, UK: Hughes & Son, 1953), 16–20.
29. Bruce, *Waziristan, 1936–1937*, 46.
30. Ibid., 45.
31. W. Barton, *India's North-West Frontier* (London: John Murray, 1939), 70.
32. Thornton, *Colonel Sir Robert Sandeman*, 19.
33. F. Tönnies, *Community and Society*, trans. Charles P. Loomis (East Lansing: Michigan State University Press, 1957), pp. 2–45.
34. "The Changing Frontier: Check to Wazir Blood Feuds," *Times* (London), 31 March 1930.
35. Bruce, *The Forward Policy and Its Results*, 43.
36. L/P&S/7/136 W. R., Merk to the Chief Secretary to Government, Punjab, Shekh Budin, 12 June 1901.
37. An observation substantiated in Trench, *The Frontier Scouts*, 46.
38. E. Cadogan, *The India We Saw* (London: John Murray, 1933), 272.
39. These were replaced by petrol engine lathes, although fuel remained in short supply.
40. Warren, *Waziristan, The Faqir of Ipi, and the Indian Army*, 70–71.
41. Nevill, *North-West Frontier*, 366.
42. T. C. Coen, *The Indian Political Service* (London: Chatto & Windus, 1971), 183.
43. C. C. Trench, *Viceroy's Agent* (London: Jonathan Cape, 1987), 60.
44. *Operations in Waziristan, 1919–1920*, 41.
45. Moore, *Just as Good as the Rest*, 38.
46. Caroe, *The Pathans, 550 B.C.–A.D. 1957*, 405.
47. T. R. Moreman, "The Arms Trade and the North-West Frontier Tribes," *Journal of Imperial and Commonwealth History* 2, no. 22 (1994): 187–216.
48. T. A. Heathcote, *The Indian Army* (London: David & Charles, 1974), 170.
49. *Frontier and Overseas Expeditions from India*, 2:2.

50. L/PS/12/3171, PZ2435, Report of Tribal Defence and Control Committee Meeting, June 1931, 5.
51. Nevill, *North-West Frontier*, 366.
52. Ibid., 367.
53. These included novel measures such as stopping the manufacture of rifles in the Kohat Pass by the simple means of "buying-up" the factories (WO 106/6027, D.D.M.I. to D.M.O.I. and D.D.M.O., 29 August 1937).
54. de Watteville, *Waziristan, 1919–1920*, 172.
55. "Waziristan Operations," *Times* (London), 17 November 1937.
56. *Operations in Waziristan, 1919–1920*, 140.
57. B. Robson, *Crisis on the Frontier* (London: Spellmount, 2004), 223.
58. Trench, *The Frontier Scouts*, 47.
59. A. Wilson, *Sport and Service in Assam and Elsewhere* (London: Hutchinson & Co., 1924), 279–280.
60. C. E. Callwell, *Small Wars — Their Principles and Practice* (London: Harrison & Son, 1906), 290.
61. A. C. Yate, "North-West Frontier Warfare," *Journal of the Royal United Services Institution* 42, no. 248 (1898): 1173.
62. Nevill, *North-West Frontier*, 368.
63. "Shpagwishtama," "The Changing Aspect of Operations on the North-West Frontier," *Journal of the United Service Institution of India* 66, no. 283 (1936): 105.
64. Moore, *Just as Good as the Rest*, 28.
65. "Afghanistan and the North-West Frontier: The Green Howards during the Third Afghan War 1919, and the Waziristan Campaigns of 1936–1937, 1937–1939," *The Friends of the Green Howards Regimental Museum Newsletter*, no. 14, September 2002, 7.
66. *Operations in Waziristan, 1919–1920*, 146.
67. Trench, *The Frontier Scouts*, 47.
68. "The Other Indian Frontier," *Times* (London), 13 August 1942.
69. de Watteville, *Waziristan, 1919–1920*, 26; *Operations in Waziristan, 1919–1920*, 126–127.
70. Trench, *The Frontier Scouts*, 139.
71. "The Other Indian Frontier," *Times* (London), 13 August 1942.
72. F. T. C. Williams, "Exciting Times and Narrow Squeaks" (Blandford, UK: Royal School of Signals Museum, 1937), 6–7.
73. "N.W. Frontier Fight," *Times* (London), 27 November 1936.
74. Richards, *The Savage Frontier*, 181.
75. Royal School of Signals Museum, Blandford, 915, Comment on Inter-Communication Waziristan Operations, 1936–37, Waziristan District Signals, Historical Records, 1938–1939.
76. O. D. Bennett, "Some Regrettable Incidents on the N.-W.F.," *Journal of the United Service Institution of India* 63, no. 271 (1933): 194.
77. de Watteville, *Waziristan, 1919–1920*, 23.
78. *Operations in Waziristan, 1919–1920*, 6.
79. Bruce, *The Forward Policy and Its Results*, 321.

80. A. Skene, *Passing It On—Short Talks on Tribal Fighting on the North West Frontier of India* (Aldershot, UK: n.p., 1932), 52.
81. G. MacMunn, *The Martial Races of India* (London: Sampson Low, Marston, & Co., 1933), 245.
82. Trench, *The Frontier Scouts*, 27.
83. Ibid., 68.
84. *Frontier and Overseas Expeditions from India*, 2:3.
85. C. C. Davies, *The Problem of The North-West Frontier, 1890–1908* (London: Cambridge University Press, 1932), 180.
86. F. Leeson, *Frontier Legion* (Ferring: Selwood Printing, 2003), 69.
87. Moore, *Just as Good as the Rest*, 50.
88. Ibid.
89. Pettigrew, *Frontier Scouts*, 68.
90. *Operations in Waziristan, 1919–1920*, 142.
91. Heathcote, *The Indian Army*, 382.
92. Royal School of Signals Museum, Blandford, 937.14, B. E. Hughes, "Waziristan Expedition," June 1920, 6.
93. J. Prendergast, *Prender's Progress—A Soldier in India, 1931–47* (London: Cassell & Co., 1979), 67.
94. F. T. C. Willimas, "The Indian Argosy" (Blandford, UK: Royal School of Signals Museum, 1936), 1:4.
95. R. C. B. Bristow, *Memories of the British Raj* (London: Johnson, 1974), 54–57.
96. de Watteville, *Waziristan, 1919–1920*, 20.
97. T. H. Holdich, *The Indian Borderland, 1880–1900* (London: Methuen & Co., 1901), 56.
98. *Operations in Waziristan, 1919–1920*, 3.
99. Trench, *The Frontier Scouts*, 93.
100. C. Lindholm, *Generosity and Jealousy: Swat Pukktun of Northern Pakistan* (New York: Columbia, 1982), 123.
101. Barton, *India's North-West Frontier*, 10.
102. Thornton, *Colonel Sir Robert Sandeman*, 13.
103. "Afghanistan and the North-West Frontier," 4.
104. Moore, *Just as Good as the Rest*, 28.
105. Ibid., 29.

CHAPTER 2. BLOOD FOR BLOOD: THE TRIBAL CULTURE OF CODE

1. Although the remainder of the chapter is written principally using historians' sources, the following anthropological and social theory works have provided useful balance: M. Banerjee, *The Pathan Unarmed: Opposition and Memory in the North-West Frontier* (Oxford: Oxford University Press, 2000); H. W. Bellow, *A General Report on the Yusufzais* (Lahore: Government Printing Press, 1864); J. Biddulph, *Tribes of the Hindoo Kush* (Calcutta: Office of Department of Government Printing, 1880); L. Dupree, *Afghanistan* (Princeton, NJ: Princeton University Press, 1973); R. Guha, *Elementary Aspects of Peasant Insurgency in Colonial India* (Durham, NC: Duke University Press, 1999);

G. S. Robertson, *The Kafirs of the Hindu-Kush* (London: Lawrence & Bullen, 1896); and A. Stein, *On Alexander's Track to the Indus* (London: Macmillan, 1929).

2. H. Beattie, *Imperial Frontier: Tribe and State in Waziristan* (Richmond, UK: Curzon Press, 2002), 4.

3. A. Akbar, *Religion and Politics in Muslim Society* (Cambridge: Cambridge University Press, 1983), 27.

4. T. H. Holdich, *The Indian Borderland, 1880–1900* (London: Methuen & Co., 1901), 68.

5. C. C. Trench, *The Frontier Scouts* (London: Jonathan Cape, 1985), 118.

6. *Frontier and Overseas Expeditions from India*, vol. 2, *North-West Frontier Tribes between the Kabul and Gumal Rivers* (Simla, India: Government Monotype Press, 1908), 365.

7. A. Calvin, "Indian Frontiers and Indian Finance," *Nineteenth Century* 38 (1895): 881–882.

8. C. C. Davies, *The Problem of The North-West Frontier, 1890–1908* (London: Cambridge University Press, 1932), 49.

9. M. Barthorp, *The North-West Frontier: British India and Afghanistan* (Poole, UK: Blandford Press, 1982), 12.

10. "Pushtunwali: Honour amongst Them," *Economist*, 23 December 2006, 39.

11. W. S. Churchill, *The Story of the Malakand Field Force* (London: Longmans, Green, 1898), 87.

12. W. Barton, *India's North-West Frontier* (London: John Murray, 1939), 17.

13. W. R. Hay, "The Blood Feud in Waziristan," *Journal of the Royal Central Asian Society* 19 (1932): 304.

14. Beattie, *Imperial Frontier*, 8.

15. Hay, "The Blood Feud in Waziristan," 310.

16. Trench, *The Frontier Scouts*, 3.

17. T. H. Thornton, *Colonel Sir Robert Sandeman—His Life and Work on Our Indian Frontier* (London: John Murray, 1895), 303.

18. R. Baden-Powell, *Memories of India: Recollections of Soldiering and Sport* (Philadelphia: D. McKay, 1915), 164.

19. Trench, *The Frontier Scouts*, 17–18.

20. C. Miller, *Khyber: British India's North-West Frontier* (London: MacDonald & Jane's, 1977), 99.

21. Davies, *The Problem of The North-West Frontier, 1890–1908*, 49.

22. G. Pfeffer and D. K. Behera, eds., *Concept of Tribal Society* (New Delhi: Concept Publishers, 2002), 265–282.

23. A. S. Ahmed, *Religion and Politics in Muslim Society: Order and Conflict in Pakistan* (Cambridge: Cambridge University Press, 1983), 18.

24. O. Caroe, *The Pathans, 550 B.C.–A.D. 1957* (London: Macmillan, 1965), 403.

25. R. I. Bruce, *The Forward Policy and Its Results* (London: Longmans, Green, & Co., 1900), 18.

26. G. Moore, *Just as Good as the Rest* (Bedford, UK: Jaycopy, 1979), 21.

27. G. N. Curzon, "The 'Scientific Frontier' an Accomplished Fact," *Nineteenth Century* 23 (1888): 904.

28. Thornton, *Colonel Sir Robert Sandeman*, 22.

29. "Mahsud Rebel's House Destroyed," *Times* (London), 14 June 1937.
30. Trench, *The Frontier Scouts*, 135.
31. Caroe, *The Pathans, 550 B.C.–A.D. 1957*, 402.
32. C. C. Trench, *Viceroy's Agent* (London: Jonathan Cape, 1987), 58.
33. F. T. C. Williams, "Exciting Times and Narrow Squeaks" (Blandford, UK: Royal School of Signals Museum, 1937), 9–10.
34. Moore, *Just as Good as the Rest*, 39.
35. J. Lionel, *The Indian Frontier War: Being an Account of the Mohmund and Tirah Expeditions, 1898* (London: William Heinemann, 1898), 5.
36. F. Yeates-Brown, *Martial India* (London: Eyre & Spottiswoode, 1945), 38.
37. Caroe, *The Pathans, 550 B.C.–A.D. 1957*, 390–412.
38. W. R. Lawrence, *The India We Served* (London: Cassell & Co., 1929), 42.
39. C. A. L. Graham, *The History of the Indian Mountain Artillery* (Aldershot, UK: Gale & Polden, 1957), 75.
40. B. Robson, *Crisis on the Frontier* (London: Spellmount, 2004), 158.
41. *Frontier and Overseas Expeditions from India*, 2:123.
42. Beattie, *Imperial Frontier*, 9.
43. Thornton, *Colonel Sir Robert Sandeman*, 13.
44. A. S. Ahmed, "An Aspect of the Colonial Encounter in the North-West Frontier Province," *Asian Affairs* 65 (1978): 319–327.
45. F. Leeson, *Frontier Legion* (Ferring: Selwood Printing, 2003), 19.
46. H. L. Nevill, *North-West Frontier: British and Indian Army Campaigns on the North-West Frontier, 1849–1908* (1912; reprint, London: Tom Donovan Publishing, 1992), 10.
47. *Frontier and Overseas Expeditions from India*, 2:334.
48. *Operations in Waziristan, 1919–1920*, compiled by the General Staff, Army Headquarters, India (Calcutta, 1921), 3.
49. Nevill, *North-West Frontier*, 10.
50. H. de Watteville, *Waziristan, 1919–1920* (London: Constable & Co., 1925), 207.
51. Caroe, *The Pathans, 550 B.C.–A.D. 1957*, 409.
52. Beattie, *Imperial Frontier*, 6.
53. Moore, *Just as Good as the Rest*, 40.
54. Trench, *The Frontier Scouts*, 14.
55. Nevill, *North-West Frontier*, 10.
56. *Frontier and Overseas Expeditions from India*, 2:364.
57. Ibid., 450.
58. *Operations in Waziristan, 1919–1920*, 19–20.
59. E. E. Oliver, *Across the Border; or Pathân and Biloch* (London: Chapman & Hall, 1890), 121.
60. Leeson, *Frontier Legion*, 7.
61. Ahmed, "An Aspect of the Colonial Encounter in the North-West Frontier Province," 322.
62. Beattie, *Imperial Frontier*, 7.
63. E. Howell, "Mizh: A Monograph on Government Relations with the Mahsud Tribe," manuscript (Oxford, 1979), preface.
64. M. Hauner, "One Man against the Empire: The Faqir of Ipi and the British

in Central Asia on the Eve of and during the Second World War," *Journal of Contemporary History* 16, no. 1 (1981): 188.

65. G. Dunbar, *A History of India* (London: Ivor Nicholson & Watson, 1936), 568.

CHAPTER 3. SECURING THE FRONTIER: POLITICS, POLICY, AND TRIBAL REALITIES

1. E. Howell, "Some Problems of the Indian Frontier," *Journal of the Royal Central Asian Society* 21 (1934): 185.
2. G. Dunbar, *A History of India* (London: Ivor Nicholson & Watson, 1936), 503.
3. W. S. R. Hodson, *A Soldier's Life in India,* ed. G. H. Hodson (London: John W. Parker & Son, 1859), 89.
4. *Frontier and Overseas Expeditions from India,* vol. 3, *Baluchistan and the First Afghan War* (Calcutta: Superintendent Government Printing, 1910), 93.
5. C. C. Davies, *The Problem of the North-West Frontier, 1890–1908* (London: Cambridge University Press, 1932), 187.
6. W. Barton, *India's North-West Frontier* (London: John Murray, 1939), 56.
7. P. Woodruff, *The Men Who Ruled India: The Guardians* (London: Jonathan Cape, 1954), 139.
8. M. Barthorp, *The North-West Frontier: British India and Afghanistan* (Poole, UK: Blandford Press, 1982), 49.
9. Davies, *The Problem of the North-West Frontier, 1890–1908,* 2.
10. G. N. Curzon, "The 'Scientific Frontier' an Accomplished Fact," *Nineteenth Century* 23 (1888): 902.
11. Davies, *The Problem of the North-West Frontier, 1890–1908,* 1–16.
12. Ibid., 4.
13. Lord Curzon of Kedleston, "Text of the 1907 Romanes Lecture on the Subject of Frontiers," http://www.dur.ac.uk/resources/ibru/resources/links/curzon.pdf.
14. Debate in the House of Lords, 7 March 1898; quoted in Davies, *The Problem of the North-West Frontier, 1890–1908,* 6.
15. Davies, *The Problem of the North-West Frontier, 1890–1908,* 17.
16. Curzon, "The 'Scientific Frontier' an Accomplished Fact," 901–917.
17. J. J. H. Gordon, R. Temple, J. Hills Johnes, Dr. Blanford, and Captain Younghusband, "The Geography of the North-West Frontier of India," *Geographical Journal* 17, no. 3 (1901): 475.
18. H. L. Nevill, *North-West Frontier: British and Indian Army Campaigns on the North-West Frontier, 1849–1908* (1912; reprint, London: Tom Donovan Publishing, 1992), 151.
19. *Frontier and Overseas Expeditions from India,* 3:285–453.
20. C. E. Bruce, *Waziristan, 1936–1937* (Aldershot, UK: Gale & Polden, 1938), 2–3.
21. Nevill, *North-West Frontier,* 21.
22. D. Dichter, *The North West Frontier of West Pakistan* (Oxford: Clarendon Press, 1967), 127.
23. P. Mason, *A Matter of Honour* (London: Ebenezer Baylis & Son, 1974), 335.

24. H. Beattie, *Imperial Frontier: Tribe and State in Waziristan* (Richmond, UK: Curzon Press, 2002), 25.
25. H. C. Wylly, *Tribes of Central Asia: From the Black Mountains to Waziristan* (London: Macmillan & Co., 1912), 5.
26. *Frontier and Overseas Expeditions from India*, 3:49.
27. Ibid., 2:355.
28. Mason, *A Matter of Honour*, 336.
29. G. F. MacGunn, *The Armies of India* (London: Adam & Charles Black, 1911), 212.
30. "Mauser," "A Forgotten Frontier Force," *English Review* 52 (1931): 70.
31. Levies, or *kassadars*, as they were known later, were armed un-uniformed retainers of chiefs and headmen who, in return for certain allowances, provided protection for certain roads and districts.
32. W. S. R. Hodson, *A Soldier's Life in India*, 146.
33. A. Lyall, *British Domination in India* (London: John Murray, 1920), 360.
34. Davies, *The Problem of the North-West Frontier, 1890–1908*, 23–24.
35. C. Miller, *Khyber: British India's North-West Frontier* (London: MacDonald & Jane's, 1977), 257.
36. F. S. R. Roberts, *Forty-One Years in India* (London: Richard Bentley & Son, 1897), 248.
37. J. G. Elliot, *The Frontier, 1839–1947* (London: Cassell & Co., 1968), 77.
38. Barton, *India's North-West Frontier*, 58–59.
39. *Frontier and Overseas Expeditions from India*, 2:386–387.
40. Beattie, *Imperial Frontier*, 49.
41. *Frontier and Overseas Expeditions from India*, 2:387.
42. Beattie, *Imperial Frontier*, 26.
43. J. Slessor, *The Central Blue* (London: Cassell & Co., 1956), 55.
44. Barton, *India's North-West Frontier*, 60.
45. D. S. Richards, *The Savage Frontier* (London: Pan Books, 1990), 182.
46. A blockade consists in preventing a certain tribe from holding any interaction with the inhabitants of British territory. It also prohibited them from grazing their flocks in neighboring districts.
47. W. H. Padget, *Record of Expeditions against the North-West Frontier Tribes since the Annexation of the Punjab*, rev. A. H. Mason (London: Whiting, 1884), 527.
48. Davies, *The Problem of the North-West Frontier, 1890–1908*, 25.
49. Barton, *India's North-West Frontier*, 59.
50. C. A. L. Graham, *The History of the Indian Mountain Artillery* (Aldershot, UK: Gale & Polden, 1957), 10.
51. B. Farwell, *Queen Victoria's Little Wars* (London: W. W. Norton & Co., 1972), 148–149.
52. R. I. Bruce, *The Forward Policy and Its Results* (London: Longmans, Green, & Co., 1900), 366.
53. W. S. Churchill, *The Story of the Malakand Field Force* (London: Longmans, Green, 1898), 96.
54. *Frontier and Overseas Expeditions from India*, 2:343.
55. W. S. Churchill, *My Early Life* (London: Thornton Butterworth, 1930), 145.

56. *Frontier and Overseas Expeditions from India*, 2:368–410.
57. Woodruff, *The Men Who Ruled India*, 141.
58. Nevill, *North-West Frontier*, 21.
59. *Frontier and Overseas Expeditions from India*, 2:455–456.
60. Ibid., 359.
61. Ibid., 359–360.
62. B. Balfour, *History of Lord Lytton's Indian Administration* (London: Longmans, Green & Co., 1899), 177–178.
63. Bruce, *Waziristan, 1936–1937*, v.
64. Bruce, *The Forward Policy and Its Results*, 14.
65. Ibid.
66. T. H. Thornton, *Colonel Sir Robert Sandeman—His Life and Work on Our Indian Frontier* (London: John Murray, 1895), 20.
67. Bruce, *Waziristan, 1936–1937*, 3.
68. Dunbar, *A History of India*, 569.
69. *Frontier and Overseas Expeditions from India*, 2:366.
70. T. H. Holdich, *The Indian Borderland, 1880–1900* (London: Methuen & Co., 1901), 64.
71. J. Martineau, *Life of Sir Bartle Frere* (London: John Murray, 1895), 1:363–368.
72. FO 371/23628, Government of India External Affairs Department, F. D. Cunningham, Esq., Commissioner and Superintendent, Peshawar Division, to the officiating Chief Secretary to Government, Punjab, 11 May 1895, Foreign Office, National Archive, Kew, Surrey.
73. Mason, *A Matter of Honour*, 337.
74. Thornton, *Colonel Sir Robert Sandeman*, 21.
75. E. W. Sheppard, *A Short History of the British Army to 1914* (London: Constable & Co., 1929), 240.
76. Davies, *The Problem of the North-West Frontier, 1890–1908*, 26.
77. Bruce, *The Forward Policy and Its Results*, 369.
78. Davies, *The Problem of the North-West Frontier, 1890–1908*, app. B.
79. Woodruff, *The Men Who Ruled India*, 142.
80. A. Fraser, *Plain Tales from the Raj*, ed. C. Allen (London: Abacus, 1977), 197.
81. T. A. Heathcote, *The Indian Army* (London: David & Charles, 1974), 28.
82. Beattie, *Imperial Frontier*, 185.
83. Nevill, *North-West Frontier*, 380.
84. Bruce, *Waziristan, 1936–1937*, 3.
85. Barton, *India's North-West Frontier*, 61.
86. M. Diver, *The Unsung: A Record of British Services in India* (London: William Blackwood & Son, 1945), 104.
87. Bruce, *The Forward Policy and Its Results*, 25.
88. Beattie, *Imperial Frontier*, 41.
89. Thornton, *Colonel Sir Robert Sandeman*, 20.
90. G. W. Gilbertson, *First Pakkhtoo Book* (Benares, India: Medical Hall Press, 1901), preface.
91. Davies, *The Problem of the North-West Frontier, 1890–1908*, 263.
92. Bruce, *The Forward Policy and Its Results*, 355.
93. Ibid., 358–359.

CHAPTER 4. THE FORWARD POLICIES:
BRITISH INFLUENCE, POLITICAL CONTROL,
AND THE *MALIKI* SYSTEM

1. The British, determined that a common frontier with the Russians should not exist, negotiated an agreement in July 1895 that left a long finger of Afghan territory, the "Wakhan corridor," stretching between the two empires from Badakhshan to the border with China. Abdur Raham had no wish to assume responsibility for the corridor, but his objections were outweighed by the offer of an annual subsidy to cover the cost.

2. J. P. Misra, *The Administration of India under Lord Lansdowne, 1888–1894* (New Delhi: Sterling Publishers, 1975), 7–8.

3. *Frontier and Overseas Expeditions from India*, vol. 3, *Baluchistan and the First Afghan War* (Calcutta: Superintendent Government Printing, 1910), 3.

4. W. Barton, *India's North-West Frontier* (London: John Murray, 1939), 167.

5. A. Swinson, *North-West Frontier—People and Events, 1939–1947* (London: Hutchinson, 1967), 127.

6. G. Dunbar, *A History of India* (London: Ivor Nicholson & Watson, 1936), 570.

7. F. Leeson, *Frontier Legion* (Ferring: Selwood Printing, 2003), 56–57.

8. CAB 37/39/30, no. 214, Dispatch from F. D. Cunningham, Esq., Commissioner and Superintendent, Peshawar Division, to the Officiating Chief Secretary to Government, Punjab, 11 May 1895.

9. M. Ewans, *Afghanistan: A Short History of Its People and Politics* (London: HarperCollins Publishers, 2002), 108.

10. *Frontier and Overseas Expeditions from India*, 2:414.

11. W. Barton, "Waziristan and the Frontier Policy," *Fortnightly Review* 142 (1937): 194.

12. K. Wigram, "Defence in the North-West Frontier Province," *Journal of the Royal Central Asian Society* 24 (1937): 73.

13. *Operations in Waziristan, 1919–1920*, compiled by the General Staff, Army Headquarters, India (Calcutta, 1921), 20.

14. Ewans, *Afghanistan*, 108.

15. Leeson, *Frontier Legion*, 16.

16. J. W. Spain, *The Pathan Borderland* (The Hague: Mouton & Co., 1963), 159.

17. Swinson, *North-West Frontier*, 251.

18. A. Warren, *Waziristan, the Faqir of Ipi, and the Indian Army* (Oxford: Oxford University Press, 2000), 23.

19. M. Hauner, "One Man against the Empire: The Faqir of Ipi and the British in Central Asia on the Eve of and during the Second World War," *Journal of Contemporary History* 16, no. 1 (1981): 187.

20. A. Lyall, *British Domination in India* (London: John Murray, 1920), 364.

21. C. E. Bruce, *Waziristan, 1936–1937* (Aldershot, UK: Gale & Polden, 1938), 2.

22. These were predominantly non-Pathan: Baluchis, Bugtis, Marris, and other tribes known to be more obedient to their chiefs than the hill tribesmen of Waziristan.

23. O. Caroe, *The Pathans, 550 B.C.–A.D. 1957* [London: Macmillan, 1965], 398.

24. C. C. Davies, *The Problem of the North-West Frontier, 1890–1908* (London: Cambridge University Press, 1932), 124.

25. Ibid., 126.
26. C. C. Trench, *The Frontier Scouts* (London: Jonathan Cape, 1985), 14.
27. *Frontier and Overseas Expeditions from India*, 2:437.
28. Trench, *The Frontier Scouts*, 401.
29. E. Howell, "Mizh: A Monograph on Government Relations with the Mahsud Tribe," manuscript (Oxford, 1979), 25–26.
30. Bruce, *Waziristan, 1936–1937*, 52–54.
31. Caroe, *The Pathans, 550 B.C.–A.D. 1957*, 404.
32. T. H. Holdich, *The Indian Borderland, 1880–1900* (London: Methuen & Co., 1901), 341.
33. D. Dilks, *Curzon in India* (London: Rupert Hart-Davis, 1969), 59.
34. P. Mehra, *A Dictionary of Modern Indian History, 1707–1947* (Delhi: Oxford University Press, 1985), 521.
35. Davies, *The Problem of the North-West Frontier, 1890–1908*, 91–95.
36. FO 371/23628, Government of India External Affairs Department, Examination of the Present Policy on the North-West Frontier of India, Government of India to the Secretary of State for India, Simla, 22 July 1939.
37. Curzon to Broderick, 17 April 1900, in Dilks, *Curzon in India*, 227.
38. T. A. Heathcote, *The Military in British India* (Manchester: Manchester University Press, 1995), 183.
39. Dunbar, *A History of India*, 578.
40. V. A. Smith, *The Oxford Student's History of India* (Oxford: Clarendon Press, 1921), 350.
41. Trench, *The Frontier Scouts*, 15.
42. H. L. Nevill, *North-West Frontier: British and Indian Army Campaigns on the North-West Frontier, 1849–1908* (1912; reprint, London: Tom Donovan Publishing, 1992), 368–369.
43. Caroe, *The Pathans, 550 B.C.–A.D. 1957*, 393.
44. Swinson, *North-West Frontier*, 252.
45. Dilks, *Curzon in India*, 225.
46. Lord Curzon of Kedleston, "Text of the 1907 Romanes Lecture on the Subject of Frontiers," http://www.dur.ac.uk/resources/ibru/resources/links/curzon.pdf.
47. C. Miller, *Khyber: British India's North-West Frontier* (London: MacDonald & Jane's, 1977), 288.
48. Military expenditure fell from £4,584,000 in 1894–1898 to £248,000 during 1899–1905 (Dilks, *Curzon in India*, 230).
49. Barton, *India's North-West Frontier*, 72.
50. Smith, *The Oxford Student's History of India*, 351.
51. Of the 1,800 tribesmen in the South Waziristan Militia at Wana, 1,100 deserted and another 100 were killed.
52. Barton, *India's North-West Frontier*, 80.
53. G. Moore, *Just as Good as the Rest* (Bedford, UK: Jaycopy, 1979), 9.
54. Caroe, *The Pathans, 550 B.C.–A.D. 1957*, 397.
55. WO 106/58, B.M. 119 from C-in-C to D.M.O.&I., 25 August 1922.
56. J. Slessor, *The Central Blue* (London: Cassell & Co., 1956), 68.
57. P. Woodruff, *The Men Who Ruled India: The Guardians* (London: Jonathan Cape, 1954), 291.

58. Leeson, *Frontier Legion*, 75.
59. Maffey's hypothesis was that deprived of the opportunity to raid the lowlands, their innate intelligence and aggressiveness would have driven the tribesmen to adapt and find other (peaceful) outlets for their energies.
60. M. Barthorp, *Afghan Wars and the North-West Frontier, 1839–1947* (London: Cassell & Co., 2002), 162.
61. Ibid.
62. C. E. Bruce, "The Indian Frontier Problem," *Asiatic Review* 35 (1939): 504.
63. Barton, "Waziristan and the Frontier Policy," 200.
64. W. K. Fraser-Tytler, *Afghanistan* (Oxford: Oxford University Press, 1967), 269.
65. A. Calvin, "Indian Frontiers and Indian Finance," *Nineteenth Century* 38 (1895): 885.
66. J. Coatman, *Years of Destiny* (London: Jonathan Cape, 1932), 130–131.
67. Bruce, *Waziristan, 1936–1937*, 36.
68. M. C. T. Gompertz, "The Application of Science to Indian Frontier Warfare," *Army Quarterly* 10 (1925): 126.
69. "Waziristan Operations," *Times* (London), 17 November 1937.
70. K. Wigram, "Defence in the North-West Frontier Province," *Journal of the Royal Central Asian Society* 24 (1937): 77.
71. Bruce, *Waziristan, 1936–1937*, 10–11.
72. R. Coupland, *The Indian Problem, 1933–1935* (Oxford: Oxford University Press, 1943), 121–123.
73. C. W. Gwynn, *Imperial Policing* (London: Macmillan, 1934), 255.
74. Bruce, "The Indian Frontier Problem," 496.
75. Ibid., 497.
76. M. Diver, *The Unsung: A Record of British Services in India* (London: William Blackwood & Son, 1945), 156–157.
77. Bruce, *Waziristan, 1936–1937*, 59.
78. Barton, "Waziristan and the Frontier Policy," 194.
79. Woodruff, *The Men Who Ruled India*, 291.
80. D. S. Richards, *The Savage Frontier* (London: Pan Books, 1990), 181.
81. Bruce, "The Indian Frontier Problem," 505.

CHAPTER 5. 1930S WAZIRISTAN: THE BRITISH ADMINISTRATIVE APPARATUS

1. L. S. S. O'Malley, *The Indian Civil Service, 1601–1930* (London: Frank Cass & Co., 1965), 160.
2. J. W. Spain, *The Way of the Pathans* (Oxford: Oxford University Press, 1972), 25.
3. C. C. Trench, *Viceroy's Agent* (London: Jonathan Cape, 1987), 66.
4. Indian army officers who had passed their promotion examinations to captain, were unmarried, and were under twenty-six could apply for a permanent transfer to the Indian Political Service. Likewise, Indian Civil Service officers who had passed their departmental examinations, followed by a selection board, were unmarried, and had less than five years service could similarly apply. Both had to possess good reports from their regiments and provinces.

5. The foreign consulates were Aden, the Persian Gulf, parts of Persia, Afghanistan, Nepal, Bhutan, and Tibet.

6. M. C. C. Seton, *The India Office* (London: G. P. Putnam's Sons, 1926), 178.

7. A. S. Ahmed, "Tribes and State in Central Asia," *Asian Affairs* 68 (1981): 323.

8. Trench, *Viceroy's Agent*, 11.

9. A. Kirk-Greene, *Britain's Imperial Administrators, 1858–1966* (London: Macmillan Press, 2000), 74.

10. T. C. Coen, *The Indian Political Service: A Study in Indirect Rule* (London: Chatto & Windus, 1971), 44.

11. O'Malley, *The Indian Civil Service, 1601–1930*, 256.

12. O. Caroe, *The Pathans, 550 B.C.–A.D. 1957* (London: Macmillan, 1965), 394.

13. B. J. Gould, *The Jewel in the Lotus* (London: Chatto & Windus, 1957), 138.

14. Spain, *The Way of the Pathans*, 130.

15. H. R. C. Pettigrew, *Frontier Scouts* (Selsey, Sussex: privately printed, 1964), 88.

16. Barton, W. "The Problems of Law and Order under a Responsible Government in the North-West Frontier Province," *Journal of the Royal Central Asian Society* 19 (1932): 13.

17. In 1901 Lord Curzon changed the title of "political officer" to "political agent."

18. C. C. Trench, *The Frontier Scouts* (London: Jonathan Cape, 1985), 134.

19. Coen, *The Indian Political Service*, 56.

20. Ibid.

21. K. Wigram, "Defence in the North-West Frontier Province," *Journal of the Royal Central Asian Society* 24 (1937): 80.

22. C. W. Gwynn, *Imperial Policing* (London: Macmillan, 1934), 271.

23. While there were clear advantages to such an approach, there were also serious shortcomings with which senior military officers found difficult to come to terms. This approach challenged unity of effort and control. Decisions were generally made by a committee of three. The chairman, being the civilian and the authority, had to rely on the advice of the two technical members: the senior Army and Royal Air Force officers. This arrangement had clear ramifications for the speed of the decision-making process.

24. C. E. Bruce, *Waziristan, 1936–1937* (Aldershot, UK: Gale & Polden, 1938), 41.

25. F. Baines, *Officer Boy* (London: Eye & Spottiswoode, 1971), 118.

26. F. Leeson, *Frontier Legion* (Ferring: Selwood Printing, 2003), 23.

27. MSS EUR D879/1, [Lowis Collection] Diaries, 1936–1937, Manuscripts, India Office Library, London.

28. P. Woodruff, *The Men Who Ruled India: The Guardians* (London: Jonathan Cape, 1954), 291.

29. Bruce, *Waziristan, 1936–1937*, 38.

30. A. S. Ahmed, *Religion and Politics in Muslim Society: Order and Conflict in Pakistan* (Cambridge: Cambridge University Press, 1983), 36.

31. W0106/1594 A, A List of Leading Mullahs on the Border of the North-West Frontier Province Corrected to 31 December 1932, O. K. Caroe, Chief Secretary to Government, North-West Frontier Province, War Office Papers, National Archive, Kew, Surrey.

32. Trench, *The Frontier Scouts*, 134.

33. D. S. Richards, *The Savage Frontier* (London: Pan Books, 1990), 1821.
34. Spain, *The Way of the Pathans,* 134.
35. Pettigrew, *Frontier Scouts,* 47.
36. Trench, *Viceroy's Agent,* 56.
37. Ibid., 58.
38. Pettigrew, *Frontier Scouts,* 21.
39. Woodruff, *The Men Who Ruled India,* 293.
40. Caroe, *The Pathans, 550 B.C.–A.D. 1957,* 409.
41. Coen, *The Indian Political Service,* 208.
42. Trench, *The Frontier Scouts,* 136; L/P & S/12/3265 Memorandum by Viceroy, 22 July 1939, Political and Secret Department, India Office Records, India Office Library, London.
43. C. Tripodi, "Peacemaking through Bribes or Cultural Empathy? The Political Officer and Britain's Strategy towards the North-West Frontier, 1901–1945," *Journal of Strategic Studies* 31, no. 1 (2008): 144.
44. Ahmed, "Tribes and State in Central Asia," 319.
45. P. Mason, *A Matter of Honour* (London: Ebenezer Baylis & Son, 1974), 337–338.
46. Trench, *The Frontier Scouts,* 135.
47. E. Howell, "Mizh: A Monograph on Government Relations with the Mahsud Tribe," manuscript (Oxford, 1979), 98.
48. Bureau of Public Information, *India in 1927–28* (Calcutta: Bureau of Public Information, 1928), 284.
49. *Kassadars* were paid set rates of pay according to their rank.
50. Woodruff, *The Men Who Ruled India,* 291.
51. Pettigrew, *Frontier Scouts,* 21.
52. Leeson, *Frontier Legion,* 117.
53. For example, for road protection between Dosalli and Ghariom, a distance of fourteen miles, there were five permanent *kassadar* picquets.
54. IOL MSS EUR D 879/1, [Lowis Collection] Diary, 28 May 1937, Manuscripts, India Office Library, London.
55. E. Howell, "Some Problems of the Indian Frontier," *Journal of the Royal Central Asian Society* 21 (April 1934): 194–195.
56. L/PS/12/3232, A. E. B. Parsons, 25 June 1937, Political and Secret Department, India Office Records, India Office Library, London.
57. Gould, *The Jewel in the Lotus,* 140.
58. Pettigrew, *Frontier Scouts,* 21.
59. Ibid., 22.
60. "The Other Indian Frontier," *Times* (London), 13 August 1942.
61. Leeson, *Frontier Legion,* 12.
62. WO 208/773, Tribal Cooperation in the NWF, War Office Papers, National Archive, Kew, Surrey.
63. J. Masters, *Bugles and a Tiger* (London: Cassell & Co., 1956), 202.
64. *Pioneer* (Allahbad), 23 February 1937.
65. L/PS/12/3171, note by Sir D. Bray, 27 March 1934, Political and Secret Department, India Office Records, India Office Library, London.
66. Trench, *Viceroy's Agent,* 71.

67. Leeson, *Frontier Legion,* 117.

68. R. C. B. Bristow, *Memories of the British Raj* (London: Johnson, 1974), 39.

69. Report on the Administration of the Khyber 1920–21, in file of the Office of the Chief Commissioner, NWFP, no. 5/18, 1921.

70. Howell, "Some Problems of the Indian Frontier," 195.

71. G. Macmunn, "A Study in Martyrdom," *Blackwoods Magazine* 241 (February 1930): 290.

72. J. Prendergast, *Prender's Progress—A Soldier in India, 1931–47* (London: Cassell & Co., 1979), 82.

73. Trench, *The Frontier Scouts,* 51.

74. Pettigrew, *Frontier Scouts,* 20.

75. "Mauser," "A Forgotten Frontier Force," *English Review* 52 (1931): 70.

76. Trench, *The Frontier Scouts,* 134.

77. V. Schofield, *Afghan Frontier: Feuding and Fighting in Central Asia* (London: Tauris Parke Paperbacks, 2003), 163.

78. T. H. Angus, "Operations in the Lower Shaktu Valley 16th–18th November 1937," *Journal of the United Services Institution of India* 68, no. 292 (July 1938): 336.

79. Trench, *The Frontier Scouts,* 51.

80. Pettigrew, *Frontier Scouts,* 33.

81. However, desertions did occur—some with serious consequences. F. T. C. Williams recalls: "We settled down in Shawali Camp [on the night of 14 August 1937], and in the evening most of us were gambling in little groups round a hurricane *bhutti* (oil lamp), while I was scribbling these notes by candlelight on a box. There was a sudden crash of machine-gun fire followed by the hiss of bullets close overhead from the village just above our camp. I blew out the candle and dropped down behind the box. One of our fellows had been hit in the head and didn't last long. The shots they say were fired by a renegade *subadar* from the Tochi Scouts" (F. T. C. Williams, "Exciting Times and Narrow Squeaks" [Blandford, UK: Royal School of Signals Museum, 1937], 8).

82. Trench, *The Frontier Scouts,* 70.

83. "Light Infantry," "Mobility," *Journal of the United Services Institution of India* 62, no. 266 (1932): 15–16.

84. Gould, *The Jewel in the Lotus,* 140.

85. A reality not unconnected with the modest travel allowance that officers drew for twenty or more miles.

86. Angus, "Operations in the Lower Shaktu Valley 16th–18th November 1937," 341.

87. "Borderer," "Essay," *Journal of the United Services Institution of India* 64, no. 274 (1934): 14.

88. Trench, *The Frontier Scouts,* 109.

89. Prendergast, *Prender's Progress,* 83.

90. "Light Infantry," "Mobility," 17.

91. Howell, "Some Problems of the Indian Frontier," 195.

92. Pettigrew, *Frontier Scouts,* 57.

93. Leeson, *Frontier Legion,* 46.

94. Prendergast, *Prender's Progress,* 83.

95. Gould, *The Jewel in the Lotus*, 139.
96. Pettigrew, *Frontier Scouts*, 48.
97. There were large vegetable gardens in Jandola, Sararogha, and Sarwakai.
98. Trench, *The Frontier Scouts*, 68.
99. P. Griffiths, *To Guard My People: The History of the Indian Police* (London: Ernest Benn, 1971), 388.
100. Ibid., 387.
101. Frontier Constabulary, *Fortieth Anniversary Reunion Booklet* (Simla, India: n.p., n.d.), 13–14.

CHAPTER 6. THE MAILED FIST IN THE VELVET GLOVE:
THE ARMY OF INDIA AND THE ROYAL AIR FORCE

1. Although numbers varied, the Army of India's approximate composition and strength were about 50,000 British troops; about 180,000 Indian troops; and some 20,000 Gurkha infantry recruited from Nepal. E. Howell, "Some Problems of the Indian Frontier," *Journal of the Royal Central Asian Society* 21 (1934): 191.
2. In total there were nine brigades operating on the North-West Frontier supported by the field army of four divisions and four cavalry brigades held in reserve in India. Seven of the eight Royal Air Force squadrons in India were also stationed along the frontier.
3. "Light Infantry," "Mobility," *Journal of the United Services Institution of India* 62/266 (1932): 10–11.
4. T. R. Moreman, *The Army in India and the Development of Frontier Warfare, 1849–1947* (London: Macmillan, 1998), 147.
5. C. C. Trench, *The Frontier Scouts* (London: Jonathan Cape, 1985), 174.
6. To make matters worse, the 2nd Battalion, Green Howards, was undermanned initially. The battalion left Meercut with 570 officers and soldiers; the minimum expected strength on the frontier was 650. *Green Howards' Gazette* 45, no. 525 (1937): 163.
7. C. W. Gwynn, *Imperial Policing* (London: Macmillan, 1934), 7.
8. H. R. C. Pettigrew, *Frontier Scouts* (Selsey, Sussex: privately printed, 1964), 46.
9. The cost of maintaining a British unit was approximately equivalent to that of three Indian units. W. Birdwood, "Recent Indian Military Experience," *United Empire*, no. 22 (1931): 248.
10. R. Chapman, "Afghanistan and the North-West Frontier: The Green Howards during the Third Afghan War 1919, and the Waziristan Campaigns of 1936–1937, 1937–1939," *Friends of the Green Howards Regimental Museum Newsletter*, no. 14, September 2002.
11. Moreman, *The Army in India and the Development of Frontier Warfare*, 145.
12. A. Warren, *Waziristan, the Faqir of Ipi, and the Indian Army* (Oxford: Oxford University Press, 2000),110.
13. Moreman, *The Army in India and the Development of Frontier Warfare*, 147.
14. D. E. Robertson, "The Organisation and Training of the Army of India," *Journal of the Royal United Service Institut* 69, no. 474 (1924): 327–328.
15. C. C. Davies, *The Problem of the North-West Frontier, 1890–1908* (London: Cambridge University Press, 1932), 13.
16. Chapman, "Afghanistan and the North-West Frontier," 12.

NOTES TO PAGES 126–130 [ 275 ]

17. Moreman, *The Army in India and the Development of Frontier Warfare*, 166.
18. This included the light machine (Lewis) gun and the heavy (Vickers) gun. The latter had developed into a powerful addition to the artillery, capable of providing a predictable fall of shot at ranges of up to 2,500 yards.
19. Waziristan's austere terrain often precluded the employment of artillery. Unless a target was close to the road network, the mountainous country precluded the allocation of all but a small number of small caliber guns to an expedition.
20. Trench, *The Frontier Scouts*, 106.
21. "The essence of Frontier warfare was to command the high ground, which could mean first having to dislodge the enemy from well-sited, strongly-held positions" (T. Pocock, *Fighting General: The Public and Private Campaigns of General Sir Walter Walker* [London: Collins, 1973], 45).
22. G. Moore, *Just as Good as the Rest* (Bedford, UK: Jaycopy, 1979), 15.
23. "The Advance to Arsalkot: Eye-Witness's Impressions of *Fakir's* Headquarters," *Civil and Military Gazette*, 10 June 1937.
24. "Mouse," "Babu Tactics," *Journal of the United Service Institution of India* 61, no. 262 (1931): 62.
25. Ibid.
26. Relations between the scouts and regulars were important, and dinner nights were a regular occurrence. Frank Baines recalls: "They [dinner nights] were utilised in the realistic pursuit of frontier politics and their ensuing military strategy and tactics, for at any minute during punitive operations of this kind, which did not involve an actual declaration of hostilities, the moment might arrive when a junior officer like myself might find himself alone and confronted by a bunch of tribals, say several headmen from a group of villages. It would be no use his mowing them down in cold blood; that would not solve anything. He would be expected, on the contrary, equally by the senior officers of his own side as well as by those of the enemy, to be capable of sitting down with them, drinking tea, and parleying like a Political Officer. On this account, even the humblest of us had to have the essentials of local politics, such as unresolved grievances and their proposed amelioration, at our finger tips" (F. Baines, *Officer Boy* [London: Eye & Spottiswoode, 1971], 151).
27. O. D. Bennett, "Some Regrettable Incidents on the N.-W. F.," *Journal of the United Services Institution of India* 63, no. 271 (1933): 202.
28. C. H. T. MacFetridge and J. P. Warren, eds., *Tales of the Mountain Gunners* (Edinburgh: William Blackwood, 1973), 109–110.
29. J. Prendergast, *Prender's Progress—A Soldier in India, 1931–47* (London: Cassell & Co., 1979), 40–41.
30. Ibid., 58–59.
31. Moreman, *The Army in India and the Development of Frontier Warfare*, 177.
32. Ibid., 60–61.
33. Of note, only Rs. 5.8 *lakh* was spent on allowances and political staffs. Warren, *Waziristan, The Faqir of Ipi, and the Indian Army*, 110.
34. "There is little doubt that this raid was an important factor in producing a desire for peace at the Headquarters of the Afghan Government" (Despatch by His Excellency General Sir Charles Carmichael Monro on the Third Afghan War, 1 November 1919 [Simla, India, 1919]).

35. B2690, RAF Museum, Salmond Papers, Report by Air-Marshal Sir John Salmond K.C.B., C.M.G., C.V.O., D.S.O. on the Royal Air Force in India, August 1922, Royal Air Force Museum, Hendon.

36. C. F. Andrews, *The Challenge of the North-West Frontier* (London: George Allen & Unwin, 1937), 115.

37. H. M. Brock, "Air Operations on the NWF 1930," *Journal of the Royal Central Asian Society* 19 (1932): 42.

38. J. Slessor, *The Central Blue* (London: Cassell & Co., 1956), 61.

39. B22, Air Staff (India) Memorandum No. 1, April 1935, Tactical Methods of Conducting Air Operations against Tribes on the North-West Frontier of India, Royal Air Force Museum, Hendon.

40. From 25 November 1936 to 16 January 1937 the hours flown by the RAF were the following: tactical reconnaissance, 535 hours; distant reconnaissance, 162 hours; close support, 147 hours; photography, sixty-five hours; supply dropping, thirty-five hours; other operational flying (including artillery cooperation, reconnaissance by military and political officers, postal flying, picking up and dropping off orders, dropping pamphlets, travel flights, etc.), 270 hours; and bombing flights, sixty-six hours. R. A. Cassels, *London Gazette,* supplement, 29 October 1937, 6815.

41. Slessor, *The Central Blue,* 66.

42. Tribesmen were routinely given twenty-four hours from the time of delivery of the notice before bombing commenced. This rule was not applied against hostile *lashkars.*

43. WO 106/5446, Tribal Disturbances in Waziristan 25 November 1936–14 June 1937, War Office Papers, National Archive, Kew, Surrey.

44. A. S. Ahmed, "An Aspect of the Colonial Encounter in the North-West Frontier Province," *Asian Affairs* 65 (1978): 324.

45. Not all tribesmen could relocate. According to Captain Munford, "Air-bombing of villages strikes hardest at the poor—the weak, the aged, the sick—who stay at home. It hits the innocent and spares the guilty" (Andrews, *The Challenge of the North-West Frontier,* 124).

46. C. C. Trench, *Viceroy's Agent* (London: Jonathan Cape, 1987), 41.

47. F. S. Keen, "To What Extent Would the Use of the Latest Scientific and Mechanical Methods of Warfare Affect Operations on the North-West Frontier of India?" *Journal of the United Service Institution of India* 53, no. 233 (1923): 400.

48. D. Omissi, *Air Power and Colonial Control: The Royal Air Force, 1919–1939* (Manchester: Manchester University Press, 1990), 155.

49. "Mauser," "A Forgotten Frontier Force," *English Review* 52 (1931): 71–72.

50. Gwynn, *Imperial Policing,* 280.

51. H. de Watteville, *Waziristan, 1919–1920* (London: Constable & Co., 1925), 197.

52. Slessor, *The Central Blue,* 66.

53. Ibid., 66–67.

54. Andrews, *The Challenge of the North-West Frontier,* 120–121.

55. MacFetridge and Warren, eds., *Tales of the Mountain Gunners,* 118.

56. Omissi, *Air Power and Colonial Control,* 166.

57. Keen, "To What Extent?" 401.

58. G. Torpy, "Counter-Insurgency Echoes from the Past," *Journal of the Royal United Services Institute* 152, no. 5 (2007): 20–21.

59. This tactic was not new. According to an official report, "Two aeroplanes, finding good targets finished their bombs and ammunition some time before their reliefs were due to arrive. The enemy was then harassing our troops and the aviators knew that the departure of the aeroplanes would be the signal for the renewal of the attack. They therefore remained and by continually diving low at the enemy succeeded in pinning him to the ground thus preventing the development of any offensive movement against our hard pressed troops" (*Operations in Waziristan, 1919–1920*, compiled by the General Staff, Army Headquarters, India [Calcutta, 1921], 118).

60. R. A. Cassels, *London Gazette*, 29 October 1937, 6815.

61. Brock, "Air Operations on the NWF 1930," 33.

62. "Mauser," "A Forgotten Frontier Force," 71.

63. Gwynn, *Imperial Policing*, 296.

64. AILO, "Close Support by Aircraft on the North-West Frontier," *Journal of the United Service Institution of India* 74, no. 16 (1944): 15.

65. However, preventing the tribesmen returning at night proved to be a significant challenge. Lieutenant Colonel L. Lawrence-Smith cites a useful example: "The villages in the immediate vicinity of Nahakki had all been evacuated by the tribesmen, but during reconnaissances signs were seen of their occupation by night and even ploughs and other agricultural implements were noticed in the fields which had obviously been used during the hours of darkness" (L. Lawrence-Smith, "Cavalry and Tanks with Mohforce, 1935," *Cavalry Journal*, no. 26 [1936]: 555).

66. Brock, "Air Operations on the NWF 1930," 25.

67. Slessor, *The Central Blue*, 54.

68. Brock, "Air Operations on the NWF 1930," 25.

69. Prendergast, *Prender's Progress*, 88.

70. H. L. Davies, "Military Intelligence in Tribal Warfare on The North-West Frontier of India," *Journal of the United Services Institution of India* 63, no. 272 (1933): 289–291.

71. Moore, *Just as Good as the Rest*, 23.

72. Brock, "Air Operations on the NWF 1930," 25.

73. P. Chetwode, "The Indian Army," *Journal of the Royal United Service Institution* 82, no. 525 (1937): 12.

74. 915, Comments on Inter-Communication Waziristan Operations 1936–37, Waziristan District Signals, Historical Record, 1938/39, Royal School of Signals Museum, Blandford.

75. Report of Intercommunications—Waziristan Operations 1937, Royal School of Signals Museum, Blandford.

76. Popham panels were made of wood and cloth, with movable panels. A canvas screen would be spread on the ground and black and white strips arranged in patterns to convey a message. For ground strip codes, see AILO, "Close Support by Aircraft on the North-West Frontier," 21.

77. Trench, *The Frontier Scouts*, 109.

78. Ibid., 132–133.

79. L. James, *Imperial Rearguard: Wars of Empire, 1919–85* (London: Brassey's Defence Publishers, 1988), 51.
80. B. Robson, *Crisis on the Frontier* (London: Spellmount, 2004), 260.
81. Slessor, *The Central Blue*, 121.
82. "Mauser," "A Forgotten Frontier Force," 71.
83. de Watteville, *Waziristan, 1919–1920*, 195.
84. MacFetridge and Warren, eds., *Tales of the Mountain Gunners*, 126.
85. AILO, "Close Support by Aircraft on the North-West Frontier," 19. However, Colonel H. R. C. Pettigrew recounts a shortfall to this tactic: "With their machine-guns firing furiously, the empty .303 cartridges cases were raining over the surrounding countryside like a July storm. Gratefully, wonderingly, the tribesmen broke off the cases to be taken to Kaniguram and elsewhere to be refilled with powder and bullet" (Pettigrew, *Frontier Scouts*, 96).
86. "Royal Air Force," *Times* (London), 10 April 1939.
87. Pettigrew, *Frontier Scouts*, 89.
88. Chapman, "Afghanistan and the North-West Frontier," 7.
89. "The Action of the 1st (Abbottabad) Infantry Brigade Near Damil on the 29th March 1937," *Journal of the United Services Institution of India* 68, no. 290 (1938): 34.
90. de Watteville, *Waziristan, 1919–1920*, 194–195.
91. "Mauser," "A Forgotten Frontier Force," 71.
92. F. Leeson, *Frontier Legion* (Ferring: Selwood Printing, 2003), 195.
93. The letter *X* indicated the position of the picquet or troops nearest the enemy; *V* signified that the enemy was in the direction the apex of the V pointed; and *T* was the SOS signal. This was a call for help when a picquet was likely to be overwhelmed or a sign that the enemy was following up a withdrawal so closely that it was impossible to get away. *X* was only used in extremis.
94. Robson, *Crisis on the Frontier*, 260.
95. Trench, *Viceroy's Agent*, 41.
96. Keen, "To What Extent?" 400.
97. M. C. T. Gompertz, "The Application of Science to Indian Frontier Warfare," *Army Quarterly* 10 (1925): 122.
98. Colonel Khushwaqt Ulmulk to A. M. Roe, e-mail, 5 November 2007.
99. C. N. Barclay, *The Regimental History of the 3rd Queen Alexandra's Own Gurkha Rifles* (London: William Clowes & Son, 1953), 11.

CHAPTER 7. A CAUSE CÉLÈBRE, THE FAKIR OF IPI,
AND THE BRITISH RESPONSE: THE TRIAL CASE
OF ISLAM BIBI AND THE 1936–1937 CAMPAIGN

1. According to Geoffrey Moore, "This part of the frontier [Waziristan] had been quiet for 13 years" (G. Moore, *Just as Good as the Rest* [Bedford, UK: Jaycopy, 1979], 10).
2. F. Baines, *Officer Boy* (London: Eye & Spottiswoode, 1971), 143.
3. WO 106/6027 Tribal Disturbances in Waziristan, 25 November 1936–14 June 1937, War Office Papers, National Archive, Kew, Surrey.
4. "Tribal Force Raised on N.W. Frontier," *Times* (London), 21 April 1936.

5. F. Leeson, *Frontier Legion* (Ferring: Selwood Printing, 2003), 82.

6. "Tribal Force Raised on N.W. Frontier."

7. A. Warren, *Waziristan, the Faqir of Ipi, and the Indian Army* (Oxford: Oxford University Press, 2000), 82.

8. IOR/L/PS/12/3230, PA NW to RW, 1 May 1936, CS NWFP to FS FPD, 8 June 1936, RW, "Agitation in Lower Dawar—April 1936" to CS NWFP, 13 May 1936, Political and Secret Department, India Office Records, India Office Library, London.

9. *Official History of Operations on the N. W. Frontier of India, 1936–37* (Delhi: Government of India Press, 1943), 4; F. G. Baqai, "Fakir of Ipi: A Brief Review of the anti-British Activities of a Waziri Mujahid," *Pakistan Journal of History and Culture* 20, no. 1 (1999): 23.

10. WO 208/773, Note on the Fakir of Ipi, 24 June 1937, War Office Papers, National Archive, Kew, Surrey.

11. M. Hauner, "One Man against the Empire: The Faqir of Ipi and the British in Central Asia on the Eve of and during the Second World War," *Journal of Contemporary History* 16, no. 1 (1981): 189.

12. T. R. Moreman, *The Army in India and the Development of Frontier Warfare, 1849–1947* (London: Macmillan, 1998), 159.

13. Warren, *Waziristan, the Faqir of Ipi, and the Indian Army*, 86.

14. "Warning to Troublesome Tribe," *Times* (London), 25 April 1936.

15. IOR/L/PS/12/3230, PA NW to RW, "Agitation in Lower Dawar April 1936."

16. Ibid.

17. Leeson, *Frontier Legion*, 82.

18. R. A. Cassels, *London Gazette*, supplement, 29 October 1937, 6811.

19. IOR/L/PS/12/3192, NWF Intelligence Summaries, no. 41, 12 October 1936, Political and Secret Department, India Office Records, India Office Library, London.

20. C. C. Trench, *The Frontier Scouts* (London: Jonathan Cape, 1985), 149; IOR/L/PS/12/3230, India Office interview with C. A. G. Savidge, Political and Secret Department, India Office Records, India Office Library, London.

21. Warren, *Waziristan, the Faqir of Ipi, and the Indian Army*, 88–89.

22. C. C. Trench, *Viceroy's Agent* (London: Jonathan Cape, 1987), 68.

23. This was not the first visit to the area after the 1935 agreement. In February 1936, the Razmak and Bannu Brigades visited the Khaisora Valley and spent two days together at Bichhe Kashkai. The operation passed without incident.

24. J. Slessor, *The Central Blue* (London: Cassell & Co., 1956), 130; "N.W. Frontier Fight," *Times* (London), 27 November 1936.

25. *Official History of Operations on the N. W. Frontier of India, 1936–37*, 23.

26. R. A. Cassels, *London Gazette*, supplement, 29 October 1937, 6811.

27. Ibid.

28. *Official History of Operations on the N. W. Frontier of India, 1936–37*, 9–10.

29. "The Khaisora Fighting," *Times* (London), 30 November 1936.

30. "N.W. Frontier Fight."

31. Trench, *The Frontier Scouts*, 150.

32. Slessor, *The Central Blue*, 134.

33. *Official History of Operations on the N. W. Frontier of India, 1936–37,* 11.
34. Trench, *Viceroy's Agent,* 68.
35. "N.W. Frontier Fight."
36. "The Khaisora Fighting."
37. *Official History of Operations on the N. W. Frontier of India, 1936–37,* 17.
38. Slessor, *The Central Blue,* 131.
39. *Official History of Operations on the N. W. Frontier of India, 1936–37,* 17.
40. Early in December, 600 Madda Khel tribesmen were collocated with the Fakir; by mid-December, this figure had fallen to approximately 150. IOR/L/PS/12/3230, India Office minute paper, December 1936, Political and Secret Department, India Office Records, India Office Library, London.
41. R. A. Cassels, *London Gazette,* supplement, 29 October 1937, 6811.
42. Ibid.
43. Slessor, *The Central Blue,* 134.
44. The aim of this extension was to provide a direct route from Bannu to the Biche Kashkai area; to enable troops to be moved quickly to the Biche Kashkai area from Bannu; to act as a deterrent to future hostile actions by tribes of the Sein area who had been a potential source of trouble in the past; to provide a means of egress for the inhabitants of the Shaktu and Khaisora Valleys; and to provide a means of lateral movement for the frontier constabulary, and thus enable them to deal rapidly with raids in that area.
45. IOR/R/12/73, file 514/VIII, J. A. Robinson, 27 June 1937, Records Received in London, India Office Records, India Office Library, London.
46. *Official History of Operations on the N. W. Frontier of India, 1936–37,* 30.
47. Leeson, *Frontier Legion,* 84.
48. IOR/L/PS/12/3232, R. A. Cassels, "Report on Operations in Waziristan," 25 November 1936–16 January 1937, Political and Secret Department, India Office Records, India Office Library, London.
49. R. A. Cassels, *London Gazette,* supplement, 29 October 1937, 6811.
50. Ibid.
51. Moore, *Just as Good as the Rest,* 21.
52. R. A. Cassels, *London Gazette,* supplement, 29 October 1937, 6811; IOR/R/12/69, file 514/IV, NWFP to FPD, 13 February 1937, Records Received in London, India Office Records, India Office Library, London.
53. R. A. Cassels, *London Gazette,* supplement, 29 October 1937, 6811.
54. *Official History of Operations on the N. W. Frontier of India, 1936–37,* 39; Trench, *Viceroy's Agent,* 68.
55. *Official History of Operations on the N. W. Frontier of India, 1936–37,* 40.
56. *Pioneer* (Allahabad), 16 March 1937.
57. R. A. Cassels, *London Gazette,* supplement, 15 February 1938, 1058.
58. "N.-W. Frontier Unrest," *Times* (London), 15 April 1937.
59. "The Action of the 1st (Abbottabad) Infantry Brigade Near Damil on the 29th March 1937," *Journal of the United Services Institution of India* 68, no. 290 (1938): 33–40.
60. D. A. L. Mackenzie, "Operations in the Lower Khaisora Valley, Waziristan, in 1937," *Journal of the Royal United Service Institution* 82, no. 528 (1938): 805.

61. The Shahur Tangi is a long and narrow gorge commanded on both sides by steep hills, which, in accordance with normal practice, the *kassadars* were expected to dominate. As the majority of *kassadars* had vacated their posts, it is probable that they were aware of the impending attack on the convoy. *Official History of Operations on the N. W. Frontier of India, 1936–37,* 55–56; "Attack on the Convoy at Shahur Tangi on the 9th April 1937," *Journal of the United Service Institution of India* 67, no. 288 (July 1937): 262.

62. Trench, *Viceroy's Agent,* 70.

63. MSS EUR C308, Account of the Shahur Tangi Affair by Lt Col Bolam, April 1937, Manuscripts, India Office Library, London.

64. H. R. C. Pettigrew, *Frontier Scouts* (Selsey, Sussex: privately printed, 1964), 26.

65. IOR/L/MIL/5/1066, EAD to SSI, 12 April 1937 and 18 April 1937, Manuscripts, India Office Library, London.

66. R. A. Cassels, *London Gazette,* supplement, 15 February 1938, 1059.

67. 915.3, 1st (Indian) Division Operation Order No. 4, 23 April 1937, Royal School of Signals Museum, Blandford.

68. "On the North-West Frontier," *Times* (London), 18 June 1937.

69. Warren, *Waziristan, the Faqir of Ipi, and the Indian Army,* 161.

70. IOL MSS EUR D 670/13 (Cunningham Collection) an appreciation, 19 April 1937, India Office Library, London.

71. Mackenzie, "Operations in the Lower Khaisora Valley, Waziristan, in 1937," 808–809.

72. This was the first time since 1895 that tribesmen attempted to rush a camp.

73. *Official History of Operations on the N. W. Frontier of India, 1936–37,* 73–76.

74. R. A. Cassels, *London Gazette,* supplement, 15 February 1938, 1060.

75. Trench, *The Frontier Scouts,* 90–93.

76. Leeson, *Frontier Legion,* 86.

77. J. Prendergast, *Prender's Progress—A Soldier in India, 1931–47* (London: Cassell & Co., 1979), 100.

78. R. A. Cassels, *London Gazette,* supplement, 15 February 1938, 1060.

79. "Fakir of Ipi Forced from Retreat," *Times* (London), 26 May 1937.

80. "The Advance to Arsalkot," *Civil and Military Gazette,* 10 June 1937.

81. Leeson, *Frontier Legion,* 88.

82. *Official History of Operations on the N. W. Frontier of India, 1936–37,* 102.

83. "Frontier Truce Terms," *Times* (London), 7 June 1937.

84. "Terms of Peace in Waziristan," *Times* (London), 10 June 1937.

85. J. Masters, *Bugles and a Tiger* (London: Cassell & Co., 1956), 243.

86. R. A. Cassels, *London Gazette,* supplement, 15 February 1938, 1068.

87. L/MIL/5/1065, Supplement 3 to Intelligence Summary 6, 17–23 June 1937, Security Services, National Archive, Kew, Surrey.

88. "Frontier Tribesmen Taken Unawares," *Times* (London), 1 July 1937.

89. R. A. Cassels, *London Gazette,* supplement, 15 February 1938, 1068.

90. Trench, *The Frontier Scouts,* 175.

91. L/MIL/5/1065, Supplement 1 to Intelligence Summary 7, 8–14 July 1937, Security Services, National Archive, Kew, Surrey.

92. "Waziristan Fighting," *Times* (London), 26 July 1937.

93. Leeson, *Frontier Legion,* 91.

94. FO 371/21065. Central Asia, General Correspondence (Waziristan) 1937, Code 97, Files 10-14.{AU: is citation correct as given? If not, please clarify.}
95. WO 106/5446, Memo on Pacification of Waziristan, 22 July 1937, War Office Papers, National Archive, Kew, Surrey.
96. R. A. Cassels, *London Gazette,* supplement, 15 February 1938, 1061.
97. "Waziristan Fighting." However, should an opportunity present itself for combat on favorable terms, the tribesmen would not be against engaging in a prolonged fight. Private Williams recalls: "We were up at 0400 hours [14 August 1937] to load our mules in the starlit darkness. All was quiet as we marched away from Coronation Camp, except for the tiny cheep-cheep of Morse signals from the pack wireless set. Dawn broke as we followed the track down into the Shaktu Valley. Suddenly a perfect storm of rifle fire burst upon us from both sides of the wooded valley, and there we were, a completely open target, not knowing from Adam where the enemy lay. Two of our men dropped, to die of stomach wounds later. A bullet-hole suddenly appeared in the right flank of the mule just ahead of me. Amazingly it didn't drop but trotted on to the next halt, where it finally collapsed. We opened fire with everything we had, but the attack continued all day until evening, when the enemy ceased fire at last we hastily dug ourselves in at Shawali" (F. T. C. Williams, "Exciting Times and Narrow Squeaks" [Blandford, UK: Royal School of Signals Museum, 1937], 8).
98. IOR/L/MIL/5/1065, supplement 2 to Intelligence Summary 7, 8–14 July 1937, Security Services, National Archive, Kew, Surrey.
99. *Official History of Operations on the N. W. Frontier of India, 1936–37,* 170.
100. IOR/L/MIL/5/1065.
101. Leeson, *Frontier Legion,* 93.
102. R. A. Cassels, *London Gazette,* supplement, 15 February 1938, 1061.
103. *Official History of Operations on the N. W. Frontier of India, 1936–37,* 174; "Indian Frontier Peace," *Times* (London), 14 September 1937.
104. IOR/L/PS/12/3233, DDIP, H. J. Vickers, 17 June 1937, Political and Secret Department, India Office Records, India Office Library, London.
105. *Green Howards' Gazette* 45, no. 525 (December 1937): 182.
106. Warren, *Waziristan, the Faqir of Ipi, and the Indian Army,* 210.
107. T. H. Angus, "Operations in the Lower Shaktu Valley 16th–18th November 1937," *Journal of the United Service Institution of India* 68, no. 292 (1938): 335.
108. IOR/L/PS/12/3234, EAD to SSI, 5 November 1937, Political and Secret Department, India Office Records, India Office Library, London.
109. *Official History of Operations on the N. W. Frontier of India, 1936–37,* 217.
110. Ibid., 218–219.
111. Angus, "Operations in the Lower Shaktu Valley," 340.
112. Ibid., 340–341.
113. *Official History of Operations on the N. W. Frontier of India, 1936–37,* 230.

CHAPTER 8. KEEPING THE FLAME OF INSURRECTION ALIGHT, 1938–1947

1. F. Leeson, *Frontier Legion* (Ferring: Selwood Printing, 2003), 98.
2. WO 106/6027, "Waziristan," Army Headquarters (India), General Staff Branch, 10 February 1938, War Office Papers, National Archive, Kew, Surrey.

3. AIR 2/4263, participation of Air Forces in the operations in Waziristan, January 1938–May 1939, Air Ministry Papers, National Archive, Kew, Surrey.
4. "Waziristan," *Times* (London), 18 July 1938.
5. "Waziristan Unrest," *Times* (London), 21 May 1938.
6. C. C. Trench, *The Frontier Scouts* (London: Jonathan Cape, 1985), 186–187.
7. Leeson, *Frontier Legion*, 100.
8. KV 2/531, Saadi Kailani "The Shami Pir," 1937–47.
9. "A New Agitator in Waziristan," *Times* (London), 25 June 1938.
10. IOR/L/PS/12/3258, "Note on the Case of the Shami Pir up to 1938," Political and Secret Department, India Office Records, India Office Library, London.
11. O. Caroe, *The Pathans, 550 B.C.–A.D. 1957* (London: Macmillan, 1965), 409.
12. FO 371/23630, Afghanistan Annual Report 1938, Foreign Office, National Archive, Kew, Surrey.
13. "Better Outlook in Waziristan," *Times* (London), 1 July 1938; "Shami Pir Deported to Syria," *Times* (London), 2 July 1938.
14. L/PS/12/3234, NWF Intelligence Summaries, no. 30, 25 July 1938, Political and Secret Department, India Office Records, India Office Library, London.
15. "Royal Air Force," *Times* (London), 10 April 1939.
16. Leeson, *Frontier Legion*, 101.
17. A. Warren, *Waziristan, the Faqir of Ipi, and the Indian Army* (Oxford: Oxford University Press, 2000), 241.
18. "Question of Co-operation by Afghan Government in Operation against the Fakir of Ipi," *Evening Standard*, 31 May 1939.
19. L/WS/1/1526-WS 13031, "Report on Operations in Waziristan 1 January 1940–24 May 1940," War Staff Papers, India Office Records, India Office Library, London.
20. "A Clean-Up in Waziristan," *Times* (London), 22 February 1940.
21. Leeson, *Frontier Legion*, 101.
22. CAB 21/1078, GOI, External Affairs Department to Secretary of State for India, 7 March 1940, Cabinet Office Papers, National Archive, Kew, Surrey.
23. T. C. Coen, *The Indian Political Service* (London: Chatto & Windus, 1971), 193.
24. Warren, *Waziristan, the Faqir of Ipi, and the Indian Army*, 252.
25. Trench, *The Frontier Scouts*, 239.
26. KV 2/2290, Nazi Activity in the North-West, 26 July 1941, Security Services, National Archive, Kew, Surrey.
27. KV 2/2290, Foreigners in Afghanistan, ~~14 August~~ 7 June 1941, Extract from Military Attaché, Kabul, intelligence summary, No. 23.
28. KV 2/2290, Nazi Activity in the North-West, 26 July 1941.
29. M. Hauner, *India in Axis Strategy* (Stuttgart: Klett-Cotta, 1981), 316–317; L/PS/12/1844, Military Attaché's Diary, 25 July 1941, Political and Secret Department, India Office Records, India Office Library, London.
30. KV 2/2290, Nazi Activity in the North-West, 26 July 1941.
31. M. Hauner, "One Man against the Empire: The Faqir of Ipi and the British in Central Asia on the Eve of and during the Second World War," *Journal of Contemporary History* 16, no. 1 (1981): 193.
32. WO 208/26, GOI to IO, No. 5889, 27 October 1941, War Office Papers, National Archive, Kew, Surrey.

33. Leeson, *Frontier Legion*, 106.
34. WS/1/1269-WS 19056, NWF and Afghan Summaries 1942, War Staff Papers, India Office Records, India Office Library, London; "The Other Indian Frontier," *Times* (London), 13 August 1942.
35. Hauner, "One Man against the Empire," 394.
36. H. R. C. Pettigrew, *Frontier Scouts* (Selsey, Sussex: privately printed, 1964), 71–72.
37. Warren, *Waziristan, the Faqir of Ipi, and the Indian Army*, 257.
38. Leeson, *Frontier Legion*, 106.
39. L/MIL/17/13/45, "Report on Air Operations on the NWF, 1944."
40. L/MIL/17/13/46, "Report of the Frontier Committee 1945," India Office Records, India Office Library, London, Military Department Records.
41. Leeson, *Frontier Legion*, 109.
42. Warren, *Waziristan, the Faqir of Ipi, and the Indian Army*, 259.
43. "Bombing of Waziristan Villages," *Times* (London), 10 September 1946.
44. Leeson, *Frontier Legion*, 110.
45. "North-West Frontier Control," *Times* (London), 16 September 1946.
46. R. E. C. Peirse, "Bombing in Waziristan," *Times* (London), 23, 30 September and 5 October 1946.
47. Trench, *The Frontier Scouts*, 264–265.
48. Warren, *Waziristan, the Faqir of Ipi, and the Indian Army*, 260.
49. L/PO/6/123, Rear Admiral Viscount Mountbatten of Burma's Personal Report no. 17, 16 April 1947, Private Office Papers, India Office Records, India Office Library, London.
50. Hauner, "One Man against the Empire," 398; Thomas Harding, "How the British Empire Failed to Tame the Terrorist Fakir of Ipi," *Daily Telegraph* (London), 15 November 2001.
51. FO 371/152245, British Embassy, Kabul, 22 April 1960 1014/60, Letter from Chancery to South East Asia Department, Foreign Office, London.
52. C. Miller, *Khyber: British India's North-West Frontier* (London: MacDonald & Jane's, 1977), 362.
53. Colonel Khushwaqt Ulmulk to A. M. Roe, email, 5 November 2007.
54. L/PS/12/3255, Lord Brabourne to Zetland, 14 July 1938, Political and Secret Department, India Office Records, India Office Library, London.

CHAPTER 9. THE HARD-EARNED LESSONS
AND REALITIES OF THE BRITISH EXPERIENCE
IN WAZIRISTAN, PART I

1. P. Woodruff, *The Men Who Ruled India: The Guardians* (London: Jonathan Cape, 1954), 297.
2. P. Musharraf, *In the Line of Fire* (New York: Free Press, 2006), 201–204; M. W. Williams, "The British Colonial Experience in Waziristan and Its Applicability to Current Operations," School of Advanced Military Studies Monographs, Combined Arms Research Library, 26 May 2005, Fort Leavenworth, KS, 42.
3. W. Barton, *India's North-West Frontier* (London: John Murray, 1939), 58–59.
4. W. R. Hay, "The Blood Feud in Waziristan," *Journal of the Royal Central Asian Society* 19 (1932): 305.

5. C. C. Trench, *The Frontier Scouts* (London: Jonathan Cape, 1985), 4.

6. P. Titus, "Honour the Baloch, Buy the Pathan: Stereotypes, Social Organisation and History in Western Pakistan," *Modern Asian Studies*, vol. 3, no. 32 (1988): 657–687.

7. J. Masters, *Bugles and a Tiger* (London: Cassell & Co., 1956), 18.

8. Woodruff, *The Men Who Ruled India*, 291.

9. Masters, *Bugles and a Tiger*, 18.

10. F. T. Stockdale, *Walk Warily in Waziristan* (Devon: Arthur H. Stockwell, 1982), 19.

11. "Waziristan Operations," *Times*, 17 November 1937.

12. N. H. Bottomley, "The Work of the Royal Air Force on the North-West Frontier," *Journal of the Royal United Services Institute* 193 (1939): 769.

13. A. S. Ahmed, *Religion and Politics in Muslim Society: Order and Conflict in Pakistan* (Cambridge: Cambridge University Press, 1983), 102–105.

14. C. Tripodi, "Cultural Understanding: Its Utility and Influence: The British Experience on the North-West Frontier, 1918–1939," *British Army Review*, no. 144 (Spring 2008): 27.

15. For example, the 1936 Arab Revolt in Palestine resulted in the garrison increasing from two battalions to twenty-two battalions.

16. A. G. Boycott, *The Elements of Imperial Defence* (Aldershot: Gale & Polden, 1936), 249.

17. A. Warren, *Waziristan, the Faqir of Ipi, and the Indian Army* (Oxford: Oxford University Press, 2000), 56.

18. Woodruff, *The Men Who Ruled India*, 295.

19. Barton, *India's North-West Frontier*, 199.

20. C. E. Bruce, *Waziristan, 1936–1937* (Aldershot, UK: Gale & Polden, 1938), 52.

21. Ahmed, *Religion and Politics*, 102, 185.

22. Bruce, *Waziristan, 1936–1937*, 27.

23. *Official History of Operations on the N. W. Frontier of India, 1936–37* (Delhi: Government of India Press, 1943), 230.

24. C. E. Bruce, "The Indian Frontier Problem," *Asiatic Review* 35 (1939): 508.

25. G. Moore, *Just as Good as the Rest* (Bedford, UK: Jaycopy, 1979), 25.

26. This included the boundaries of each clan and tribal area; the names and dispositions of religious and tribal leaders; tribal habits and allegiances; economic dependence; employment figures; antigovernment activities; population flow; and local concerns and issues.

27. Prior to the establishment of the North-West Frontier Province, decisions had taken a long time to reach the frontier. The establishment of the province prevented hesitation and delay and negated the difficulties associated with policy execution.

28. O. Caroe, *The Pathans, 550 B.C.–A.D. 1957* (London: Macmillan, 1965), 410.

29. "Light Infantry," "Mobility," *Journal of the United Services Institution of India* 62, no. 266 (1932): 15–16.

30. R. T. Strickland, "The Way of the Pashtun: Pashtunwali," *Canadian Army Journal* 10, no. 3 (2007): 48.

31. "Waziristan," *Times*, 18 July 1938.

32. Nonetheless, such activities caused serious disruption at minimal cost to the tribesmen.

33. C. Lindholm, "Images of the Pathan: The Usefulness of Colonial Ethnography." Available at http://www.bu.edu/anthrop/faculty/lindholm/Pathan1A .html.
34. Strickland, "The Way of the Pashtun: Pashtunwali," 49.
35. J. Prendergast, *Prender's Progress—A Soldier in India, 1931–47* (London: Cassell & Co., 1979), 86.
36. Warren, *Waziristan, the Faqir of Ipi, and the Indian Army*, 133.
37. F. G. Baqai, "Fakir of Ipi: A Brief Review of the anti-British Activities of a Waziri Mujahid." *Pakistan Journal of History and Culture* 20, no. 1 (1999): 23–31, esp. 28; L/PS/12/3236, Dated 11 November 1937, Political and Secret Department, India Office Records, India Office Library, London.
38. H. R. C. Pettigrew, *Frontier Scouts* (Selsey, Sussex: privately printed, 1964), 85.
39. Ibid., 86.
40. T. L. Pennell, *Pennell of the Afghan Frontier: The Life of Theodore Leighton Pennell* (London: Seely, Service & Co., 1922), 400–402.
41. C. A. L. Graham, *The History of the Indian Mountain Artillery* (Aldershot, UK: Gale & Polden, 1957), 38.
42. Warren, *Waziristan, the Faqir of Ipi, and the Indian Army*, 61.
43. Bruce, "The Indian Frontier Problem," 508.
44. Trench, *The Frontier Scouts*, 93.
45. Pettigrew, *Frontier Scouts*, 88.
46. For example, Waziristan possessed two primitive X-ray machines in the 1940s.
47. Pettigrew, *Frontier Scouts*, 86.
48. F. Leeson, *Frontier Legion* (Ferring: Selwood Printing, 2003), 26–27.
49. J. Clobby, *The History of the Royal Army Veterinary Corps, 1919–1961* (London: J. A. Allen & Co., 1963), 30.
50. Pettigrew, *Frontier Scouts*, 87.
51. WO 208/773, Intelligence Report on NWF, 24 June 1937, War Office Papers, National Archive, Kew, Surrey.
52. NDC, Islamabad, "Selections from the NWFP Archives," acc. no. 486, "NWFP Police Abstract of Intelligence, 2/8/1937," quoted in Warren, *Waziristan, the Faqir of Ipi, and the Indian Army*, 203.
53. *Official History of Operations on the N. W. Frontier of India, 1936–37*, 86.
54. F. Baines, *Officer Boy* (London: Eye & Spottiswoode, 1971), 147. The Rani of Jhansi was an infamous central Indian "princeling" involved in the insurrection of 1857.
55. Ibid.
56. *Green Howards' Gazette*, October 1938, 124.
57. W. R. Lawrence, *The India We Served* (London: Cassell & Co., 1929), 43.
58. Bruce, "The Indian Frontier Problem," 510.
59. Warren, *Waziristan, the Faqir of Ipi, and the Indian Army*, 22.
60. V/16/68, Financial and Revenue Accounts of the Government of India 1936–1937, India Office Records Official Publication Series.
61. Bruce, *Waziristan, 1936–1937*, 26.
62. E. Howell, "Some Problems of the Indian Frontier," *Journal of the Royal Central Asian Society* 21 (1934): 194.

63. Pettigrew, *Frontier Scouts*, 21.

64. Ibid.

65. M. Crawshaw, "Running a Country: The British Colonial Experience and Its Relevance to Present Day Concerns," *Shrivenham Papers*, no. 3 (April 2007), 8.

66. Bruce, *Waziristan, 1936–1937*, 14.

67. C. Tripodi, "Peacemaking through Bribes or Cultural Empathy? The Political Officer and Britain's Strategy towards the North-West Frontier, 1901–1945," *Journal of Strategic Studies* 31, no. 1 (2008): 145.

68. Woodruff, *The Men Who Ruled India*, 292.

69. Leeson, *Frontier Legion*, 110.

70. Trench, *The Frontier Scouts*, 135.

71. Pettigrew, *Frontier Scouts*, 85.

72. *Official History of Operations on the N. W. Frontier of India, 1936–37*, 286.

73. Masters, *Bugles and a Tiger*, 218.

74. D. E. Robertson, "The Organisation and Training of the Army of India," *Journal of the Royal United Service Institut* 69, no. 474 (1924): 319.

CHAPTER 10. THE HARD-EARNED LESSONS AND
REALITIES OF THE BRITISH EXPERIENCE
IN WAZIRISTAN, PART 2

1. T. R. Moreman, *The Army in India and the Development of Frontier Warfare, 1849–1947* (London: Macmillan, 1998), 147–150.

2. C. E. Callwell, *Small Wars — Their Principles and Practice* (London: Harrison & Son, 1906), 33.

3. "Afghanistan and the North-West Frontier: The Green Howards during the Third Afghan War 1919, and the Waziristan Campaigns of 1936–1937, 1937–1939," *The Friends of the Green Howards Regimental Museum Newsletter*, no. 14, September 2002, 14.

4. "Mauser," "A Forgotten Frontier Force," *English Review* 52 (1931): 72.

5. "Mouse," "Babu Tactics," *Journal of the United Service Institution of India* 61, no. 262 (1931): 64.

6. J. Masters, *Bugles and a Tiger* (London: Cassell & Co., 1956), 252.

7. H. R. C. Pettigrew, *Frontier Scouts* (Selsey, Sussex: privately printed, 1964), 46.

8. Moreman, *The Army in India and the Development of Frontier Warfare*, 132.

9. Lieutenant Colonel O. D. Bennett posits, "In vain do we turn to our training manuals; they deal with the subject [of mountain warfare] on too broad a scale to be of assistance" (O. D. Bennett, "Some Regrettable Incidents on the N.-W.F.," *Journal of the United Service Institution of India* 63, no. 271 [1933]: 202).

10. C. W. Gwynn, *Imperial Policing* (London: Macmillan, 1934), 6.

11. G. Moore, *Just as Good as the Rest* (Bedford, UK: Jaycopy, 1979), 20.

12. E. M. Spires, "Gas and the North-West Frontier," *Journal of Strategic Studies* 4, no. 6 (1983): 109.

13. "Mouse," "Babu Tactics," 65.

14. Callwell, *Small Wars*, 346.

15. T. E. Moreman, "The Army in India and Frontier Warfare, 1914–1939," www .king-emperor.com/article4.htm.

16. C. Allen, ed., *Plain Tales from the Raj* (London: Abacus, 1977), 197.

17. L. James, *Imperial Rearguard: Wars of Empire, 1919–85* (London: Brassey's Defence Publishers, 1988), 31.

18. Moreman, *The Army in India and the Development of Frontier Warfare,* 171.

19. J. A. Nagl, *Learning to Eat Soup with a Knife* (Chicago: University of Chicago Press, 2005), 219.

20. A. M. Roe, "To Create a Stable Afghanistan: Provisional Reconstruction Teams, Good Governance, and a Splash of History," *Military Review* 85 (November– December 2005): 20–21.

21. Masters, *Bugles and a Tiger,* 216–217.

22. Bennett, "Some Regrettable Incidents on the N.-W.F.," 194.

23. Gwynn, *Imperial Policing,* 2.

24. N. H. Bottomley, "The Work of the Royal Air Force on the North-West Frontier," *Journal of the Royal United Services Institute* 193 (1939): 778.

25. Ibid., 780.

26. C. C. Trench, *Viceroy's Agent* (London: Jonathan Cape, 1987), 6.

27. For example, with the independence of the RAF threatened by cuts in defense expenditure, Chief of Air Staff Sir Hugh Trenchard suggested the idea of controlling the tribesmen by airpower alone.

28. Trench, *Viceroy's Agent,* 77.

29. J. Slessor, *The Central Blue* (London: Cassell & Co., 1956), 130.

30. Ibid., 656.

31. Bottomley, "The Work of the Royal Air Force," 772.

32. R. A. Cassels, *London Gazette,* supplement, 29 October 1937, 6815.

33. D. A. L. Mackenzie, "Operations in the Lower Khaisora Valley, Waziristan, in 1937," *Journal of the Royal United Service Institution* 82, no. 528 (1938): 822.

34. James, *Imperial Rearguard,* 47.

35. H. L. Davies, "Military Intelligence in Tribal Warfare on The North-West Frontier of India," *Journal of the United Services Institution of India* 63, no. 272 (1933): 290.

36. Moore, *Just as Good as the Rest,* 20–25.

37. Callwell, *Small Wars,* 54.

38. J. Prendergast, *Prender's Progress—A Soldier in India, 1931–47* (London: Cassell & Co., 1979), 88.

39. F. Leeson, *Frontier Legion* (Ferring: Selwood Printing, 2003), 39.

40. *Official History of Operations on the N. W. Frontier of India, 1936–37* (Delhi: Government of India Press, 1943), 234.

41. Ibid., 90.

42. WO 106/5446, Tribal Disturbances in Waziristan, 25 November 1936–14 June 1937, War Office Papers, National Archive, Kew, Surrey.

43. Slessor, *The Central Blue,* 132.

44. *Official History of Operations on the N. W. Frontier of India, 1936–37,* 233.

45. Prendergast, *Prender's Progress,* 180.

46. *Frontier and Overseas Expeditions from India,* vol. 3, *Baluchistan and the First Afghan War* (Calcutta: Superintendent Government Printing, 1910), 343.
47. C. E. Bruce, *Waziristan, 1936–1937* (Aldershot, UK: Gale & Polden, 1938), 25.
48. A. G. Boycott, *The Elements of Imperial Defence* (Aldershot: Gale & Polden, 1936), 261.
49. "Waziristan Fighting," *Times* (London), 26 July 1937.
50. For planning purposes, it was assumed that a three-ton lorry could carry roughly between fifteen and thirty camel loads and had twice the radius of action. *The Army in India and Its Evolution* (Calcutta: Government Printing Press, 1924), 224.
51. M. C. T. Gompertz, "The Application of Science to Indian Frontier Warfare," *Army Quarterly* 10 (1925): 125.
52. Ibid., 127.
53. Ibid., 128.
54. Moreman, *The Army in India and the Development of Frontier Warfare,* 164.
55. Ibid., 166.
56. Leeson, *Frontier Legion,* 177.
57. *Green Howards Gazette,* December 1937, 182.
58. James, *Imperial Rearguard,* 45.
59. Davies, "Military Intelligence in Tribal Warfare," 295.
60. C. E. Bruce, "The Indian Frontier Problem," *Asiatic Review* 35 (1939): 495.
61. Moreman, *The Army in India and the Development of Frontier Warfare,* 158.
62. Colonel Khushwaqt Ulmulk to A. M. Roe, e-mail, 5 November 2007.
63. Moreman, *The Army in India and the Development of Frontier Warfare,* 163.
64. A weekly magazine that contained caustic comment on current affairs.
65. Prendergast, *Prender's Progress,* 89.
66. Chapman, "Afghanistan and the North-West Frontier," 19.
67. R. A. Cassels, *London Gazette,* supplement, 29 October 1937, 6815.
68. R. A. Cassels, *London Gazette,* supplement, 15 February 1938, 1062.
69. A. Warren, *Waziristan, the Faqir of Ipi, and the Indian Army* (Oxford: Oxford University Press, 2000), 212.
70. Colonel Khushwaqt Ulmulk to A. M. Roe, e-mail, 10 April 2008.
71. Prendergast, *Prender's Progress,* 81.
72. M. Hauner, "One Man against the Empire: The Faqir of Ipi and the British in Central Asia on the Eve of and during the Second World War," *Journal of Contemporary History* 16, no. 1 (1981): 389–397.
73. R/12/73, file 514/VIII, J. A. Robinson, 27 June 1937, Records Received in London, India Office Records, India Office Library, London.
74. "Waziristan," *Times* (London), 18 July 1938.
75. "North-West Frontier Engagement," *Times* (London), 18 March 1939.
76. A deserter from a Punjab regiment of the Indian army.
77. "A Clean-Up in Waziristan," *Times* (London), 22 February 1940.
78. Moreman, *The Army in India and the Development of Frontier Warfare,* xviii.
79. Richard Cobbold, "RUSI Interview with General David Richards," *Journal of the Royal Artillery* 134, no. 2 (2007): 57.
80. Major General Jonathan Shaw recalls, "I have yet to meet any soldier or civil

servant who has served in Afghanistan who has ever heard of it [O. Caroe, *The Pathans, 550 B.C.–A.D. 1957* (London: Macmillan, 1965)], let alone read it" (J. Shaw, "Don't Fight the Soil," speech on cultural understanding delivered to the Defence Academy, Shrivenham, 11 June 2008).

81. Caroe, *The Pathans, 550 B.C.–A.D. 1957*, 404.

82. M. Banerjee, *The Pathan Unarmed: Opposition and Memory in the North-West Frontier* (Oxford: Oxford University Press, 2000), 154.

83. However, to be balanced, there was considerable professional interest among British officers regarding tactics, techniques, and the use of new equipment against the frontier tribesmen.

## CHAPTER 11. CONTEMPORARY PARALLELS AND PROGNOSTICATIONS

1. A. Warren, *Waziristan, the Faqir of Ipi, and the Indian Army* (Oxford: Oxford University Press, 2000), 236.

2. At the time of the British withdrawal Kashmir was invaded by tribesmen from the North-West Frontier Province and regular Pakistani soldiers.

3. S. S. Harrison, "Beware Pashtunistan," *Newsweek*, 3 November 2007, available at http://www. newsweek.com/id/67966/output/print.

4. C. C. Trench, *The Frontier Scouts* (London: Jonathan Cape, 1985), 280.

5. H. R. C. Pettigrew, *Frontier Scouts* (Selsey, Sussex: privately printed, 1964), 100.

6. U. Ansari, "Cobras over the Frontier," in *Air Forces Monthly*, April 2008, 60.

7. See D. Edwards, *Before the Taliban: Genealogies of the Afghan Jihad* (Berkeley: University of California Press, 2002); B. Rubin, *The Fragmentation of Afghanistan* (New Haven: Yale University Press, 1995); and K. Lohbeck, *Holy War, Unholy Victory* (Washington, DC: Regnery Gateway, 1993).

8. M. Ewans, *Afghanistan: A Short History of Its People and Politics* (London: HarperCollins Publishers, 2002), 238–260.

9. Ibid., 266.

10. J. L. Anderson, *The Lion's Grave: Dispatches from Afghanistan* (New York: Grove Press, 2002).

11. See A. Rashid, *Taliban: Militant Islam, Oil, and Fundamentalism in Central Asia* (New Haven, CN: Yale University Press, 2000); and P. L. Williams, *Osama's Revenge the Next 9/11* (New York: Prometheus Books, 2004).

12. "Pakistani Intelligence Hunting for Bin Laden," *Washington Post*, 17 September 2001.

13. A. H. Sinno, *Organizations at War in Afghanistan and Beyond* (New York: Cornell University Press, 2008), 255.

14. According to the 9/11 Commission, the advantages that a "sanctuary" provide include "time, space, and ability to perform competent planning and staff work; a command structure able to make necessary decisions and possessing the authority and contacts to assemble needed people, money, and materials; opportunity and space to recruit, train, and select operatives with the needed skills and dedication, providing the time and structure required to socialize them into the terrorist cause, judge their trustworthiness, and hone their skills; a logistics network able to securely manage the travel of operatives, move

money, and transport resources where they need to go; access; reliable communications between coordinators and operatives; and opportunity to test the workability of the plan." *The National Commission on Terrorist Attacks upon the United States Report*, 22 July 2004, 365–366, available at http://www.9-11commission.gov/.

15. Ansari, "Cobras over the Frontier," 62.
16. S. M. Maloney, *Enduring the Freedom* (Washington, DC: Potomac Books, 2005), 294; P. Musharraf, *In the Line of Fire* (New York: Free Press, 2006), 201–204; D. Markey, "A False Choice in Pakistan," *Foreign Affairs* 86, no. 4 (2007): 88.
17. It is alleged that a small number of U.S. Special Forces conducted operations in North Waziristan.
18. R. Yusufzai, "Analysis: Pakistan's Army in the Tribal Areas," *BBC News*, 25 June 2003, available at http://news.bbc.co.uk/1/hi/world/south_asia/3020552.stm.
19. J. Rupert, "Where the Taliban Still Rule," *Newsday.com.*, 9 February 2006, available at http://www.newsday.com/news/nationworld/world/ny-wotalio546187 26feb09.
20. E. Blanch, "Pakistan: A Major Stepping Stone in Al Qaeda's Global Strategy," *Middle East*, April 2008, 6.
21. Pettigrew, *Frontier Scouts*, 100.
22. However, a significant number of tribesmen have left the frontier to become manual laborers in the Arab States (especially Libya and Saudi Arabia).
23. B. R. Rubin and A. Siddique, "Resolving the Pakistan-Afghanistan Stalemate," *Special Report 176*, United States Institute of Peace, October 2006, 13.
24. At least 200 tribal *maliks* have been killed since mid-2006.
25. S. Tanner, *Afghanistan: A Military History from Alexander the Great to the Fall of the Taliban* (New York: Da Capo, 2002), 134.
26. C. Tripodi, "Cultural Understanding: Its Utility and Influence: The British Experience on the North-West Frontier, 1918–1939," *British Army Review*, no. 144 (Spring 2008): 26.
27. T. Harding, "How British Empire Failed to Tame the Terrorist Fakir of Ipi," *news.telegraph*, 15 November 2001, available at http://news.telegraph.co.uk/news/main.jhtml?xml=/news/2001/11/15 wipi15.xml; M. Hirsh, "A Troubled Hunt," *Newsweek*, 30 May 2005, available at http://www.newsweek.com.id/52193?tid=relatedcl.
28. I. Tharoor, "History: The Original Insurgent," *Time*, 19 April 2007, available at: http://www.time.com/time/printout/0,8816,1612380.
29. Musharraf, *In the Line of Fire*, 220.
30. S. A. Nasir, "Baitullah Mehsud: South Waziristan's Unofficial Amir," in *Terrorism Focus* 3, no. 26 (2006): 3–4.
31. T. Moss, "Afghanistan has 'right' to launch cross-border attacks, says Karzai," *Jane's Defense Weekly* 45, no. 26 (2008): 25.
32. R. T. Strickland, "The Way of the Pashtun: Pashtunwali," *Canadian Army Journal* 10, no. 3 (2007): 44.
33. Ibid., 53.
34. M. McFate, "The Military Utility of Understanding Adversary Culture," *Joint Forces Quarterly* 38, no. 3 (2005): 42–48.

35. S. S. Thorburn, *Bannu: Our Afghan Frontier* (Whitefish, MT: Kessinger Publishing, 2004), 166.

36. T. H. Johnson and M. C. Mason, "No Sign until the Burst of Fire," *International Security* 32, no. 4 (2008): 64.

37. Ibid., 68.

38. Maloney, *Enduring the Freedom*, 294.

39. Ansari, "Cobras over the Frontier," 66.

40. R. Kaplan, *Soldiers of God: With Islamic Warriors in Afghanistan and Pakistan* (New York: Vintage Books, 2001), 22.

41. Robert F. Baumann recalls that in the early 1980s "the government [of Afghanistan] employed tribal volunteer units to prevent the free movement of guerrillas and their supply trains from Pakistan. . . . For example, the Ahmadzar tribe in Paktia supposedly raised 1,000 fighters for a 2,500-man regiment to be supported jointly with the men of another tribe. In some instances, the DRA [Democratic Republic of Afghanistan] offered payments to tribes such as the Shinwari along the Pakistan border or sought to exploit tribal antagonisms by recruiting a given tribe to curb the activities of a traditionally hostile neighbor. The approach met with some success" (R. F. Baumann, "Russian-Soviet Unconventional Wars in the Caucasus, Central Asia, and Afghanistan," *Leavenworth Papers*, no. 20, Combat Studies Institute, U.S. Army Command and General Staff College, 1993, p. 167).

42. S. S. Harrison, "Pashtunistan: The Challenge to Pakistan and Afghanistan," Real Instituto Elcano, 2 April 2008, 3.

43. For example, the nascent Afghan border police.

44. Musharraf, *In the Line of Fire*, 271.

45. Richard Cobbold, "RUSI Interview with General David Richards," *Journal of the Royal Artillery* 134, no. 2 (2007): 57.

46. Ibid., 56.

47. R. Stewart and S. Cowper-Coles, "Are We Failing in Afghanistan?" *British Army Review* 144 (Spring 2008): 10.

48. The U.S. provided approximately $10.5 billion in aid to Pakistan from 2002 to 2007. Just over $5.5 billion was earmarked by Islamabad for the tribal territory, but only 4 percent was used on nonmilitary projects.

49. The Pashtuns constitute the largest ethnic group in the world without a nation-state.

50. For example, five ethnolinguistic regions make up Pakistan.

51. Harrison, "Pashtunistan," 5.

52. *Official History of Operations on the North-West Frontier of India, 1920–35* (Delhi: Government of India Press, 1945), vii.

53. G. N. Curzon, *Speeches as Viceroy and Governor-General of India 1898–1905* (London: Macmillan, 1906), 43.

# SELECTED GLOSSARY

| | |
|---|---|
| *amir* | a ruler or king |
| *badal* | revenge |
| *badragga* | tribal escort |
| *bandish* | blockade |
| *baniya* | shopkeeper |
| *barampta* | seizure of men, animals, or property to enforce reimbursement for an offense |
| *burqa* | enveloping outer garment worn by women |
| *chaplis* | sandals |
| *charas* | drug made from hemp; hashish |
| *chigha* | pursuit party |
| *fakir* | a holy man; a first name |
| *feranghi* | foreigner or outsider |
| *gasht* | armed patrol (also used as a verb) |
| *ghazi* | follower of Islam |
| *ghwa* | cow |
| *Haj* | pilgrimage to Mecca |
| *hamsaya* | a tribesman or outlaw who resides under a *maliks*'s protection |
| *havildor* | sergeant |
| *hujra* | house or hostel for men |
| *jemadar* | a viceroy's commissioned officer (second lieutenant) |
| *jezail* | long-barreled matchlock rifle |
| *jihad* | a Muslim or holy war |
| *jirga* | assembly or parliament of tribal representatives |
| *jowar* | Indian millet |
| *kaches* | alluvial deposits |
| *kassadar* | tribal levy or policeman |
| *kot* | walled village |
| *lakh* | a hundred thousand |
| *langer* | food kitchen |
| *lara* | road |
| *lashkar* | tribal armed force |
| *loose-wallah* | professional rifle thief |
| *madrassa* | Islamic religious school |
| *malang* | religious leader |
| *malik* | a tribal leader or elder |
| *melmastia* | hospitality |
| *mian* | a religious leader |
| *mujahadeen* | (literally "struggler") a person involved in a *jihad* |
| *mullah* | a religious leader who takes prayers |
| *munshi* | language teacher |
| *muwajib* | tribal allowance |
| *naik* | corporal, master, or landlord |

| | |
|---|---|
| *namus* | the protection of female relatives as well as a tribesman's land |
| *nanawatai* | sanctuary |
| *nang* | honor |
| *nikat* | nonnegotiable law of tribal division |
| *nullah* | ravine |
| *pagri* | turban |
| *pakol* | flat squat hat |
| Pashtu | tribal language |
| Pashtun | generic name for the tribesmen of the North-West Frontier |
| Pashtunistan | a theoretical Pashtun homeland independent of Afghan and Pakistani authority |
| *Pashtunwali* | austere moral concept of tribal honor |
| picquet | also piquet; a flanking patrol or a manned fortified outpost |
| *pir* | a tribesmen with religious distinction |
| Powindah | nomad |
| *purdah* | gender separation |
| *qalang* | rent or tax |
| *qanun* | law |
| Raj | kingdom; used to denote British rule in India 1858–1947 |
| *riwaj* | custom |
| *sangar* | stone breastwork defense wall |
| *saristita* | alternative name for *nikat,* the nonnegotiable law of tribal division |
| *sayyid* | a religious leader |
| sepoy | infantry soldier |
| *shalwar kamiz* | loose shirt |
| Sharia | Islamic law |
| *sharm* | shame |
| *subedar* | a commanding lieutenant (company commander) |
| Taliban | seekers of truth (originally students from religious schools) who assumed political authority over Afghanistan |
| *tangi* | defile or gorge |
| *tarbur* | first cousin |
| *tuman* | allowances payable to a tribe |

# BIBLIOGRAPHY

GOVERNMENT DOCUMENTS
National Archive, Kew, Surrey
Air Ministry Papers
AIR 2/2516, Operations in Waziristan, 1937.
AIR 2/4263, Participation of Air Forces in the Operations in Waziristan, January 1938–May 1939.
AIR 2/9393, Immediate Awards: Waziristan Operations, 1938.

CABINET OFFICE PAPERS
CAB 21/1078, GOI, External Affairs Department to Secretary of State for India, 7 March 1940.
CAB 37/39/30, no. 214, Dispatch from F. D. Cunningham, Esq., Commissioner and Superintendent, Peshawar Division, to the Officiating Chief Secretary to Government, Punjab, 11 May 1895.
CAB 37/53/72, North-West Frontier of India.
CAB 67/4/23, Situation in Waziristan, 1940.
CAB 79/3/23, Situation in Waziristan, 1940.
CAB 80/8/5, Situation in Waziristan, 1940.

FOREIGN OFFICE
FO 371/15224, British Embassy, Kabul, 22 April 1960, 1014/60. Letter from Chancery to South East Asia Department, Foreign Department, London.
FO 371/21065, Central Asia, General Correspondence (Waziristan), 1937.
FO 371/23628, Government of India External Affairs Department. F. D. Cunningham, Esq., Commissioner and Superintendent, Peshawar Division, to the Officiating Chief Secretary to Government, Punjab, 11 May 1895.
FO 371/23628, Government of India External Affairs Department. Examination of the Present Policy on the North-West Frontier of India. Government of India to the Secretary of State for India, Simla, 22 July 1939.
FO 371/23630, Afghanistan Annual Report, 1938.

WAR OFFICE PAPERS
WO 32/4152, Operations in Waziristan from November 1936 to January 1937.
WO 32/4640, Waziristan Operations, 1938.
WO 106/58, B.M. 119 from C-in-C to D.M.O.&I., 25 August 1922.
WO 106/1594 A, A List of Leading Mullahs on the Border of the North-West Frontier Province Corrected to 31 December 1932.
WO 106/5446, Waziristan: Military and Political Matters, 1933–1938.
WO 106/5446, Memo on Pacification of Waziristan, 22 July 1937.
WO 106/6027, Tribal Disturbances in Waziristan, 25 November 1936–14 June 1937.
WO 106/6027, "Waziristan," Army Headquarters (India), General Staff Branch, 10 February 1938.

WO 106/6027, D.D.M.I. to D.M.O.I. and D.D.M.O., 29 August 1937.
WO 208/773, Tribal Cooperation in the NWF.
WO 208/773, Note on the Fakir of Ipi, 24 June 1937.
WO 208/773, Intelligence Report on NWF, 24 June 1937.
WO 208/26, GOI to IO, No. 5889, 27 October 1941.


TREASURY
T 301/9, Waziristan, 1939–1941.


SECURITY SERVICES
KV 2/530, Muhammad Saadi Al Gailani, Alias The Shami Pir.
KV 2/531, Saadi Kailani, "The Shami Pir," 1937–1947.
KV 2/2290, Nazi Activity in the North-West, 26 July 1941.


INDIA OFFICE LIBRARY, LONDON
MSS EUR C308, Account of the Shahur Tangi Affair by Lt. Col. Bolam, April
    1937.
MSS EUR C393, Tochi Scouts 1938–1941, T. J. Phillips.
MSS EUR D 670/13, [Cunningham Collection], 1937–1946 and 1947–1948.
MSS EUR D 879/1, [Lowis Collection] Diaries, 1936–1937.


INDIA OFFICE RECORDS, INDIA OFFICE LIBRARY, LONDON
*Military Department Records*
L/MIL/5/1065, Supplement 1 to Intelligence Summary 7, 8–14 July 1937.
L/MIL/5/1065, Supplement 2 to Intelligence Summary 7, 12–18 August 1937.
L/MIL/5/1065, Supplement 3 to Intelligence Summary 6, 17–23 June 1937.
L/MIL/5/1066, EAD to SSI, 12 April 1937 and 18 April 1937.
L/MIL/17/13/45, Report on Air Operations on the NWF, 1944.
L/MIL/17/13/46, Report of the Frontier Committee, 1945.


*Private Office Paper*
L/PO/6/123, Rear Admiral Viscount Mountbatten of Burma's Personal Report no.
    17, Secretary of State for India, 16 April 1947.


*Political and Secret Department*
L/PS/7/136, W. R. Merk to the Chief Secretary to Government. Punjab, Shekh Bu-
    din, 12 June 1901.
L/PS/12/1844, Military Attaché's Diary, 25 July 1941.
L/PS/12/3171, Note by Sir D. Bray, 27 March 1934.
L/PS/12/3171, PZ2435, Report of Tribal Defence and Control Committee Meeting,
    June 1931.
L/PS/12/3192, NWF Intelligence Summaries, no. 41, 12 October 1936.
L/PS/12/3230, PA NW to RW, 1 May 1936, CS NWFP to FS FPD, 8 June 1936, RW
    "Agitation in Lower Dawar—April 1936" to CS NWFP, 13 May 1936.
L/PS/12/3230, India Office Interview with C. A. G. Savidge.
L/PS/12/3230, India Office Minute Paper, December 1936.
L/PS/12/3232, A. E. B. Parsons, 25 June 1937.

L/PS/12/3232, R. A. Cassels, Report on Operations in Waziristan, 25 November 1936–16 January 1937.
L/PS/12/3233, DDIP, H. J. Vickers, 17 June 1937.
L/PS/12/3234, EAD to SSI, 5 November 1937.
L/PS/12/3234, NWF Intelligence Summaries, no. 30, 25 July 1938.
L/PS/12/3236, Dated 11 November 1937.
L/PS/12/3255, Lord Brabourne to Zetland, 14 July 1938.
L/PS/12/3258, Note on the Case of the Shami Pir up to 1938.
L/PS/12/3265, Memorandum by Viceroy, 22 July 1939.

*War Staff Papers*
L/WS/1/1269-WS 19056, NWF and Afghan Summaries, 1942.
L/WS/1/1526-WS 13031, Report on Operations in Waziristan, 1 January 1940–24 May 1940.

RECORDS RECEIVED IN LONDON
R/12/69, file 514/IV, NWFP to FPD, 13 February 1937.
R/12/73, file 514/VIII, J. A. Robinson, 27 June 1937.

INDIA OFFICE RECORDS OFFICIAL PUBLICATION SERIES
V/16/68, Financial and Revenue Accounts of the Government of India, 1936–1937.

CENTRE OF SOUTH ASIAN STUDIES, UNIVERSITY OF CAMBRIDGE, CAMBRIDGE
BIA-6, Afghanistan—Frontiers General, 1908–1941.
BIA-8, Afghanistan—Frontiers, Waziristan, 1907–1940.

ROYAL AIR FORCE MUSEUM, HENDON
B22, Air Staff (India) Memorandum No. 1, April 1935, Tactical Methods of Conducting Air Operations against Tribes on the North-West Frontier of India.
B2690, Salmond Papers, Report by Air-Marshal Sir John Salmond K.C.B., C.M.G., C.V.O., D.S.O. on the Royal Air Force in India, August 1922.

ROYAL SCHOOL OF SIGNALS MUSEUM, BLANDFORD
915, Comments on Inter-Communication Waziristan Operations 1936–1937, Waziristan District Signals, Historical Record, 1938–1939.
915.3, 1st Division Operation Order No. 4, 23 April 1937.
937.14, B. E. Hughes, Waziristan Expedition, June 1920.

NATIONAL ARMY MUSEUM, ARCHIVES, LONDON
6605-24, Notes by Colonel George Brown on the Military History of Waziristan.
6909-8, Miscellaneous Reports on Waziristan.
7306-67, Autobiography of General Sir Eric de Burgh, GOC 1st Division, 1937.

PUBLISHED GOVERNMENT SOURCES
Cassels, R. A. *Supplement to the London Gazette,* HMSO, London, no. 34449, 29 October 1937.

————. *Second Supplement to The London Gazette,* HMSO, London, no. 34484, 15 February 1938.

Dispatch by His Excellency General Sir Charles Carmichael Monro on the Third Afghan War (Simla, India, 1919).

Report on the Administration of the Khyber 1920–21, in file of the Office of the Chief Commissionaire, NWFP, no. 5/18, 1921.

*The Army in India and Its Evolution.* Calcutta, 1924. London: HMSO.

*Frontier and Overseas Expeditions from India.* Vol. 2, *North-West Frontier Tribes between the Kabul and Gumal Rivers.* Simla, India: Government Monotype Press, 1908.

*Frontier and Overseas Expeditions from India.* Vol. 3, *Baluchistan and the First Afghan War.* Calcutta: Superintendent Government Printing, 1910.

*India in 1927–28.* Calcutta: Bureau of Public Information, 1928.

*Military Report on Waziristan, 1935.* London: HMSO, 1936.

*Official History of Operations on the North-West Frontier of India, 1920–35.* Delhi: Government of India Press, 1945.

*Official History of Operations on the North-West Frontier of India, 1936–37.* Delhi: Government of India Press, 1943.

*Operations in Waziristan, 1919–1920.* Calcutta: Superintendent Government Printing, 1921.

*Report of the Frontier Committee, 1945.* Tucker Committee. Delhi: Government of India Press.

*Report of the Frontier Watch and Ward Committee, 1936.* New Delhi: HMSO, 1937.

*The Third Afghan War, 1919: Official Account.* Calcutta: Government of India Central Publishing Branch, 1926.

MINISTRY OF DEFENSE PUBLICATION

*Army Field Manual.* Vol. 1. *Combined Operations Part 10: Counter-insurgency Operations.* London: Ministry of Defense, 2001.

THESES, PAPERS, AND SPEECHES

Bailes, H. R. "The Influence of Continental Examples and Colonial Warfare upon the Reform of the Late Victorian Army." Ph.D. diss., University of London, 1980.

Baumann, R. F. "Russian-Soviet Unconventional Wars in the Caucasus, Central Asia, and Afghanistan." *Leavenworth Papers,* no. 20, April 1993.

Crawshaw, M. "Running a Country: The British Colonial Experience and Its Relevance to Present Day Concerns." *Shrivenham Papers,* no. 3, April 2007.

DeNeufville, P. B. "Ahmad Shah Massoud and the Genesis of the Nationalist Anti-Communist Movement in Northern Afghanistan, 1969–1979." Ph.D. diss., King's College, London University, 2006.

Harris, L. "British Policy on the North-West Frontier of India, 1889–1901." Ph.D. diss., University of London, 1960.

Howell, E. "Mizh: A Monograph on Government Relations with the Mahsud Tribe." Master's thesis, Oxford University, 1979.

Shaw, J. "Don't Fight the Soil." Speech on cultural understanding delivered to the Defence Academy, Shrivenham, 11 June 2008.

Williams, M. W. "The British Colonial Experience in Waziristan and Its Applicability to Current Operations." School of Advanced Military Studies Monographs, Combined Arms Research Library, 26 May 2005, Fort Leavenworth, KS.

NEWSPAPERS
*Daily Telegraph* (London)
*Evening Standard* (London)
*Imperial Gazetteer of India*
*London Gazette*
*Pioneer* (Allahbad)
*Saturday Evening Post* (London)
*Times* (London)
*Washington Post*
*Washington Times*

BOOKLET
Frontier Constabulary. *Fortieth Anniversary Reunion Booklet.* Simla, India: n.p., n.d.

BOOKS
Adamec, L. W. *Historical Dictionary of Afghanistan.* Metuchen, N.J.: Scarecrow Press, 1991.
Akbar, A. S. *Religion and Politics in Muslim Society.* Cambridge: Cambridge University Press, 1983.
Anderson, J. L. *The Lion's Grave: Dispatches from Afghanistan.* New York: Grove Press, 2002.
Andrews, C. F. *The Challenge of the North-West Frontier.* London: George Allen & Unwin, 1937.
Ascoli, D. *A Companion to the British Army, 1660–1983.* London: Harrup Publishers, 1983.
Baden-Powell, R. *Memories of India: Recollections of Soldiering and Sport.* Philadelphia: D. McKay, 1915.
Baines, F. *Officer Boy.* London: Eye & Spottiswoode, 1971.
Balfour, B. *History of Lord Lytton's Indian Administration.* London: Longmans Green & Co., 1899.
Banerjee, M. *The Pathan Unarmed: Opposition and Memory in the North-West Frontier.* Oxford: Oxford University Press, 2000.
Barclay, C. N. *The Regimental History of the 3rd Queen Alexandra's Own Gurkha Rifles.* London: William Clowes & Son, 1953.
Barthorp, M. *The North-West Frontier: British India and Afghanistan.* Poole, UK: Blandford Press, 1982. Republished as *Afghan Wars and the North-West Frontier, 1839–1947.* London: Cassell, 2002.
Barton, W. *India's North-West Frontier.* London: John Murray, 1939.
Beattie, H. *Imperial Frontier: Tribe and State in Waziristan.* Richmond: Curzon Press, 2002.
Beckett, I., ed. *The Roots of Counter-Insurgency: Armies and Guerrilla Warfare, 1900–1945.* London: Blandford Press, 1988.

Bellow, H. W. *A General Report on the Yusufzais.* Lahore: Government Printing Press, 1864.

Biddulph, J. *Tribes of the Hindoo Kush.* Calcutta: Office of Department of Government Printing, 1880.

Boycott, A. G. *The Elements of Imperial Defence.* Aldershot: Gale and Polden, 1936.

Brett, G. A. *History of the South Wales Borderers and the Monmouthshire Regiment, 1937–52, Part 1.* Pontypool: Hughes & Son, 1953.

Bristow R. C. B. *Memories of the British Raj.* London: Johnson, 1974.

Bruce, C. E. *Waziristan, 1936–1937: The Problems of the NWFI and Their Solutions.* Aldershot: Gale and Polden Ltd, 1938.

Bruce, R. I. *The Forward Policy and Its Results.* London: Longmans, Green & Co., 1900.

Cadogan, E. *The India We Saw.* London: John Murray, 1933.

Callwell, C. E. *Small Wars—Their Principles and Practice.* London: Harrison & Son, 1906.

Caroe, O. *The Pathans, 550 B.C.–A.D. 1957.* London: Macmillan & Co., 1965.

Churchill, W. S. *My Early Life.* London: Thornton Butterworth, 1930.

———. *The Story of the Malakand Field Force.* London: Longmans Green, 1898.

Clobby, J. *The History of the Royal Army Veterinary Corps, 1919–1961.* London: J. A. Allen & Co., 1963.

Coatman, J. *Years of Destiny.* London: Jonathan Cape, 1932.

Coen, T. C. *The Indian Political Service: A Study in Indirect Rule.* London: Chatto & Windus Ltd., 1971.

Cordesman, A. *The Ongoing Lessons of Afghanistan: Warfighting, Intelligence, Force Transformation, and Nation Building.* Washington, DC: Centre for Strategic and International Studies, 2004.

Coupland, R. *The Indian Problem, 1933–1935.* Oxford: Oxford University Press, 1943.

Curzon, G. N. *Speeches as Viceroy and Governor-General of India, 1898–1905.* London: Macmillan, 1906.

Davies, C. C. *The Problem of the North-West Frontier, 1890–1908.* London: Cambridge University Press, 1932.

de Watteville, H. *Waziristan, 1919–1920.* London: Constable & Co., 1925.

Dichter, D. *The North West Frontier of West Pakistan.* Oxford: Clarendon Press, 1967.

Dilks, D. *Curzon in India.* London: Rupert Hart-Davis, 1969.

Diver, M. *The Unsung: A Record of British Services in India.* London: William Blackwood & Son, 1945.

Dunbar, G. *A History of India.* London: Ivor Nicholson & Watson, 1936.

Dupree, L. *Afghanistan.* Princeton: Princeton University Press, 1973.

Edwards, D. *Before the Taliban: Genealogies of the Afghan Jihad.* Berkeley: University of California Press, 2002.

Elliot, J. G. *The Frontier 1839–1947.* London: Cassel, 1968.

Ewans, M. *Afghanistan: A Short History of Its People and Politics.* London: HarperCollins Publishers, 2002.

Farwell, B. *Queen Victoria's Little Wars.* London: W. W. Norton & Co., 1972.

Featherstone, D. *India: Victorian Colonial Warfare*. London: Blandford Publishers, 1993.

Fraser, A. *Plain Tales from the Raj*. Ed. C. Allen. London: Abacus, 1977.

Fraser-Tytler, W. K. *Afghanistan*. Oxford: Oxford University Press, 1967.

Galula, D. *Counterinsurgency Warfare: Theory and Practice*. Westport, CT: Praeger, 1966.

Gardner, B. *The East India Company: A History*. New York: McCall Publishing Co., 1972.

General Staff Army Headquarters, India. *A Dictionary of the Pathan Tribes in the North-West Frontier of India*. New Delhi: Mittal, 2005.

Gilbertson, G. W. *First Pakkhtoo Book*. Benares: Medical Hall Press, 1901.

Gordon, A. *The Rules of the Game*. London: John Murray, 1966.

Gould, B. J. *The Jewel in the Lotus*. London: Chatto & Windus, 1957.

Graham, C. A. L. *The History of the Indian Mountain Artillery*. Aldershot: Gale & Polden, 1957.

Gregorian, V. *The Emergence of Modern Afghanistan: Politics of Reform and Modernisation, 1880–1946*. Stanford: Stanford University Press, 1969.

Griffiths, P. *To Guard My People: The History of the Indian Police*. London: Ernest Benn, 1971.

Guha, R. *Elementary Aspects of Peasant Insurgency in Colonial India*. Richmond: Duke University Press, 1999.

Gwynn, C. W. *Imperial Policing*. London: Macmillan, 1934.

Hauner, M. *India in Axis Strategy*. Stuttgart: Klett-Cotta, 1981.

Heathcote, T. A. *The Indian Army*. London: David & Charles, 1974.

———.*The Military in British India*. Manchester: Manchester University Press, 1995.

Hodson, W. S. R. *A Soldier's Life in India*, ed. G. H. Hodson. London: John W. Parker & Son, 1859.

Holdich, T. H. *The Indian Borderland, 1880–1900*. London: Methuen & Co., 1901.

James, L. *Imperial Rearguard*. London: Brassey's Defence Publishers, 1988.

Johnson, T. *Imperial Britain: A Comprehensive Description of the Geography, History, Commerce, Trade, Government and Religion of the British Empire*. London: Imperial Press, 1898.

Kaplan, R. *Soldiers of God: With Islamic Warriors in Afghanistan and Pakistan*. New York: Vintage Books, 2001.

Kirk-Greene, A. *Britain's Imperial Administrators, 1858–1966*. London: Macmillan Press, 2000.

Kitson, F. *Bunch of Five*. London: Faber & Faber, 1977.

———. *Low Intensity Operations: Subversion, Insurgency, Peace-Keeping*. London: Faber & Faber, 1971.

Lawrence, W. R. *The India We Served*. London: Cassell & Co., 1929.

Leeson, F. *Frontier Legion*. Ferring: Selwood Printing, 2003.

Lindholm, C. *Generosity and Jealousy: Swat Pukktun of Northern Pakistan*. New York: Columbia, 1982.

Lionel, J. *The Indian Frontier War*. London: William Heinedmann, 1898.

Lohbeck, K. *Holy War, Unholy Victory*. Washington, DC: Regnery Gateway, 1993.

Lyall, A. *British Domination in India*. London: John Murray, 1920.

MacFetridge, C. H. T. and J. P. Warren, eds. *Tales of the Mountain Gunners.* Edinburgh: William Blackwood, 1973.

MacGunn, G. F. *The Armies of India.* London: Adam and Charles Black, 1911.

———. *The Martial Races of India.* London: Sampson Low, Marston & Co., 1933.

Majumdar, R. C. *An Advanced History of India.* Part 3. London: Macmillan & Co., 1951.

Maloney, S. M. *Enduring the Freedom.* Washington, DC: Potomac Books, 2005.

Martineau, J. *Life of Sir Bartle Frere.* Vol. 1. London: John Murray, 1895.

Mason, P. *A Matter of Honour.* London: Ebenezer Baylis & Son, 1974.

Masters, J. *Bugles and a Tiger.* London: Cassell & Co., 1956.

Matinuddin, K. *The Taliban Phenomenon: Afghanistan, 1994–1997.* Karachi: Oxford University Press, 1999.

Mehra, P. *A Dictionary of Modern Indian History, 1707–1947.* Delhi: Oxford University Press, 1985.

Miller, C. *Khyber: British India's North-West Frontier.* London: MacDonald & Jane's, 1977.

Misra, A. *Afghanistan: The Labyrinth of Violence.* Cambridge, UK: Polity Press, 2004.

Misra, J. P. *The Administration of India under Lord Lansdowne, 1888–1894.* New Delhi: Sterling Publishers, 1975.

Mockaitis, T. R. *British Counterinsurgency, 1919–1960.* London: Macmillan, 1990.

Molesworth, G. *Afghanistan 1919.* London: Asia Publishing House, 1962.

Moore, G. *Just as Good as the Rest.* Bedford: Jaycopy, 1979.

Moreman, T. E. *The Army in India and the Development of Frontier Warfare, 1849–1947.* London: Macmillan, 1998.

Musharraf, P. *In the Line of Fire.* New York: Free Press, 2006.

Nagl, J. A. *Learning to Eat Soup with a Knife.* Chicago: University of Chicago Press, 2005.

Newton, A. P. *A Hundred Years of the British Empire.* London: A. R. Mowbray & Co., 1942.

Nevill, H. L. *North-West Frontier: British and Indian Army Campaigns on the North-West Frontier of India, 1849–1908.* London: Tom Donovan Publishing, 1912.

Norris, J. A. *The First Afghan War, 1838–1842.* Cambridge: Cambridge University Press, 1967.

Oliver, E. E. *Across the Border; or Pathân and Biloch.* London: Chapman & Hall, 1890.

O'Malley, L. S. S. *The Indian Civil Service, 1601–1930.* London: Frank Cass & Co., 1965.

Omissi, D. E. *Air Power and Colonial Control: The Royal Air Force, 1919–1939.* Manchester: Manchester University Press, 1990.

———. *The Sepoy and the Raj: The Indian Army, 1860–1940.* London: Macmillan Publishers, 1994.

Padget, W. H. *Record of Expeditions Against the North-West Frontier Tribes since the Annexation of the Punjab.* Revised by A. H. Mason. London: Whiting, 1884.

Pennell, T. L. *Pennell of the Afghan Frontier: The Life of Theodore Leighton Pennell.* London: Seely, Service & Co., 1922.

Pettigrew, H. R. C. *Frontier Scouts.* Selsey, Sussex: privately printed, 1964.

Pfeffer, G., and D. K. Behera, eds. *Concept of Tribal Society.* New Delhi: Concept Publishers, 2002.

Philips, C. H., with H. L. Singh and B. N. Pandey, eds. *The Evolution of India and Pakistan, 1858 to 1947: Selected Documents on the History of India and Pakistan.* London: Oxford University Press, 1962.

Pocock, T. *Fighting General: The Public and Private Campaigns of General Sir Walter Walker.* London: Collins, 1973.

Poullada, L. *Reform and Rebellion in Afghanistan, 1919–1929.* New York: Cornell University Press, 1973.

Prendergast, J. *Prender's Progress—A Soldier in India, 1931–47.* London: Cassell, 1979.

Rashid, A. *Taliban: Militant Islam, Oil, and Fundamentalism in Central Asia.* New Haven: Yale University Press, 2000.

Richards, D. S. *The Savage Frontier.* London: Pan Books, 1990.

Roberts, F. S. R. *Forty-One Years in India.* Vol. 2. London: Richard Bentley & Son, 1897.

Robertson, G. S. *The Kafirs of the Hindu-Kush.* London: Lawrence & Bullen, 1896.

Robson, B. *Crisis on the Frontier.* London: Spellmount, 2004.

———. *The Road to Kabul: The Second Afghan War, 1978–1881.* London: Spellmount, 1975.

Rodd, J. R. *Social and Diplomatic Memories.* Vol. 3. London: Edwards Arnold & Co., 1925.

Rubin, B. *The Fragmentation of Afghanistan.* New Haven: Yale University Press, 1995.

Schofield, V. *Afghan Frontier: Feuding and Fighting in Central Asia.* London: Tauris Parke Paperbacks, 2003.

Seton, M. C. C. *The India Office.* London: G. P. Putnam's Sons, 1926.

Sinno, A. H. *Organizations at War in Afghanistan and Beyond: A Short History of Its People and Politics.* New York: Cornell University Press, 2008.

Skene, A. *Passing It On—Short Talks on Tribal Fighting on the North West Frontier of India.* Aldershot, UK: Gale & Polden 1932.

Skyes, P. *The Right Honourable Sir Mortimer Durand—A Biography.* London: Cassell & Co., 1926.

Slessor, J. *The Central Blue: Recollections and Reflections.* London: Cassell & Co., 1956.

Slim, W. *Unofficial History.* London: Cassell & Co., 1959.

Smith, V. A. *The Oxford Student's History of India.* Oxford: Clarendon Press, 1921.

Spain, J. W. *The Pathan Borderland.* The Hague: Mouton & Co., 1963.

Stein, A. *On Alexander's Track to the Indus.* London: MacMillan & Co., 1929.

Stockdale, F. T. *Walk Warily in Waziristan.* Devon: Arthur H. Stockwell, 1982.

Subrahmanyam, G. *New Perspectives on the British Imperial State, Effortless Rule and Military Realities: The British Imperial State in 1891.* London: London School of Economics and Political Science, 2002.

Swinson, A. *North-West Frontier—People and Events, 1939–1947.* London: Hutchinson, 1967.

Tanner, S. *Afghanistan: A Military History from Alexander the Great to the Fall of the Taliban.* New York: Da Capo, 2002.

Thompson, R. *Defeating Communist Insurgency: The Lessons of Malaya and Vietnam.* New York: Praeger, 1966.

Thorburn, S. S. *Bannu, Our Afghan Frontier.* Whitefish, MT: Kessinger Publishing, 2004.

Thornton, T. H. *Colonel Sir Robert Sandeman—His Life and Work on Our Indian Frontier.* London: John Murray, 1895.

Tönnies, F. *Community and Society.* East Lansing: Michigan State University Press, 1957.

Trench, C. C. *The Frontier Scouts.* London: Jonathan Cape, 1985.

———. *The Indian Army and the King's Enemies 1900-1947.* London: Thames and Hudson, 1988.

———. *Viceroy's Agent.* London: Jonathan Cape, 1987.

Vogelsang, W. *The Afghans.* Oxford: Blackwell Publishers, 2002.

Warren, A. *Waziristan, The Faqir of Ipi, and the Indian Army.* Oxford, UK: Oxford University Press, 2000.

Williams, F. T. C. *Exciting Times and Narrow Squeaks.* Blandford: Royal School of Signals Museum, 1937.

———. *The Indian Argosy.* Vol. 1. Blandford, UK: Royal School of Signals Museum, 1936.

Williams, P. L. *Osama's Revenge the Next 9/11.* New York: Prometheus Books, 2004.

Wilkinson-Latham, R. *North-West Frontier, 1837-1947.* London: Osprey Publishers, 1977.

Wilson, A. *Sport and Service in Assam and Elsewhere.* London: Hutchinson & Co., 1924.

Woodruff, Philip. *The Men Who Ruled India: The Guardians.* London: Jonathan Cape, 1954.

Wylly, H. C. *Tribes of Central Asia: From the Black Mountains to Waziristan.* London: Macmillan and Co., 1912.

Yeates-Brown, F. *Martial India.* London: Eyre & Spottiswoode, 1945.

ARTICLES

"The Action of the 1st (Abbottabad) Infantry Brigade Near Damil on the 29th March 1937." *Journal of the United Services Institution of India* 68, no. 290 (1938): 33–40.

Ahmed, A. S. "An Aspect of the Colonial Encounter in the North-West Frontier Province." *Asian Affairs* 65 (1978): 319–327.

———. "Tribes and State in Central Asia." *Asian Affairs* 68 (1981): 152–188.

Air Intelligence Liaison Officer. "Close Support by Aircraft on the North-West Frontier." *Journal of the United Service Institution of India* 74, no. 16 (1944): 15–25.

Angus, T. H. "Operations in the Lower Shaktu Valley 16th–18th November 1937." *Journal of the United Service Institution of India* 68, no. 292 (July 1938): 335–342.

"An Infantry Soldier." "Collective Training in a Battalion." *Journal of the United Service Institution of India* 60, no. 259 (1930): 126–132.

Ansari, U. "Cobras over the Frontier." *Air Forces Monthly* 241 (April 2008): 60–66.

"Attack on the Convoy at Shahur Tangi on the 9th April 1937." *Journal of the United Service Institution of India* 67, no. 288 (1937): 261–277.

"Auspex." "A Matrimonial Tangle (or Mountains and Machine Guns)." *Journal of the United Service Institution of India* 63, no. 272 (1993): 367–374.

Baqai, F. G. "Fakir of Ipi: A Brief Review of the anti-British Activities of a Waziri Mujahid." *Pakistan Journal of History and Culture* 20, no. 1 (1999): 23–31.

Barton, W. "The Problems of Law and Order under a Responsible Government in the North-West Frontier Province." *Journal of the Royal Central Asian Society* 19 (1932): 5–21.

———. "Waziristan and the Frontier Policy." *Fortnightly Review* 142 (1937): 194–203.

Bennett, O. D. "Some Regrettable Incidents on the N.-W. F." *Journal of the United Services Institution of India* 63, no. 271 (1933): 193–203.

Birdwood, W. "Recent Indian Military Experience." *United Empire*, no. 22 (1931): 243–253.

Blanch, E. "Pakistan: A Major Stepping Stone in Al Qaeda's Global Strategy." *Middle East,* April 2008, 6–10.

"Borderer." "Essay." *Journal of the United Services Institution of India* 64, no. 274 (1934): 9–26.

Bottomley, N. H. "The Work of the Royal Air Force on the North-West Frontier." *Journal of the Royal United Services Institute* 193 (1939): 769–780.

Brock, H. M. "Air Operations on the NWF 1930." *Journal of the Royal Central Asian Society* 19 (1932): 22–44.

Bruce, C. E. "The Indian Frontier Problem." *Asiatic Review* 35 (1939): 492–514.

Calvin, A. "Indian Frontiers and Indian Finance." *Nineteenth Century* 38 (1895): 870–888.

Chetwode, P. "The Indian Army." *Journal of the Royal United Service Institution* 82 (1937): 6–16.

Curzon, G. N. "The 'Scientific Frontier' an Accomplished Fact." *Nineteenth Century* 23 (1888): 901–917.

Davies, H. L. "Military Intelligence in Tribal Warfare on The North-West Frontier of India." *Journal of the United Services Institution of India* 63, no. 272 (1933): 289–300.

Editorial. *Journal of the United Service Institution of India* 61, no. 262 (1931): 1–9.

Farrell, T. D. "The Founding of the North-West Frontier Militias." *Journal of the Royal Central Asian Society,* June 1972, 165–178.

Gompertz, M. C. T. "The Application of Science to Indian Frontier Warfare." *Army Quarterly* 10 (1925): 122–133.

Gordon, J. J. H., R. Temple, J. Hills Johnes, Dr. Blanford, Captain Younghusband. "The Geography of the North-West Frontier of India." *Geographical Journal* 17, no. 3 (1901): 473–482.

Hauner, M. "One Man against the Empire: The Faqir of Ipi and the British in Central Asia on the Eve of and During the Second World War." *Journal of Contemporary History* 16, no. 1 (1981): 374–404.

Hay, W. R. "The Blood Feud in Waziristan." *Journal of the Royal Central Asian Society* 19 (1932): 304–310.

Howell, E. "Some Problems of the Indian Frontier." *Journal of the Royal Central Asian Society* 21 (1934): 181–198, 238–257.

Jacob, A. G. "Waziristan." *Journal of the Royal Central Asian Society* 14 (1927): 238–257.

Johnson, T. H., and M. C. Mason. "No Sign until the Burst of Fire." *International Security* 32, no. 4 (2008): 41–77.

Kasprowicz, M. D. "1857 and the Fear of Muslim Rebellion on India's North-West Frontier." *Small Wars and Insurgencies* 8, no. 2 (1997): 1–15.

Keen, F. S. "To What Extent Would the Use of the Latest Scientific and Mechanical Methods of Warfare Affect Operations on the North-West Frontier of India?" *Journal of the United Service Institution of India* 53, no. 233 (1923): 393–415.

Lawrence-Smith, L. "Cavalry and Tanks with Mohforce, 1935." *Cavalry Journal*, no. 26 (1936): 552–561.

"Light Infantry." "Mobility." *Journal of the United Services Institution of India*, 62, no. 266 (1932): 9–29.

Lindholm, C. "Images of the Pathan: The Usefulness of Colonial Ethnography." *Archives Europeennes de Sociologie* 21 (1980): 350–361.

Mackenzie, D. A. L. "Operations in the Lower Khaisora Valley, Waziristan, in 1937." *Journal of the Royal United Service Institution* 82, no. 528 (1938): 805–822.

Macmunn, G. "A Study in Martyrdom." *Blackwoods Magazine* 241 (February 1930): 282–293.

Markey, D. "A False Choice in Pakistan." *Foreign Affairs* 86, no. 4 (2007): 64–78.

"Mauser." "A Forgotten Frontier Force." *English Review* 52 (1931): 69–72.

McFate, M. "The Military Utility of Understanding Adversary Culture." *Joint Forces Quarterly* 38, no. 3 (2005): 42–48.

Moreman, T. R. "The Arms Trade and the North-West Frontier Tribes." *Journal of Imperial and Commonwealth History* 2, no. 22 (1994): 187–216.

Moss, T. "Afghanistan Has 'Right' to Launch Cross-Border Attacks, Says Karzai." *Jane's Defence Weekly* 45, no. 26 (2008): 25–26.

"Mouse." "Babu Tactics." *Journal of the United Service Institution of India* 61, no. 262 (1931): 60–65.

Nasir, S. A. "Baitullah Mehsud: South Waziristan's Unofficial Amir." *Terrorism Focus* 3, no. 26 (2006).

"Pushtunwali: Honour amongst Them." *Economist*, 23 December 2006, 38–41.

Richards, C. "The Origins of Military Aviation in India and the Creation of the Indian Air Force, 1910–1932." *Air Power* 10, no. 3 (2007): 56–75.

Robertson, D. E. "The Organisation and Training of the Army of India." *Journal of the Royal United Service Institute* 69, no. 474 (1924): 316–333.

Roe, A. M. "Friends in High Places: Air Power on the North-West Frontier of India." *Air Power Review* 11, no. 2 (2008): 30–42.

———. "To Create a Stable Afghanistan: Provisional Reconstruction Teams, Good Governance, and a Splash of History." *Military Review* 85 (November–December 2005): 20–26.

Rubin, B. R., and A. Siddique. "Resolving the Pakistan-Afghanistan Stalemate." *Special Report 176*. United States Institute of Peace, October 2006, 1–20.

"RUSI Interview with General David Richards." *Journal of the Royal Artillery* 134, no. 2 (2007): 56–62.

Shapland, J. D. "North-West Frontier Operations—Sep/Oct 1935." *Journal of the Royal Artillery* 24, no. 2 (1937–1938): 206–211.

"Shpagwishtama." "The Changing Aspect of Operations on the North-West Frontier." *Journal of the United Service Institution of India* 66, no. 283, (1936): 102–110.

Simpson, F. C. "Review of N. W. Frontier Policy from 1849–1939." *Journal of the United Services Institution of India* 74, no. 16 (1944): 50–60.

Spires, E. M. "Gas and the North-West Frontier." *Journal of Strategic Studies* 4, no. 6 (1983): 94–112.

Stewart, R., and S. Cowper-Coles. "Are We Failing in Afghanistan?" *British Army Review*, no. 144 (2008): 7–11.

Strickland, R. T. "The Way of the Pashtun: Pashtunwali." *Canadian Army Journal*, no. 10.3 (fall 2007): 44–58.

Titus, P. "Honour the Baloch, Buy the Pathan: Stereotypes, Social Organisation and History in Western Pakistan." *Modern Asian Studies* 3, no. 32 (1988): 657–687.

Torpy, G. "Counter-Insurgency Echoes from the Past." *Journal of the Royal United Services Institute* 152, no. 5 (2007): 18–22.

Tripodi, C. "Cultural Understanding: Its Utility and Influence: The British Experience on the North-West Frontier 1918–1939." *British Army Review*, no. 144 (2008): 24–31.

———. "Peacemaking through Bribes or Cultural Empathy? The Political Officer and Britain's Strategy towards the North-West Frontier, 1901–1945." *Journal of Strategic Studies* 31, no. 1 (2008): 123–151.

Wigram, K. "Defence in the North-West Frontier Province." *Journal of the Royal Central Asian Society* 24 (1937): 73–89.

Yate, A. C. "North-West Frontier Warfare." *Journal of the Royal United Services Institution* 42, no. 248 (1898): 1171–1193.

Young, J. R. "Royal Air Force, North-West Frontier of India, 1915–39." *Journal of the Royal United Services Institute* 127 (1982): 59–64.

REGIMENTAL MAGAZINES/GAZETTES

R. Chapman, "Afghanistan and The North-West Frontier: The Green Howards during the Third Afghan War 1919, and the Waziristan Campaigns of 1936–1937, 1937–1939." *Friends of the Green Howards Regimental Museum Newsletter*, no. 14, September 2002.

*Green Howards' Gazette*, vol. 45, no. 525, December 1937; vol. 46, no. 531, June 1938; vol. 46, no. 535, October 1938.

*Journal of the Royal Artillery*, vol. 134, no. 2, Autumn 2007.

INTERNET

Harding, T. "How British Empire Failed to Tame the Terrorist Fakir of Ipi," *news .telegraph*, 15 November 2001. Available at http://news.telegraph.co.uk/news/main .jhtml? xml=/news/2001/11/15 wipi15.xml.

Harrison, S. S. "Beware Pashtunistan." *Newsweek*, 3 November 2007. Available at http://www. newsweek.com/id/67966/output/print.

Hirsh, M. "A Troubled Hunt." *Newsweek*, 30 May 2005. Available at http://www .newsweek.com.id/52193?tid=relatedcl.

Lindholm, C. "Images of the Pathan: The Usefulness of Colonial Ethnography." Available at http://www.bu.edu/anthrop/faculty/lindholm/Pathan1A.html.

Lord Curzon of Kedleston. 1907 romances lecture on the subject of frontiers. Available at http://www.dur.ac.uk/resources/ibru/resources/links/curzon.pdf.

Rupert, J. "Where the Taliban Still Rule." *Newsday.com*, 9 February 2006. Available at http://www.newsday.com/news/nationworld/world/ny-wotali 054618726feb09.

Tharoor, I. "History: The Original Insurgent." *Time*, 19 April 2007. Available at http://www.time.com/time/printout/0,8816,1612380.

National Commission on Terrorist Attacks upon the United States. Report, 22 July 2004, 365–366. Available at http://www.9-11commission.gov/.

Yusufzai, R. "Analysis: Pakistan's Army in the Tribal Areas." *BBC News*, 25 June 2003. Available at http://news.bbc.co.uk/1/hi/world/south_asia/3020552.stm.

# INDEX

administrative border, 63, 65, 67
Afghanistan, 1–2, 6, 62
    Axis nationals expelled, 185
    political propaganda, 34
Afghan National Army, 252
Afghan tribesmen in Waziristan, 164–166,
    170–171, 175, 202–203. *See also*
    Fakir of Ipi: reinforcements from
    Afghanistan
Ahmed, Akbar, 11, 105
allowances, incentives and subsidies, 13,
    102, 239
    as a peacemaker, 210–211
    benefits to Wazirs, 159
    called into question, 86–87
    paid to *maliks*, 5, 86, 195
    profitable to misbehave, 211
    for route security, 84
al-Qaeda, *See* Qaeda, al-
Amanullah, Amir, 26, 94
Anglo-Afghan Treaty, 93
Anglo-Afghan War, First, 2
Anglo-Afghan War, Second, 2, 65, 82–83
annexation of the Punjab, 7, 60, 62
Anzilotti, Enrico, 185
armaments, tribal
    accuracy, 29
    arms factories, 24
    arms race, 23–34
    artillery, 30, 179–180, 183, 189, 208, 231
    cost, 25
    government issue, 25
    modern rifles, 28
    Sadde Khan's gun, 30
    scarcity of ammunition, 28
    *See also* gunrunning
Army of India, 5, 108, 123, 130
    advantages, 128–129
    cost, 130, 210
    duties/roles, 123–124, 126–127
    1st (Abbottabad) Infantry Brigade, 167, 176
    4/2nd Gurkhas, 186
    government service, tribal, 33
    9th (Jhansi) Infantry Brigade, 169
    Probyn's Horse, 162
    2nd (Rawalpindi) Infantry Brigade, 164,
    169

6th Battalion, 13th Frontier Force Rifles,
    161
3rd Battalion (Duke of Connaught's
    Own), 7th Rajput Regiment, 162
3rd (Jhelum) Infantry Brigade, 166, 168
    training and transformation, 127–128,
    217–218
24th and 26th (Beluchistan) Regiments, 33
    weaponry, 125
    *See also* British Army
Arsal Kot, 164, 166–167, 169
    capture of Ipi's headquarters, 171
    food kitchen, 164

Balochistan, 4 (map), 87
Bannu
    Basin, 15, 19, 58
    City, 18
Barnes, Major H. A., 180–181
Barthorp, Michael, 10
Beattie, Hugh, 10
Beatty, Captain Roy, 166
Bhittani, Din Fakir, 172, 234
Bhittani tribe, 39, 55, 87
Biche Kashkai, 31, 158, 161–162, 169
bin Laden, Osama, 6, 246
Birmal, 17, 164
blockades, 21, 70–71
blood feuds, 24, 58, 111, 114, 194, 246
Bolan Pass, 18
Bowring, Captain J. B., 44
British Army
    1st Battalion the South Wales Borderers,
    176
    King's Own Scottish Borders, 30
    2nd Battalion, Argyll and Sutherland
    Highlanders, 124
    2nd Battalion The Green Howards, 29,
    124, 175
    *See also* Army of India
British Raj, 103

Caroe, Sir Olaf, 10, 87, 94
casualties, 78
    government forces, 101, 161–162, 164–
    165, 168, 176, 179, 183, 185, 229
    tribal, 74, 164, 168–169, 185, 232

caves, 37, 132, 164, 173, 175
Churchchill, Sir Winston, 72–73
Civil Service of Pakistan, 105, 250
closed border policy, 65–74, 82, 92, 197
    advantages, 79
    criticism, 75–81
coalition, 13, 235
coalition support fund, 254
conglomerate scheme, 89
counterinsurgency, 7
Crawshaw, Michael, 6
cultural understanding, 200–203, 248–250
Cunningham, Sir George, 166, 193
Curzon, Lord (Viceroy), 3, 50, 63, 90–95

Datta Khel, 30, 179, 185
Dawar tribe, 39, 55–56, 87, 156
Deane, Major H., 72, 92
decorations and honors, 81
Deeds, Major General R. B., 30, 185
Deputy Commissioners, 81
Dera Ismail Khan, 18
Dil, Mehn, 181, 234
Din, Fazal, 157
Donald, Major John, 187–188
Durand, Sir Mortimer, 84
Durand Delimitation Commission, 3, 86
Durand Line, 21, 50, 92, 191, 254
    challenges, 203–204
    demarcation, 85–86
    description, 15, 64
    establishment of border, 3, 64, 203
    limits, 57

East India Company, 257n4
education, 23, 58, 198
    schools, 96
Edwards, David, 11
European agents, 184–185. See also German
    agents
Ewans, Sir Martin, 12, 84
expeditions, punitive, 71–75, 163

fakir, 50–51
Fakir of Ipi, 5, 7, 9, 13, 101, 154 (photo), 246
    activities 1936–1947, 155–192
    background, 101, 157
    call to arms, 157
    cost to Treasury, 178
    death, 190
    demands, 158

letter to Afghan government, 174
Mirza Ali Khan, 51, 101, 157
mystical powers, 208, 233
plan to bomb hideout, 187
reinforcements from Afghanistan, 164–
    166, 170–171, 175, 202–203 (see also
    Afghan tribesmen in Waziristan)
reported ill, 209
fines, tribal, 27, 70, 174
foreign fighters, 244
forward policy, 83–87, 194, 197, 235
    reintroduction of a forward policy,
    96–101
frontier constabulary, 5, 121
Frontier Corps, 251–252
Frontier Crimes Regulation, 68–69, 194
Frontier Defense Committee, 187
frontier posts, 67

Gee, Herbert (Political Officer), 90
German agents, 184–185. See also European
    agents
Germany, 2, 182
Ghazni (Afghanistan), 18
Gomal
    Pass, 18, 54, 86
    River, 15
    Valley, 55, 69
Great Game, 1
Gul Zamir Kot, 172
gunrunning, 27. See also armaments, tribal
Gurkhas, 21
Gwynn, Major General Sir Charles W., 10,
    133

Habibullah, Amir, 93
hamsaya, 22
Hindu populace, 35
hostages, 70

Iblanke Pass, 170
independence, Pakistan's, 193, 241
    tribal control 1947, 193
India Act of 1919, 99
Indian Army Service Corps, 126
Indian Civil Service, 104
Indian National Congress, 189
Indian Political Service, 104, 110, 112, 236
    language training, 106
    responsibilities, 108–109, 111
    selection, 105

structure, 107
   *See also* political officers
Indian States, 13
Indian Subcontinent, 1, 58
Indus
   River, 19, 60, 62
   Valley, 63
injuries, general, 31
intermediaries, middlemen, 70, 79, 88
Inter Service Intelligence, 242
Islam, 49
Islam Bibi (Ram Kori), 155–156, 159, 190.
   *See also* Jehan, Noor

Jehan, Noor, 155. *See also* Islam Bibi; Kori,
   Ram
*jihad,* 50
*jirga,* 46–48, 69–70, 74, 89, 111, 147 (photo)

Kabul, 130
Kabul Khel, 74
Kaitu Pass, 18
Kaniguram, 30, 35, 41
Karzai, President Hamid, 244
*kassadars,* 5, 14, 92, 95, 107, 112–115,
   148 (photo), 194
   cost, 210
   dismissals, 165
   hereditary *kassadars,* 115
   shortfalls, 113–114
   size, 112
   structure, 113
Keogh, Captain J. A., 166
Khaisora River and Valley, 31, 158, 160
Khan, Abdul Ghaffar, 99–100, 188, 241
Khan, Amir Sher Ali, 82
Khan, Bahram, 48
Khan, Firqa Mishar Mohammed, 174
Khan, Hayat, 138
Khan, Khonia, 167–168
Khan, Sahdullah, the Mad Mullah, 90
Khan, Shah Nawaz (Nawab of Tank), 80
Khan, Sher Ali, 172, 174–176, 179, 234
Khan of Kalat, 62
Kharre Mountains, 181
Khel, Malik Khonia, 20, 172, 234
Khojak Pass, 18
Khudai Khidmatgaran, 99. *See also* Redshirts
Khyber Pass, 18, 94
Khyber Rifles, 94
kidnappings, 21, 94, 156, 187

Kohat Pass, 24
Kori, Ram, 101, 155. *See also* Jehan, Noor
Kurram Valley, 15

Lansdowne, Lord, 83–84
*lashkar,* 48–49, 58, 172, 178–185, 230
Lawrence, Lord, 63, 65
leadership, 233–234
learning approach, 215–219
Lohbeck, Kurt, 11
*loose-wallahs,* 26
Lyall, Sir Alfred, 2
Lytton, Lord (Viceroy), 2, 64

Madda Khel, 87, 179
Maffey, Sir John, 96
Mahsud tribe, 5, 39, 53–55, 69, 168, 171
   allowances, 87
   clans, 53
Makin, 35
Malakand Field Force, 42
*maliki* system, 87–90, 103
*maliks,* 5, 46, 209
   asked to leave government service,
      166
   intimidated or killed, 246
   reduced cooperation, 191
   respect, 202
   rewards, 34, 86, 158, 191
   roles, 158–160, 168–169, 173
   shortcomings, 171
   support to politicals, 109–110
   See also *maliki* system
medicine, 23, 58
   ailments, 106, 206
   healthcare, 96, 205
   medical assistance, 204–207
   treatment, 68, 102
Mehsud, Baitullah, 246–247
Merk, W. R. H., 23, 89
*mians,* 50
militias, 92–94, 102
Mir, Azal, 172, 234
Mir Ali, 161–162, 169
Miranshah, 138, 171
Mirsa, Amalendu, 12
missionaries, 23
modified forward policy, 90–95, 197
Mohammed, Faqir, army deserter, 234
Moreman, T. R., 10
Mountbatten, Earl, 189

Muhammed, Fakir Din, 175
*mujahadeen,* 242
*mullahs,* 49–50
Musharraf, President Pervez, 12, 194, 243, 253

*nang* tribes, 39, 41
Nawaz, Gul, 234
Nevill, H. L., 20, 27, 29
Newton, A. P., 10
*nikat,* 46, 89, 210
North Atlantic Treaty Organization, 235
Northern Alliance, 242
North-West Frontier, 60, 101
North-West Frontier Province, 4 (map),
    10, 93
    creation, 3, 92
    political agencies, 3, 92
    settled districts, 3, 92

Omar, Mullah, 243
Orakzai tribe, 173
outlaws, 22

Pakistan, 6, 189, 242
Pashtun, tribesmen, 2
Pashtunistan, 101, 189, 194, 241, 254
Pashtun tribal belt, 14
*Pashtunwali,* code of behavior, 7, 61, 102
    assessment, 51
    autonomy of adult male, 45
    compliance to Islam, 49, 246
    honor/revenge, 42–44
    hospitality, 44–45, 132
    leadership, 45–47
    origin, 41–42
    protection of females, 44
    sanctuary, 45
    standard of behavior, 195, 236
    understanding of, 112, 201–202
    See also *jirga*
Persia, 1
picquets, 126, 149 (photo)
*pir,* 50
political agents, 45, 47, 212
political officers, 13, 71, 104–112, 200
    assistant political officers, 107, 201, 212
    See also Indian Political Service
Powindah, Mullah, 50, 157
powindahs, 21, 41, 54
Prendergast, John, 10
Punjab Frontier Force, 67, 71
Punjab government, 2, 91

Punjab Irregular Force, 67
*purdah,* 205–206

Qaeda, al-, 5, 243–244, 250, 254
*qalang* tribes, 39

Rahman, Amir Abdur, 2, 82, 84
Raiding, tribal, 20–23, 94
Razmak, 95–96, 125, 152 (photo)
Redshirts, 99–100, 103. *See also* Khudai
    Khidmatgaran
Richards, General Sir David, 253
road construction, 68, 90, 97–98,
    150 (photo), 163, 173, 199
    cost, 228
    strategic advantages, 228
road opening days, 167, 229
    "picquetting the heights," 229
roads, 227–230
Roberts, Field Marshal Lord, 63
Robertson, Major General D. E., 161
Rodd, Sir Rennell, 1
Roos-Keppel, Sir George, 99
Royal Air Force, 5, 130, 141, 161
    air blockade, 135, 166
    air reconnaissance, 135
    challenges, 134–135, 138–140
    close air support, 222
    cooperation, 136–137
    employment, 131, 133
    fratricide, 140
Royal Army Medical Corps, 106
Russia, 1, 64

Sandeman, Sir Robert, 21, 47, 87
*sayyids,* 50
scientific frontier, 63
scouts (militias), 5, 115, 122, 147 (photo),
    201
    advantages, 119
    ailments, 121
    desertions, 33
    duties, 117
    equipment, 120
    *gashting,* 119, 138
    numbers, 116, 118
    structure, 116–117
    transformation, 218
September 11, 194
settled districts/areas, 121, 196
Shah, Sayyid Amir Noor Ali, 101, 155
Shahidganj Mosque, Lahore, 158

Shahur Tangi, 167
Shaktu River and Valley, 157, 186
Shami Pir, Muhammad Saadi al Kailani,
     180–181, 192, 234, 239
*Sharia,* Islamic law, 49
Shaw, Major General Jonathan, 7
Sikh rule, 61
     "old Sikh line," 63
Sinno, Abdulkader, 11
Slessor, Sir John, 70
South Waziristan Scouts, 11, 29, 96, 118, 167
     encircled, 179
Soviet invasion, 242
Soviets, 251
Sudan, 90
Suliman Khel tribe, 21
Suliman Mountains, 60
superstition, 49, 207–210, 226
surprise, 223–227

Taliban, 5, 242–243, 250, 254
Talibanization, 246
Third Afghan War, 5, 94, 130, 191
Tochi River and Valley, 16, 18, 55
Tochi Scouts, 96, 118, 158, 161, 170
Tori Khel Wazirs, 31, 157, 165, 171
tribal areas, 40 (map)
tribal villages, 144 (photo)
     children, 38
     description, 35–37
     relocation, 69, 102
     role of women, 37–38
     watch towers, 36, 44, 73, 145 (photo)

*tuman,* 89
Turkey, 2, 54

Ulmulk, Colonel Khushwaqt, 11, 142
unified action, 219–223

value of political/military structure, 212–214
viceroy's commissioned officers, 129

Wana, 95–96
Warburton, Sir Robert, 80
Warren, Alan, 6, 10
Waziritsan, 5–7, 45, 85
     agriculture, 19
     climate, 18, 197
     geography, 15
     investors/contractors, 98–99, 199
     natural resources, 18
     profit, 197
     terrain, 16, 197, 245
     trade, 19
     transportation network, 8 (map), 16
Wazirs, Darwesh Khel, 5, 39, 52–53, 66
     clans, 53
     numbers, 52
World War I, 33
World War II, 187, 192, 217

Zaman, Sher, Fakir of Ipi's brother, 157–158,
     172–173, 234
Zarinai (Fakir's townhouse), 163
Zawahiri, Ayman Al, 247